Yellow Ribbon

Yellow Ribbon

The Secret Journal of Bruce Laingen

AMBASSADOR L. BRUCE LAINGEN

BRASSEY'S (US), Inc.

A Division of Maxwell Macmillan, Inc.

WASHINGTON · NEW YORK · LONDON

Brassey's (US), Inc.

Editorial Offices
Brassey's (US), Inc.
8000 Westpark Drive
First Floor
McLean, Virginia 22102

Order Department
Brassey's Book Orders
% Macmillan Publishing Co.
100 Front Street, Box 500
Riverside, New Jersey 08075

Brassey's (US), Inc., books are available at special discounts for bulk purchases for sales promotions, premiums, fund-raising, or educational use through the Special Sales Director, Macmillan Publishing Company, 866 Third Avenue, New York, New York 10022.

LIBRARY OF CONGRESS CATALOGING-IN-PUBLICATION DATA

Laingen, L. Bruce.
    Yellow ribbon : the secret journal of Bruce Laingen / L. Bruce Laingen.
        p.   cm.
    Includes index.
    ISBN 0-02-881030-9
    1. Iran Hostage Crisis, 1979–1981—Personal narratives.
2. Laingen, L. Bruce—Diaries. 3. Ambassadors—United States—Diaries. I. Title.
E183.8.I55L35   1992
955.05′4—dc20   92-5377
                                                       CIP

Designed by Robert Freese
10 9 8 7 6 5 4 3 2 1

PRINTED IN THE UNITED STATES OF AMERICA

Contents

Preface

It would have been beyond my comprehension had someone suggested to me when I first joined the Foreign Service in 1949 that I would someday become the only head of an American diplomatic mission abroad to lose his embassy and its entire staff to political terrorists and then be held hostage for political purposes for more than a year. Yet that distinction became mine on November 4, 1979, in Tehran, Iran—a city and country where a quarter century earlier I had served with youthful enthusiasm in an earlier diplomatic assignment.

It was not, however, the first time that a diplomat in Tehran had lost his diplomatic mission. In January 1831, as a consequence of political disturbances triggered by problems in implementation of the Treaty of Turkomenchai between Iran and Russia, a mob stormed the Russian Legation and massacred everyone inside but one, including the minister heading the legation. We were to be more fortunate in that we survived. But in stark contrast with that earlier incident that saw the Shah then on the Persian throne act immediately against the culprits and dispatch his grandson to Moscow on a mission of apology, this time what passed for government in Tehran promptly gave its blessing to those committing the act and became in effect partners in the crime. As the U.S. government's brief noted in its successful appeal to the World Court at The Hague: "From the 16th century down to the present time, no receiving state has authorized or condoned a breach of a diplomat's personal violability. . . . That great tradition of recognizing and honoring the inviolability of Embassies and diplomats has now been shattered, for the first time in modern history."

This book is a personal account of that dramatic event, as seen from and experienced in the diplomatic reception rooms of the Iranian Ministry of Foreign Affairs, where I and two colleagues spent our captivity until three weeks before our release, when we were turned over to the student terrorists and placed in solitary confinement. It is based on excerpts from a journal I maintained during this period and secreted out by a variety of means, usually in mail sent out via the Swiss Embassy or hidden on my person while in solitary, and on letters to senior Iranian government officials, all "cleared" via the Office of Protocol in the ministry. Until the formal break in diplomatic relations in

April of 1980, I wrote and signed such letters (*appeals* would be a better word) in my capacity, however theoretical under the circumstances, as chargé d'affaires of the United States in Iran.

The book is therefore a reactive account to developments as they occurred rather than a definitive history of the crisis, its origins, and consequences. The account is inevitably incomplete, in that at no time during our captivity was I fully informed as to all the details of efforts by individuals and governments to achieve our release. Our sources of information were a mixed bag at best, dependent on occasional visits by resident ambassadors, access to Iranian radio and TV for much of the time, sporadic telephone contact with the Department of State in Washington, and exchanges with what we called the grass roots— those who guarded and fed us in the ministry. We knew enough to wish we knew more.

The account is particularly reactive in that it reflects the impact that human emotions—triggered by the traumatic events of November 4 and the many frustrations that followed—had on the judgment and assessments of a hostage-participant in those events. I make no apology. The seizure of the embassy and the Iranian authorities' response were wrong on every count—legally, politically, morally—whatever grievances those responsible felt. These acts were unworthy of Iran, its Revolution, and people whose historical experiences have often been difficult and who have suffered more than anyone else from the consequences of this tragic episode in their long history.

Time has a way of easing those emotions, of putting events in a deeper and broader perspective than is possible in their immediate aftermath, and it is now more than a decade since we returned to freedom. Regrettably, however, that period has seen political terrorism continue in Iran and elsewhere in the Middle East, with other Americans held hostage far longer and in more grievous hurt than were we. Only now do the successors of the Ayatollah Khomeini appear to be coming to an appreciation that their identification with terrorism in Beirut and elsewhere is prejudicial to any hopes of their Revolution having any social and economic benefit for the people of that long-troubled country.

Having known a different Iran during an earlier assignment, one with proud traditions that include a warmth of hospitality to foreigners, I remain convinced that what is in place in Tehran today must inevitably evolve to something more compatible with those traditions and with the more tolerant values of Islam. That, I believe, will again permit a relationship with the United States that is different from that of the past but includes a mutual recognition of the power realities of the Persian Gulf region. It is, after all, unnatural, given our earlier relationship, for us to remain indefinitely at odds. A decade of revolutionary vitriol against the United States surely has not wholly erased the memory of historic American humanitarian and educational involvement with Iran. Moreover, a future relationship will inevitably find strength in one of the most enduring by-products of the Iranian Revolution—the United States is today the second largest Persian-speaking country in the world.

Acknowledgments

No American chief of mission could have been better served than was I in the men and women of the embassy in Tehran. They were a cohesive, resourceful, and good-spirited group in the months of stress and uncertainty prior to our seizure. Their conduct as hostages, with the rarest of exceptions, was exemplary—most especially that of the two women, Ann Swift and Katherine Koob. The entire group richly deserves the Award for Valor presented them by Secretary of State Alexander Haig on our release. I am proud to have served with them. My special affection and respect for Victor Tomseth and Michael Howland, unexpected roommates for all but the last weeks of the crisis, is documented in the pages of this book.

I am in debt as well to many members of the diplomatic corps in Tehran at that time. None sensed more keenly the total abuse of diplomatic immunity suffered by my embassy. My gratitude goes especially to Switzerland's resident ambassador, Erik Lang, a distinguished example of his country's professionalism in diplomacy and its long tradition of effectiveness as a protecting power of the interests of an absent mission—as was the case for us in Tehran after relations were formally severed in April 1980. But well before that and throughout the crisis, Ambassador Lang's personal regard (and that of his wife) for the three of us in the ministry helped keep our spirits and hopes alive. That regard, evident in his personal visits to us, was often extended at personal risk; his anger and his disapproval of making diplomats hostages were never in question.

That same feeling was evident in other ambassadors as well—the British, Swedish, German, Dutch, Norwegian, Turkish, and, above all, the papal nuncio, Archbishop Annibale Bugnini. That truest of Christian humanity, a rotund and gentle Italian, was constant in his efforts to remind us, his "colleagues of solitude," of the promise of faith; I will always regret that his untimely death shortly after our release prevented me from embracing him in freedom. British Ambassador John Graham was another good friend, whose distinction in diplomacy was later recognized by Queen Elizabeth II when she made him Sir John. Later, of course, the diplomatic skills and political perceptiveness of the Algerian intermediaries would become key elements in the process that eventually restored us to freedom.

Canadian Ambassador Kenneth Taylor and his wife, Pat, merit more thanks than I can express. Their help, and that of their government, for six American diplomats at risk in Tehran extended to the point of sacrificing all of their country's interests in Iran to bring them home to freedom and dramatically reminded all Americans of their good fortune to have Canada as a neighbor.

Uncertainty about their personal safety precludes my identifying the many Iranians, including some who also supported the Revolution, who found ways to tell us that they shared our feelings. Most of those who fed and guarded us made little secret of their view that what had been done to the hostages was wrong and contrary to Iran's traditions. And among Iran's professional diplomats working in the ministry where we were held, one in particular—a diplomat of the old school and the epitome of Persian courtesy—will forever be my friend. He will know whom I mean.

To attempt to thank Americans at home would be an unending task. Probably no single group of Americans in recent history experienced the warmth of national affection as did we in Tehran. No one benefited from more prayers per capita than we did. Each of us had his own special group to thank, and for me that began with my neighbors in Bethesda, Maryland, and particularly Helen and Russell Chapin. They and mutual friends Joyce and Congressman Clarence Brown (R-Ohio) were a foursome whose support sustained my wife, Penne, throughout the special hurt, fear, and anger that only families of hostages can know. Vera Jensen, Marion Perry, Curtis Steuart, Carolyn White, and Patricia Young were prominent among the countless others who reached out to my family and me on my return.

The Naval Academy at Annapolis, where my son Bill was then in his second and third years, was another place of special support. Its superintendent, Vice Adm. William Lawrence, had been almost seven years a POW in Vietnam, making him and his wife, Diane, highly credible counselors to my wife and to Bill. The same was true for two other former POW families on the academy staff: Capt. Richard Stratton and his wife, Alice, and Cdr. Paul Galanti and his wife, Phyllis. This book gives me an opportunity to say again how grateful my family is for the role the Naval Academy has played in our lives.

Equally supportive was the rector of my parish church, the Rev. Dr. Stuart Irvin, and indeed all of its parishioners. Dr. Irvin's own deep faith caused him to believe that my return and that of all my colleagues was nothing less than a miracle. If so, it also had help from another special group—those members of that parish and others, led by Bob Alyward and Joe and Jodi Keyerleber, whose leadership in Sunday night vigils on Massachusetts Avenue across from the Iranian Embassy kept the faith of a host of others alive. My special gratitude also goes to Frank Crawford, an old friend whose diplomatic service included Iran, who did not fail each weekend to join in a ritual ringing of the bell in the tower of my church. Finally there is my former secretary at the Department of State, Gladys Decker, whose support for me and my wife included typing an unknown number of often almost indecipherable handwritten pages of this journal. Gladys Decker is a shining example of the expertise and dedication that make the Department of State function.

In that department and in the Foreign Service abroad, my colleagues and I had that special kind of support that comes naturally from comrades in arms. Many of them had personally experienced the dangers of terrorism that in recent years has so endangered diplomats abroad. I am personally in debt to countless numbers of them for the support they communicated, both during and after the crisis, beginning with then Secretaries of State Cyrus Vance and Edmund Muskie, Undersecretary David Newsom, Assistant Secretary Harold Saunders, his deputy, Peter Constable, and many others down through the ranks. None sweated it out more than my immediate counterpart in the department, Iran Country Director Henry Precht, and later his successor, Ralph Lindstrom. Sheldon Krys was tireless in coordinating the department's outreach efforts to our families. A host of friends staffed the Iran Working Group, headed by Marion Precht, that was magnificent in coping with the hopes and fears of our families.

One additional person in the department deserves special mention: Deputy Secretary of State Warren Christopher, whose indefatigable diplomatic endurance made possible the Algiers Accord that saw our release—an accord that he himself rightly has termed a singular example of the art of diplomacy.

I want to record as well my gratitude to Carmella LaSpada, founder of No Greater Love, an organization that reaches out to children of Americans in distress, beginning with the POWs in Vietnam. Carmella has been unceasing ever since in that role, and the families of all of us in Tehran are in her debt for what she did for us. When my wife began the yellow ribbon effort, no one worked harder than Carmella did to make that symbol the powerful force for unity and caring that it has since become.

Most of all, I am grateful to my family, beginning with all of them in Minnesota; my parents-in-law, Fred and Margaret Babcock, in Washington; and above all my wife, Penne, and my three sons, William, Charles, and James—all of whom opted for public service of their own in the U.S. Navy. My family served with me in Karachi, Kabul, and Valletta. They knew the rewards and the costs of foreign service. They were never with me physically in Tehran, but I felt their presence in every waking moment. Nothing mattered more to me than knowing I had their love and support. I join with my hostage colleagues in recognizing that families at home also become hostages when terrorism strikes.

As my wife and as founder of FLAG (Family Liaison Action Group) and the originator of the yellow ribbon campaign, Penne has my special thanks and respect for the role she played in this crisis. Public attention focused on me; I got the awards and the recognition. She deserved them in equal measure. She has them in my mind and heart.

1

Assignment Tehran

It was already dusk when my plane landed in Tehran on June 16, 1979, but not dark enough to obscure the familiar massif of the Elburz Mountains, which loom above the city that sprawls down its lower slopes and out onto the dusty, arid plain so typical of the central Iranian plateau. Whatever else may have changed with the Iranian Revolution, they had not. The magnificent Elburz Mountains are today as before the saving grace of a city that has few redeeming features in urban design or architecture. The glories of Persian architecture are elsewhere. In the far provinces are the magnificent examples of Persian art and architecture, in Isfahan and Meshed, the gardens of Shiraz, the caravan crossroads of Tabriz and Hamadan, the ruins of the palaces of Darius and Xerxes at Persepolis, and everywhere the vistas of mountain and desert-clad horizon, sometimes relieved by the lush fertility of surprisingly green valleys.

Tehran today has little beyond the earlier Qajar dynasty's Persian baroque Gulistan Palace and the misplaced opulence of the last Shah's palatial residences. Even its bazaar, however sprawling, cannot approach that in Isfahan for color and character. But Tehran is unchallenged among Iranian cities for its size—in both area and population—and for the ill-organized momentum of its growth under the Shah's modernization effort. This Persian megalopolis, one of the world's least attractive capitals, has endless blocks of banks and office buildings almost devoid, even in its newer sections, of architectural merit. It is a place of grime and misery in the burgeoning slums of south Tehran, which

1

contrast starkly with the Shah's palaces and the nouveau riche mansions and swimming pools in the mountain suburbs of north Tehran. From those congested slums had come that mass of volatile humanity that the leaders of the Revolution had used so effectively to face down the Shah's military might on the city's streets.

I had lived in Tehran once before—for two years just after the collapse of the Mossadegh regime in 1953. Having completed my first tour in the Foreign Service in Hamburg, Germany, and having been assigned as consular officer in Kobe, Japan, I was on leave on my family's farm in southern Minnesota, with all my household effects already on their way by sea, when a telephone call from the Department of State canceled my Kobe orders. I was to go instead to Tehran. There the embassy was expanding in the aftermath of the restoration of the Shah to his throne, and there I spent two very exciting years as a participant—however junior—in the beginning of an American relationship with Iran that would become one of remarkable and ultimately disastrous proportions. But while I was there I had time to enjoy Iran's celebrated hospitality and the splendor of places like Isfahan, Hamadan, and Meshed. As a consequence of that twist of fate, moreover, I met my wife, who then lived in suburban Washington next door to the home of Minister of Embassy Bill Rountree. He and I had completed our tours in Iran and transferred to Washington, and one day in 1955 he said, "Come out to dinner and meet the girl next door."

Now as my plane landed at Mehrabad Airport, history for me was ironically repeating itself. Only two weeks before I had been preparing to depart for South America as head of a Foreign Service inspection team and was on leave at that same family farm in Minnesota, when I received a call from Washington telling me that the secretary of state wanted me to go instead to Tehran, forthwith. I was to go as chargé d'affaires while Washington decided how to respond to the Iranian regime's sudden rejection of the ambassador it had nominated (Walter Cutler) to be our first ambassador to the provisional government of the Revolution. That rejection had followed the U.S. Senate's adoption in May of a resolution sharply critical of the regime's posture toward the Jewish minority in Tehran. Large anti-American demonstrations had also taken place. I was to serve for "only four to six weeks" while Washington decided whether to accredit someone else as ambassador or to temporize further with a long-term chargé. In either case, such a designee, I was assured, would be someone other than I.

This assurance mattered to my wife, whose views on my assignment and on the revolutionary leadership in Tehran were jaundiced at best. Never enamored with Iran, having formed a very negative opinion of Iranian treatment of women in her two visits there, she was skeptical of the outlook in Tehran. She counseled against my going, telling me the United States would be better off putting a kind of figurative fence around the country and leaving it to its own devices while the revolutionary turmoil sorted itself out. Yet she reluctantly saw me off. She understood full well my excitement at returning to a country where I had known the adventure of the Foreign Service at its best, the challenge of managing a diplomatic mission in the midst of revolutionary upheaval, and the sense of duty I felt when the secretary of state pointed a finger at me. Moreover, in this instance, I was going out to take over from an old friend, Charlie Naas, who had served as deputy chief of mission in Tehran for two years and then as chargé himself since shortly after the Revolution.

This time I was returning to a very different Iran, symbolized by the brief seizure of the embassy compound on Valentine's Day only four months earlier, in the midst of the Islamic Revolution, and the drastic reduction in the embassy staff that had followed. Some things appeared the same as Charlie and I drove into the city: traffic like dodgem cars loose on the streets and traffic police who seemed to confirm rather than control the noisy pandemonium. Unchanged, too, was a singularly joyless street populace with little to smile about in a city choking on pollution and made irritable by grossly inadequate public services.

What was different along those streets were the boarded-up office fronts and smoke-blackened facades of banks and theaters, evidence of revolutionary zeal in toppling the Shah's regime. In the north of the city was more change— imperial palaces that now stood empty, and the mansions of the rich, now closed or sequestered by the Poor People's Foundation. Young men in Komiteh (committee) groups, vigilantes of sorts who manned roadblocks at night, were everywhere. The Ayatollah Mohammad Beheshti had in mind these changes when he later told me that the 34 million of the oppressed were now in charge, and the 1 million of the aristocracy and nouveau riche would have to accept the consequences or leave.

The American Embassy Compound to which Charlie and I drove—once almost isolated in the outskirts and by now in the heart of the city—was still there, but a platoon of some 30 revolutionaries headed by an unprincipled swashbuckler named Mashallah roamed it at will, supposedly at Khomeini's orders for the embassy's "protection" after its seizure in February. Tension was often high between the American staff, especially the Marine guards, and these gun-toting young men, who flaunted their power and presence. The compound, my home for the next five months, would become for me symbolic of everything that went wrong in Iran. Too large and too centrally located, its scattered buildings were almost impossible to defend; it was also a chancery devoid of aesthetic appeal. For Iran's revolutionaries during the Shah's later years, it had symbolized what was wrong in terms of a visual presence and influence propping up a hated regime, just as the similarly large compounds of the British and Soviet embassies had symbolized perceived wrongs in earlier Iranian history and had contributed to the scapegoat syndrome so endemic in the Iranian psyche.

This official American presence, which it had now become my responsibility to lead and represent, faced an awesome substantive challenge, hunkered down as it had been within its graffiti-laden walls since the February seizure. That challenge was to convince a skeptical revolutionary leadership and the indoc-trinated street masses that the United States, despite its identification with the ancien régime, was prepared and indeed eager to accept the new realities in Iran. I did not doubt the difficulty of my challenge; the fact that my embassy was still "protected" by a band of revolutionary zealots rather dramatically symbolized the limited progress we had made with the new cast of characters in Tehran.

But one's attitude toward problems is always conditioned by personal experience. In my case, that included the still vivid and positive memory of the Iran I had known, an Iran that had captured the fascination of generations of American diplomats, missionaries, educators, and adventurers. Like them, I had been enamored by the stark beauty of its landscape and the translucent blue of its skies. I had delighted in the Persian love of gardens, the special appeal of the sound of fountains within them, and the penchant for poetry among so many Iranians. I had come to understand how the starkness of the Persian landscape was relieved by the rich color and form of Persian carpets and architecture, above all by the majestic mosques with the special appeal of blue so evident in their intricate tile work and mosaics—mosques that also spoke of the role of Islam in Iran's history and in the fabric of life for every Iranian.

My memory of Iran included as well the grinding poverty of the mass of its people, the way village conditions and life seemed forever embedded in the past, and the contrast of the ruling elite's wealth and arrogance then and indeed throughout Persian history. Yet I had sensed too how that gulf in some ways was bridged by the pride of all Persians in the real or imagined glories of a distant past, as well as by that split personality all Persians have in their attitude toward foreigners—on one hand an aloofness and suspicion born of unhappy experiences with invading or otherwise intruding outsiders, and on the other hand a tradition of hospitality toward foreigners that no one who has lived and traveled in that country can forget.

I also recalled the considerable dimensions of America's Point Four and subsequent economic assistance to that country, the role of American investment in the Shah's grandiose modernization drive, and the pervasive presence of the American military role. On my first tour in Tehran, I had served for a time as an aide in the office of the director of the Point Four program and met in that office Ardeshir Zahedi, later the Shah's last ambassador to Washington.

Nevertheless, my subsequent assessment of what was happening in Iran had been necessarily as a distant observer. Watching Iran from assignments in Pakistan and Afghanistan, which had had so much less apparent success in modernization and nation-building, I had been impressed by the Shah's strong leadership, his innovative programs in areas such as literacy training, his seeming progress in land reform, the evidence of industrialization and growth in Tehran and in provincial cities as well, and the Shah's seeming success in building vested interests among many elements of the body politic in a continuation of his rule.

But like others, I had not appreciated the costs and weaknesses: the deficiencies in the industrial infrastructure and land reform support system; the unmet economic expectations of the explosive urban slums, especially after the inflationary spiral that accompanied the massive oil price increases of the mid-1970s; and above all the growing alienation of many Iranians from a regime that seemed to identify with American political purposes and culture to a degree that was corrosive to Iran's own cultural and religious traditions. Nor had I sensed the frustration of the secular elite with the Shah's reluctance to entrust an organized political opposition with a legal framework for such opposition— and ultimate participation. Like too many others, I had also allowed an ingrained prejudice toward a seemingly anachronistic clerical class to affect my judgment of the potential influence and attitudes of that class, representatives of which were soon so profoundly to affect my personal well-being.

Change had been too rapid, a traditional culture was being eroded, and economic aspirations could not be met. A frequently well-meaning Shah could not overcome his imperial pretensions, his isolation, and his distrust of his own people to act forcefully and imaginatively when he might have done so. Withal, his regime's perceived identification with American policy and culture was effectively used by a revolutionary leadership, secular and clerical, to make America the Great Satan behind every figurative tree of misfortune.

All of that was symbolized by the collapse of American influence and presence in Tehran and, for me, as I drove into the compound, by its beleaguered appearance. But I had not taken on this new assignment to revel in regret or retribution. I had been reminded that one of my major responsibilities was to strengthen the morale of the small band of Foreign Service personnel who now represented American interests, and I was keenly aware that in the hierarchical structure of a diplomatic mission its head has substantial influence; in a besieged embassy compound like ours, a chargé's impact on morale and the perceived direction of things could be considerable. So I had good reason to bring what confidence and cheer I could to the scene. In any event, I was excited by the kind of challenge that comes only occasionally in a diplomatic career, and I intended to make the most of it. As for my friend, Charlie Naas, less than 48 hours later I would see him off from the airport VIP lounge, he embracing in the Iranian fashion, but with a wink of relief in my direction as he did so, each of that band of ruffian revolutionaries whose "protection" had been his fate and, at times, good fortune in the months of tension since February. Escorted fore and aft by that same group back into turbulent Tehran, the responsibility was now mine, and my prospects uncertain.

Describing all this in my first letters home, I commented:

It probably sounds slightly mad to you. And perhaps it is. But don't be alarmed. We are reasonably confident it [the February 14 attack] won't happen again—not like that, in any event. Our chancery is well protected with massive steel doors, sand-filled steel barriers at each window, and bulletproof glass in the reception area. We call it Fort Apache from without. It would take a massive effort to get in, if we have advance warning. Today, as added protection against any rioters trying to scale the building to the second floor, the rather handsome stone balcony outside my office window was totally removed . . . even the flagpole out front has the lanyard taped to the pole about 25 feet up and the pole covered with a mixture of grease and Ben-Gay to stop flag snatchers. The flag flies round-the-clock.

The ambassador's residence in Tehran is a few minutes' walk from the chancery through a grove of towering pine trees. An immense if architecturally uninteresting place, it was defended around-the-clock by Marines, my bedroom doors lined with thick steel plates strong enough to resist a G-3 rifle bullet. The walls of the great salon were still pockmarked from gunfire during its occupation in the Valentine's Day attack. It was destined to suffer the abuse of intruders again when it would serve for a time as a prison for some of those taken hostage in the November attack.

In the chancery I was to occupy the office of the ambassador, where as a junior officer 25 years earlier I had observed in awe the diplomatic skills of one of the giants of American diplomacy, Ambassador Loy Henderson. Now I sat at his desk, marveling at the workings of fate that had brought me to this place. There and in scattered other compound buildings, about 100 Americans—and perhaps as many Iranians—now worked, greatly reduced from a much bigger cast during the Shah's time. Their numbers would decline further over the next several months, with 72 Americans to be taken hostage (or escape, as six would) on that fateful day in November. All served without dependents, their families having left during the Revolution.

My official guidance from Washington instructed me to do essentially three things: report my own assessment for the prospects of building a relationship with this new Iranian regime, including the outlook for American business interests affected by revolutionary takeovers; restore American security within the embassy compound; and provide leadership for a dispirited embassy staff who were largely restricted to living and working within the compound since the Revolution. I was also encouraged to do what I could to begin a frank dialogue about the thorniest of the issues remaining from the Shah's period— the billions of dollars in military supply contracts, all suspended because of the changed political relationship. In all that I did I was also to project the central theme of American policy toward the new Iran: that the United States fully recognized the reality of the Islamic Revolution and was prepared to work with its provisional government to develop a new, if vastly different, U.S.-Iranian relationship.

That message was one we would eventually learn the more radical elements of the Revolution were simply not prepared to hear. In a letter that autumn to my family, noting a long talk with a leading mullah, I said,

> I came away with a new appreciation of how much of a communications gap exists between the West and the clerical leadership of this place. Suspicion of us is deep indeed, a product of our support of the Shah and of Israel and of a perception of American society as a materialist one generally hostile to Islam. However much I tried to emphasize that Americans too were a people with strong spiritual values, I found that we were talking past each other most of the time.

The mullahs were centered in the Revolutionary Council, which had real political power, but they operated largely behind the scenes, and we would rarely reach this group. Within that circle sat the Ayatollah Khomeini, whom I was never to see; a regrettable gap but on reflection it was one that probably could never have been closed in any event, his anathema toward the United States a total one.

The ministers of the provisional government, including Prime Minister Mehdi Bazargan, however, were always accessible, over endless cups of tea. Bazargan was a veteran protagonist for political change in the Shah's years and a man of great personal charm and decency, but he was constantly undercut by Khomeini, leaving him, in Bazargan's own words, like a knife without the blade. His ministers, especially Foreign Minister Yazdi, seemed to regard my assignment as chargé but with a personal title of ambassador as a signal of our good intentions toward the Revolution. At the embassy's Fourth of July reception, its first major social event after the Revolution and my first as chargé, Yazdi, three other ministers, and several senior military officers attended. That seemed to me, as I wrote to my family, "clearly a signal of sorts that Iran is prepared to have some sort of resumed relationship."

My observation should have added the proviso that others in the collective leadership might feel differently, yet progress that summer and fall suggested otherwise and contributed to what in the final analysis proved to be an excess of wishful thinking. Most visibly, security gradually seemed to improve in the city, especially along the streets outside the residence, with fewer of the running firefights among contending revolutionary groups that so often disturbed my sleep. We encouraged American businessmen to return at least long enough to determine the outlook for settling their claims, and a good many did. Officers of the embassy traveled to Tabriz and Shiraz to test the outlook for reopening consular offices in those cities.

For security reasons I did not travel far beyond the inner city, but in a mid-July letter to my family, I described a drive into the slums of south Tehran in an unmarked car with an American security officer:

> I came back reminded that for a great many Iranians, life is damned tough. . . .
> The picture is one of grinding misery and drabness for most of the people who live down there and there are several millions of them . . . most of whom look tired, grouchy, and out of sorts with the world. I don't blame them.
> The Shah used to talk of Iran being one of the top six or seven powers of the world by the end of the century . . . what I saw today reminded me of how grandiosely wrong he was. This is a poor country and will be for a long time, except for the lucky few who were at the top of the heap under the Shah . . . but beyond that is the distance this society has yet to go to develop its technological skills, its capacity for government, a sense of social order and responsibility . . . these and many other things that go with being a major power. . . . And involved as well, in the massive task this place faces, is finding a way to adapt its Islamic fervor with modern requirements.

By mid-August, we had persuaded the regime to remove the "protecting" force from our compound and restored a happy Marine unit to full control, except for regular police units outside the walls. The protecting forces did not leave willingly, however—they having come to regard the place as their personal fiefdom. The government sent in 35 to 40 Revolutionary Guards to force them out with a brief firefight within the compound. Having had no precise word from the government as to the timing of the operation, I found myself involved as well when I opened my bedroom door at 7:00 A.M. to find two Revolutionary Guards confronting me with G-3 rifles. They looked as surprised as I. Deadly serious in their purpose, they were not at all happy at finding a swimsuit-clad chargé en route to the residence's swimming pool. I was summarily ordered to sit down while they searched my closets and then escorted me to the lobby below. There was another group of revolutionaries, confronting a singularly angry and embarrassed pair of Marines, who had failed to detect this early morning intrusion through the residence's kitchen windows. It took some time to sort things out.

As for the arms supply issue—a substantive area as important as any if U.S.-Iranian trust was to be restored—enough progress had been made by autumn to see a limited amount of urgently needed military spare parts, owned and paid for by the Iranians but held in the United States, to be shipped. Agreement was also reached for the Iranians to designate a team to go to Washington and review in detail and on the spot the incredibly complex accounting affecting billions of dollars' worth of contracts—an agreement stillborn by the events of November 4. No issue dominated more of my time and that of my military liaison head, Maj. Gen. Phil Gast, USAF, and no issue aroused so much suspicion in the minds of the Iranian ministers and generals, who were thoroughly convinced, good rug merchants as Iranians tend to be, that Iran had essentially been had in these contracts signed with the Shah. Not understanding the intricacies of an arms supply process involving hundreds of private American suppliers, they argued that if the U.S. government were genuine in its professed acceptance of the Revolution it could easily cut a deal at a vastly reduced figure.

Meanwhile my original assignment of four to six weeks had become something else, Washington apparently pleased enough to ask me to stay on as chargé. On August 6, by coincidence also my birthday, I was summoned to the telephone from the compound's tennis courts to be told the secretary of state wanted to put my name to the president as ambassador to Iran that very day. That call triggered a series of cable exchanges and ultimately a trip to Washington for consultations. My own view had been that "retreading" a chargé to become ambassador would not best serve U.S. interests in Iran. Moreover for me it posed an agonizing personal decision, involving painful prospects of further family separation. As I later wrote my 13-year-old son:

> A Dad ought to be around when a boy is growing up, and I hope you understand why I am not there now. The Foreign Service for me, after 30 years, is something I take seriously, because I am serving my country—your country—and I think I should respond when I'm asked to do this work in Iran. . . . I'll be thinking of you a lot, proud of what you do and what you are . . . and I hope you will be proud of me for doing what I think I must do.

I returned to Tehran in late September with the issue still undecided, though I had committed myself to stay on as chargé for as long as necessary and even to serve as ambassador if that decision were made. But in October a message from the Department of State indicated that my name was no longer under consideration because naming me "would not be the right signal" at that point. In retrospect, had I or someone else then been named as ambassador—thus signaling publicly our acceptance of the Revolution—events surrounding the Shah's later admission into the United States might conceivably have been different.

During my September consultations I had taken a cautiously optimistic view of things in Tehran. Security conditions had improved to the point where, by mid-October, we were recommending that adult dependents be allowed to return on a case-by-case basis. We had also gotten sufficient regime cooperation to complete a modern visa-issuing facility. With its opening came the crowds, more than 3,000 on day one. The place became a kind of tourist attraction, with street vendors outside and police to help keep order. I commented in a letter to my wife about this paradox: "We are not the most popular people in Iran these days . . . even our friends are cautious about being seen too close to us . . . and yet there is this picture of sometimes thousands of Iranians outside our embassy each day, obviously desperate to get to the United States!"

On October 22, my optimism began to waiver. Relaxing over a Sunday morning breakfast, I was called by the Marine on duty to come immediately to the chancery to read a secret NIACT message, the department's maximum designation of urgency. It told me the Shah was in the process of being admitted into the United States for urgent medical treatment and instructed me to so inform the prime minister and to seek the regime's understanding and its assurance of security for the embassy. The message was hardly a welcome one.

Twice during the preceding months I had been asked, in highly sensitive messages from Washington, to provide my judgment about the impact on the embassy's security were the Shah, then living in Mexico, to be admitted for medical treatment of what was described as a seriously deteriorating physical condition. On both occasions I had responded (in messages later seized and published by the student militants occupying our embassy) that I thought we should eventually provide him sanctuary but only when the Iranians had replaced the provisional government with a permanent structure and, more important, when we had formally signaled our acceptance of the Revolution by naming an ambassador. Failing that, I said, we risked the same kind of assault on our embassy as had occurred in February should the Shah be admitted. Neither of my stated preconditions was in place when I was instructed to inform the prime minister of the Shah's entry for "urgent humanitarian treatment" at a New York hospital.

Less than two weeks later the embassy would become a prison for those who served there. On November 1, three days before the seizure of the embassy, large and angry demonstrations swirled all day around the compound walls. But still larger crowds were diverted elsewhere, and good police protection limited the danger to shouts and graffiti. In a letter to my wife written that evening, I wrote of the "mounting irritation" over the admission of the Shah, adding: "We are going to have some heavy weather for a while. Pity, because up to now, we have been making some progress, however slowly, in gaining confidence here, in what is a real uphill struggle." This letter, on my desk and ready for mailing on November 4, instead became yet another of the hundreds of documents seized and published by those who took the embassy.

On November 1, in distant Algiers, Prime Minister Bazargan met with Zbigniew Brzezinski at the 25th anniversary celebrations of the Algerian revolution—a meeting I had actively encouraged to begin dialogue for the first time at that level. But in Tehran it was a red flag for the radical clerics behind the scenes and deepened their determination to act to undermine Bazargan's provisional government, which they sensed was allowing the Revolution to drift from its moorings back into a relationship with the Great Satan.

We had in effect become the victims of our own success. We had made enough progress in rebuilding a relationship with Iran as represented by the provisional government to force the hand of the radicals. Our admission of the Shah provided the issue on which they could act. Those in the small circle that took the action against our embassy did not really expect to force his return to Iran for trial. But they sensed, and they would be proven right, that it could be made an issue of sufficient emotional appeal to radicalize the Revolution's politics, discredit Bazargan and his more secular colleagues, and in time accomplish a second Iranian revolution. We had failed adequately to realize where the real power rested in Tehran. Bazargan's earlier assurance to me, however genuine, that his government "would do its best" to ensure the embassy's security with the Shah's admission, would prove useless, given the determination of the more radical elements of the Revolution to bring his government down.

2

The Embassy Is Taken

On Sunday morning, November 4, we were a reasonably confident group at the embassy's 9:00 A.M. staff meeting, having relaxed over a holiday weekend in the aftermath of the large demonstrations around the compound walls three days earlier. We noted that more demonstrations had been announced in the press for that day, but these were targeted at the university grounds some miles away to commemorate the martyrdom of students who had died a year earlier in demonstrations there as well as to mark the anniversary of Khomeini's forced exile to Turkey in 1964. We sensed no imminent danger to us, though we agreed to remain on alert, and I decided to keep a long-scheduled morning appointment at the Foreign Ministry with its director general for political affairs.

The American Embassy's Roosevelt Gate opens rather grandly through high wrought-iron portals directly into the intersection of two of Tehran's busiest thoroughfares. (Ironically, I had joined the rest of the diplomatic corps the previous evening at a command performance showing of a new documentary on the Revolution in February, with particularly graphic shots of violence on the streets outside that very gate.) No one seemed to take special notice of my limousine and its follow car, filled with mufti-clad Iranian police, as we ventured into the heavy traffic and occasional groups of demonstrators. With me were my deputy and political counselor, Victor Tomseth, and one of the embassy's two security officers, Michael Howland. Unlike other chiefs of mission in the city, I avoided flying the American flag from its fender standard, the Stars and Stripes likely to trigger more trouble for us than respect on Tehran's clogged and chaotic streets.

At the Foreign Ministry our conversation was amicable, over traditional glasses of Iranian tea, but would also prove ironic on two counts. I took the opportunity to convey Washington's appreciation for the good cooperation we had had from the police in dealing with the demonstrations three days earlier. But even more ironic, the subject of my conversation with the director general that morning was the diplomatic immunity status of our six-man Defense Liaison Office, a new element in the embassy staff, intended to replace the cast of hundreds who during the Shah's rule had implemented an enormous arms sales program and advised on its use. An hour later, that new group would be seized and held hostage, in total contempt of the very concept of diplomatic immunity.

Returning to my limousine in the courtyard below we found that Mike Howland had just received a radio call from his counterpart at the embassy, Alan Golacinski, telling him that there was trouble at the motor pool gate. Within seconds Alan was back on the radio telling us that "at least 500" demonstrators, apparently students, were pouring through the gates and over the walls and that we should return to the ministry to seek help rather than attempt to return. Racing back up the stairs into the ministry, Tomseth and I spent the next several hours pleading for security forces of whatever kind that could prevent a complete takeover of the compound or, failing that, remove the demonstrators, as had ultimately been done after the Valentine's Day seizure of the compound. This time, no such force was ever to come.

Theoretically, assistance should have been more available than in February, only three days following the ouster of the Shahpour Bakhtiar government, the last under the Shah. Now a government, admittedly still provisional, was in place. The Revolution was nine months old. But, in reality, the government had little authority over its divergent parts, and the security forces were preoccupied with other problems. The prospects for action were hardly furthered by the coincidence that on that day much of the government's leadership was unavailable. Prime Minister Bazargan, just back from attending the independence anniversary celebrations in Algiers, could not at first be reached; Foreign Minister Yazdi was variously reported still in Algiers, still airborne, or en route from the airport; the defense minister was in Kurdistan; and the chief of police was concentrating on the university demonstrations. Closeted with acting Foreign Minister Kamal Kharrazi (now Iran's ambassador at the UN), we listened with deepening worry and frustration to hurried phone calls supposedly soliciting help from the police and other security forces, reassured all the while by a nervous chief of protocol that of course help was on its way.

Meanwhile, our colleagues in the besieged chancery—in sporadic touch with us by radio and telephone—reported seeing among the milling mob below their windows only a few police at the motor pool gates, a lone Revolutionary Guard at one point, and allegedly a fire truck or two following reports of smoke from the other side of the barricaded entrance to the chancery's second floor. At one point we broached the idea that I would try to reach the compound to talk it out with the demonstrators, but poor communications left this idea stillborn—fortunately, perhaps, because in retrospect the result would have been my being held at the compound as well.

By this time my initial shock had turned into a deepening anger and an anguish over the safety of my staff, relieved only partially by the impressive calm and courage evident in the voices of Political Officer Ann Swift and others at the other end of our phone lines. Aware that hundreds of militants were in the compound, I declined to order the use of firearms by the Marine guards, authorizing only the use of tear gas and that only in *extremis*. The Marines were there, as in any embassy, not to fight "Custer's last stand" operations but to buy time while the Bazargan government came to our assistance pursuant to its obligations under international law. Some two and a half hours after that first call of alarm to us on the limousine radio, it became clear that there would be no help from the regime's security forces. The embassy clearly had no alternative but to surrender, especially when word reached us that Golacinski, Political Officer John Limbert, and one or more of the Marines had been taken captive outside the barricaded second floor and were being threatened with death if that door was not opened. It was midafternoon when I gave my concurrence; my last words to a staff I would not see again for 444 days were that in surrendering they "do it in style" and only when they themselves judged that to concede control was their only alternative.

As I did so, I looked in pained disbelief at my two colleagues, each of us aware that what we had feared most had now happened, with the three of us powerless to relieve the situation. But neither we nor probably any of our colleagues in the chancery thought then that the affair would be anything more than a symbolic occupation that would be terminated and somehow put right within a matter of hours, as had happened in February. That expectation, incidentally, contributed to regrettable delays in the destruction of classified documents—as did inadequate shredding facilities and excessive files—leading to their seizure and subsequent public release by the student militants, including many that were shredded but then laboriously pieced back together, strip by strip. For all of that I bear full responsibility.

Foreign Minister Yazdi—his exact location during much of this time still a mystery, possibly deliberately so—at last received us. My first words to him were a strong expression of protest at the seizure of my embassy and an urgent request for action to restore the status quo ante. His response, at no point including an expression of regret, was essentially, "I told you so." He had, he said, told me earlier there would be a strong emotional reaction from the public to the Shah's entry into the United States. I should calm down, my anxiety increasingly evident; action would be taken to deal with the situation. But his attitude and action throughout that long afternoon and evening belied his words. Unlike February, when he had himself gone to the compound to oversee its return to us and the placement of security forces to maintain the situation, this time his authority would prove irrelevant. Then, only recently arrived from Paris with the Ayatollah and named a deputy prime minister, he could act with confidence. Now, though foreign minister, he was keenly conscious of new and contending centers of power—above all that of the ascendant clerical forces. So his authority was limited, a fact that became increasingly apparent as the afternoon wore on into the evening. At several points I reminded him of the contrast between his action then and what I saw now, and I pleaded that he again go directly to the compound and use his influence to achieve a restoration of the situation. His answer was that in February there was immediate risk of violence; now there was none, and I should relax. The matter was "under control."

By midafternoon a Washington telephone connection reached me on one of a bank of telephone receivers on a small table next to the minister's desk, and from then on I maintained a determined sit-in at the minister's left hand. His own telephone rang frequently, including the red one I had earlier dubbed his "sacred line" (to Khomeini). This phone produced Dr. Yazdi's only positive statement, when he put down the receiver and said, "We will solve this tonight; I have just had some good news." What the news was he declined to say. Despite the lack of action or results, the minister maintained a facade of normalcy and a relaxed air of confidence that the matter would be resolved, "probably tonight but at the latest by tomorrow." Discussions to accomplish this, he assured me with some irritation, were under way, involving the government, the Revolutionary Council, and the Ayatollah himself. I need not worry about the safety of my colleagues; the embassy was not damaged, his contacts had reported; tear gas fumes were still strong, but no one had been hurt; those held would be released unharmed, and our embassy would be returned to us.

We had no lack of such assurances. I could so inform President Carter, who, as morning broke in Washington, was asking for information on the outlook. As for what the White House could say to the press, the Iranian government had assured us it would do its best to see that the matter was resolved in an early and satisfactory manner. The words "it would do its best" were a further indication of the limitations on the prime minister's authority that had so bedeviled him for months and that he would cite as the principal rationale for his resignation less than 48 hours later.

All the while, the foreign minister, noting his own state of exhaustion—he had had no sleep since his overnight arrival from Algiers that morning—kept reminding me that he would have to leave for "a meeting to deal with this situation." He asked, "Where do you and your colleagues propose to go?" That, I shot back, was for the minister to decide, in that his government had an obligation to provide for our security, which was clearly now at risk were we to venture into the streets. Reports were already reaching us that representatives of the "students" were at the ministry's guarded doors, asking about our whereabouts. To his credit that night Yazdi, although dismissing these reports as fabrications, put no pressure on us to leave the ministry, solicitous to see that we would be well cared for and responsive to our refusal to move from his immediate office until another direct telephone line with Washington was established in our overnight quarters. It was almost midnight when he escorted us personally to a room in the diplomatic reception area, where we expected to spend that one night but where instead we were to stay for all but the last three weeks of the crisis.

I was to talk only twice again with the minister—the first time early the following morning about a phone message to me from the department containing the text of a medical bulletin on the former Shah, and the second time that same evening, when he and his aides came to hear from me the text of another message delivered via the ministry's telex connections with Washington. That message was that Secretary of State Vance wanted the minister to know that I would be available to meet with the Ayatollah's son, Hojjatol-Islam Ahmed Khomeini, to facilitate communications looking toward the prompt release of our personnel and the restoration of the compound to our control. Meanwhile, however, that key figure had already gone to the embassy compound, where he was so swept up by popular enthusiasm that he lost his turban and a slipper in the crush and was lifted bodily over the embassy wall. There he pronounced: "This is not an occupation, in fact, we have thrown out the occupiers. . . . The entire nation supports this action." By the next morning, with the announcement of the Bazargan government's resignation, Dr. Yazdi was out of office.

Thus began our stay in the Foreign Ministry—a stay that none of the three of us conceived, even in our worst dreams as we tried to sleep that awful night, would continue for more than a year. Thus began as well a permanent stay within our embassy compound of those young Iranians who termed themselves "Students following the Line of the Imam." What they themselves contemplated that night about the duration of their stay in that compound must await the first of their memoirs. But evidence suggests that most of them envisaged only a temporary takeover along the lines of the February 14 seizure, designed to demonstrate their strong opposition to the Bazargan regime's dalliance with the United States.

Whatever their intention, within hours they had massive support from quarters that mattered—not simply the masses in the streets but very quickly key figures within the Revolutionary Council, a body that now began to move from its shadowy background role to one of full governmental authority. But that authority had perforce to be shared with the Ayatollah, of course, but in no small way with the "Students following the Imam's Line" as well. That this could be their role was quickly apparent to the "students," and certainly to their mentors, as they saw from the compound walls the intensity of mass support that swirled around them. Thus these "students" began what was to become for them a dramatic success story—the forcible use of American diplomats as pawns in a political process that would institutionalize clerical radicalism in the Iranian Revolution and exorcise the influence of that Great Satan, the United States.

At the outset we became a kind of mini-embassy within the Foreign Ministry, restricted to the two rooms of the diplomatic reception area but allowed telephone and telex contact with Washington and access to TV and shortwave radio. A ministry messenger would bring us printed copies of the telex messages, usually routine inquiries about our situation and our assessment of the prevailing mood. These messages amounted to formal instructions, as if we remained a functioning embassy of sorts, including a series of messages in which we were asked to seek assurances regarding the Clark-Miller mission; former Attorney General Ramsey Clark and former Foreign Service Officer William Miller (a friend of many in the revolutionary government since his days on assignment in Tehran and Isfahan) having been asked by President Carter within the first 24 hours of the crisis to go to Tehran in an effort to end the embassy seizure. That effort went nowhere. The assurances conveyed to us in the ministry about aircraft landing rights and meetings at senior levels of the Revolutionary Council were subsequently vetoed by Khomeini. Clark and Miller never got closer than Istanbul.

Our quasi-official status during those first days was reflected as well in my being allowed contact with other members of the diplomatic corps, both by telephone in a limited way at the outset and occasionally in person. A ministry messenger would inform us that at a certain time the ambassador from a given country would come to call, we would put on our best appearance, the ambassador would join us for tea, and our visitor would do his best to inform us of the mood of the city and what he knew of the scene at the embassy compound and listen patiently to our expressions of mixed confidence, frustration, and—most often—concern about the well-being of our colleagues. Those diplomatic callers included even the dean of the corps, the Czech ambassador. That gentleman—we would learn later from our friends promoting a unanimous appeal from the diplomatic corps to release the hostages in accordance with Iran's obligations under international law—was instead faithfully responding to Soviet pressure behind the scenes to ensure that no such appeal was possible.

Until the collapse of the Clark-Miller mission, the Foreign Ministry's readiness to deal with us more or less officially was also evident in our telephone contact with Iranian diplomats in the American affairs part of the ministry and even one visit to us in our quarters by acting Foreign Minister Kamal Kharrazi after the Bazargan government fell and before Bani-Sadr became minister for several weeks. During one visit about the Clark-Miller mission, I made this appeal, according to Victor Tomseth's notes:

> I implore you, with all the conviction I can command, let's take this first step. I came to Iran as a friend—as a friend of the people of Iran and as a friend of the Revolution. That is my government's policy. That has been the policy of the American people. Because whatever the past, it was clear to my people that this was a genuine, popular, mass revolution. My instructions from my government since I came here have been to seek to demonstrate that policy, by word and deed. We want to continue that effort. But neither I nor any other American can understand or appreciate what has now happened. It is totally unacceptable to the American people that their representatives should be taken prisoner and held captive and that their Embassy should be taken from them. . . . It is contrary to human decency and to the traditions of mercy and compassion which are *central to Islam.*

That demarche reflected my mood—a determination to preserve the respect that I felt was due to me, a conviction that justice was on our side, and a reluctance to believe that what had happened could not be undone. My optimism rested as well on my good fortune in companions. Vic was a Farsi language officer, deeply knowledgeable of Iran and its people after three years of duty in the embassy, as consul at Shiraz, and an earlier Peace Corps assignment in Nepal. A sensitive, soft-spoken man uncomfortable with chitchat, his keen analytic mind had produced some of the embassy's best reporting. Mike, by contrast, had been in Tehran only several months but had close Iranian friends who would secretly prove helpful to us later in the crisis. His own perception of the Iranian character came partly from having to deal directly, at all hours of the day and night, with the revolutionary hotheads who had occupied the embassy compound. Mike's professional focus on the problems of security and his macho image did not always hide a gentle and sensitive inner self, open to friendship, humorous, and quick with a smile.

Vic rarely displayed his emotions, except when he talked of his family, particularly his two children. Mike's emotions were closer to the surface, especially in flashes of temper in response to our guards. Vic could converse at length with the guards, who were also bored much of the time. Mike and Vic grew close during the long crisis. Both were respectful to me, even when they did not share my generally more optimistic views, and by good fortune, our personalities were remarkably compatible. When tensions arose or one of us was down in spirits, another almost instinctively moved to introduce some balance. For more than a year we were to live at closer quarters than most men ever do. The mutual respect and friendship that time cemented are still strong today.

When the crisis struck and in the days that followed, we found ourselves in effect picking up our professional purposes, even in these different circumstances. Both Vic and Mike saw me as still in charge, Vic became the principal drafter of telexes and other messages, and Mike was constantly alert to our new security situation and to the possibility of escape. His disdain for the competence of our guards and the soldiers in the courtyard below our third-floor rooms was only barely concealed. The three of us went about our business in a way that said to our guards the crisis would work out to our advantage and that our confidence was undiminished.

Yet each of us was well aware of cold reality. I faced a failed mission, often sick at heart knowing that my chancery and residence had become the prison of my entire staff, the seat of much of revolutionary power in Iran, and a crisis of large and apparently growing dimensions at home. As news reached us of the president's reactions and the international impact of the issue, we sensed we had become bit players in a drama far larger than even the painful one of Iranian TV pictures (in the adjacent guards' room) of immense, shouting crowds swirling around the walls of the embassy compound and our colleagues bound hand and foot, denied the right to speak, and often blindfolded. With those at the other end of the telex and telephone links to Washington, we were determined not to come across as pessimists, but our optimism struggled with a roller coaster of emotions, especially in the first weeks of uncertainty, occasional fear, frequent anger, and ongoing frustration.

And the "what ifs." What if the Shah had not been admitted? What if we had pressed the department to close the embassy at that time? What if we had been at the embassy when the attack began? Would that have made any difference? What if I had ordered the Marines to fire against the first "students" penetrating the compound?

For me there was special irony. In these same rooms 26 years before—now more elegant as a result of the Pahlavi dynasty's imperial pretensions—younger and wide-eyed with enthusiasm, I was among hundreds of guests at a glittering reception in honor of visiting Vice President Richard Nixon and his wife, Pat. Part of that evening's entertainment included a magnificent display of fireworks in the ministry's garden. This time we would also see fireworks, but on this occasion they celebrated the first anniversary of the *overthrow* of the Pahlavi regime.

3

November 1979: Involuntary Guests

DAY 5, *November 8, 1979*—Late afternoon of a fine fall day in Tehran. . . .
We are three involuntary guests of the Foreign Ministry for the past four days,
quartered in the aging splendor of the Foreign Ministry's diplomatic reception
area. Well-proportioned rooms, magnificent Czech chandeliers, fine—if a bit
worn—Persian carpets on creaky floors. Easy chairs slipcovered in a dusty
beige. Occasionally a Foreign Ministry servant comes in to serve tea, or perhaps to sit and watch the TV himself.

The three of us pass the time by reading newspapers and a few magazines
provided by the staff. We find time—and the need—to wash out socks and
underwear, drying them from the chandeliers. We are caught with only the
clothes we wear, except for a change of socks and underwear provided by a
sympathetic soul in the Protocol Office. For the past two days, our phones have
been cut, so we neither call in nor call out—depriving us of, among other
things, any link with Washington. Our only outside contact is via the telex of
the Foreign Office, which occasionally allows us to exchange routine messages
with the State Department.

When the news comes on the TV and radio, we are treated to long recitations
of our sins by the students who now hold our embassy, plus readings of messages of support for the students from countless groups all around the country.

One marvels at the number of detractors we have, but, even more, one worries about the manner in which all of this is spreading and deepening the public's hostility toward us.

Why? To what end? What purpose is served? We have tried by every available means over the past months to demonstrate, by word and deed, that we accept the Iranian Revolution, indeed, that we wish it well—that a society strongly motivated by religion is a society we, as a religious nation, can identify with. Far from wishing to see this nation, this government, stumble, we wish it well and hope it can strengthen Iran's integrity and independence. . . .

———

Dear Jim [13-year-old son, the only son still living at home],

I love you, and I don't want you to worry about me. I'll be all right, thanks to the support I know I've got from you and Mom and Bill and Chip. . . .

I look forward to telling you all about this escapade we're in—hopefully that won't be too long from now. I'm praying that all is well with you and Mom. You really have to be the man of the house now, until I get back. That means carrying in wood for the fireplace once in a while. Don't forget to open the draft inside the chimney before you use it. And close it when you're *not* using it, because you lose heat up the chimney when it's not in use.

Better have someone check the antifreeze in the car sometime, to be sure it's good enough for winter. And Mom should be sure to turn off the outside house faucet (from inside) before it freezes. . . .

I'm tired of my clothes. Been wearing them for days now. Oh, we do wash out our socks and underwear, and someone very kindly gave us an extra set of underwear and socks each. But I'm sure tired of my suit, shirt, and tie! No shower either, so we take kitty baths, in cold water.

But don't worry, all will be well. This adventure will be worth several chapters in my memoirs! Think what I can tell my grandchildren! Join the Foreign Service and see the world!

Love to you all, Dad

DAY 6, *November 9, 1979*

Dear Bill [20-year-old son, second-year midshipman, U.S. Naval Academy],

Mom told me over the phone today that you were going to be home for the weekend. That was good news because your being there at this time helps both me and Mom. Our talk was brief—someone stood beside me to put the phone down as soon as I had spoken for two minutes. And I fear I sounded emotional, which I *was* in talking to Mom because of my concern for her. But I have *no* trouble in standing up to this, however sad it is and however reprehensible it is what happened to all those now hostage at the embassy compound. It will haunt me all the rest of my life.

But I will try not to focus on that in this brief letter. I will wait to see you—hopefully soon—to fill you and the family in on all the pain that this has meant to so many people, for which I must take ultimate responsibility.

Tonight was to have been the Marine Ball at the residence! What an ironic turn of events for those wonderful men I respect so much. To me they are like sons, each and every one of them. . . .

Men are wiser with experience, Bill, and this will certainly be true for all of us here. I fear we have judged poorly what we do not know well. Mom has been a better judge than I, if I am to conclude from her letters. I am an optimist, who has tried to focus on what is best in human behavior, however much it may be obscured from time to time. I stilll think that is the best approach in life—to do otherwise, in any event, would be hard for me. It would make life too dreary and hopeless. I will go on looking at the bright side, and that's what I'm doing now. . . .

All this will end. Or, as they say, this, too, will pass. I remain a total optimist about our people over there, providing we keep our heads about us, here and especially in Washington. I'm proud, so far, of the restraint our people and government are showing. It is vital that this continue, if things are to be kept from worsening. . . .

Dad

DAY 7, *November 10, 1979*—It is morning of the seventh day, and still no progress on any front—except perhaps in a chance for a group of four ambassadors to visit the compound to see the condition of the hostages. We are visited routinely by Protocol Department officers, and one of them is assigned to spend the night with us. . . . We have little to complain about, compared to the crowded and difficult and psychologically depressing situation that must be the hourly fare of my 66 colleagues over at the compound. . . . We feel compelled and obliged to watch the TV news, even though the constant barrage of anti-American propaganda becomes hard to take after a while. What is it doing to public opinion out there? What's behind it? What is its purpose? Clearly it is the product of something more by now than an "unanticipated" attack by a crowd of students. Others have clearly seized upon it and are carrying this to ends not then planned or seen. Or is our assessment of this place again flawed, as it has been so often in the past?

We speculate among ourselves what will come of this when it's over. What does it mean for a future relationship? Is any such possible? Why have our efforts over the past five months to show that we *accept* the Revolution gone so unnoticed among the public and those who make decisions here? Why does that provide no cushion now?

The radio notes that the UN Security Council has adopted a "strongly worded resolution" appealing for the urgent release of the hostages. The Pope supposedly sent a personal envoy to see the ARK [Ayatollah Ruhollah Khomeini]. The PLO is involved somehow; the president's mission (Clark and Miller) wait in Istanbul. I feel totally irrelevant, in protective custody without outside contact. Meanwhile, hostility and bitterness reportedly grow in the United States, which could further aggravate the atmosphere in which room for reason and discussion must be found. . . .

Washington sends us copies of texts of yesterday's statements by the White House and by the family members of hostages who met with him yesterday. They are magnificent expressions of support, appealing for restraint at a time of national crisis, urging the American people to find strength in uniting and in the power of prayer. We are buoyed in spirit and proud—one message notes that Penne helped draft the one from the families. I'm doubly proud.

DAY 8, *November 11, 1979*—A week today, and no movement, only a digging in of position here and the danger of a poisoning of the public atmosphere in the U.S. Some way *must* be found to make contact possible. And that is possible if one man will permit it. . . .

It is a beautiful fall day outside—but when did I last spend a full week indoors with no exposure to the outside air? In a way I marvel that the time has passed as fast as it has. But we are bored, not so much with each other as with the limited variety in what we do. Last night we watched footage on TV showing four ambassadors, accepted by the occupiers of the compound, walking through the rooms where the hostages are held. The place appeared to be embassy prefabs. The ambassadors were those of Sweden, France, Syria, and Algeria. The Swede acted as spokesman, but what he said was not carried on TV. They reportedly said they found no evidence of harassment or illness (except colds), but that the hostages were tired. No pictures of women. We recognized about ten, and all looked reasonably well, if determinedly unsmiling. Who can blame them!

DAY 9, *November 12, 1979*—It is late in the day of yet another day—without progress—but a day that saw some hope back in our lives simply because we have suddenly again been given access to the telephone—for a telecon with the Department of State's Iran Task Force and, through them, a patch call to each of our families. What a boost it was to talk to Penne. . . . I fear my voice breaks on occasion, from the sheer joy of talking to family again after these days of isolation and of wondering how family is taking the total lack of progress, so far as we can see. I suspect Penne and Jim and Bill and Chip are taking this well. They are strong and close-knit, and that's what matters at times like this. I find myself discouraged but not without hope. I am too much of an optimist for that. Late today the papal nuncio came by. He is acting as the Pope's special representative and has seen the Imam. He also saw our hostages yesterday and gave us a firsthand report in his limited English. He is a gentle man who is also an optimist, a man who professes to see in the occupiers of the compound youthful idealism sufficient to bring this yet to a peaceful solution. I hope he's right.

At midmorning the diplomatic corps was invited to the ministry to meet the acting foreign minister, Mr. Bani-Sadr, and to hear a statement from him on the crisis. Since we live in the diplomatic reception rooms, we had to be spirited out to the main dining room, where the three of us spent a couple of hours seated at the end of a dining table that seats 40—one playing solitaire, one reading, and the third pacing around and around the vast room trying to keep his sanity and gaining a little exercise at the same time. I have not had substantive contact with anyone in the ministry since November 8. Not clear whether this is deliberate. One assumes it must be, even though I remain the president's representative in this country, technically, at least.

DAY 11, *November 14, 1979*
Dear Penne [wife of 22 years; at home],

Today, as yesterday, we are moved for a couple of hours to the state dining room, a room perhaps 40 by 60 feet, so that we will be out of sight during a press conference by the PM. . . . We are like fugitives, a feeling I never thought I would have in the diplomatic service! . . .

I send you, Penne and the boys, my warmest love. I miss you all terribly, but I am confident that all will be well, however long this takes. Be patient, be forgiving, we must be—however upside down this whole thing seems now. . . .

Bruce

DAY 13, *November 16, 1979*—We are outraged, angry, frustrated, and bored, in roughly that order. The hardest part is living here day after day with a feeling of irrelevance, of being involved and responsible and yet having virtually no way of affecting or influencing events. To the extent we can, we channel ideas and reactions to Washington via the telex, but we cannot speak of sensitive subjects on this open channel. Since our immediate concern is the safety and welfare of the hostages, we also do what we can to contribute to some improvement in their conditions, by talking with Protocol and ambassadors allowed to see us.

We have access to Iranian radio and television, and since one of my colleagues here with me speaks Farsi, we have continuing access to developments locally. The tenor of these broadcasts continues to be bitterly and endlessly anti-American, tragic in terms of the bitterness and hatred that is being impressed on local public opinion. Our telephones to the outside have been cut, apparently as a result of some understanding with the occupiers of the embassy, since 10 days ago. But once a day, or occasionally every other day, a call from Washington is allowed. That helps. . . .

We admire and applaud the restraint and dignity and support shown by the American people so far, in the face of this outrageous situation. Pray God this will continue. No one stands to suffer more from all this than Iran and the Iranian people; I marvel that no one in the leadership here seems to appreciate this.

We term ourselves prisoners in a gilded cage. Prisoners in the sense that we do not have freedom to move out of these rooms; a gilded cage in the sense that, like beautiful canaries, we are well treated and suffer no physical discomfort. Our "cage" is the central salon of the diplomatic reception rooms, a room perhaps 40 by 70 feet, handsomely proportioned and decorated in a French style. Large windows, curtained in damask, look out toward the Elburz mountain range (rarely visible, however, because of the smog of this city). Off to the side of this central salon is an equally long but narrow dining room, where we sleep on sofas that improvise as beds. They are tolerably comfortable. Large windows in this much narrower room flood the place with sunlight and make it our favorite place; afternoons and evenings in the vast salon are frankly gloomy. Down the center of this dining room runs a long dining table and on it, upside down, are extensions to the table, their Duncan Phyfe legs offering useful places to hang and dry our laundry. We spend part of the day usually sitting in the windows to get some sun—happily the weather is consistently sunny—rain and clouds would deepen the gloom.

We are unhappy about our relative comfort in the sense that we know our colleagues in the compound are infinitely less well-off. We understand their hands are still bound, the windows in their rooms are curtained or papered over to ensure they do not see out, and they are not—according to several reports— allowed to speak to each other. We do not know (but doubt) whether they have access to newspapers, although they apparently do have books. One recent report would suggest they are given fresh air five to ten minutes daily, but we are not sure of this. Daily, according to TV reports, there are massive demonstrations on the streets outside the compound, with noisy chants denouncing Carter, the United States, and the embassy—the last as a den of spies and espionage. The hostages, who can hear this shouting, must be subject to very severe mental and psychological strain and stress. It is almost unbelievable that all this should be happening. It is wrong on every possible count—morally, politically, psychologically. It is contrary to all standards of human decency; it is unprecedented in all annals of diplomatic history. It is incredible, but it is true.

Somewhere there must be a strain of decency, or realism, that must be found and brought to bear. We know where it must begin, Iran being what it is today, but that beginning is not yet—even 13 days after. I am sick at heart, but I remain an optimist, too, confident that human decency will ultimately prevail. Then we will have a long, long time in which to reflect on this tragedy and gradually, perhaps, to rebuild on a stronger basis. . . .

DAY 14, *November 17, 1979*
Dear Penne,

Your letter of November 12—got it last night. And Jim's!! Many thanks, big son.

What magnificent letters! I've read them three times, and I feel better every time I read them. What magnificent support from so many wonderful people! It is almost incredible, and yet it isn't, because there is every reason that so many good people would react that way to what is so wrong, so wrong from every conceivable point of view.

Someday I look forward to thanking all of them personally. For now, to the extent you can, please thank them all and send them my warmest regards. It's all been worth it, this Foreign Service experience, when the response is like that at a time of difficulty.

Bill, Chip, Jim [Chip, or Charles, 18-year-old freshman at the University of Minnesota in NROTC (Naval Reserve Officers' Training Corps)]—what great sons they are, each of them. They and you, more than anything else, give me the confidence and optimism that I need here. . . . I wrote Chip a letter the other day and slipped it unobtrusively to a visiting ambassador, which is what I hope to do with this one. Not quite sure yet, however, when I can do so. I hope Chip, in particular, since I'm sure he has some contact with Iranian students there, will keep an open and mature mind about them.

The *Herald Tribune* that we saw last night carried an editorial on the Iranian student issue from the *Washington Post*, clearly written in Meg Greenfield's style. She is reminding us to keep our heads, to keep our perspective, and that matters so *much* as we deal with this problem. We have *got* to show that we are mature enough to keep our heads and our cool, despite the understandable anger and frustration that we all feel. That is why the statement that you families made after the meeting with the president was so good. . . .

Two weeks after the embassy's seizure, and reportedly as a result of Yassir Arafat's intervention, Khomeini announced that the women and blacks among the hostages would be released as a gesture of support for the black minority and American women "suffering the oppression of American society." That magnanimity fell short; three of them were not released: First Secretary Ann Swift in the Political Section, Director Kate Koob of the Iran/America Society, and Charlie Jones, a communicator.

Quoting from a message sent by me via the Foreign Ministry telex, Secretary of State Vance issued the following statement on November 21:

On the eve of the return to America of the first group of released hostages, I would like to share with all Americans a message to us from Bruce Laingen, our Chargé d'Affaires in Tehran:

> "In our prayers of thanks for the safe return of the first of the hostages, of hope for the early release of those who remain, and for strength in standing firm for what we believe is right, let us also pray that a process can begin that will ultimately permit the restoration of the traditional friendship between the American and the Iranian peoples. Let us ask God's guidance that the two countries, in all they do and say, will act on that basis and from a posture of humanity and restraint, so that both our peoples and governments can again look to a future of restored understanding and cooperation.
>
> "Let the nation's church bells ring with that message and that hope."

The families of the hostages are requesting that this message be read across the nation; that wherever possible church bells, town sirens, college bells or carillons toll out every day from 12:00 noon to 12:15 until the hostages are released. The events of the past few weeks have been dark days for America, for the Foreign Service, and for the Marine Corps, but we are hoping for a ground swell reaction from the people of the United States which will prove to the Iranians that we are united, strong, and resolute in our beliefs of what is right.

This appeal from Secretary Vance and the hostages' families to show national resolve with symbols drew from the American people a remarkable response that would grow and prevail throughout the crisis. That ground swell in time would also involve what became the most ubiquitous of symbols, the yellow ribbon. The hostages' awareness of that symbol would be apparent on the tarmac in Algiers when two freed women hostages, proudly wearing yellow ribbons in their hair, would lead their colleagues down the ramp of the aircraft.

DAY 15, *November 18, 1979*—We are much buoyed in spirit today by news that the women and blacks are to be released, two weeks to the day since that fateful morning. . . . What a blessing it will be that the women will be free from their nightmare! And the blacks—I know them all personally, and they are all fine representatives of our country. "Forced to come to Iran," nonsense! They were all volunteers, and in any event doing a first-class job here. I'm proud of every one of them. One is an air force captain, graduate of the Air Force Academy. I wish Bill could meet him—he's a great person. . . . Still not clear what the arrangements will be to move this group out—we count seven women and ten blacks. Hopefully today. Thank God. Prayer works—it *must.* . . .

DAY 17, *November 20, 1979*
Dear Penne,
  On my desk in the office, now occupied by wild-eyed extremists who pretend to be students, lies a letter to you. There were other letters there as well, that I had written over a three-day weekend. Alas, I assume I will never see those letters, nor will you, the occupiers probably having seized them to add to their outrageous allegations that the embassy was a "center of espionage and a nest of spies.". . .

In time I did again see this particular letter. It would eventually appear, complete with Farsi translation, in one of the 50-plus volumes of captured embassy documents published by the students, many laboriously pieced back together, strip by shredded strip. In my letter I described popular reaction to the admission of the Shah to the United States for medical treatment: "There is mounting irritation over this, and we are in for some trouble if the Shah stays for further treatment on an outpatient basis . . . where this will end is unclear at the moment but we are going to have some heavy weather for a while I fear. . . ."
  At the end of that typed letter was my handwritten postscript: "We called on a leading Mullah at the Senate building last week—an interesting conversation with a man apparently prepared to listen. . . . But perhaps the most interesting part

of the call involved the 12–14-year-old girl who saw our black Chrysler limousine waiting outside and who asked of my security officer: 'Whose car is this?' When told that it was that of the American chargé, she said, 'But I thought all of the Americans had left—we're going to chase them out!' "

DAY 20, *November 23, 1979*

Dear Penne,

This is a quiet morning—Ministry is closed for Friday; we are listening to Friday prayer sermons (by radio) at University in the hope that just perhaps they will reflect some beginning of effort at moderation, at calming the public fervor here. We have not seen it yet. It could, if someone would only wish it. . . .

Henry [Precht, country director for Iran in the Department of State] told me on the phone last night that Liz [my secretary] had sent a message saying that she and the other hostages kept in the residence have "used every stitch of clothes" from my closets and drawers. I sent back word that I couldn't imagine any group of people I'd rather have wear my clothes! Hope they also enjoyed the chocolates in my room that had come via Henry and which I hadn't eaten.

One wonders what we will ever see of *any* of our personal things again—we assume none. One of the things that periodically haunts me is Andy Sens's dog, Tom, which he brought with him from Oslo and which is the most totally loyal dog I've ever seen. Even when Andy was there, Tom would roam the compound looking sad-eyed and deserted. Or he would sneak into the embassy and lie in his office, or, if he couldn't get in, he would lie outside a chancery door, watching everyone come and go. Now, assuming he's still alive, he must be desperate in his daily search for his missing master. We had a cat at the residence—wonder who's feeding him.

We sit back and marvel once in a while about this entire drama—so bizarre in some respects as to make a plot along these lines almost unbelievable for a novel or a movie plot. But, in other respects perhaps, a marvelous plot for just that kind of thing. A whole embassy stolen, its entire staff held hostage, "students" occupying the place and issuing daily press bulletins, outside the walls daily processions in the tens and hundreds of thousands, a government falls, daily pronouncements come from distant quarters. The press, radio, and TV mount thunderous attacks against the U.S. and us here, the government in Washington at the highest level gets into the act, our local employees here appeal to us for their pay(!), many Iranians upset by lack of access to our visas—it goes on and on. And last night, a Republican congressman from Idaho [George Hansen] becomes yet another character in the cast—the first congressman *ever* to come here since the February Revolution. Unannounced, he descends on the scene to try to facilitate dialogue, even walking into our quarters here late last night with an entourage of two journalists, an MFA [Ministry of Foreign Affairs] escort, and two security types. They arrive totally unannounced and their number makes us wonder, as we hear their footsteps on the stairs, whether we are being picked up and taken else-where. The congressman in haste announces he is allowed "only five min-utes" with me, whereupon he is off, hopefully to see the remaining hostages. I say, God bless you. You're the only game in town at the moment, and I wish you luck. . . .

                              Much love, Me

DAY 23, *November 26, 1979*

Dear P,

Hope to send this out via a visiting ambassador. . . . No change here—but UNSC is meeting today and that may open things up.

Good ambassadorial friends help by occasional visits. They bring books, a sweater, after-shave lotion, even fruit and food that help break the monotony. But the daily routine is dull and weighs heavily some days—compounded by the frustration of sitting here and feeling so irrelevant. But we try, in every small way we can, to get views across here—including letter writing to local leaders, which I tried today, uncertain that they'll ever reach the address-ees. . . .

The atmosphere of venom, officially promoted, is something I have never ever experienced—and I hope I never will again.

                              Love, Love, Love, B

DAY 24, *November 27, 1979*

Dear Bill,

I'd like to believe that by the time you get this (by whatever mail carrier I can locate surreptitiously), it will be overtaken by events—that is, that I and all my colleagues will be home. But I have no assurance of that and indeed nothing to go on at the moment but hope—and confidence. I've got lots of that, even on the worst days.

I'm learning a good deal of how precious one's freedom is. We are treated well and not suffering, except psychologically, but we do feel, painfully, the denial of freedom. We recall what a painful experience that must have been for the POWs [prisoners of war] in Vietnam. . . . I have resolved to myself that when this is all over, I intend to insist with the Foreign Service Institute that I be asked to speak to every new Foreign Service officer class. I have learned a lot from this tragedy—much that I had not sufficiently focused on before. It is the one good thing in this terrible mess that I *have* gained, and I want to impress these things on the minds of new officers from the very first months of their careers. Perhaps our country—and government—as a whole has learned something. I think we have. But so often we forget, and go back to our old routines. Like oil. There is one thing that should redound to our benefit as a people—getting along without the 4 percent of our needs that Iranian oil represented before. If we can do that, as individuals and as a people, then we have gained much. We *must* find a way to reduce our dependence (for oil) on uncertain and unstable regimes such as this one.

Well, there will be a lot to talk about when we see each other again. I hope that's soon. . . . I know you're behind me and that's all that matters.

Warm regards, Dad

DAY 25, *November 28, 1979*

Dear Penne,

You won't get this by your birthday, but I want you to know I'll be thinking of you on that day. I had plans to send you something I'd seen advertised in a magazine—all that is now lying on my desk in the residence and is past history.

Don't have much to tell you—life goes on, day after day. There are times when we get pretty depressed, but not for long. A visiting ambassador comes by, and that helps. Especially a jolly one like the Dutch yesterday, who brought us Droste-Haarlem chocolate. Wow, did that relieve the monotony of our food!

I reflect occasionally where this affair will take me—us—when it's all over. Do I retire? Will I have much alternative? Or do I spin it out a while in some corner of the department? If I retire, what then? Live off the royalties of the book you'll write? Maybe I should write a book about my experiences here! Certainly I want to talk to every new FSO over the next few years; I've learned a lot from this tragedy. Wish I could relive the past six months. . . .

Perhaps I'll be home before you get this, but there will be much we need to talk about. I have no idea what this affair will mean in terms of another assignment, at home or abroad. Someone will have to bear responsibility, and I'm quite prepared to take a lot of it. . . . And what if I had accepted assignment as ambassador here when it was first suggested by telephone in early August? I wonder whether that would have changed anything. I probably would long since have seen the ARK, which might have helped. I probably wouldn't have been in the ministry that fateful morning; I'd have sent my DCM [deputy chief of mission], in which case I'd have been a hostage over there. Who can say, but isn't it interesting the way Iran has so massively affected our lives—both in 1953–55, as a result of which you and I met, and now this!

I'm so proud of the way you are working back there, with the department and other families. Know the boys are proud of you, too. We are a stronger family because of this, so thank God for small favors.

Love, B

DAY 26, *November 29, 1979*

Dear Jim,

. . . I hope, Jim, that you're as proud as I am of the dignified way that our country is standing up to the crisis here. A powerful country, as ours is, doesn't need to throw its weight around. We can afford to be restrained. There is dignity and decency in restraint—and our country will come out of this a strong and better and more respected country because we are seeking a solution of this problem through peaceful means. We will be stronger, too, because of what we have learned. And *we'll* succeed, because *right* is on our side.

Warm regards to you and Duchess [the family dog] and Mom, Dad

DAY 26, *November 29, 1979*—The 26th day, dark and gloomy and rainy. Appropriate for the season, this being Tasua and tomorrow is Ashura, the most important days of the first ten days of the mourning month of Muharram. You know what it's like—much wearing of black and much beating of breasts and much wailing and gloom. So happily it's raining; we rather welcome it, even if it brings gloom into these cold rooms, too. There is no heat, the central heating system having apparently not worked since before the Revolution. We have a portable electric heater that we carry around with us, but generally we stay in the narrow dining room, where sun normally helps warm and cheer us on better days. The stairs are now closed to us, except when we ask to be allowed to use the stairs for exercise.

I am in not much mood for anything today. The oppression caused by awareness that our friends are now in their fourth week of mistreatment gets a bit heavy at times. . . . The two o'clock radio news (Farsi) is on, and what with all the fervent denunciation of U.S. imperialism, it manages to go on for more than an hour! One of our less attractive times of the day. Our Farsi speaker listens and gives us the gist; the rest of us have to listen to the seemingly endless references to "American imperialism" in news read out in turn by a woman and a man newscaster. Then there is blissful silence until the 8:30 P.M. TV news, when the entire business is run through again, this time with pictures.

We try to keep our sense of humor about the whole business, but there are times when our wisecracks fall flat. Part of the news today included the reading of some telegrams from our files as stolen by the occupiers of the compound. These cables concerned visa cases where we supposedly issued visas to corrupt types of one sort or another, one cable signed by some fellow named "Lain-gin" and the other by a "Cirus Vance." All of which is appalling and aggravating, but we take it reasonably well. Vast processions are promised for tomorrow (we hope it rains generously), most of which are conveniently to pass by the embassy. There will be much praying and we hope some sense of love is imparted to them in response, but one would doubt that, however much one hopes it. . . .

There is a new foreign minister, Sadegh Ghotbzadeh, announced at midnight last night. His predecessor, Bani-Sadr, lasted less than three weeks. We wonder what it might mean and rather shy away from speculation because we really haven't a clue, or is it because we are reluctant to face up to reality? Where does all this end? How do we pick up the pieces again? And when? Where does emotion—however understandable it might be from a certain perspective—end and where does some rationality begin, at least on the part of leadership? What is the point, when there is so much else to be done? The answer, obviously, lies in a conviction, based on stubborn conviction many times over, that the past was wrong and someone must pay for it, and Western rationality in this case doesn't apply. It's all there, and the picture can be drawn, but surely there must be an end to it, too, because there are others of a lesser age who perhaps see this country's future in slightly different dimensions and possibilities. But I fear that still more time has to pass and more psychological hurt suffered on the part of our captive compatriots, and that is hard to take.

DAY 27, *November 30, 1979*—It is Friday, the tenth day of Muharram—Ashura, the commemoration of the martyrdom of Imam Hussein. The ministry is as quiet as a tomb, perhaps symbolic for this day of mourning in the Shia religious calendar. But the day dawns clear and beautiful, after rain and cold and gloom the preceding day, which was Tasua, the day commemorating Hussein's march, with his band of only 72 followers, out onto the scorching plains of Karbala, there to meet the vastly larger forces of Yezid, king of Damascus, and there to meet also his inevitable martyrdom, together with all his cohorts.

Still early in the day, and the air washed clean by rain, the city's pollution has yet to rise, as it inevitably will, from the urban conglomerate that is Tehran, to obscure the massive range of the Elburz Mountains. From our third-floor windows, these magnificent mountains stand out clear and cold above the city, covered almost to their foothills with a blanket of snow for the first time this season.

At this early hour the streets below our windows, normally a chaos of noise and movement, are quiet, the only movement an occasional lonely figure returning from the bakery with sheaves of Iran's flat, unleavened bread, *nan*, the staple food for everyone's breakfast, supplemented by tea and cheese and sometimes jam. The only other movement that we can see is a "jube" dog (so named for the open causeway or gutters that line every Tehran street) barking aimlessly as her brood of pups scamper in and out of the jubes. We wonder how long she can possibly keep them alive during the weekday traffic.

Suddenly there is the sound of a helicopter approaching, the sound increasing, indicating an intention to land on the helicopter pad in the ministry's garden, which is visible from the windows on the other side of the diplomatic reception area in which we spend our time. It is soon apparent that the helicopter is back from an overnight trip to Qom, where the foreign minister—appointed only the night before—and probably other ministers have gone to seek the Ayatollah's guidance on the crisis at the embassy compound. The minister does not enter the deserted ministry, walking directly instead to his waiting Mercedes and speeding off, followed by that Tehran classic—the follow car.

He is in a hurry, probably, because the minister, too, this morning must prepare for his weekly obligation—especially on Ashura—to attend Friday prayers at the university, seated cross-legged on carpets in the first row along with other ministers, leading clerics, and possibly a visiting revolutionary figure from abroad.

In our rooms, our ever-present security officers are clearly more nervous today than usual because of the crowds expected in the streets. They check the locks and chains that restrict us to the rooms we occupy and urge that we not make ourselves visible from the windows; we are told to take our laundry out of the windows and hang it elsewhere. We can see enough from the windows to sense the gradual increase of tempo on the streets below, as one or two, then small knots of people, and then large groups of demonstrators move steadily in the direction of the city's center and on to the university grounds.

The people are mostly family groups—the father in working dress, the mother hurrying along, always a few steps behind, wrapped in a black chador and fussing with a baby in arms or one slightly older pushed along in a stroller; often a young boy energetically skips along in front of his father, sometimes followed by a ten- or twelve-year-old sister already skilled in wearing a chador or at least a shawl around her head. Everyone hurries, the more fortunate (until the traffic clogs, as it inevitably must) in cars and small vans and trucks, all in one direction. Small pickup trucks, open at the rear, speed by, packed with women clinging to each other and to the trucks, their black chadors streaming out behind them like a pack of blackbirds in flight.

Occasionally a large and obviously organized group moves past—boys with placards proclaiming revolutionary or anti-American slogans, others with framed photos or paintings of Khomeini or allegorical representations of the tragedy at Karbala, still others carrying fringed velvet and towering circular standards, obviously brought out from places of honor in neighborhood mosques for these annual processions. Fortunately for the marchers, the weather is good, if crisp, and the atmosphere as the crowds move to their gathering points is eager and festive.

Restricted to our quarters in the ministry, we cannot follow the crowds beyond sight of our windows. But within an hour our transistor radio brings us the high-pitched voice of the Friday (*Jomeh*) preacher, the Ayatollah Montazeri, lecturing, cajoling, beseeching the crowds that by now jam every square foot of the university grounds and spread out on adjoining streets in all directions. The radio speaks of a million, possibly two, citizens of Tehran listening, remarkably attentive and orderly. The women are carefully segregated, the children surely restless, yet there is little evidence of this to our ears. The preacher, bearded and turbaned, stands with a bayonet and rifle in one hand, gesticulating with the other, without notes. His rostrum is a stage erected at one end of the main plaza of the university grounds. White cloth banners, emblazoned with black revolutionary and religious slogans, completely cover the outlines of this elevated stand. The backdrop is a vast drawing on cloth of the face of the Ayatollah Khomeini, gazing unsmiling and stern at the crowds below. At the very mention of the name Khomeini, the vast throng erupts in sound with thundering repeats of his name and then subsides into respectful and quiet attention.

Then the main sermon ends, followed today by a short but impassioned and revolutionary call for support from the same rostrum by a representative of the students occupying the embassy compound. He invites the throng to march to the embassy for a further rally when the prayer service ends. Occasionally he is interrupted by shouts of "Carter is vanquished—Khomeini is victorious" or other slogans of anti-American fervor. Then the prayers begin, the preacher switching now to Arabic while a separate prayer leader of rich and commanding voice intones the instructions "Sujoud" (kneel) and "Allah O'Akbar" (God is great), the latter taken up by the crowd with particular enthusiasm and unison.

Reminded thus of the emotional appeal of Islam and the capacity of the regime to bring its supporters onto the streets, we spend a long and quiet afternoon, after mechanically eating yet another lunch of thick cabbage soup, chicken kabob, and rice. We find little to say to each other at most such meals, having now enjoyed our meals together and alone for three long weeks.

At night we see and experience it all again, this time in extensive coverage on the evening TV news, the crowds impressive in their size and order at prayers, those in the plaza below the Jomeh preacher in row after endless row of men and boys, seated on their haunches, standing and then kneeling in unison to touch their foreheads on the ground in front of them. Later we see coverage of these same crowds, now whipped into almost mass hysteria, passing in the street before our embassy and raising their fists in angry unison to emphasize their unity against American imperialism and support of Khomeini and the Revolution.

All of this climaxes with a mass response to a call from Khomeini to go to the rooftops of the city and shout "Allah O'Akbar" for 15 minutes. We hear the frenzied calls in all directions from our windows but especially from the teeming southern quarters of the city. "Allah O'Akbar!"

Through it all we are reminded of our colleagues inside the embassy compound, now almost four weeks in confinement, often bound and sometimes blindfolded and threatened, without knowledge of any kind of what their government may be doing to try to relieve them of their agony. Daily they are beset by the rolling, pressing sound of thousands of voices from the streets around them, calling for death to America, Carter, and imperialism. We are sick at heart, always fearful that mass hysteria of this kind could erupt into violence that endangers the lives of our colleagues. We are saddened and depressed by this deliberate fostering of hate and venom and bitterness. We dread the thought of trying to sleep—sleep is almost impossible to achieve because of the pain and worry about how and where this tragedy will end. We long for morning, bringing at least the cheer that sunshine can provide and the hope that another day may yet bring some break in the crisis.

4

December 1979:
The Hope of Christmas

By early December, a month had passed without movement in the confrontation. Dates such as Thanksgiving that we hoped might trigger some Iranian flexibility had come and gone without result. A referendum on the new Iranian constitution, designed to help institutionalize clerical dominance in the structure of government, won overwhelming endorsement. To the radicals, this was the first "success" from the embassy seizure and their use of the hostages as pawns in the revolutionary process.

Ignored by the regime was the UN Security Council's resolution of December 7, calling on Iran to release the hostages forthwith and to enter into discussions with the United States. Equally ignored and vilified would be the preliminary but unanimous judgment of the World Court at The Hague, endorsing the position of the United States. My growing frustration was evident in what I wrote.

DAY 29, *December 2, 1979*
Dear Penne,

You sounded down last night. I'm not surprised, and it probably doesn't help much for me to tell you not to be. But that's what I must tell you. It will take time, honey, but in the end everything will be all right. I'm convinced of that. If I weren't, I couldn't go on myself. I think I have never known more painful days, but neither I nor you can dwell on it. Certainly you shouldn't. . . . You and all the American people are conducting yourselves with great composure and restraint and we must not lose that. . . .

My routine continues essentially unchanged. I do 10 to 15 minutes of calisthenics in the morning and half an hour on the stairs in late afternoon. That seems to keep me in reasonably good shape. We sleep reasonably well; how we sleep usually is best determined by how good or bad the evening news is. . . . The Canadian ambassador brought in more paperbacks yesterday, and the Swiss ambassador brought in a round tin of freshly baked cakes from his wife. What wonderful people! There is also a lady in Protocol who sends us things occasionally. And many more, I know, who would if they could!

How I miss you! How I miss the boys! How wonderful it will be to see you all again! I'll try to make the *Messiah* on the 16th, but if I'm not back, please go. I'll be there in spirit, you can be sure of that. Bill, I know, has many friends at the Naval Academy, and I'm sure they're standing squarely behind him now.

I send you all my warmest love, B

DAY 36, *December 9, 1979*—It is Sunday, the ninth of December, five weeks to the day since the theft of the embassy. I wonder had I been told that dreadful day that five weeks later we would still be here and still without much prospect of release what I would have said or done. Looking back, I can recall feeling that we were in for some real problems in recouping the embassy, but I'm sure I did not, in my darkest moments, expect it to take this long.

And still it continues. Now, with the *third* foreign minister since the takeover (Sadegh Ghotbzadeh), there is, if anything, more rigidity than then. But time and responsibility of office did have some impact on his predecessors; perhaps it will yet in this case. (I wish I could write that with more confidence than I do!)

The pattern is unchanged. Whatever expressions of give or moderation are made from whatever quarter, the real hard-liners, the "students" at the embassy, shoot them down with rigidity surpassing their own. "The Shah must be returned!" However unlikely even they know that must be, they continue to demand it. . . . What kind of "students" are they, anyway? Intensely ideological, even idealistic, yes. To the point of unreality, apparently. What we see of them on TV suggests the most unsmiling and inflexible kind of youthful zeal and commitment—an apparent commitment and conviction that they alone now stand tall in defense of the original elements of Khomeini's revolution. They alone can be depended on, by Khomeini, to ensure that the Revolution is put back on its original tracks. They alone, in Iran's society, are untainted and uncorrupted from the past and will not be swayed by dangerous compromise and concession to "reality." If they do not stand firm, they apparently see pernicious Western, especially American, political, economic, and cultural influence again becoming a corrosive, creeping rot that will undermine any hope of achieving their revolutionary ideals—whatever they are at this point.

DAY 37, *December 10, 1979*

Dear Penne,

Two weeks till Christmas Eve. . . . We are beginning to reconcile ourselves to still more time being required. That hurts, but our confidence in ultimate release remains strong; indeed, it remains certain. Rejoining you and the boys will be all the sweeter when it comes—there will be pain and hurt and wrong in what is said and "revealed" in the course of the process that now seems about to begin. But what cannot be expunged from the record is the effort that an embassy and its *entire* staff demonstrated over the past nine months, and especially the past six, to build a good relationship with the new Iran. That is fact, however tragic it is that it failed.

Love, B

Sadegh Ghotbzadeh, who became foreign minister on November 29 and who would figure so large in American public impressions of the hostage crisis, hardly looked the part of an Islamic revolutionary. Instead, he was a kind of walking fashion plate. He was in his late thirties, always in Western suit and tie, clean-shaven, suave, and handsome. He claimed and seemed to have a uniquely personal link with Ayatollah Khomeini. The American television audience was his prime target. On the one hand, he was glib, smooth, so unyielding in his arguments with American TV interviewers that he symbolized the difficulty of achieving any rational dialogue that would take into some account the American side in the crisis. But in time he would also be seen and remembered as an Iranian leader who seemed to appreciate more than most that the crisis was hurting Iran as much as anyone else and needed to be brought to early resolution. This insight would eventually lead to his political downfall and then his execution, victim of revolutionary infighting with the more radical elements.

The three of us in the Foreign Ministry were to talk with him only twice, but even that interaction suggested some political courage on his part, given the anathema that we represented to the student militants. When he first assumed office, he made publicly clear that he would have nothing to do with us, that we were as guilty as our colleagues of espionage. At the same time, in his first press conference as foreign minister, he was quoted as saying that we were free to leave, and Washington advised me by telex (again via the ministry's facilities) to leave if offered the opportunity and not to decline departure in deference to any "captain of the ship" syndrome. Our own preparations over several nervous hours included a written request to Ghotbzadeh that our departure be facilitated. It included as well a painstakingly worded draft of my "departure statement," however improbable it appeared at the time and however ludicrous it appears now in retrospect.

Reality, however, quickly prevailed. Ghotbzadeh made it clear in a speedily issued "clarification" that while the three of us were free to leave he could not assure our security outside the Foreign Ministry building. So ended what was fantasy from the outset.

My own feelings were mixed. Ordered by the department to leave, I would have had no option but to do so, but doing so would have been deeply painful, knowing that my colleagues were still held—at that time held in especially harsh circumstances. Among some observers at home, the affair gave rise to a myth of sorts that I had been offered a chance to leave and had refused, out of concern for my colleagues. In fact, the option was not real then and never became so. Yet this dilemma would not leave the back of my mind, affecting thereafter any and all notions of possible escape plans. Where would such plans take us in a place as chaotic and isolated as Tehran? What would such an effort, if successful, mean for the welfare of our colleagues still held? How would it complicate the atmosphere in which Washington was pursuing an end to the crisis? The pain that any of us would understandably have felt at leaving our colleagues behind was evident in the case of Richard Queen, who in mid-1980 would be released with an illness later diagnosed as muscular sclerosis. Richard's courageous strength in those circumstances did not hide the pain he felt at knowing that his colleagues in Tehran remained at risk.

DAY 38, *December 11, 1979*—There is always much scurrying about among the staff, especially by Hajji, the principal custodian of these rooms and a man always concerned about our welfare—both physical and psychological. The reasons for the activity today are a press conference scheduled by the new foreign minister in the adjacent formal dining room this afternoon and a meeting with the diplomatic corps tomorrow.

So the Persian carpets are vacuumed, the slipcovers removed from the French style furniture, the marble-topped sideboys are dusted, and—most important of all—we are instructed to make ourselves scarce. We joke with Hajji that perhaps the minister would like to present us as exhibits during his press conference. After all, we are easily and quickly available, and we would, no doubt, make good copy. Surely many of the reporters, being enterprising types, must know in any event that these are the rooms where we are being held—one can imagine some of them surreptitiously peeking behind drapes to see if we can be detected. It would not be hard if they would glance behind the drapes along one side of the main salon, because behind these drapes is the long, narrow dining room that we have littered to the point where a quick cover-up for the hours of the press conference would be almost impossible. Washed socks and underwear hang on the furniture; playing cards, books, and magazines litter a felt-covered portion of the dining tables; sofas converted to beds are rarely made up; teacups and orange peels lie about. The place is a mess, but it's home for the present. . . .

So we are taken to the dining room, where, for the duration of the minister's revelations of the truth and justice of the Iranian position, we will pace the floors, pass the time with solitaire, or read yet another mystery or more serious book of the many that our diplomatic colleagues have made available to us.

Like one by Lawrence Durrell called *Sauve Qui Peut*, a sprightly, more clever by half book of less than a hundred pages spoofing diplomatic life. The first chapter ends with, "In diplomacy, it is so often a case of 'sauve qui peut,' " which translated means "every man for himself."

Hajji appears to find the whole business a bit unsettling—the business, that is, of our being held here and all the pronouncements of American imperialism being responsible for Iran's ills. With seven children, he appears to find much of this an unwarranted diversion from his and Iran's real problems. The sentiment varies, presumably, among the staff that look out for us here. There was the one who, within the first day or two of our arrival here, asked why we didn't turn ourselves in with the other hostages at the compound.

There is one woman among them, presumably chador-clad outdoors but in these rooms wearing only a head scarf as her recognition of her Islamic duties. She is quiet, but seemingly friendly. Few speak any English, so it is difficult to know how they feel. Occasionally other workers come in briefly, to repair light fixtures or to check on the heating; they glance furtively at us, curious no doubt as to what we look like and what we may be doing. Some wonder probably why indeed we are not packed off with the rest of the hostages, others possibly appalled at the whole business—as we assume many, if not most, of the professionals in this building feel.

We are fed well, if a bit much of the same, day after day. . . . Almost without fail, a fourth guest arrives for these meals, the smell of meat, especially fish, attracting a cat—but a cat well out of reach, having found over the years a way to get up into a recessed part of the ceiling in this large room where indirect lighting and a loudspeaker system are installed. The cat is black, but happily with a spot of white at the neck—a formal cravat as it were. She speaks to us with clear signals that we are to feed her—which we do (out of sight of the staff) by tossing up chicken bones, fish heads, and whatever else is tossable. . . . She (or he) is described as "Hoveyda's cat," Hajji telling us that she has appeared in this fashion ever since Amir Hoveyda's years as prime minister whenever large banquets were held in these halls. We choose to regard her as a friend and a good luck omen and in any event a diversion in days sometimes tedious indeed with boredom and, above all, frustration.

Within days of our seizure, determined to take every opportunity I could to demonstrate to Iranian officials that I retained some kind of official status, I had begun a practice of expressing my concern in formal letters signed as chargé d'affaires ad interim. However futile those communications proved to be, the exercise helped occupy my time and bolster my morale. Written in draft, then discussed with my two colleagues (they occasionally exercising a veto), and then written formally on whatever paper was available, they were hand carried by guards or kitchen staff to the Office of Protocol below and to whatever fate awaited them; possibly they went into one of the ministry's "circular" files, but evidence from time to time indicated most reached their destinations. Rarely did a recipient respond and then only indirectly and orally, lest word reach the militant students.

With news of Ghotbzadeh's appointment as foreign minister, I sent the following message:

Dear Mr. Minister,

My government remains deeply troubled by the persistent lack of knowledge of the welfare, both physical and psychological, of our Embassy personnel now in their 40th day as hostages.

In this connection, Mr. Minister, our concern has been sharply intensified by what is clear from the comments by Corporal William Gallegos, USMC, in an interview allowed to NBC/TV by the occupiers of my Embassy.

According to what I have read of the interview in the *Tehran Times* of December 12, Corporal Gallegos, while noting that he was physically well, also notes that his hands, like those of the other hostages, are kept loosely tied. He adds that the hostages are not allowed to speak, either to each other or to their guards. . . .

Surely, Mr. Minister, this is cruel and unnecessary psychological harassment. . . . Not even prisoners of war are subjected to such treatment. . . . Only someone of the strongest body and mind can take such treatment without harm.

Perhaps I am wrong. I fervently hope so. But let the world know, let the parents and the families of these hostages know, through some impartial third party, that they are well.

Why, Mr. Minister, is there no recognition of this elementary humanitarian consideration?

DAY 44, *December 17, 1979*—Let us look at truth as seen in Tehran these days and as reported faithfully in the columns of the *Tehran Times*. Today, for example:

Admiral Madani, Governor General of Khuzistan, asked concerning the relevance of the Geneva Convention and diplomatic immunity to the situation at the American Embassy in Tehran, replied that "the U.S. Embassy in Tehran was not a diplomatic mission. It was staffed by American spies and it was actively engaged in espionage activities against Iran. They abused the diplomatic immunity granted to them and they should be tried for this trespass and betrayed."

The admiral, of course, offers no proof. There is none. He knows that every man and woman in that embassy was charged with the task of *building* a relationship with the new Iran and in no way undermining it or sabotaging anything.

Who should be tried?

- Who has stolen an entire embassy and all its property and possessions?
- Who has rifled diplomatic correspondence, correspondence endowed with immunity from seizure and search for centuries because it is correspondence involving another sovereign state?
- Who has taken prisoner and denied life's most precious gift, freedom, to the entire staff of this embassy?

- Who is now denying them even the right to speak? Who keeps them bound after six long weeks of confinement?
- Who denies them correspondence with their families?
- Who ignores the voice and conscience of the world community as represented by the United Nations?
- Who rejects the unanimous call of the Security Council for the release of the hostages and commencement of talks?
- Who is refusing dialogue on the very subjects on which Iran seeks reassurance and relief?

A further example of truth, from the same paper of today's date:

> The students at the embassy compound "also denounced the International Court of Justice as a 'dictated court.' " The foreign minister termed it a "unilateral judgment . . . unacceptable to Iran" and instructed his mission in The Hague "not to pay attention to it."

Who is dictating to whom in this instance? What kind of international comity and community can exist when any state concludes it can make its own judgments on international law and practice, regardless of their impact on others?

Can the minister or students honestly say that the members of this court are dictated to by anyone except by the rule of law itself? Consider its members: Judges from the United Kingdom, Argentina, Brazil, Egypt, West Germany, France, India, Italy, Japan, Nigeria, Poland, Senegal, Syria, the USSR, and the United States. All present and voting. A "dictated to" bunch indeed! . . .

Elsewhere, yet further claims to truth: the foreign minister, for example, says that the hostages are "well, they're O.K., they're fine." The facts are:

- He does not know; he has never seen them.
- Most have not been seen by *any* outside observer since the first week.
- The "students" themselves have allowed one of the hostages to speak to the press and say, publicly, in the sixth week, that their hands are still loosely bound and they are allowed to speak to no one!
- No one, the foreign minister or anyone else, can say in the face of this evidence of inhumanity and cruel psychological harassment that the hostages are "O.K., they're fine."
- That is an insult to humanity and human intelligence and a grave offense to human rights.

Yet another example: Penne reports that when she and Kate Koob's sister took a wreath to the Iranian Embassy last night and made a short statement along the lines of "let our people go," she was reminded that Iranian students were being unfairly harassed in the United States. But how do the two situations compare? In Iran, our people and embassy have been taken in clear violation of all established diplomatic practice and international law. In the

United States, by contrast, Iranian students are simply being asked to respect American immigration laws and regulations and are protected in the process by the courts and Constitution, as demonstrated by the fact that a federal court has declared unconstitutional the president's order to the INS to determine whether all Iranian students are adhering to law and practice. . . .

DAY 45, *December 18, 1979*
Dear P,

No visitors since last Wednesday. Some nervousness here on the subject of visits to us by ambassadors, obviously. Don't know what's behind it—possibly people on the staff here complaining about too many favors to us? Or possibly the "students" at the embassy complaining about calls on us, after they'd heard the press reports of the Canadian ambassador seeing us. Don't know. In any event, it reduces our knowledge of the outside world, and it further adds to the monotony, which hangs very heavy sometimes, especially today, the start of the seventh week. But we will not be bullied or cowed by the regime, and we are proud of our colleagues who have not cracked to our knowledge. . . . We don't dwell only on the madness we see and hear around us. There are real friends, decent people, on the housekeeping staff here who are genuinely helpful to us. We are strongly buoyed by the awareness we have of such overwhelming support and friendship from the American public. That's the best Christmas present we could have.

Warmest best wishes and love, B

P.S. Save gas!

DAY 46, *December 19, 1979*—Someone sent me this marvelous cartoon of a couple in a travel bureau, picking up tickets. The man behind the counter says, "And in case trouble breaks out, here's the address of the U.S. Embassy . . . stay away from there."

How true. And how the world has changed. . . .

The ARK has today described Carter as an "animal." How can a man of God say that about another human being, a man whom he *knows* to be a decent man whose fault is probably that he is *too* human, too decent, not tough enough in some respects. In another interview, the USG [U.S. government] is described by the ARK as a bully that "skins alive the meek ones wherever it finds them, rains bombs on them whenever it can, and strips nations of their resources wherever it can." Elsewhere the "students" have a lovely name for the United States: "this Satan and corruption," or, as we are frequently described, "world-devouring ghouls." Their lexicon of hate is boundless—it is also purposeful, of course, and that is apparently to paint us publicly as so barbaric and hostile as to preclude any wavering here on the part of the government and, of course, to "expose" us as a corrupt, mean, hostile state that cannot be trusted by Iran or indeed any self-respecting country in the developing world. They can carry that only so far before they begin to look ridiculous, and surely they have long since passed that point as far as most of the world is concerned.

Maggie Thatcher—isn't she something? We need more women prime ministers! That's the kind of friend we need.

———

Later—What ironies this year has brought, what strange turns of the wheel of fate! Twenty-six years ago, in the fall of 1953, I was a young Foreign Service officer enjoying home leave with my parents on the farm in Minnesota, looking forward to my tour as a consular officer at the American Consulate in Kobe, Japan. My second tour, after two years in visa work at Hamburg, Germany. Kobe was not a post I would have sought, but Japan's an interesting place; I was young and ready for anything. Perhaps less than a week before I was supposed to leave for Kobe, Washington called with a change in orders; I was to go to Tehran as an economic officer. . . . If I had not gotten that call 26 years ago, breaking those orders to Japan? Obviously my life would have been totally different. I would not be here at this moment. But thank God that call came. I would have made a lousy Japanese expert and an even lousier consular officer. And most important, I wouldn't have met Penelope Lippitt Babcock!

DAY 47, *December 20, 1979*

Dear Penne,

You sounded *down* tonight, Honey. I'm so sorry. Why did I ever get you into this? Why, why, why? There are so many questions that begin with *why*. I can only say I *will* get out of this, I *will* be home again. We *can* make up this difficult year. *Hasn't* it been a difficult year? A crazy year, I guess you'd call it. Ambassador to Malta, bounced from there, bounced back to Malta for an international conference, bounced to the Inspection Corps, then to Iran. Four to six weeks, remember? Then this—"this"—how can I refer to it that way? "This" indeed. A nightmare, a bad dream at least—would that I could dream, and then I might sleep more. Forty-eight days today, 48 days for those poor colleagues of mine at the compound, now "generously" promised that "clergymen" will visit them for Christmas. How generous, how thoughtful! Perhaps they'll be free of their bindings for an hour or two. Perhaps the crowds will stop chanting long enough for the clergymen (are they to be Islamic, perhaps?) to say a prayer!

But I do so hope that you and the boys will find some way to take your minds off of me—to have some degree of normalcy about the holidays. I feel so sorry that I've offered so little—not even much in the way of ideas as to what you and/or the boys can do. God grant that you *will* find some solace and peace in at least the conviction that this *will* end, and end safely for all concerned. It must.

I'm not sure when or how this will get mailed—we've been isolated now since a week Wednesday. Keeps us harmless apparently, and keeps the militants satisfied.

Love, Bruce

Christmas 1979—For 53 American hostages in Tehran, a Christmas that would be long remembered, unequaled except perhaps by yet another that would follow in 1980. But 1979 would be remembered most of all, I suspect, for what at that stage in the crisis was our feeling of incredulity about the whole affair. An entire American Embassy staff held hostage within their own chancery, denied contact with their government and their families at home by fervent practitioners of another religious faith, denied that promise of "peace on earth, good will toward men" so much a part of the most joyous of times in the Christmas calendar. How could such an incongruous affair be real? Certainly it could not go on, however real it was. Few of us had become such convinced pessimists at that early stage as to fail to hope that maybe, just maybe, the notion of a Christmas gesture of releasing at least a few more of the remaining hostages would strike our hosts as an opportunity to win themselves some sympathy on the world stage. But our optimism was hardly in peak form either, and a reluctance to put too much faith in that hope saw me send off Christmas "gifts" in the form of letters to my sons.

DAY 48, *December 21, 1979*

Dear Bill,

Christmas 1979. What can I send you and my other sons for Christmas this year but a letter! And my very best wishes and prayers that Christmas will be for you what it is for me, above all a reminder of the enormous gift we have as a family.

I have known that before, but I have never known it so deeply as I have known it these past weeks as a hostage in distant Iran. I know it because of the support and love and prayers I have felt from all of you, wherever you are and whatever you may be doing at any given time. For me, for the moment, life is stationary—all the more reason for me to know almost every hour of the day what each of you is doing. Or at least I know where you are and I can imagine what you are doing.

As the expression goes, all this, too, will pass. I am confident of that. I remain convinced that there is decency in every human being and that it will yet prevail here. Then we will all have the opportunity to reflect on what has happened, to think about what we have all learned, and certainly many of us have learned a good deal. Above all, I hope our country, our people, have learned the strength of unity, the good feeling of genuine patriotism, the dignity and worth of the least of us.

And there are material lessons—not the least the folly of further drift in our national energy policy. Surely we have learned by now the need to reduce our thoughtless dependency on foreign sources, unstable ones at best, for so much of our oil.

You have this world ahead of you, Bill. And I am proud indeed of the way you are preparing yourself for your role in it. Never lose your pride in doing something well, whatever it is, however small or big. Never lose your pride in yourself, so long as it is a sense of pride born in doing things well and in being helpful to others. You have always had that in your character, and I am impressed by the way your life and experience and training at the academy are strengthening you in this respect.

Never lose your sense of tolerance and openness to others. I've just read a book by Djilas, the famous Yugoslav communist whose eyes were opened to the rigidity and dogmatism in that ideology. Several lines impressed me in that book: "Tyranny begins with ultimate truths about society and man. . . . There are no ultimate truths about man, any more than there are about the world. The truth about man is boundless and unforseeable. . . . The future is known only to the Gods and to dogmatists."

These lines could well apply to this place, where I have served these past six months. Where is tolerance and compassion? Where is recognition that perhaps the ultimate truth is not known here either? Where is love?

And I guess that is what has impressed me most in these five silent weeks: realizing what danger there is in hate, especially when it is fanned and encouraged as a virtual national tonic or dogma. There is good in every man, and nothing brings it out more surely and fully than love, respect, and a demonstrated decency and kindness.

Naiveté, no. That's foolish. Firmness—but a firmness that is based on genuine knowledge and understanding—and convictions tested by experience. Again, that is yet another satisfaction in what I sense of the American mood, or most of it at least, in the present crisis. There *is* firmness in support of what we think is right, but it is firmness resting on a sense of restraint—restraint worthy of a country with power that should be used only as a last resort in a world that so desperately needs peace. Restraint also that reflects some understanding for what troubles the Iranians—or some of them at least—so that when this is all over, we can go on inhabiting this globe together in some degree of friendship again.

So, Bill, I send you the warmest regards for Christmas, best wishes for a magnificent year ahead, and my prayers for peace and good will among all men—and women!

Sincerely, Dad

P.S. Save gas!

DAY 49, *December 22, 1979*

Dear Jim,

Since I can't send you a present, big son at home, I'll send you a letter! . . . This is no way to spend Christmas, Jim! I wish I were home with you and Mom and Bill and Chip. But since I'm not, I have to depend on you and your brothers, but especially *you*, to make sure that there is lots of Christmas spirit around. Christmas is for everyone, but it's especially for young people like you. A time of love and good will and good cheer and regard for others. I know you will think a lot about the hostages over at the compound. If you and more than 200 million other Americans think hard about them, and send them their love in that way, I know they'll feel it.

These have been bad days for our country, Jim, but they've been good days, too. And proud days. . . . Because our country is standing strong and tall for what is right and that matters a lot. It matters even more that the American people are solidly behind their government and showing it by the things you and everyone else are doing—like saving gas, and ringing church bells, and signing petitions, and, above all, by keeping our cool. We can best win this fight by keeping our powder dry and showing the rest of the world in that way that when your cause is right, you can succeed without using force or bluster.

We will win this one, Jim, wait and see. Nothing that is done or manufactured as fact here will change the *solid* fact that international law and practice is on our side. *And* that it is *Iran* that has failed to see that our government and our embassy were actively working to build a relationship with the *new* Iran and to put the past behind us.

I know I've got your support, Jim, and that's going to help a lot. You will look back on all this someday, when you're older, and be proud of your country for what it stood for. I'm proud of you for standing by Mom. You're her man about the house these days, and I'm counting on you a lot.

Merry Christmas! Best wishes for the best New Year ever. See you *soon.*
                                Sincerely, Dad
P.S. Save gas! (Use a sled!)

DAY 50, *December 23, 1979*—The day has been uneventful for us. A wicker basket full of plastic boxes of various kinds of Iranian candy and decorated with a large pink bow arrived from the Spanish ambassador and his wife, two people who served twice in Washington and cannot tell you enough how warmly they feel toward the United States. . . . I had my 30 minutes of stair walking in the ceremonial entrance to this building, an area where we are now admitted by special request only. Try walking stairs for 30 minutes sometime; it's boring, but it helps keep me in reasonable shape. That plus my calisthenics in the morning manages to keep me tolerably fit. . . .

Our friendly chief of protocol came by, as always, late in the day. Today I found it hard to carry on a conversation—we have exhausted almost every conceivable topic of conversation long since. So after he describes briefly what his day was like and kindly asks after ours, there isn't much left to say. Depending on my mood, I sometimes grouch a bit about what this government is doing to us, and to itself, and to the hostages, but there is little point to this—and I then quiet myself. . . .

Christmas: the radio reports that various clerics have been invited by the Iranians to visit the hostages—and presumably us as well. Our feelings are mixed—gratitude for any variation in our routine and special gratitude that the 50 will hopefully now *all* be seen by the outside world, but less than gratitude when one focuses on the fact that there is cynicism in the way the whole thing is being orchestrated and the hostages exploited. You, my dear P, are quoted in the *Herald Tribune* that arrived today as saying that American patience will begin to run out if something doesn't happen by Christmas, and I'm sure you are entirely right. . . .

The whole thing is unconscionable, outrageous, depressing—that a government that professes to be guided by spiritual considerations should demonstrate such cruelty and inhumanity. It boggles my mind and depresses my spirit. I grieve at what this is doing to Islam's image among our people—and this during the year-long celebrations in the United States of the 14th centenary of Islam! . . .

DAY 53, *December 26, 1979*

Dear Penne,

The second day of Christmas, in the most unusual Christmas that I will ever spend, God willing. It is snowing—a day late for a white Christmas—heavy, wet snowflakes that melt quickly, though surely in the mountain suburbs the snow is heavy. On the ski slopes of Dezin it must be magnificent—pity, that was an area where we might have skied this year.

Christmas Day, yet another day in captivity, and yet it could not be just another day. Christmas is never just another day. We did what we could to make it special. We even put on ties! Happily, sensitivities in the Foreign Ministry over access to us by other ambassadors have apparently cooled to the point where such visits are again being allowed. So on Christmas morning the British ambassador arrived with a box full of good things to relieve the monotony of our meals: a variety of tinned pâtés, chocolates, catsup and relish, a tin of ham, olives, pistachios, and, in his briefcase, a bottle of "cough syrup" from which the label had been carefully removed. It was red wine, which we hid behind a decorative pot in the corner and secretly drank with dinner. . . . Late in the day we discovered two candles, lit them, drank our forbidden things, and manfully sang a few Christmas carols after being put in the mood to do so by a beautiful program of lessons and carols from Kings College Chapel at Cambridge, broadcast over BBC. It was hauntingly beautiful, reminding me of Christmasses past with my family at home. . . .

Christmas day dawned with the *Tehran Times*, which headlined "Ring Bells for God" over a story and text of the Imam's new blast at the United States and Carter as a kind of Christmas present, the reference to the bells being that the United States "rings bells for hostages . . . when it should be ringing bells for God." Carter is denounced in the Imam's "Christmas message" as "the ringleader of the oppressors of the world," after quotations from the Koran and even the Sermon on the Mount. The message calls on all Christians to rise and "save Jesus from the jaws of these executioners."

As if that were not enough, the Christmas editorial in the *Times* includes this monumental idiocy: "For the first time since the Renaisance [*sic*], Western Christians are being exposed to an official government situation [Iran presumably!] which is devoted to putting into practice the word of God as preached by Jesus Christ."

You may wonder how we survived the day after that! Well, we did, by keeping Christmas in our hearts, which is where it should be. And late in the day the three clerics—Coffin, Howard, and Gumbleton—invited by the student occupiers at the embassy to celebrate Christmas services with the hostages came by to see us for a couple of hours.* We were torn between irritation with them for allowing themselves to be exploited in this fashion by the students and our satisfaction at their willingness to come on short notice to give the hostages at least some indication at last that Americans care, which, of course, they do. We found the clerics sobered by the experience, clearly surprised by the rigidity of the zealots holding the hostages, and perhaps that is enough to make the trip worthwhile—so that people like these three, too, see what fanaticism is abroad in Iran.

Love, B

DAY 56, *December 29, 1979*—Today we are rousted out of bed early (7:40 is early for us in this place) because we are told that the foreign minister is to give a press conference in one of the adjoining two large dining rooms and we are to be squirreled away and out of sight before 8:00 A.M. . . . to the second of the two rooms, the doors chained shut, and a small table brought in so we can be given lunch here. We joke that perhaps we might sit at opposite ends of the immensely long dining table in this room already—a table that sits 45 or 50 easily—a table almost lost, even at that size, in a room that must be 40 by 60 feet in size. A terrible room for us—too big and cold and gloomy. We pace the floor, play solitaire, read, write (as I am doing), or stretch out on a row of four or five chairs and try to get some sleep. Mike stands at the chained doors, listening carefully through the cracks for what he can hear, which seems to be more of the same, i.e., tough talk about standing up to American threats, etc. . . .

DAY 57, *December 30, 1979*
Dear P,

Eight weeks today—almost incredible, but we look at the calendar and know it's true. Eight weeks since we were brought down to these rooms by the then foreign minister, "to spend the night." . . . Had we known—or been told at the time—that it would be eight weeks plus? No, we would not have believed it.

Today we are told that the secretary has asked the UNSC to impose sanctions, but only after Kurt Waldheim has been out here to make some effort on the spot for some flexibility. So far there is no indication that such a visit will be rejected—in today's climate, the absence of negativism is a positive development. The morning paper quotes the FM [foreign minister] as saying that sanctions would be a "move in the wrong direction." He is quoted as telling a press conference that Iran is "running out of concessions" and when asked what these have been, he cites the visit by clergymen to the hostages for Christmas

* The Rev. William Sloane Coffin, Jr., Riverside Church, New York City; the Rev. William Howard, Jr., president, National Council of Churches of Christ; Monsignor Thomas Gumbleton, Auxiliary Roman Catholic bishop of Detroit.

and Iran's willingness to switch from trials of the hostages to an international tribunal where the hostages would be witnesses.

So much for "concessions." Words take on the meaning that their users want them to have. Concessions indeed! But we sense, in all this, perhaps some growing appreciation on the part of those at the level below the ARK that this can't go on indefinitely. One wonders, in this connection, what effect the Soviet coup in Afghanistan will have on the Iranians—a coup so blatant as to make everyone sit up and take notice. Now Babrak Karmal's predecessor in Kabul, Hafizullah Amin, is termed an "imperialist lackey" and is forthwith executed. An uncertain destiny, being on top in Kabul. Ah, but this time the Soviets have come in with, reportedly, 15,000–20,000 troops and that suggests that Babrak has enough backing to keep his seat secure for a time. The Brits tried imposing their chosen rulers on Kabul once, but that was long ago—in the 19th century—and it failed rather miserably. The Soviets have the power to do it more decisively, but precedents are against them and the Afghans don't take such very well for very long.

DAY 58, *December 31, 1979*—I loved a remark that one of the hostages apparently made to one of the three clergymen when they visited the compound. His first remark on seeing this visiting American was, "Isn't this *absurd?*" How right he is—it is absurd. So unnecessary and so costly for both countries, not least for Iran, which has so many other problems on which it should be focusing, especially now that Afghanistan has become southern Asia's Czechoslovakia. I wonder why the Russians thought they had to go quite this far, and so blatantly. It seems unnecessary, given the control they already had there. But they apparently felt Amin wasn't up to coping with the insurrection. . . .

Penne amazes me—all the activity she manages. But I am reassured, too, by all the love she generates, for herself, the boys, and for us. I wonder sometimes what all this is doing to each and every one of us. I know one thing, and that is that I have come to appreciate and love my family more than ever before. I have come anew to realize what matters, and nothing matters more than having family that love and support you when you're down. . . .

5

January 1980: A Canadian Caper

January, the start of a new year—surely, we told ourselves, things could not get worse. We were soon to learn that they could, and would, evident in the failure of the visit of UN Secretary General Kurt Waldheim. His aborted mission, the ouster late in the month of all remaining American journalists, and other signs of deepening Iranian rigidity saw the three of us losing whatever optimism we may have had during the Christmas season that the crisis would end soon. But the month would end with a big boost to our morale when news reached us of the "Canadian caper"—freedom for those six of our colleagues who had eluded capture on November 4 and had spent the following three months hiding out with our Canadian friends.

Nothing for me was a heavier burden throughout the crisis than the sense of helplessness and frustration I personally felt in not being in a position to ease the conditions for my staff in the embassy compound. Only a mile or two from us across the city, they suffered in silence the abuse of their captors and the shouted passion of the mobs on the streets outside. Almost every television newscast carried coverage of the militant students addressing some new "crime" on our part. Occasionally there were glimpses of my colleagues bound hand and foot; at the outset even the women were bound to their chairs.

This was my embassy, my staff, my charge, my colleagues—as supportive a staff as I had ever known, including those proud and tough Marines, mature

49

beyond their years, reminding me of my own sons at home. Ultimately the responsibility was mine; their pain and abuse were the consequences of a failed mission. Nothing in my experience in life compared to the pain I felt at this, a hurt and a frustration that brought me often to quiet but angry tears as I sat and watched what I saw on the television screen and then tried to overcome my reactions by pacing the floor of our room. I remember swearing to myself, looking down at the worn but fine Persian carpets on which I paced, that I could never again stomach walking on such carpets (an emotion I have since overcome).

DAY 59, *January 1, 1980*—I think tonight I have learned to hate. Certainly I have felt bitterness in ways that I never have before.

Tonight the local TV carried a half-hour film of the visit to the embassy compound of Catholic Bishop Gumbleton of Detroit and Cardinal Duval of Algiers for Christmas services with our captive hostages. The film was put together by the student militants who hold the hostages; put together obviously as a blatant propaganda exercise, it was a shocking exploitation of the Christmas festival to serve the political purposes of the militants.

We saw a largish room, the walls of which were covered with revolutionary, anti-U.S. slogans, plus dozens of photographs of maimed or dead Iranians—presumably victims of the violence that accompanied the late months of the Shah's regime. Superimposed on all this were Christmas decorations—lavish decorations, even a decorated tree, below which were heaped some of the thousands (million perhaps) of Christmas cards sent by the American public to the hostages. In the middle of the room, a table covered with Christmas sweets to eat and candles lit.

The two priests were in vestments, and there were scenes of the four hostages taking communion. But far and away the bulk of the film was of these hostages reading a prepared statement, praising the revolutionary zeal of their captors, reciting the misdeeds of the embassy in supporting the Shah, citing documents discovered in the embassy to suggest "espionage," and calling on the U.S. government to return the Shah to Iran. All this was done in what appeared to be a rehearsal reading, seriatim, by the hostages of their statement, the desk in front of them displaying "evidence" of one kind or another. Only one (Steve Lauterbach) of the four seemed in any way hesitant in what he was reading. The hostage who seemed to preside, Joe Subic, clearly was, or seemed to be, relishing his role. A young Marine, Kevin Hermining, too, seemed relaxed and at ease. The fourth, the businessman named Jerry Plotkin, read a separate statement, and he, too, seemed in control of himself.

All of this culminated in young Subic displaying a Christmas card from which he read a special greeting to Imam Khomeini on behalf of the hostages. All of this is incredible. I have heard of brainwashing and mind control. I have read of such and recognize that in all hostage situations this is commonplace. But here is an example involving people I *know* and whom I *respect.* . . . And here they were, shown to the world as Americans from within the embassy itself who have come to recognize the "rightness" of the militants' cause, even to defend the takeover of the embassy, and to voluntarily (or so it would appear) describe and cite examples of embassy "espionage."

I know all but Plotkin, who was visiting the embassy that morning. They are dedicated, patriotic Americans, proud of their assignments and enjoying their work in Tehran. They could not possibly have voluntarily turned in this way against their own country. Each of them *is* young, *is* impressionable, and probably feels genuinely, even before being taken captive, that the Revolution in Iran was right for Iran, as many of us, if not all of us, did. But the militants have seized on this, in a hostage situation, and eight weeks of confinement and harassment by sound from the crowds in the streets brought the hostages to the point of apparent servitude to their captors' purposes. And all this in a setting of Christmas with the two priests sitting docilely, watching and listening to the entire charade.

Hate for the militants for what they have done. Sympathy for the hostages for what they have suffered. I do not judge them. How does any one of us know how we might behave in similar circumstances? Guilt I must confess, too, in good measure—how can I avoid it?—I was in charge of that embassy. I kept it functioning, despite the risks that were there, before and after the Shah's entry into the United States. I was absent on that fateful morning of November 4, resulting in a leaderless embassy, my deputy being with me here in the ministry, too. I gave the go-ahead to surrender. Who knows what might have happened had we tried to hold out longer? What might have been different today if I had not been in the ministry? Certainy we would have focused more on destruction than we did. Perhaps, perhaps—there is so much that might have been. . . .

Yet where does one begin when you start down that road? If someone else had been tapped to come here in June to give the place temporary leadership? If I or someone else had been designated ambassador long before? If the trend in our relationship had been down instead of the up that it was? If the Shah had not been admitted? If the gates had not been so easily penetrated by the mob? If the security officer on the scene had not been captured early on, further weakening the leadership situation? If the government had sent security forces to help? If, if, if—where does it end?

Some of it ends in scenes like those on TV tonight, of young Americans used by captors whose zeal and commitment are total and intense (I grant them that, in spades). Now these Americans, one a member of the U.S. Marines, must live with this situation on their release. How do they react then? How are they treated by their colleagues?

One of the priests told us later that one of the four, Steve Lauterbach, had conceded in a whispered conversation with the priest that the whole thing was "staged." But why? Why did Steve and his colleagues do it, in that case?

DAY 60, *January 2, 1980*—Today's big event is that UNSYG (UN Secretary General) Waldheim is in town. The student militants are denouncing him as having "kissed the hand of the Shah." The foreign minister says he is welcome to "collect information," but there will be "no negotiations" relating to the hostages. We assume at least some of this is bluster; one would not think, at this point in the crisis, that the Iranians could ignore the chief officer of the UN. It matters a lot, given the UNSC resolution that will move to sanctions if we are not released by January 7.

So we three have a rather special interest in all this. We were wakened this morning to the sound of megaphones from police cars directing traffic in anticipation of Waldheim's visit here in the ministry. And this afternoon, his schedule included a stop at the former Officers' Club (now the Revolutionary Club) across the street, where he was to meet with Iranians crippled during the Revolution. Before that event, a demonstration was put together in the street between us and the club, so we had grandstand seats to watch its formation. . . . The people dutifully went through their drill, shouting slogans about imperialism and us and Khomeini. At one point I felt they noticed me watching from the window so I drew back quickly, lest the demonstration turn into one against us.

Today the phones are cut again for the third day running. Reportedly the students have contacts here in the ministry and are insisting that the clamps be put on us a bit. We complain to the chief of protocol, who rolls his eyes to the ceiling and throws up his hands—making it fairly clear that he is powerless to do much about it. Our visits from ambassadorial colleagues are also cut sharply. Except for the Australian on New Year's Eve day, and the Dane, British, and Swiss at Christmas time, we have had none since December 12. That complicates getting mail out, and it generally diminishes our lives, because such visits have given us some occasion to think beyond our four walls, to have some diversion from ourselves, to know what's going on. But, again, it is reportedly the militants who are behind the cutback, irritated by reports that reached the press that we had had visitors.

Today I had the first really warm shower since getting here. The shower worked and for once it was warm. . . . But we need haircuts badly—none now for almost three months in my case. It saves money, but I was not meant for long hair. The chief of protocol worries about our safety, should he bring in just any barber, and the American barbers we know from the embassy aren't available. Perhaps we should forget it—and walk out of here with our long hair as our own "badge of honor." . . .

I'm tired. I need to go to bed, though I dread it because I don't sleep well. The sofa "bed" is damned uncomfortable. I find myself tossing and turning and thinking, missing my family and home.

DAY 61, *January 3, 1980*—One would have to describe today as a memorable day. The secretary general of the United Nations came to see us. I had sent a note to the foreign minister saying I hoped to see him. But apparently Waldheim himself asked to see us, and well, one doesn't say no to the UN's secretary general very easily. He was ushered in around noon.

He is a soft-spoken man, exactly as the press photos suggest—gaunt and tall, clearly dedicated and tireless—a diplomat who knows the ropes, unhurried and unruffled. A man with a lot of experience and thus a man who knows he's got a very tough problem here. His first concern was our condition—how we were, how we felt—with sympathy for our frustration. As he said, "We're all diplomats, we understand the problem, we know how you feel."

Here is an opportunity that the Iranians must not fail to grasp—that none of us can fail to grasp. If this thing can't be sorted out through the UN, then we've all got problems—big ones. He stayed for an hour. It did wonders for our morale—whatever the obstacles, large as they were, for anything coming of his visit. My own morale got a special boost when his deputy for political affairs made a special point of telling me of the strong and favorable impression Penne was making in her several appearances in TV interviews—an impression of quiet strength and confidence.

Two days later Waldheim left Tehran, ahead of schedule, his visit seen as a failure. Press reports suggested that he had left because of threats against him and his inability to see either the Ayatollah or the hostages held at the embassy compound. Meanwhile, Iran continued to ignore the preliminary but unanimous judgment of the World Court at The Hague to release the hostages, branding the court as a creature of imperialism designed to interpret international law to the benefit of its own interests.

News of the Shah's departure from the United States to live in Panama (after having been denied reentry by Mexico) triggered new threats from the student militants that trials of the hostages would "definitely begin." The Iranian government formally asked Panama to arrest the Shah for extradition to Iran. On January 13 the Soviet Union vetoed a UN Security Council (UNSC) resolution calling for economic sanctions against Iran.

DAY 64, *January 6, 1980*—Today is Epiphany, . . . and for me it is also my dad's birthday. I'm glad, I suppose, that neither of my parents is alive today to experience this crisis. Neither would have understood it. My mother would have worried to death. My dad would have fussed and fumed. I can hear him now! . . . For us it is the beginning of the tenth week. What does one say that hasn't been said? Nothing. Except to commit oneself to go on with it, finding things to occupy one's mind and time. That gets harder with the cutoff of visitors. But it's all relative, and we remind ourselves that 50 of our colleagues experience the same problems, only much worse, and apparently are weathering it well.

The news reports constantly call for unity and for demonstrations to show that unity. But it also reports the unrest that exists in many quarters of this tormented country. One is reminded how little one really knows of this country, its far-flung regions, and the differences that seem still to divide them, a full year into a successful revolution.

Among the differences, of course, is the hostage issue—and, we presume, the varying points of view in the several power centers as to how to deal with us. Today's *Tehran Times* reports, under a caption "Laingen issue referred to Imam," that the foreign minister is seeking orders as to how to respond to demands from the student militants that I (we) be turned over to them for questioning. And tomorrow is the deadline set by the last UNSC resolution for release of the hostages, failing which economic sanctions are to be imposed—or at least the council must face up to that possibility as a next step.

DAY 65, *January 7, 1980*

Dear P,

It is nearly midnight, but I will try to write a bit before trying to sleep on my lumpy sofa. I've asked for a mattress but they don't seem to exist. We normally don't get to sleep till midnight, hoping to be tired enough to sleep. I've just walked the floor for 15 minutes; that helps tire me out a bit.

Today was a good day, in the sense that the Swiss ambassador finally brought around a pouch of mail for hostages, and us. . . . So life goes on. Some days are better than others. Some days we are all "down"; it depends in part on what we read in paper and hear on news, the kind of weather we see outside, the visits we have. Fridays, when the ministry is empty, it is like a tomb. We read a lot, I try to write a lot (please keep my letters as a kind of diary). . . . Food is getting terribly monotonous and frankly, in recent days, pretty poor. Vegetables are either cold carrots and peas or soggy cabbage. Soup isn't too bad, except when the same soup comes around again at night, sometimes reheated to the point of being burned. Mystery meats #1, 2, 3, and 4 we now tolerate, thanks to several bottles of catsup sent in by the Dutch ambassador. We went through a jar of his peanut butter rapidly and wish we had more. . . . There is never any dessert, except canned fruit occasionally.

All we need, besides more peanut butter, is two things: a haircut and our freedom. We can do without the former if necessary. . . . We are angry, but stoical—we have little choice. We have no complaints about our government's actions; we think they are right. We would like to think the Afghan tragedy will help here, in terms of attitudes, but there is little evidence of that yet. . . . I know I have your love and support, and that of Jim and the older boys. That makes all this bearable, knowing that I have all of you to come home to.

B

DAY 67, *January 9, 1980*—Today is the 40th day after Muharram. There

are again vast demonstrations planned, focusing on martyrdom and against imperialism. . . . We grieve for our colleagues, who have become nonpersons—so little is heard of them. Since Christmas, again, not one has been seen. . . . Another week, another ten days, the days go by, and they sit there in silent isolation. What gross inhumanity, especially when the press frequently refers to them as being cared for with "Islamic humanity"! Time goes by and the focus on their plight inevitably lessens, as does public interest in the United States and the willingness of international public opinion to stand firm. We feel frustrated more than ever by our helplessness sitting here. . . .

Later—It is late afternoon, of a clear and cold January day. I put on my sweater and open wide the windows looking down from our third-floor room to the ministry's garden below. It is a large garden, pierced by driveways, in the center a large pool and fountain, and in the far corner a helicopter pad. The garden is deserted as I open the windows, except for the flock of pigeons gathered on the sill to eat the barley bread we've put there, but who clatter away in fright, and the lone sentry far off by the gate who paces back and forth in bored solitude. At least he has solid ground beneath his feet. I look at the grass, dry now and covered with hoarfrost in the mornings, and I long to walk on it again, after two months and more of pacing on creaking wooden floors and Persian carpets and, when we ask, the marble stairs of the entrance way. Traffic is light (for Tehran) on the street that I can see in the distance. It has been remarkably quiet today, a day when we expected large crowds to move by here en route to the demonstrations. All we heard were a few early this morning—and, in the distance, the chanting of a mullah's call to prayer several times during the day. Even the one guard and one servant (for meals) who are with us on this floor today ignore us. So we are left to ourselves and our devices, with which generally we are bored by this time. Vic is reading on one of the sofas in the big salon. Mike is doing his hour of pacing the floor. I manage an hour and find it too much. . . .

I find myself wondering how our colleagues are coping—if it is heavy going for us, what can it be like for them? I wonder how some of them are. It seems an eternity since I left them that morning of November 4. Tom Schaefer, for example—I wonder if he's lost his smile, which he was rarely without. A warm and decent man who could be firm but, I suspect, never unkind. Indeed, I find it difficult to think of him as capable of anger. Yet surely he must feel it now. A man who enjoyed people and now must be silent, who loved sports but now must sit, day after day, week after week.

And Kate Koob, as warmhearted a person as ever walked the earth, picked up at her Iran-America Society as a "spy"! And now held these many weeks and kept from doing what she loved doing and that was meeting and talking with and loving Iranians.

My housemate—Col. Chuck Scott, USA—or at least my housemate until a day or two before this happened, when he had moved to an apartment a short walk from the embassy. I remember counseling him that walking was not a good idea—as a military man he was too much a target. And yet he loved to walk (and jog) and especially to walk alone on the streets, using his Farsi (rather good) on shopkeepers and sidewalk vendors, fascinated by a country he knew well from a previous assignment. How does he tolerate this enforced idleness and silence?

DAY 69, *January 11, 1980*

Dear P,

Well, we are still in place, though there is a great deal of nervousness, as reflected in our limited access to Bell's invention. . . .

It has become a sort of test of wills, between the MFA [Ministry of Foreign Affairs] and the militants. What happens to us as people is beside the point—the MFA's stance in support of our staying here is its way of standing up with a bit of authority of its own, in a place where authority is not easily come by—unless you've seized it, as the militants have, by taking over the embassy and blithely ignoring all challenges, while speaking with the backing of the popular "will," as reflected by the masses in the streets outside the compound.

But as the British ambassador said in a note that arrived (together with some milk chocolate balls and chocolate-covered raisins), "What amazes me is that it is all so irrelevant to the real problems." How right he is. . . . From the viewpoint of the militants, however, it has not been irrelevant at all. Their purpose is to deepen the roots of the Revolution, to imbue the masses with greater Islamic and revolutionary zeal, to serve a warning that is indelible to the would-be leaders of this country that the Revolution can brook no identification with or acceptance of American purposes or policies in this region. But even they, after more than two months of this, must now be wondering where it is to lead, or at least whether their holding the compound and the hostages will not become a diminishing resource, and a bother at that.

I fear, however, that with elections on January 25 and February 15, there will be a compulsion to keep this charade going. . . . We are probably too prickly a subject for anyone to dispose of *before* the elections. And in the meantime, the hostage issue and that dramatically visible, slogan-festooned compound can continue to serve the political purpose of keeping the street masses agitated and the atmosphere sufficiently revolutionary to ensure the election of only those with genuine revolutionary zeal and credentials.

Oh, yes, I must note down my quote for the day from the *Tehran Times*—this one from a column about candidates for the presidential election:

> If Islam is not viewed as the vivid, inspiring, dynamic existential force which thundered out of the lips of Gabriel and was born to the world out of the womb of the Cave of Hira on the Night of Power, when the Qoran was revealed to the Prophet, so surged forth into a motion, the waves of which are still radiating outward, and when several decades later, Ali, the leader par excellence, being the first and foremost disciple of the Prophet and the master of both the material and spiritual worlds, was martyred from material existence, then it is not the true, the Towhide [the "one God"], the Revolutionary Islam.

Try that in one breath!

                            Love, Bruce

DAY 70, *January 12, 1980*
Dear Penne,

Well, not much happened today. Oh, the press did note that the International Seminar of Liberation Movements, organized by the "students" at the embassy, concluded its session and branded the United States as the major enemy of all the oppressed nations of the world. Or perhaps that doesn't strike you as news? The choice is limited. The seminar, incidentally, even had an American participant—an Indian named John Thomas from the Rosebud Reservation of South Dakota!

There are a few interesting noises out of New York, where the UNSC has delayed its meeting on sanctions for 24 hours to hear what the Iranians may have to say. That's progress, if they're saying *anything* in N.Y.!

I do have another good quote for you—again from the *Tehran Times* editorial page, which is a daily treasure trove of revolutionary rhetoric and dialectic. I won't bore you with much of it. In one section it describes how the Islamic revolutionary

> has no choice but to be ethical and moral and a socially positive force, for he consciously and voluntarily abandoned any attachment to worldly and material things. . . . What a contrast this is with the materialists' [that's you and me, should you wonder] mechanistic conception of the human being, who is only a helpless chemical conglomerate [*sic*], forming a unit of energy being shaped by inexorable and ultimately unintelligible factors.

All this on the day that I also read a report in the *Herald Tribune* in which the "student" revolutionaries at the compound, those examples of the "moral and socially positive" types noted above, continue to keep the hands of the hostages *bound!*

That is Islamic humanitarianism for you. B.S.!

B

DAY 71, *January 13, 1980*—Today is notable for yet another accusation against the United States. This time the finger is pointed at us as responsible for the "plot" that has produced 124 candidates for president in the upcoming election on January 25. This charge began at the Friday prayers, when the celebrated mullah at the compound, Mousavi Khoeini, told the throngs that our hand was behind this. Now it is taken up by the Imam and of course by the "students" who allege, in their 91st "circular" that "the Great Demon, bloodthirsty America, . . . is now attempting to destroy the mighty revolution of this brave nation from within, or to create deviations in its path. . . . The criminal U.S. has extended the range of its conspiracy, by interfering in the nominations for Presidential candidates. . . ." The mind boggles at this. How we can possibly be responsible for the people's eagerness to get their names in print by filing for the presidential election!

Ah well, I guess one should long since have concluded that we cannot win here under present circumstances. . . .

DAY 72, *January 14, 1980*
Dear Bill,

. . . Christmas passed here as pretty much another day, although a number of ambassadors sent us things to eat that helped for a while to relieve the monotony of the food. A bottle of catsup can do wonders to hide the taste and toughness of mystery meat #3! And a jar of peanut butter from the Dutch—we went through that in a hurry. Another ambassador sent us a bottle of "cough medicine," which helped our "coughs" a great deal, and even a can of caviar, which we kept on a window sill only to discover that a crow had knocked it off as he tried to peck his way into it. Three floors below it lay, but our security officer, Michael, bulldozed his way out the door past the guards and recovered it. . . .

So, you see, we have friends. . . .

The days go on. We try not to count them any more. We'll come through this all right, Bill, because we're standing firm on a principle that matters, i.e., that the taking of diplomats as hostages is a crime, pure and simple. . . . I wish you a good year, Bill . . . don't waste your energies worrying about me. I'd rather you show your colleagues there what good stuff you're made of, as you've been doing all along.

Sincerely, Dad

DAY 72, *January 14, 1980*
Dear Jim,

So you're back at school—joy. That reminds me of the Christmas card Chip sent me—it shows a slob of a character holding a drooping poinsetta flower and looking real forlorn—you open the card and it says, "Rejoice."

Today was just another day—they don't change much. But we had a visit from the Swiss ambassador, a fine man, and that made it possible to get some mail sent. . . . Had mystery meat #3 for dinner tonight . . . and catsup does wonders on #3. And on #4, 5, and 6, too, for that matter. But there's not much you can do for mushy cabbage, cold, especially when we had it for lunch, too! Best solution? Don't eat it! We didn't.

We've got a 3,000-piece jigsaw puzzle that we've been working on for weeks. It helps pass the time!

Hope you're following the UN debates on this subject and on Afghanistan, Jim. It's a good way to learn a lot about international diplomacy.

Sure miss you and Mom and Duchess, too. Take care of them, will you?

Regards, Dad

DAY 73, *January 15, 1980*
Dear P,

. . . I've just done my 30 minutes on the stairs. It's 10:00 P.M. and that helps me sleep, though we don't get to bed till midnight. Presidential candidates began appearing on TV tonight—each of them gets half an hour. Elections on

January 25, which means, in all honesty, that nothing will move on this crisis before then. The thought is depressing, but it's reality. And there are parliamentary elections on February 15.

As Ashok is inclined to say, more frequently than he should (in *The Far Pavilions*), "It isn't fair—It just isn't fair!" It's certainly not fair for our colleagues in the compound, about whom we are reminded so often. . . . We worry that, as time drags on, the whole issue will be forgotten, and public concern and unity at home will dissipate. And that concern will turn into futile anger and irritation—with all the negative effect that can have on the public atmosphere at home. I believe the administration's policy is exactly right, but I'm not sure how long the public can hold.

Love, B

DAY 74, *January 16, 1980*—Still snowing this morning—*big*, fluffy flakes. Ski slopes must be beautiful now. . . .

U.S. press is ordered out of the country—part of the rationale is that the "students might be more relaxed." Well, there may be something to that. At least it will deprive them of a podium of sorts from which to take positions. There's something to be said, too, for the criticism that all these "media opportunities" for the leadership here cause them to get painted into corners. But on balance I think I regret it, if only because it isolates this place even more. The foreign press chief here, a man named Sadegh, discussing this says, among other things, "I think the hostages do not live in a condition worse than millions of Americans. . . ." Thanks a lot—as if *that* were the issue!

Oh, yes, . . . another good quote. The head of the Revolutionary Court in Tabriz, a mullah, is quoted in the press (on the subject of recent disturbances there) as saying, "Following the fall of the Shah's regime, and when American imperialism lost its Savak bases here, world-devouring U.S. imperialism began to implement its plots by using dependent capitalists and Iranian exploiters. . . ." He added that "remnants of Savak, Free Masons, and capitalists were the main agitators."

It's always good to have a roster of scapegoats available. . . .

Beautiful! I've just seen a photo in the *Herald Tribune* of a large Cub Scout pack, all in uniform, "outside the occupied U.S. Embassy in Tehran as part of a day's outing. [*sic*] The Cub Scouts shouted anti-American slogans." *That* is the end! What a perversion of the Scout movement!

DAY 76, *January 18, 1980*—Where does a revolution find meaning and get its support? That meaning must be articulated, and it must be supported, both by the intelligentsia and the masses.

The Iranian Revolution has a very powerful meaning in one sense—the overthrow of the Shah and the regime that he headed. But that, however much it inspired the masses, was a negative purpose, an expression of what the Revolution was *against*, rather than what it is *for* in a future sense. That may be, or seem to be, an unfair judgment, or so the leaders of the Revolution would say, since it was and is obviously designed as well, in a strongly positive sense, to establish a system, a political and economic structure, a whole way of life that is motivated by and rests on Islamic principles and beliefs.

Hence the virtual total preoccupation by the radio and TV, and much of the press, with Islam, with Khomeini, with the simple and unpretentious Islamic way of life that he epitomizes, with a turning away from "Western" values and practices. The *Tehran Times* (the only paper to which we have access) had this to say in one of its long and rather turgid editorials the other day:

> The Iranian Revolution is anti-imperialist, anti-exploitation, and anti-dictatorial and directed towards a society which is free of any distinctions of class or any other mark of privilege and is, in the fullest sense, "Towhide," observing the truth that the material and spiritual worlds are totally integrated and inseparable dimensions of human consciousness.

Perhaps a year is too soon to expect that rhetoric such as that should by now be translated into something more concrete (though God knows, the anti-imperialist line is quite concrete in the shape of our embassy seizure and all the clamor that has accompanied that!). Nonetheless, it is difficult to see what all that is to mean in practice and in ways that promise material as well as spiritual comfort to the common man. (Clearly the masses, at least, *do* appear to get a good deal of *spiritual* satisfaction in all the rhetoric—if their continued enthusiastic participation in street processions and Friday prayers is any indication!) The same editorial goes on to say:

> One advantage which the Iranian Revolution under the leadership of Imam Khomeini has over so many others is its deep commitment to and understanding of what it means to be a human being. In that respect the Imam combines the revolutionary wrath which is necessary for a great motivator of social change with the spiritual awareness of a Mahatma Gandhi.

Well, that will remain to be seen, I suppose. Again it seems that in practice, and frequently in rhetoric, the emphasis is on the *negative,* to wit the following in the same editorial:

> And like all profoundly spiritual leaders, he opts for the passive and the peaceful path if that will be effective in achieving the aims of the Revolution and fulfill the aspirations of the people who are following his lead. But, equally, he is prepared for a belt-tightening resistance against the foreigner and against the domestic members of the privileged classes and, if necessary, armed struggle, where twenty million men, women, and young people take up arms in defense of their birthright.

Exactly, again the struggle *against* something that dominates the end of that paragraph of purpose. And this time, yes, our embassy, the foreigner, the United States, that affair surely had and still has as its purpose to galvanize the masses, to reenergize them in support of the Revolution, to have at the power that is portrayed as having frustrated the interests of the Iranian nation for the past 35 years, and the power that symbolizes all the foreign and materialist and sinister cultural influence from the West that Khomeini wants Iran to be rid of.

Another article recently put this element of the Revolution this way:

> This Revolution is the Revolution of people who crystallize and sculpt all their ideas and ideals from Islam. . . . The central kernel of this Revolution and the moving force of it are the young men and women who have decided to stand upon their own feet and not fall under the force of any unwanted power, whether internal or external . . . the health of international relations is based upon each country's being able to preserve its characteristics, authenticity, identity and finally the singularity and uniqueness of its culture. The West always tried and is still trying to impose its culture and criteria and particular way of thinking upon others, whether through force, military might and politics or through propaganda, without thinking about the danger and result of these efforts.

Well, there is much more of this kind of thing. I can have sympathy for it, especially in light of the history of Iran for the past 40 years. And yet it remains essentially negative, and intellectually chauvinistic in the extreme. No doubt it is a phase, in this and any other revolution. For the sake of all of us, not least the Iranians, one hopes that that phase soon passes into something more constructive and materially tangible. But I suspect we have a good while to wait. For the chauvinism and xenophobia that have been so evident in this Revolution from the start, and that now are hurled against Carter, imperialism, and the United States, are traits in Iranian society that go back a long time. Blaming the foreigner is a time-honored ploy, not only in Iran, but in Iran it has been a constant feature of politics since World War II—first the British, and to some extent the Russians (but they are too close to blame too avidly), and now the Americans. It reflects the preoccupation of most Iranians with themselves, with their sense of insecurity, and yet also their enormous pride and sense of cultural superiority over all their neighbors. (The way the Iranians look at Afghanistan, for example; Afghanistan is Iran's Appalachia.)

All of which is reflected in the persistent theme from Khomeini, thundered from Qom, that Iranians must rid themselves of Western culture and all its invidious penetration and derogation of Iranian culture and especially the tenets and way of life of Shi'a Islam. For that matter, Iranian culture, as he and many other both religious and secular nationalists see it, has been under attack for years from Western-encouraged permissiveness among the young—pornography, pop music, and ways of dress. Hence the very substantial (and to me understandable) reaction *against* the Western physical presence in Iran that developed in the years preceding the Revolution, including some 45,000 to 50,000 Americans. Good grief, I hope we've learned that much from this tragedy—that such a presence cannot help our long-term interests in a society and culture so different from ours and with rich and proud traditions of its own.

But surely the hard-line Islamic approach by the purists from Qom is also no answer to the Iranian split personality. Indeed, it may only deepen the social and political frustrations that now bedevil this place.

DAY 80, *January 22, 1980*
Dear Bill,

Well, in case you wondered, we're still here! Not much, indeed, nothing, will happen until this place elects a president—in an election scheduled for January 25. But there are lots of candidates, and the winner must get at least 50 percent of the votes, so we expect a runoff election and more delay. Maybe, when there is a president, someone will begin to make a decision here. But don't hold your breath!

We're not holding ours. We live from day to day, some days up and some days down. The Spanish ambassador sent me a good quotation: "Patience is a bitter cup, which only the strong can drink." I like that.

And that reminds me of our colleagues who are hostages at the compound. I think it's a tribute to *their* patience and their strength that so few of them have yet been brainwashed by the "students" to make public appeals for their (the "students' ") cause. After 79 days of forced silence and inhuman treatment, I think that speaks very well for the moral fiber of our colleagues.

Haven't been able to talk much with Mom lately; the "students" have been threatening, so they've got their friends in this building to cut us off after about three to ten minutes on the phone with Washington. It's a petty, peevish game they play, but there's not much we can do about it. . . .

Warm regards, Bill. Don't lose hope; we haven't. And we don't intend to make any compromise on the basic principle involved, either. We'll sit it out as long as necessary.

Dad

DAY 83, *January 25, 1980*—A doctor is coming in to give us physicals— that will at least be a diversion. Today, Friday, as usual is a very quiet day, the ministry empty and the streets around us quiet. Friday prayers have been moved indoors, into a mosque in another part of the city—too cold to sit outside, even down here in the middle of the city, where snow normally doesn't last long. Cold enough in this building today to keep a sweater on, but very quiet and boring. Fridays we don't even have a visit from the chief of protocol, who works hard and needs a day off once in a while. During the week he walks in on us about 5:30 or 6:00 and usually stays an hour, sitting here and talking. Some days we don't feel much like talking, so the atmosphere can be a bit stiff. Other days we might have had some reason to be cheerful, or more so, and then we find the conversation easier. He is our custodian, so to speak, so he is the one who makes sure we have the toilet articles we need, checks the food, and brings in the *Herald Tribune*. He also keeps us supplied with cookies, after we once mentioned that having that kind of thing would be a diversion from our diet. . . . He is a very senior diplomat in the Iranian Foreign Service, former ambassador to Indonesia, very protocol-conscious and yet a warm and decent man who, I think, is genuinely concerned for our welfare and wants to make our situation as bearable as possible. But as a responsible official, he is very careful in what he says on political matters, including our problem, and we do not press him very much. His constant advice is "patience." Well, we've learned that long, long ago and don't really need *that* advice.

DAY 86, *January 28, 1980*
Dear P,

Today our big event was getting mattresses! Imagine! May not sound like much to you, but thank God for small favors locally. I finally got so weary of rolling about in the trough that the pillows on my sofa amount to that I wrote a note to the chief of protocol appealing to him for a mattress for each of us. That produced expressions of regret for several days running that the ministry section that dealt with such was not one that he had authority over, but he would see what could be done. Mashallah (God be praised), there appeared three mattresses today, one of which now has replaced the pillows on my sofa, and I look forward tonight to modestly better sleeping. Sleeping is not my forte here—there is too much of it in the first place (midnight to 8:30 A.M.)—and so I spend much of it tossing, turning, thinking of this and that, and no doubt keeping my colleagues awake more than they let on. There is also, invariably, one trip to the bathroom during the night, and since the parquet floors in this area are notorious for their squeaking, it is a very noisy trip to the bathroom in this silent ministry!

I'm reading *The Adventures of Hajji Baba of Isfahan*, courtesy of the British ambassador, a book I've read before, but long ago, and it remains a wonderful character study of the Persians. Even the latter will concede that, though I suspect that if we were to suggest that today, we would be accused of trying to spread some Zionist, imperialist, counterrevolutionary plot! Which reminds me, a bit, of the reply by the newly elected President Abol Hassan Bani-Sadr today to a question about how the hostage crisis is to be resolved. According to the press, he replied by saying that Iranian demands of the United States were "simple"—all that was necessary was that the "U.S. should respect our political norms, our political dignity, leave us alone and allow us to settle our affairs in the way most suitable to us."

Well, now, that's fine, we would have no problem with that. Indeed, I would have to ask him: Just what did he think we were trying to do here during the nine months preceding November 4? Exactly that, but today, instead, we are accused of all sorts of malfeasance and interference and subversion. I am depressed by the way in which our motives are maligned here, for political purposes, of course.

B

Canadian Ambassador Ken Taylor and his wife, Pat, had been good and true friends of our embassy in better times in Tehran. How meaningful their friendship would be we would not know until catastrophe struck on November 4. That day six of the embassy staff slipped out the compound's back gate and, after several harrowing days of elusive flight from one place to another, finally found refuge in the residences of Ambassador Taylor and the minister of his embassy. Vic Tomseth maintained telephone contact with them at the outset. During Ambassador Taylor's several visits, he paced the floor with us, out of earshot of our guards, he keeping us aware in general terms of his cable exchanges with both Ottawa and Washington, and we offering our own ideas, on a plan for the Americans' departure from the city.

America could not have had better counsel than his, of his equally spirited wife, and indeed of Minister and Mrs. Sheardown and the entire Canadian Embassy staff. There had not been the slightest hesitation when the six first sought refuge with them; there was none thereafter in the very serious risks that attended the three months that followed, both in keeping their presence unknown and in the complex process of arrangements among the diplomatic and intelligence communities of both governments. January 29 saw the safe departure of the six Americans, each with Canadian passports, forged Iranian visas, and the best Canadian accents they could muster. Simultaneously, Ambassador Taylor closed his embassy and departed the country with his entire staff.

Canada had demonstrated, for all Americans to see, the quality of a true good neighbor. In the ministry, our spirits had never been higher with the news that all concerned were safely out of Iran. It mattered little that for several weeks—the students and others suspicious that the three of us had been somehow involved— all visits from friendly ambassadors ceased, and telephone contact with Washington stopped for a time as well. What mattered was that our colleagues were safely out of Iran and that Canadian-American relations had a boost that we hoped would never be undone.

The next day, an American journalist who had not yet left Tehran was described in press reports as communicating the news to an armed student at the chained gates of our embassy. The student's reaction was an expression of disbelief, capped with the words, "but that's illegal!"

DAY 88, *January 30, 1980*

Dear Bill,

Got about nine letters from Mom yesterday, which made my day! Full of all kinds of news of what she's been up to. Also sent me a clipping showing you and Chip at the candlelight vigil—you are both in uniform and look sharp indeed. So many people have written to say how impressed they have been by the way you boys have conducted yourselves. And Mom was *very* grateful to you and Chip for spending time with her and Jim at Christmas time. . . . Mom tells me that you and Leah had plans to go up and visit the Lopez family. Wonder how that went. Sergeant Lopez is a *good* Marine—good humor, good spirit, tough, *and* an excellent drawer—he does cartoons that are professional indeed. . . .

Not much has changed here, with *one* exception. We now have a president-elect with almost 80 percent of the popular vote, which is remarkable and encouraging. That means there *should* be much greater decision-making capacity here. He is also a rational man, relatively moderate on the hostage issue, so I am optimistic—modestly so.

Another change, in a different sense, has to do with the big news today that six of our colleagues are now out of here. We are absolutely delighted by this news, since we have worried about them ever since the beginning. We knew they were in good hands. *How* good has now been made apparent to everyone. I hope it reminds the American people what great and good and trusted neighbors we have to the north. Too often we ignore them, or at best don't bother to think about them. Not that we mean it, or are hostile, but just that we are so preoccupied with our own problems, and so big, that we don't think often enough what massively important real estate that big stretch of land to the north is. And what basically friendly and compatible people the Canadians are. In a crunch, they are our closest and most reliable friends, and we should never forget that. And good luck, Bill, in everything you do.

Sincerely, Dad

DAY 89, *January 31, 1980*

Dear P,

The end of another month! It's a cold winter morning here, but clear and sunny. . . . Don't know when we'll get another chance to send out mail, but I'll write this in hope something will turn up. We're not getting many visitors anymore and probably will get fewer for a while as "punishment" for the Canadian caper. . . .

I'm amazed to read in your letters of the numbers of people who've written or called. What great friends—and what a great service the Foreign Service is in a time of need. Even William Rogers calling! And Kissinger sending you another note! I can't imagine how we'll ever be able to repay all this kindness. Here, too—the Brits, the Australians, Danes, Dutch, Germans, Vatican, and, of course, those lovely, magnificent people, the Canadians. I can't tell you how much Ambassador Ken and Pat Taylor did for us here. They were good friends before the takeover, and since? Well, *since*, they've been heroic. That's all one can say. There was never the slightest doubt that they would do everything they could, and do it gladly. . . .

B

6

February 1980:
Backstage Maneuvering

Among the policy options open to the Carter administration, diplomacy was consistently a favored one. The first months of 1980 saw Washington in an especially high state of diplomatic activity—some public, a good deal covert— that culminated in a long-overdue break in diplomatic relations in early April, to be followed within two weeks by a rescue mission and its tragic failure at Desert One.

Pursuing every conceivable opening, the Carter administration edged close to economic sanctions and then backed away, pronouncing veiled warnings of force—especially regarding Tehran's occasional talk of putting the hostages on trial—and then backing off and sending careful signals of a readiness to discuss differences with that regime. That was especially true after Bani-Sadr's election as president in early February, raising Washington's hopes for a more moderate power center in the chaos of Tehran.

Watching this from our vantage point in the Foreign Ministry but unaware of the details of the secret and sometimes almost cloak-and-dagger, person-to-person minuet of Ham Jordan, the French and Argentine lawyers, and eventually Foreign Minister Ghotbzadeh himself, our hopes rose and fell almost daily. We were increasingly concerned that Washington was overlooking the fact that in all this maneuvering the real power brokers, namely, the students at the compound and, above all, the Ayatollah Khomeini, were not on board.

To us Washington seemed prepared to risk conceding a prior guarantee, and prior implementation as well, of an agreed release of the hostages before considering Iran's grievances against the United States. Having already been held illegally for several months, we thought it better to sweat it out longer to preserve the principle that, whatever its "grievances" against the United States, Iran had no right on any grounds to hold diplomats as pawns to serve its own political purposes. So we took every opening available to us to get our concerns across to Washington; however, our access to the telex ceased totally following the Canadian caper, and the ambassadorial visits and other outside contacts dropped off as well. The telephone calls from Washington stopped totally for a time and never thereafter resumed on any sustained basis.

DAY 90, *February 1, 1980*—Well, no visitor today either. I suspect we are being "punished" for the Canadian caper and possibly for having had access to the phone for so long that evening. It's been dead for the 48 hours since that time. Tomorrow is Friday so there will, in any event, be no visitor then. We feel intensely frustrated to be so totally out of touch with whatever may be under way. . . . Even our telex has been unproductive for two days. Tonight on the local TV news we heard a report that the administration may be considering a deal where we are turned over to the Red Cross here while the tribunal proceeds to investigate the Shah's misdeeds. I think that would be a mistake because it would reward their blackmail without getting the hostages *totally* released. It would mean giving them what they've demanded in return for only a *partial* release! *No.* . . .

Tomorrow is Groundhog's Day. If the ARK sees his shadow, we'll be here another six weeks. Or do I have that wrong? . . .

We enjoy our little diversions, like watching the pigeons this morning breaking the ice in the fountain in the garden below. Landing on the thin ice, walking toward the edge, the ice breaking, and the birds enjoying a cold bath.

The TV tonight is full of documentary films of the ARK's return exactly one year ago today. Full also of films of processions and prayer meetings all over the country, lauding him and praying for his good health.

You wonder why he doesn't smile? Let me tell you why by quoting from *The Adventures of Hajji Baba of Isfahan*, that celebrated book about Persians from 1823, which paints a picture of a place and a people whose characteristics have not changed all that much. Hajji has sought refuge in a shrine in Qom, and his friend, a dervish, tells him this about Qom:

> This Qom is a place that, excepting on the subject of religion, and settling who are worthy of salvation and who to be damned, no one opens his lips. Every man you meet is either a descendant of the Prophet or a man of the law. All wear long and mortified faces, and seem to look upon that man as an appointed subject for the eternal fires who happens to have a rosy cheek and a laughing eye. Therefore as soon as I approach this place, I always change the atmosphere of my countenance from fair to haze, and from haze to downright clouds and darkness, according as circumstances may require. . . .

DAY 93, *February 4, 1980*
Dear P,

It is three months today. . . . It is also the Prophet's birthday . . . and so another holiday. As you said one day on the phone, don't they ever work? Well, not more than necessary. I've just finished *Hajji Baba.* I am even more amazed at how national characteristics then viewed (admittedly by an Englishmen) remain so true today. For example, Hajji talks of the "Franks," i.e., the Europeans, thus:

> The Franks talk of feelings in public life of which we are ignorant. They pretend to be actuated by no other principle than the good of their country. These are words without meaning to us; for as soon as I die, or when the Shah is no more, all that we may have done for the welfare of Persia will most likely be destroyed; and when his successor shall have well ruined the people in securing himself, the whole business of improvement and consolidation must be gone over again.

Ah, well, let us be generous. Perhaps this time, with the Revolution, things can develop differently. For Iran's sake, I hope so. I have never faulted the Revolution as a hopeful process of change, but let it focus on what Iran needs to do for *itself* rather than on foreign scapegoats who are supposedly frustrating everything the Revolution seeks to do. . . .

The evening TV news has just shown some footage of the militants at the compound doing some close-order drill with guns in our parking lot. Much chanting of revolutionary and Khomeini slogans. Penne, I get so angry watching stuff like that that I could scream and cry and bust the TV set! *Our embassy, our* property, stolen, pilfered, looted, our people held hostage. I will never get over it. I hope those "students" live to regret it some day.

Love, Bruce

DAY 94, *February 5, 1980*—My God, has this place no pride? Tonight, on the late TV, or should we say "local prime time," there being little else to watch on the boob tube here, the "students" were back on with more of their "revelations" from the plundered files of our embassy. Tonight they appeared to be reading from biographical reports on various senior Iranians, one of whom is presently a minister. Routine stuff, the kind of thing all embassies do, to build up a data base on the leadership of a country so one knows something about the actors. . . . None of the stuff was harmful to *our* interests (as if we had any interests left here!). But the shocking thing is that the leadership here allows this kind of thing to continue.

It is so degrading to *Iran.* Surely an intelligent Iranian watching this kind of performance must be repelled . . . allowing a group of "students" to claim TV time to denigrate leaders in the present government. But beyond that, allowing "students" to continue defying all standards of conduct and decency—looting a foreign embassy's files, sitting there three months after the seizure while 50

Americans wait in silent degradation. It is so outrageous that I could choke the first Iranian I see. . . . A gang of thieves, condoned by another gang of thieves. Fie on them all. . . .

DAY 96, *February 7, 1980*

Dear P,

I'm dubious that this bunch of papers that I've been writing will be going anywhere very soon, given our status these days. Telex and telephone cut since January 29 and no visitors since the 26th. . . . A contact in protocol today confirmed that these actions against us relate to the Canadian caper. I found out because I tried to send out a note to the Swiss ambassador, thanking his wife for some nut bread and saying I hoped he'd come in to see us. I was told that instructions have been issued that all such contacts were to cease. Well, we can live with that kind of pettiness . . . or, as Meg Greenfield called it, "muddled and mean." (Her *Washington Post* editorials on this hostage issue have been consistently first class.) Happily, we hope, the hostages at the compound haven't suffered for it. Such pettiness degrades the Iranians more than it hurts us.

Not sure you care for all this chitchat in my letters, but it amounts to a kind of diary, so hope you bear with it. Wrote a long letter to the new Iranian president today, calling the continued holding of the hostages something that "makes a mockery of human rights in Iran." I also gave him some detail on the kind of people who are being held there, because I'm not sure he knows, and he should. I'm not even sure the letter will ever reach him, but it did my conscience good to write it.

The news these days is full of embassy seizures and attacks in other countries—the French in Libya, several in Central America—and I suspect they are not without considerable inspiration from the situation here. That is a cost that the Iranian authorities might give some thought to, they who have condoned and encouraged an act of blackmail such as we have seen here. The result is a growing new international menace and even more evidence that this business of diplomacy is becoming a dangerous profession indeed, and *that* profession ought to be sacrosanct from such dangers because it was, and is, a profession meant to provide the means for civil communication and dialogue among governments, even in times of tension. When this crisis here is over, I think our government must take some initiative within the UN to try to get some broad international backing and consensus for stiff actions against governments that condone the abuse of diplomatic privilege and practice. . . .

This morning's *Tehran Times* had several quotes that suggest at long last that men of some courage are beginning to speak up here, especially former PM Bazargan, who among other things was quoted as saying: "Now the country is run by a bunch of kids and this is regrettable." And he said this about the "students" reading from our files: "It is not correct to devote the TV screen to the most shameful accusations against people without asking the other side to defend themselves. You jeopardize the honor and nobility of the people with this."

And Bani-Sadr's description of the "students" is magnificent: "dictators who have created a government within a government." And "How could you expect a government employee to go to work feeling secure? When there is no legal or judicial security in the country, that will undoubtedly lead to disorder."

Ah, but now what will the ARK have to say on the subject? Let us hope that he does not undercut his president, in this excellent beginning—at long last—in curbing the power of the "students."

Today we hear that all sorts of Americans are in town on private jaunts of one kind or another to promote what they describe as "reconciliation." A group promoted by a Kansas University professor commends the "students," presumably for inviting them, in these words: "We congratulate the students for the bold and courageous effort." Come on, we don't need that kind of pandering to what Bazargan rightly calls "a bunch of kids." I suppose it makes for great lecture material out in Kansas, but I'd like to believe these characters aren't representative of those solid citizens out there. This individual, Norman Forer, also is quoted as deploring the "wanton exploitation of the hostage situation by the war mongerers and money changers of the country." Good grief, if that is the way he interprets U.S. *restraint* on this issue, he isn't fit to teach kindergarten. . . .

Today I finished the 3,000-piece puzzle! I need a new diversion. The Brits sent in *War and Peace*, but I read that once, and I don't intend to stay here the length of time it would take to read *that* again.

Love, B

DAY 100, *February 11, 1980*

Dear P,

Today was the first anniversary of the Revolution. It rained *all* day. (We found it difficult not to take some psychic satisfaction in that fact.) But from the TV coverage this evening the rain appears not to have kept down the crowds at the parade, happily this time *not* along the street in front of the American Embassy. The chief guest appears to have been Yassir Arafat. The film of his arrival, together with Bani-Sadr, at the parade reviewing stand showed absolute chaos! *Masses* of military personnel, so many of *them* as to cause the most incredible security debacle you can imagine. How they got Bani-Sadr and Yassir up to the stand without them being crushed is beyond me. The parade here, as well as those in cities around the country, appeared to be heavily if not entirely military. That's a bit of a paradox, considering all the hoopla about this Revolution being against militarism, the excessive arms purchases from the West, etc. Yet there were all the tanks, howitzers, APCs [armored personnel carriers], trucks, and marching soldiers that all that money bought!

And slogans! My God, if the success of this Revolution were to depend on slogans, it would be vastly successful. The past week has been *all* Revolution on the TV, and the air is constantly rent with the screams of the crowds, the constant slogan yelling, denunciations of the United States being heard right and left, of course.

But *more* important. Tonight on VOA [Voice of America radio] we heard a report, apparently from in front of the Iranian Embassy (in Washington) during one of the prayer vigils because we could hear "The Battle Hymn of the Republic" being sung. And there was a brief exchange with Louisa Kennedy [wife of hostage Moorhead Kennedy] and a VOA reporter in which she sounded wonderfully angry about the *criminality* of this thing. Also a brief recording of Kate Koob, apparently from the time the other day when Archbishop Capucci was squired around the embassy. She spoke in very emotional terms. My heart went out to her, knowing what a wonderful, sensitive person she is, now held there like a criminal and shown off to a visiting "prince of the church" as if the place were a zoo. . . .

I've just finished a book, *The Political Elite of Iran,* by Marvin Zonis. The book reminded me, in ways that I think I had forgotten, of the extent to which Iran has been invaded, dominated, interfered with by outside powers—never to the point of losing its independence, but often losing its pride and self-respect. One of the results was that it never had a unifying war to *achieve* its independence. All of which clearly has left a deep mark on the character of these people, evident in the *intense* bitterness that has been built up—or found expression—against us over the past several months. But this rests in turn on a couple of *centuries* of foreign penetration, something that the current crowd, so determined to get at *us,* overlook. Their problems did not begin with the Shah. They are deep and historic, much more so than most of us, including myself, have fully appreciated, to our regret.

B

DAY 102, *February 13, 1980*

Dear P,

Your letters are wonderful, Honey! I feel privileged indeed. . . . I'm impressed by all your work . . . the yellow ribbon bit, your work with the families. You're wonderful, and everyone says so. Certainly agree with you too that the families have held up beautifully, or so it seems to us. We have commented frequently, the three of us, how struck we are with the apparent absence of *any* public criticism by the families of the government's approach to this crisis. Having said that, we recognize that we don't have much information here—perhaps there has been some. I've written letters to all of the families, a big job, but it gave me something to do. Problem is I have no way, apparently, of mailing them.

. . . I'm reading a book by Edward Crankshaw, *The Shadow of the Winter Palace,* on Russian history of the 19th century. Book sent to us by Brits. A fascinating study of the Romanov tsars, I am again impressed, as I was in reading *Hajji Baba* relating to Iran, to see how Soviet behavior today (and

Iranian behavior) is the product of centuries of history. Obviously all peoples, all nations, are molded by their historical experience. Thank God *U.S.* history, however blemished, was one that fostered openness and liberalism, so unlike both the Russian and Persian experiences.

As I wrote earlier, I was struck by what to me was the incongruity of the massive military tone of the first anniversary celebrations here. In that connection, the paper the next morning noted that three people were killed when they were crushed under tanks along the parade route, and others injured. And we read today that six of the celebrated 49 Americans brought here by the "students" were injured in the collapse of one of the reviewing stands when crowds got out of control. We remain appalled that Americans are prepared to come here to be *used* by the "students," but I suppose that among 220 million Americans there are bound to be *some* fools. Another vignette from reporting on the chaotic parade, this lovely line from one press report: "The parade was cancelled after it became impossible to round up the spectators."

Another aspect of the celebrations was the time-honored revolutionary gambit (here) of urging everyone to go out on their rooftops at 9:00 P.M. on the eve of the Revolution and shout "Allah O'Akbar" at the top of their lungs for 15 minutes. One supposes it does something to fire up enthusiasm. In any event that slogan, heard at virtually every gathering here, is one with which I have no problem. I agree with it.

While I'm on celebrated press quotes, here's another one, in which the "student" militants are quoted as talking about their current confrontation with Bani-Sadr: "We will help Bani-Sadr fulfill his role as President within the articles of the Constitution, but he should not interfere in issues that are not dealt with in the Constitution, such as the hostages issue." To which Vic responded, as we read this with some astonishment at breakfast today, "Well, now, the Constitution doesn't specifically deal with robbery and kidnapping either, does it?" You can see the problem that has now been created here, for which the leaders (all of them, Bani-Sadr included) have no one to blame but themselves.

Vic (who must have lettered in it at college!) and Mike play a great deal of backgammon. It's a good game, though I'm not good at it. I'll teach Jim when I'm home. He would be a whiz, too.

B

DAY 107, *February 18, 1980*—We have kept close to the shortwave to get the latest on VOA as to what is up in New York and Washington. Late in the day we hear that Iran, too, has now agreed to the five-man panel of inquiry that Waldheim has put together, and there is talk of its being in New York within 24 hours. But we are at a loss to know what else is involved, how the panel relates to the timing of our release, etc. Vance is said to have gone to NYC to see Waldheim. We fear that there are a good many loose ends to tie up, any one of which could cause a snag. And we are concerned, too, about the indications that release is *not* now likely to be coincident with the start of the panel's work, which seems to us to be a concession to blackmail that we will live to regret. But we are holding our fire until we learn a bit more.

Otherwise the day has been a normal one—heavy snow, but clear blue skies by this afternoon. How wonderful it will be to walk in fresh air again, after more than three months! An end to creaky floors and slippery Persian carpets! Some mail arrived, including three good letters from Penne, full of her own indignation over the time that has elapsed and the obduracy of the crowd here. Her spirits sound good, and her vexation is understandable. What a magnificent person she is!

My quote for the day, again from a *Tehran Times* editorial, which—commenting that in a "tolerant" mood Ghotbzadeh had said that the U.S. press might again be admitted here—wrote this about the misbehavior of the press while they were here before: "The slightest hint of a controversy, or a dissension or conflict, which Iran with all its post-revolutionary problems was trying to solve, were avidly taken up to make it look as though nearly everyone in Iran were acting like a pack of unrestrained savages."

Exactly. How else to characterize the mobs that gathered daily for weeks and weeks on end outside our embassy, encouraged to go there by the local press and authorities, to scream their hate and venom for all of Iran and all the world to see?

DAY 109, *February 20, 1980*—It is late, 11:30 P.M., and we have just heard on VOA of the formal announcement of the panel, "which it is believed will lead to a release of the hostages." Other reports earlier spoke of a "gentlemen's agreement" in the background somewhere between us and Iran and the UN on this point. Well, one would surely hope so. It cannot be simply left to a "hope" or "expectation." We hear also that the panel is delaying its arrival until the weekend, because the Iranians needed "more time." No doubt. They probably need more time to get the mobs organized who will scream and shout in the panel's hearing about the Shah's excesses and U.S. "connivance" with him. Or perhaps they need more time to get the Savak prisons and torture chambers ready and the slums in South Tehran ready for the visitors to see. Perhaps even an assassination attempt might be "discovered" to add to the tensions while the panel is here.

But *worse* is the VOA report that Waldheim has said that *at Iranian insistence* each of the hostages is to be interviewed by the panel. We are appalled that we have agreed to that, which is nothing other than the old militants' demand that the hostages be put on trial, but with the euphemism of their being "interviewed." The hostages—and that includes us three—are not relevant to the inquiry! The 50 at the compound are totally uninformed of the events of the past three and a half months! They had no part whatsoever in events during the Shah's period! They have been subjected to three and a half months of propaganda and brainwashing by their captors! How can anyone who calls himself an international lawyer agree to any such procedure? For that matter, how have legal experts agreed to even *beginning* this operation without a firm commitment that the gross illegality of the holding of diplomats as hostage be *ended* before they *begin* their inquiry? Surely they see the illegality of expecting uninformed and abused hostages to speak to the question this panel is to address. What guidance do they, the 50, or we have from our government? *None.*

We are saddened and deeply worried, more than at any time since this tragedy began. We are all to be faced with a serious moral dilemma: do we *agree* to speak to the panel, or do we refuse, and what then? If we agree to speak, what do we say? And having spoken, what is done with our "testimony"?

DAY 110, *February 21, 1980*—There is not much change today, beyond statements from various sources as to the status of the panel and much speculation, all vague, as to the relationship between the panel's work and the hostage release. VOA reported that yesterday morning in Washington the president was awakened at 3:30 A.M. on the issue and called a meeting in the Oval Office for 5:30 A.M. That apparently produced a statement to the press emphasizing, inter alia, (1) that the panel would also hear complaints from the U.S. side against Iran (not clear from whom), (2) that it was a fact-finding body and not a tribunal, and (3) that the hostages were not to be interrogated but that the panel would *see* each hostage. Where all this leaves us is not clear and probably won't be for some days; clearly, we think, there is some quiet understanding somewhere on the key aspect of timing of release, which I'm sure all agree cannot be made public now.

Indicative of the pitfalls still to be risked is the TV show being run as I write this note. The "students" have apparently been cleared by the RC [Revolutionary Council] for yet another NIRT [National Iranian Radio and Television] "show and tell" of "revelations," i.e., documents pilfered from embassy files to prove American spying and other activities against Iran. Two "students" sit there, reading *selectively* from documents, in earnest and outraged tones. Anyone with perceptive good sense would realize the documents are not being read whole and in any event give no proof of actions hostile to the Revolution. The whole business is outrageous, repulsive, degrading to *Iran.* . . . This place is truly mad. . . .

> There were many such "down" days for us in Tehran, days when it was an uphill battle to retain our confidence that time and patience would eventually work in our favor. None of those days would equal the pain and depression that we felt with news of the failed rescue mission, soon to hit us like an avalanche. But no less discouraging was the Ayatollah Khomeini's public statement in late February, with the much ballyhooed UN Panel of Inquiry airborne en route to Tehran at the very moment he spoke, that the hostage issue would be decided by the Majlis, the new parliament then expected to be elected in late March. Had we known at the time of the Ayatollah's statement that the Majlis would not begin to focus on the hostage issue until July, our frustration would have been even deeper. In any event, the Ayatollah's statement—in effect, dogma written in stone, as was the case with all his pronouncements—essentially scuttled the panel's purposes.

DAY 112, *February 23, 1980*

Dear Penne,

I feel as if I've been up before the parole board and failed! On the 2:00 P.M. news today, the ARK issued a statement that the issue of the hostages should be decided by the Majlis! The latter doesn't even yet exist—elections are not until March 14 and 21 . . . so we can't expect the issue to be even addressed until early April. And of course there is no likelihood whatsoever that the ARK's position will change, it having now been handed down from the heights. We are astounded by this, since we had brought ourselves to believe that there must be some quiet understanding on timing for release at some point during the panel's meetings here, or at least at its termination. That panel is airborne now, en route from Geneva. So far no reaction from Washington to the ARK's statement, but we assume that the U.S. government has been had.

We are sick at heart, especially for our colleagues who are now sentenced to possibly another two months of isolation. Where is compassion in this place? There clearly is none. The ARK's God must be a different one from mine. I think this is the lowest moment I have known here since the first week. We can take it, however deeply I miss you, Penne, and the boys, but I grieve for my compatriots at the embassy so cruelly treated. I think of home, of perhaps helping (trying?) Jim with homework, walking with Duchess, visiting your folks, driving over to see Bill, hearing more of Chip's discoveries of life in Minnesota. I am missing so much, and it's so *damned unnecessary* if this place were led by someone with vision, and by people with a capacity for self-criticism. Today's *Tehran Times* had a story with this headline: "If released, Hostages will go to Psychiatrists." Ha! I don't need a psychiatrist, but I know a nation that does!

Love, B

DAY 114, *February 25, 1980*—We woke this morning to rain, which turned to wet snow—much to our delight because we hoped it would complicate the preparations for the march-past in front of our embassy that today marked the end of "National Mobilization Week." What effect it had, we don't know. The affair went ahead on schedule, and we watched coverage of it on tonight's TV news show. The new president, Bani-Sadr, gave a speech from the top of the guardhouse at the embassy's motor pool gate, followed by a vitriolic anti-American harangue by one of the students. I am appalled. The very *idea* of a president of a country, standing on the walls of a stolen foreign embassy, within which members of that embassy staff are held hostage! It is beyond my comprehension, almost, though after the past four months I should perhaps not be surprised! As Vic says, these people seem to lack a sense of proportion, and today was a classic example. Did Bani-Sadr have *any* reservations himself at the propriety of such an act? Or does he feel so hard-pressed, so unsure of himself politically that he feels he must indulge in such obscene acts as this? God knows.

Today's *Tehran Times* carried a letter to it from Bruce German, B&F [budget and fiscal] officer at the embassy and now a hostage. It states the case of the students for the Shah's extradition and then appeals to the United States to act to obtain the hostages' release. One wonders if Bruce really wrote the letter. If he did, what force did he feel to do it? Or is it simply the effects of almost four months' denial of *any* knowledge of what his government and people are doing for him? How can anyone be critical of anyone in such circumstances? How can anyone feel anything but revulsion toward people who force their victims to such demeaning acts? I feel a strong sense of sympathy for Bruce's family, whom Penne knows and whom she speaks well of. What effect does such a letter have on them, especially his children? Does it occur to Bruce's captors that their actions have fallout there, too? Perhaps they do and couldn't care less.

DAY 115, *February 26, 1980*—Quiet day. I sent a letter of regret today to the president concerning his using the walls of our embassy as a podium for yesterday's affair. I wonder if my letters ever reach his office, and if so, if they have any impact. A letter to U.K. Ambassador John Graham didn't make it through the system—I knew I was getting too frank. But as I told the chief of protocol who returned it, he must expect that I will press for every opportunity I get for communication. . . .

> Dear Mr. President,
>   As you know, it is the view of my government, a view overwhelmingly supported by world legal and public opinion, that the seizure of its Embassy in Tehran and the holding of its personnel as hostages for political purposes was and is a flagrant violation of all precepts of international law and practice.
>   I must therefore record my deep sense of regret that by the use of the walls of that Embassy as a podium for yesterday's National Mobilization Week march-past, the dignity of your office was so directly and graphically linked to the situation affecting that Embassy and the personnel still forcibly held there as hostages.

It is 10:00 P.M., and the TV is carrying another hate session, this one an assembly of those allegedly disabled during the Shah's period, all of them assembled at the Hilton Hotel (where the UN Panel of Inquiry is staying) to hear fiery speeches by various mullahs—all for the benefit of the panel. As Vic calls it, another "dog and pony show" or, as I would call it, another "show and tell" session, so that the panel gets the proper picture. There have already been other gatherings of the disabled, a visit to the cemetery, another to the prisons. . . . Yesterday, on five minutes' notice, the panel (plus a UN assistant secretary general) was ushered in to see us, and we spent two hours talking with them. We made a fairly comprehensive statement in which we expressed our concerns about the very creation of the panel (a reward to blackmail that continues), the procedures they will follow, the importance of their seeing our 50 colleagues, the conditions we and they have faced, etc.

They were a good audience, listened carefully, told us to avoid substance relating to U.S.-Iranian relations (not in their mandate with us, they said), and asked a good many questions. It was high drama for us to be able to get a good many things off our chests. We learned little, however, as to how all this links up with the timing of our release, their answer essentially being that for the present that should be left to the "constructive ambiguity" within which the whole thing was agreed upon. That leaves us decidedly worried, in light of the Imam's strong statements about the Majlis, but since we have little else, we hang onto straws about this "ambiguity" and the statements we continue to hear from Waldheim and Washington that indeed there is a link between the panel's report and the timing of release.

Beheshti was quoted yesterday as saying that the Majlis probably would not get to the hostage issue until May, blithely seeming to set that human issue aside while procedures are dealt with. The callousness of statements like that, after four months of holding innocent people criminally hostage, is appalling, especially coming from someone who professes to be a man of God.

Today the news carries reports of the seizure by terrorists of the Dominican Embassy in Bogotá, along with U.S. Ambassador Diego Ascencio and 12 other ambassadors. This, obviously, is a further manifestation of the "Iranian Syndrome" and of why it is so vital that this seizure here continue to be seen for what it is, international blackmail by terrorists supported by a government and therefore a criminal act for which that government cannot escape responsibility.

It is all so callous, especially when one reads the same day in the *Tehran Times*' editorial: "[Islam] is a religion which first takes into account the nurturing of the soul to reach to the highest of spiritual endeavours, a religion that teaches gentleness, tolerance, mercy, patience and every conceivable virtue in the pursuit of divine goals." How can they possibly write such stuff in the face of the *in*tolerance and cruelty being shown to the 50 innocent men and women in the compound?

7

March 1980: UN Diplomacy Fails

March would see the apogee of the UN-led negotiating process and its eventual collapse, with its panel of inquiry leaving Tehran in seething frustration. Had the process succeeded, it would have seen our 50 colleagues from the embassy compound brought to the same rooms where we were held—removed from student control as the first step in an intricate diplomatic scenario painstakingly pursued (especially by Foreign Minister Ghotbzadeh) since the secretary general's visit in January. Its failure dramatically demonstrated that real power at that point lay with the student militants, thanks to their supporters in the Revolutionary Council and the Ayatollah's own appreciation of the students' emotional hold on the masses in the street. But the month would not end before a further effort, led by President Bani-Sadr and involving, in the background, a French lawyer, an Argentine lawyer, and a mysterious Jimmy Carter letter.

The three of us were left with our own share of frustration, always heightened—as would be the case throughout the crisis—by a sense that we knew only pieces of the total picture beyond the walls of the ministry.

DAY 119, *March 1, 1980*—We made it through Leap Year Day yesterday. The day's high point was when Mike, who spends some time occasionally sitting in a window overlooking the street (to the great vexation of our security guards), spotted Luigi (my cook) and Hicaz (my driver) in a car across the street. They had obviously driven over here to see if we could be spotted. We waved. They got out of the car, but we signaled them to get back in the car and leave before the guard at the entrance spotted them and caused them trouble. But how good it was, just to be able to wave briefly to these two fine people! . . .

We watch the news reports carefully to see if the UN panel is making any progress in seeing the hostages, which appears to be evolving as the real litmus test of whether the panel and Bani-Sadr can make any headway against the militants and conservative clerics. But nothing appeared to move today, which made for a very depressing day. We are getting a bit edgy with this endless affair. Perhaps tomorrow will prove a better day. I made another request of the foreign minister today for resumed telex and telephone contact with Washington, but expect it to be ignored. . . .

Today we read in the press that apparently the "students" *themselves* have been holding former Deputy PM Entezam prisoner since he was reported arrested "for CIA contacts" in November, . . . and they are holding the Navy's commander, also recently arrested on the basis of documents allegedly found in our embassy linking him to us. The charges are preposterous, but worse is the fact that the "students" can actually arrest and hold such people. They are a sovereign state unto themselves.

DAY 121, *March 3, 1980*—The UN panel is still here, continuing, among other things, their efforts to see the hostages. Tonight the word is that the Revolutionary Council had agreed, but the "students" say they will agree only if the ARK so directs. And apparently a further condition from the "students" is that the panel accept some documents stolen from our embassy as "evidence." What a travesty it all is! What a shabby business that a government is so throttled by a bunch of lawbreaking "students" that it becomes in effect a lawbreaker itself. But, having embarked on this panel approach, what alternative is there?

DAY 122, *March 4, 1980*—Today is four months, the 122d day, a third of a year, and the end is not yet in sight. The optimism of several weeks back is largely dissipated in the face of the reality of Iran's political structure, the power struggle of contending forces, and the continued rigidity of the ARK. Today the president, a man who no doubt wants to find a solution, is quoted as telling the press: "Until now the government has not taken over the hostages . . . I should not be responsible for the hostages." True enough, physically the "students" still hold them, "students" that the leadership here has allowed, over these past four months, to evolve into a state within a state. They occupy their own sovereign territory, territory that once was sovereign U.S. soil. They control who comes and goes; they have their own small militia that trains and marches back and forth within the compound; they issue press releases; they summon the press to read "revelations" from embassy documents, and, in the process, they condemn innocent men, Iranian and American; indeed, they even hold Iranian leaders, people like Entezam, if one is to believe press reports. They are a force that the government here must negotiate with to find a basis on which the work of the UN Panel of Inquiry can conduct its work.

So the president is absolutely and tragically right. The government has not taken over the hostages; it cannot control their captors. But the president is not right when he says *he* should not be responsible for the hostages. Governments *are* responsible for what goes on in their domain. Bani-Sadr is now president. He cannot evade responsibility. He and others who have passed for government here over the past four months *are* responsible. He has been a member of the Revolutionary Council since the beginning. That council endorsed the actions of the "students" from the very outset. That action was a crime against humanity, against all precepts of international law and practice, from the very moment it occurred. Those who aid and abet a crime are no less criminal thereafter than those who committed it. There can be no escaping that judgment. No amount of rationalizing on the basis of past alleged grievances can be allowed to set that judgment aside.

From the first moment, the action understandably, given Iran's revolutionary political climate, became a political issue, which meant that any leader or would-be leader who said or did anything bearing on the action would need to take into account the impact on his own political status or future of doing so. With parliamentary elections now only ten days off, that situation is very much a real one. Hence the president, even with his own 76 percent vote mandate, must perforce put a wet finger to the wind before making any move. Hence the extreme unlikelihood now of action that would result in early release of the hostages. With one exception—the ARK. From the very beginning it has been in his power to correct the situation. It is in his power now, without any political cost to him or his cohorts. Indeed, any rational view would suggest that his acting now to order the immediate release of the hostages would bring him support from the large number of Iranians who must find the continued holding of the hostages both inhumane and un-Islamic and also counterproductive to Iran's image abroad. But the prospects of such an act seem remote. He has spoken.

DAY 123, *March 5, 1980*—Someone (Penne!) sent me a page from a Snoopy book of "Happiness is, etc." This one reads "Happiness is knowing you've made it through another day." That pretty much says it for us, after 123 days. The days get harder as the number increases and as the days get longer and the weather better outdoors. We look down on the ministry's garden, a garden that we saw wither and die with frost last fall and that now again begins to turn green. Even a common criminal in most prisons has access to the prison yard for a daily walk. We lack that; we have not stepped on grass or soil or even urban concrete in all these long days and weeks. A small balcony just off the ministry room formerly known as the Shah's room would give us exposure to the air. We have asked the chief of protocol for access to it. He promised to look into it, but there is as yet no answer. Even reading, after four months of reading, begins to pale a bit, but we stick with it and our friends in embassies on the outside are generous in responding to our requests.

DAY 125, *March 7, 1980*—Well, today appears to have been a watershed of sorts. Around 11:00 A.M., the foreign minister, the chief of the Revolutionary Guards, and a security escort suddenly appeared in these rooms—unannounced. They did not introduce themselves, simply went ahead with an inspection that immediately suggested to us that they were making an assessment of the practicality of bringing the hostages *here*. Less than an hour later, I was summoned to see the minister in his office, where I was asked how I felt. I replied that that was a long story, but that I felt well physically. He then proceeded to tell me that the hostages will be brought here tomorrow to share our quarters. He refused to say for how long, simply referring to the Imam's referral of the issue to the Majlis, but not denying that this could be altered.

We talked for 45 minutes, mostly about arrangements. He allowed as to how he'd "heard a good deal about you" from Dick Cottam [professor at the University of Pittsburgh]. I expressed a few of my grievances on substance, but said I thought this was not the time or place for a discussion on substance. He was courteous, soft-spoken, a bit ill at ease perhaps over the kind of meeting it was. It left me very excited, however, at the prospect of tomorrow, the thought of reunion with our colleagues. But we are also a bit concerned over the kind of reunion it will be. How will our colleagues see *us?* Will they hold any grievances against us? Will they be angry at this further shift in their status as hostages, with no freedom yet? This will bring all 50 of them together for the first time. How will they interrelate? And for that matter, will they come at all? Will the "students" again frustrate progress? (But the word on the news tonight is that the "students" have announced they *are* turning over the hostages, but holding on to the compound.) I think I will not sleep much tonight; there is too much on my mind.

DAY 126, *March 8, 1980*—I did *not* sleep well, and now it is 24 hours later and I suspect I will not sleep well again. The hostages remain in place, even though this ministry's administrative people practically turned these rooms upside down today to clear space for them. *All* furniture has been removed, including carpets, from the main salon (Mossadegh Hall) and in the small dining room we use as well, save for a few tables and our three mattresses. A political power struggle continues between the "students" (with presumably their conservative clerical supporters in the background) and the Bani-Sadr–led elements on the Revolutionary Council, including FM Ghotbzadeh. The "students" claim the Imam has not yet authorized the turnover to the council. Meanwhile, the Imam sits silently, visited by other bearded, aging mullahs, and the hostages become, even more than before, hapless objects in the power struggle that goes on. There seems no concern for them as human beings; they are simply inanimate objects with which the "students" and their backers seek to hold onto political power. It is cruel, ruthless, and surely un-Islamic.

Tonight's TV had footage of one of the "students," speaking in accented and agitated English, pointing out his American wife standing next to him, and then lighting a match to a large, silk American flag that his dear American wife held as it burned. She then said in a few almost inarticulate words, but in American English, that she was from New York State, had watched all of the Revolution, and then seemed to run out of words, smiling inanely as she did so.

What a nauseating sight—that an American would stand holding a burning U.S. flag inside a compound where 50 other American citizens are held hostage in flagrant violation of international law! I hope, fervently, that that pair never again seeks entry into the United States, and if they do, that grounds are found to deny them.

DAY 127, *March 9, 1980*—Our colleagues have still not arrived. They sit, still at the compound, and presumably without any knowledge of the whole affair. Today the "students" issued conflicting noises, one saying the hostages could leave, or be turned over to the Revolutionary Council, between 10:00 A.M. and 5:00 P.M. The other corrected that to say, no, the decision on timing had yet to be made. Tonight the foreign minister was on TV and made a tough speech, in effect denouncing the "students" as *not* following the line of the Imam. In an earlier TV film, the "students" were heard saying that one of the reasons they were reluctant to turn over the hostages was that they might be taken to a hospital for a physical checkup and then who knows what might happen. They might even be freed!!

Good grief, the arrogance of those monsters—and I use the word advisedly because the authorities here have allowed them to evolve into the monsters that they are—threatening the government, taking the law into their own hands, maligning innocent people. In any event, the day passed without diversion. The large room has been completely emptied of carpets and furniture, so all is in readiness for the 50 when they come. A dining table seating 50 is ready in the room we use as a bedroom. . . .

DAY 128, *March 10, 1980*—No progress today, and possibly slippage—it's not yet clear. News reports say that the RC [Revolutionary Council] and the president met with the ARK and the latter issued a statement. It apparently said that the president and RC orders should be obeyed, which is good obviously, but it also said that the hostages should be "interrogated" by the commission, which would suggest that the students' position has been strengthened in the sense that they have said that the hostages must "testify," though they have also taken the position that they would determine *who* is seen by the commission. The students presumably now will *hold onto* the hostages and force the commission to decide whether they will go *there*, to interview the hostages on pretty much whatever conditions the students set. The alternative for the commission would be to stand firm and then leave. But much is still unclear, and we should know more by morning. Yet we doubt very much now that the hostages will be brought here. So we are on that emotional roller coaster again, way down tonight.

Our morale wasn't helped by the meager mail. . . . I do get short letters from friends in the diplomatic corps, where I have a fairly active correspondence with the British, Danish, Swiss, Norwegian, and occasionally the German ambassadors. . . . The Norweigans, God bless them, sent a copy of Kissinger's *The White House Years*. This book has 1,500 pages, and our Norweigan friends had the kindness to say they hoped we wouldn't be here long enough to read it! . . .

DAY 129, *March 11, 1980*—Today the news has been bad. The UN panel left this morning for Geneva and New York, holding to principle. They refused to accept the conditions set by the ARK, i.e., that they could "interrogate" those hostages charged with spying, then they could issue a statement in Tehran on their findings, then—and only then—they could meet with *all* the hostages. The ARK also directed the "students" to turn over to the panel any "documents" they had on U.S. spying, etc. Since the panel had prior agreement from Iran before coming here that they would see *all* the hostages, they obviously could not accept these conditions, and they rightly left. The "students" went to the airport and practically forced the panel to take their "documents," but they refused to accept them.

Tonight all concerned are trying to put the best face on this latest failure, but it is clearly another—and serious this time—example of the ARK undermining his own government officials, including the FM and president, and in effect siding with the "students." And there is something especially objectionable about this supreme leader of Iran directing the "students" to go ahead and turn over stolen diplomatic documents from a seized embassy to a body of the UN. . . .

So our days of great expectation are ended, and we sit, idle, at the bottom of that emotional roller coaster we've been on for so long. We could hardly be more depressed than we are tonight, after hoping that at least our colleagues would be out of the hands of the "students" and with us in custody here. We wonder whether they know anything of this, indeed, whether they have *any* intimation of what's been going on. We have to assume not and that they continue to be kept, cruelly, from any word whatsoever as to what their government is trying to do for them. . . .

What cruelty is abroad! And this government of Bani-Sadr is demonstrated to be powerless to impose its will. Meanwhile, clerical forces and others work behind the scenes to help the "students" retain *their* power base and thus further their political ambitions and those who work with them. How can even the most bitter anti-American describe this treatment as "Islamic"? How can those Iranians who stop to think tolerate such a performance? Are there no Iranians prepared to speak out, to warn their countrymen and their leaders what this is doing to Islam and to Iran?

I find myself wondering what my colleagues think of me, the person who headed that mission and the person who in that sense at least is responsible for this debacle. I sit here helpless and useless. I look out the windows and see Iranians going about their normal daily lives. At 2:30 P.M. the Foreign Ministry buses load up with attractively dressed ladies and Iranian diplomats and functionaries. Sometimes they see us watching them from these windows. Are they embarrassed? Amused? Do they care at all? Do they stop to think how their leaders are using 53 human beings as pawns in a psychological campaign to portray the United States as the Great Satan? Worse, do they realize that these men and women, held now for 129 days, no longer seem even to be regarded as human by their captors or indeed by the ARK? Instead they are inanimate chips to use in the political power struggle that seems endless here. But these *are* human beings, men and women with spouses and children and brothers and sisters who love them and miss them but who have so patiently accepted the restraint their government has urged on them.

How long can this go on? If these colleagues of mine are permanently disabled, psychologically at least, how can I who presided over this embassy ever come to terms with myself? Will I always ask myself these questions as to what I should have done, or might have done, to better protect that chancery and its people against attack? I find myself tonight wishing there was a way that force could be used to rescue our friends, but I know that that can only mean severe risk of loss of life for many people. Yet what alternative is there? Can we go on letting these poor people be psychologically crippled while we wait?

DAY 130, *March 12, 1980*—Amidst all the gloom, today there was at least some magnificent good news, personally. The chief of protocol brought up a note from the British ambassador in which he, the chief, is asked to tell me that "son, Chip, has won his [NROTC] scholarship. This news comes from Mrs. Laingen." Well, that *is* good news, especially for Chip. How proud he will be, and deservedly so, that he has demonstrated that he, too, like his brother Bill, is qualified to be seen by the navy as someone in whom an educational investment will do the navy, and the country, proud. And I'm proud, too, proud of two boys who are committed to advancing themselves and at the same time serving their country. That makes three of us in professional government service. I hope both boys never regret their decisions, and I hope both will continue to do well. More important than anything else, to me and I know to Penne, is that both boys see value in service and both have standards of conduct and character that our country needs so much these days. . . .

Today I sent a stout letter to the FM expressing my strong regret over the new impasse, making it clear where I thought the responsibility lay (ARK):

Dear Mr. Minister,
You will appreciate my extreme sense of disappointment and regret that yet another impasse appears to have been reached in steps to resolve the crisis between Iran and the United States.
It is clear where responsibility for this situation lies. It would seem to me that if that responsibility were to be exercised in a clear and decisive fashion, those who occupy my Embassy could no longer frustrate those understandings already reached on procedures permitting a solution fair to all.
That, however, is a matter for your government and your authorities to resolve and in expressing my own strong view above, I do not pretend that I can influence the matter.
My immediate concern, Mr. Minister, remains my 50 colleagues held hostage. I have read of your statement at the airport yesterday that "the hostages are safe and in good health." *I simply cannot accept that.* Nor can their families in the United States. They are neither "safe" when held by a group of people who are a law unto themselves nor can they be in "good health" after soon five months of confinement, under conditions often short of even those guaranteed prisoners of war! . . .
Mr. Minister, it cannot be in Iran's interest that 50 innocent men and women should be subjected any longer to confinement that risks long-term psychological impairment. That would neither be necessary, nor fair, nor — if I may say so — Islamic.
As I said in a recent letter to President Bani-Sadr, their continued confinement in itself makes a mockery of human rights in Iran. . . .

My colleagues, especially VT, are "down" today. How can they be otherwise? But what, in practical terms, can we do about it? The lack of an answer to that question heightens our sense of frustration.

DAY 132, *March 14, 1980*—The day is beautiful, it is Friday, and Iranians are enjoying probably the first real day of spring. The sky is clear and remarkably unpolluted; there is a nice breeze, the temperatures in the low 60s perhaps. The army group that guards the FM (and us, presumably) spends much of the day today playing soccer on a field of lawn that surrounds the helicopter pad in the far end of the garden. We sit in the windows, trying to absorb as much sun as possible. Some of the soldiers wave and say a few words in English. I stare at them, hoping they might conceivably have a sense of remorse that they and their country are holding 53 Americans in their 132d day of captivity. I wonder what they *do* think as they look up at us. The news today reports that in the United States a TV film has been shown (taken by the "students" during a visit by doctors to the hostages last week). It apparently suggests further that the psychological condition of the hostages is satisfactory at best, and apparently Press Attaché Barry Rosen doesn't look well at all. But for the first time, says the department spokesman, all the hostages can be accounted for on the basis of the film. That is something. I wish I could do *something* to help these people, but what? . . .

DAY 134, *March 16, 1980*—After heavy rain during the night, the day is again beautiful, the sky washed clean to a brilliant blue, with only a scattering of fluffy, white clouds. The Elburz Mountains seem to loom even closer in such weather, but who notices them except us, perhaps, to whom they seem to represent what is big and lasting and real in contrast to the tired and dirty gray of the city beneath them. The weather, signaling spring, even draws the foreign minister to the garden below our windows, where he strolls back and forth, chain-smoking, the other hand in his pocket, with an aide we don't recognize, while burly security guards walk behind him, looking very serious about their task. . . .

In marked contrast with the weather, the outlook for our release seems to recede further and further into the unclear distance. Today's press speaks of the parliament not getting around to even meeting until late May, and then who knows when the hostage issue will be taken up, or indeed what new conditions will be demanded of us by this new center of power in a city where power has so long slithered from pillar to post while the ARK looks on from his heights. First reports on the elections suggest a hefty vote for candidates of the Islamic Republic Party led by Ayatollah Beheshti, and many of the candidates are clerics themselves. We can expect little sympathy from such a group. . . .

The ultimate travesty on the facts is a statement in today's press issued by the Iranian Embassy in Washington: "We strongly condemn all conspiratorial and prejudicial provocation against Iranians in this country and distractions against the Islamic Revolutionaries in Iran. We demand that the authority clearly identify and prosecute those responsible for harming Iranians and thus breeding hostility." Good grief! How muddleheaded can one be? Where is provocation in this case, if it is not massively here in the American Embassy? Can't they see that? How can they have the gall to charge Americans for "harming Iranians" and then, the ultimate irony, to "demand" prosecution of those responsible for "breeding hostility"! Talk about truth turned upside down!

DAY 138, *March 20, 1980*—Today is *No Ruz* . . . or at least it will be, officially, at about 2:42 P.M. It is Iran's great holiday, a time for family gatherings, a time of renewal, with a year ending and another beginning. It is the New Year. . . . It makes so much more sense, as a New Year's holiday, than ours in the Western calendar, because the new year here coincides with the beginning of spring. And surely, that is better than having to celebrate New Year's in the middle of a dark, cold winter day!

. . . For the first time since January 29, we were given a chance to talk, on March 18, for a few minutes by telephone with our families. Hurried, excited talk that left me wondering what we really got said to each other, but wonderfully welcome talk nonetheless. . . . And, after weeks of pressure, we have finally prevailed on our "hosts" to give us access to a 15 by 20–foot terrace-balcony off a room on this floor, giving us a chance to stand in the open air and sunshine for the first time in almost five months. We are urged to stay out of sight and not use it during office hours, lest the "students" hear of it and cause difficulty.

In a sense, all of this charity (the term seems appropriate) paled into insignificance yesterday by contrast with the fact that the Swedish ambassador came, not alone, but with his wife! As the chief of protocol said, "I have brought you a flower for No Ruz!" And indeed he had. He could do it because the building was empty and those who saw it presumably can be trusted. The Swedes spent two hours with us, and we could have talked for hours more. . . . We joked among ourselves that we would not know how to comport ourselves in the presence of a lady, and such a very attractive and charming lady as well. But we were on our best behavior.

Today, as a result, is a day of massive anticlimax. We will be left—for some time, we suspect—with the view of the Iranian women employees of this ministry we can see from our windows, and who can be very attractive too, and with the one woman employee who works in our quarters—a solidly built, most Islamically dressed seamstress and laundry lady who trudges occasionally through the main salon here, smiling at us with genuine friendship, we think, but wary of any real contact and strongly conscious of her role.

DAY 140, *March 22, 1980*—The diplomatic corps was invited to the ministry last night. Before it ended, it became an interesting affair for us. We watch, discreetly, from our windows as the limousines sweep into the courtyard below, most of them with flags flying, and we are embarrassed to find how few of the flags we can identify. The ambassadors and chargés move quickly from their cars and up the steps and do not notice us. But the drivers, after parking their cars and lounging about, rather quickly notice us. There is no secret about our location in Tehran, and in any event no one is better informed than an embassy's head driver. The Chinese chargé's driver gets out of his car and proceeds to do some special deep-knee-bending exercises, in the midst of which he catches Michael's eye at his window, looks perplexed for a moment, and then breaks into a vigorous and knowing smiling and nodding of his head.

All the while our irritation deepens at the very idea of such an affair, with captive diplomats hidden in the room next to that of the reception. But, it appears, that perhaps the minister is not without some degree of embarrassment himself, because with the reception almost over, the chief of protocol suddenly appears and tells us that we are to join the eight chiefs of mission from the European Community (Luxembourg is not present here) whom the minister (himself departed) has asked to remain behind to meet with us!

So, sans ties and coats, but enthusiastic and a bit unbelieving, we stride into the brilliantly chandeliered salon next to this one (ours still vacant save for the 50 lockers brought in for our 50 colleagues who did not arrive) to be greeted, warmly, by the eight good friends, all of course dressed like proper diplomats. Never mind—the excitement of reunion obscures all thought of dress. And for a good hour we talk about the political atmosphere, the prospects for the hostages' release, our concerns for their condition, and—inevitable for diplomats—the comings and goings of the corps, some of whom, like the Italian (to Peking), are nearing transfer.

The whole affair is incongruous—the magnificent hall, now empty save for us and the eight, the chief of protocol staying discreetly out of earshot (he is a professional, too), our colleagues sympathetic but powerless to help. Diplomats in the ministry of the country to which they are accredited, "allowed" by a possibly embarrassed foreign minister to meet with fellow diplomats held hostage, in total violation of international law and practice, by the government to which they are accredited. Yet we conduct ourselves in a sense as if nothing had happened, sharing impressions and keeping our emotions under full control, despite our anger and frustration. After an hour or so, we bid our visitors goodbye under the enormous chandelier in the mirrored reception rotunda, acting almost as if we were the hosts of the glittering affair rather than hostages generously allowed briefly to resume our diplomatic careers!

DAY 143, *March 25, 1980*—Today is the National Day of Greece; tomorrow it is that of Bangladesh, and two days ago it was Pakistan Day—all of them days that called for attendance at receptions at one time or another in my career. To help occupy my time, I send notes of congratulation to ambassadors on their national days. I suspect they also find the exercise of interest, receiving diplomatic notes from diplomatic hostages! . . .

The Shah departed yesterday from Panama for Cairo, met at the airport by Anwar Sadat, who emphasized that the Shah was there to stay. The Shah left Panama on the very day that Iranian government lawyers were scheduled to present legal papers in support of their request for extradition. And so the immediate suspicion here is that the USG [U.S. government] has connived with the Shah, Sadat, and the Panamanians to frustrate the Iranian effort at extradition. That suspicion, say the Iranians, is heightened by the fact that Hamilton Jordan of the president's staff has been in Panama the past few days on a much-publicized visit relating to a "controversy" over medical treatment of the Shah between his American and Panamanian doctors. . . .

So much, for the three of us, is unclear. What role *did* we have in the latest move? Why did the Shah leave now for Cairo and not earlier? Was the likelihood of extradition from Panama real enough to cause him to depart? Apparently so, at least in his mind. . . . One of Bani-Sadr's stated conditions for an end to the crisis is that the United States *not* attempt to frustrate or stand in the way of Iran's effort to achieve extradition. If he were now to conclude that in fact we *did* counsel the Shah's departure from Panama, we would then be seen by him as deliberately flouting this condition. What will this mean in terms of the efforts at settlement by the more responsible elements locally? The answer to that question could be decisive for the prospects for progress in ending this tragic business. . . . It is frustrating to know a little and yet *not* know so much. There again, perhaps, the 50 hostages are better off than we; they can be said to be in blissful ignorance of all this pulling and hauling that so directly affects them. Yet they surely will hear, today, the loud slogans outside the walls again—after a period of some weeks of relative quiet—and they will be asking themselves what this will mean for them. The cruelty of it all, in terms of these people, is appalling.

DAY 145, *March 27, 1980*—Our morale is poor this morning. The weather outside is the top of spring—in the high 60s, the grass greening, the Japanese quince or redbud or whatever in new bloom. . . . But the most depressing of all is the continuing delay in completing the Majlis election vote counting, which means continued delay before it meets and takes up the hostage issue. . . .

Our fate *is* hung up in the whole affair, and that makes us angry and depressed. Does anyone here give any thought to the human aspects of it all? What is to be served anyway by continued delay in resolution of this problem? The Shah is in Egypt; nothing will remove him from there save a coup against Sadat, and pray God *that* doesn't happen! Yet the vindictiveness of the leadership here ensures that the Shah's move will simply heighten the resolve to "get at" us, and that may serve their short-term egos but does nothing to serve Iran's long-term interests, which require that this place get over its emotional binge involving us and the Shah and get to work on its real problems.

So we enter our 145th day, each of us harboring a hope in the back of our minds that a miracle may yet occur, that God in His grace might yet see to it that this man who now determines the destiny of this place might act with the "mercy and compassion" that he and his crowd constantly invoke. But we know in our hearts this is not going to happen, so we swallow hard and try to keep a smile about ourselves. It's hard, knowing that life goes on out there, that our families' activities must continue but that we are kept from participation in them, that participation that makes life worth living. I find myself becoming angry at every Iranian I see, since I feel that all are responsible for what their leadership does, and yet there must be countless Iranians who feel exactly as we do.

DAY 148, *March 30, 1980*—This morning we are baffled, wondering what sort of never-never land we inhabit here. The reason? A mysterious presidential "letter." Last night's Farsi news announced that the Swiss chargé had delivered a message dated March 26 from Carter to the Imam, describing our willingness to work with Iran to resolve the crisis, mentioning the idea of a "joint commission" to look into Iran's grievances, recalling that the United States had in other situations "like Chile" recognized past mistakes, and even indicating some understanding of the students' action against the embassy. Within two hours, VOA was carrying a denial by the White House that there has been any such letter, though conceding exchanges with Iranian leaders over the past several months during which some of the "ideas" mentioned in the "letter" had been discussed.

What does all this mean? Curious indeed, especially since the morning paper quotes an MFA source here as saying the message is genuine and saying that "documentary proofs" will be issued today. . . . Surely this will rank as one of the most bizarre aspects of this entire trauma. We have not seen evidence of the "proofs," but spokesmen of the ARK and of MFA continue to insist that there is a letter to the Imam from Carter. The ARK's son says that our refusal to admit the fact of the letter indicates how we have still not understood the Revolution, but, never mind, the whole issue of the hostages will "be decided by the people" anyway. He also indicated that Bani-Sadr will speak to the subject when he addresses the nation on April 1, Islamic Republic Day. That we find interesting. Could it conceivably be that he will announce some dramatic move that day, possibly taking over the hostages from the students as a starter?

An interesting clue regarding the celebrated letter is that the ARK's son referred to it as having been in French. Why in French? Carter doesn't use that language. Someone obviously has done a hoax. Could it be from within the regime here itself? If so, why?

All of this discussion of real or imagined or contrived—or whatever—letters reminds me again of the strong strain of self-righteousness now abroad in the ruling circles of Iran, perhaps to be expected in any society undergoing a Revolution but surely more pronounced here because of the role of religion, Islam, as the central motivating force in Iran's Revolution. . . .

Again I am torn as to how I should feel. As a human being, I am angry, indeed bitter, over what has been done to us here. But as a *rational* human being, to the extent that I am rational, should I allow that bitterness to control my actions? As a diplomat with some awareness of the patterns of political revolution, must I not concede that a good deal of what has happened here is normal and that we have, through our own inability or failure to understand what was evolving, brought this upon ourselves? In any event, should I allow bitterness to affect my attitudes toward *all* Iranians? I think not; surely it would be wrong to do so, however much it is true that all citizens of a society bear some degree of responsibility for what their government does.

I explain my bitterness to myself on grounds that there can be no justification for what was done to my 50 colleagues and for the way in which their—our— motives here have been maligned. To concede any justification for this can only give respectability to methods that, if continued, will hurt all societies and people everywhere. I am bitter because the seizure here is rationalized as something responsive to some alleged higher morality in Islam that recognizes an evil that other religions, specifically those corrupted by Western culture, cannot know. That surely is poppycock, and here I feel sorrow for an Iranian society that must bear the burden of a morality and way of life that even good practitioners of Islam must concede is regressive and stultifying.

I conclude, I suppose, with a recognition that all men are fallible, that what has happened here hopefully is an aberration, and that I cannot hold permanent bitterness or contempt for either the leadership or the average Iranian. We as a society and a government may well have been inadequately aware of Iranian sensibilities. Surely this country *has* suffered, throughout its modern history, from an excess of foreign intervention—not entirely by *any* means U.S. But they must recognize, the Iranians, that is, that they as a people and a culture also bear responsibility for allowing this to happen. Iran's shortcomings, such as they are, were not born of the past 25 years, or 50 years, or even the past century. History began some time before *that!*

I conclude, too, with a reminder to myself that bitterness can be corrosive to anyone's spirits. And I suppose bitterness in a sense is also a reflection of defeat. And I don't feel—I don't want to feel—any sense of defeat. So there is no point in harboring bitterness, however much I feel it in the short term.

8

April 1980:
Tragedy at Desert One

Two major events marked the month of April. On the sixth, Jimmy Carter's own sense of frustration saw him formally break diplomatic relations and order the departure of the Iranian chargé and his staff from their handsome and still free embassy on Massachusetts Avenue. Three weeks later Carter would receive the telephone call in the Oval Office informing him that a rescue mission had failed and, worse, that eight men had lost their lives in the effort. Probably no day in his presidency was so grim and so personally painful.

Nor would there be a darker day for me and my two colleagues, immensely proud that our countrymen were ready to put their lives on the line to restore us to freedom but sick at heart at this ultimate evidence in human terms of the cost of the continuing crisis to our country. If there was any sense of satisfaction for me personally in an otherwise down time, it was that my counterpart at the Iranian Embassy in Washington had gotten his departure notice. The discrepancy between his freedom and my lack of it was at least diminished.

DAY 150, *April 1, 1980*—The 150th day. A kind of zero hour is approaching as I write this. At noon today, Bani-Sadr is scheduled to speak to the country at a ceremonial march-past celebrating Islamic Republic Day. Reports are that he will announce steps relating to the hostages, most probably a transfer to the control of the Revolutionary Council. . . . Carter is also scheduled to speak today, *after* he has heard what they have to say here. How much this is a coordinated affair we don't know; are we then primed to respond in a cooperative way to whatever is said here? Or, if the statement is inadequate here, will we announce further punitive measures? There is talk of that.

Our own efforts to make some kind of contribution to the planning failed again yesterday when, despite my oral pleas and two penned notes, the CP (chief of protocol) felt he could not bring the Norwegian ambassador in to see us. So we had no way of sending our views to anyone. The CP describes the atmosphere as "very hot out there." . . . I did take the opportunity when a phone call came through from Mark Johnson [Iran Desk, State Department] to say that 148 days were too many, that it was too much to ask the American people to wait yet another two months while Iran sorted out its archaic electoral procedures, and that something had to give. We would need, I said, to take measures that *hurt*, going well beyond simply asking a few more Iranian diplomats to leave the United States, which wasn't going to hurt anyone. In response, Mark assured me that he understood, that such sentiment was strong in the United States too, and that he thought we would see evidence of that in USG actions over the next several days.

Well, we'll see. . . . I feel a sense of such futility and irrelevance, not being able to make any kind of sustained input into the process of trying to resolve this. We have written several messages now over the past several weeks that simply sit here because we can find no way to send them. . . .

Yesterday when the CP came to see us, he was in a clearly subdued mood, and the reason became evident when he told us he had been informed that day that he and others with more than 30 years of service are to be retired as of this week. . . . We assume he has been serving on borrowed time, so to speak, for some time. He is probably considered by those who have the upper hand now in this ministry as too closely identified, in manner if nothing else, with the ancien régime. He said that he was genuinely sorry that he would no longer be around to be helpful to us in whatever way he could, and we have no doubt he means that. He is an enormously decent man—for us he has been a link to decency and civility here, a man to whom we could vent our complaints, however much we also knew that he could do nothing about them, beyond assuring that to the maximum degree possible we are physically comfortable here. On the substance of the issue, he has been scrupulously aloof. . . . We understand that and respect him for it. We think we know how he feels in his heart, but we know we embarrass him by pressing him to take any position on or give any expression to substance. It has been a hard role for him to play, but he has played it with great distinction and decency. He is a credit to Iran.

We hear that some of the hostage families have formed an action group to try to bring pressures to bear where appropriate to expedite things. Penne tells me she is actively involved. We hear too they have an acronym of some kind to label the group, though we're not clear what it is. [We learn later it is the Family Liaison Action Group, or FLAG.) Vic suggests one: FAITH, "Families Against Islamic Terrorism and Harassment." This reminds us of the one he thought up earlier for the exclusive club we propose to form when we leave here to be made up of *all* the hostages and their families and that would gather every November 4 in reunion—that was SPIES, "Society for the Prevention of Islamic Espionage and Subversion"!

DAY 151, *April 2, 1980*—Yesterday, at a massive rally (this will be remembered as a revolution of street rallies and slogans!) Bani-Sadr read a letter from Carter and then responded publicly that the government was prepared to take over control of the hostages, subject to assurances that no further punitive measures would be imposed by the United States and that there would be no further public "provocations" or statements against Iran. Shortly thereafter, Carter announced that the United States regarded the Bani-Sadr statement as a positive development and was therefore suspending any further imposition of sanctions against Iran. This morning the news is that Bani-Sadr does not regard the Carter statement as adequate; the White House says they do not know *what* Iran wants but that there is a limit beyond which any president can go. The Bani-Sadr response may reflect irritation with the Carter public speech later in the day yesterday in which Carter expressed strong concern about the issue and put Iran on notice again about limits to U.S. patience. . . . Our own reactions yesterday to the first Bani-Sadr speech varied from strong irritation to a sense of resignation that we had little alternative but to go along with the Iranian position if we want the hostages released unharmed. The constant temptation to get mad, to strike back with the force that we have avoided all along, is awfully attractive. And yet there is the constant awareness that this might not work, or at least that it would probably do little good now except to complicate the atmosphere in which the Majlis makes its decision. A different president perhaps, but J.C. [Jimmy Carter] and the secretary are men whose concern for human life and dignity and decency is very strong, reflected in the priority evident from the beginning of this affair that securing the hostages' safe release is of paramount concern.

But there is the other side of the coin, respect for the principle that was violated so grossly here at the beginning—i.e., that diplomats and their embassy are immune from assault—violated the more here because the Iranian government endorsed the takeover. Where is the limit of our restraint in the face of that indignity? Where and when do we lose our credibility if we do not stand tougher in the face of the drift and continued demands from here? When does a country's prestige and self-respect require that the regard for these hostages become secondary? The government here is still using those hostages for political purposes, an egregious violation of all standards of international law and practice.

But one must deal with the reality that exists. Accepting the latest Bani-Sadr conditions will at least remove the hostages from "student" control. In human terms, that is a vast improvement. It should also improve *slightly* the atmosphere in which the Majlis makes its decision, which will surely involve new demands, but perhaps the demands will be less this way. Meanwhile, we can leave our own sanctions in place, and one hopes that we are encouraging our European and other friends to drag their feet as much as possible, quietly, in their own relationships here. Our only hope is that the hurt for Iran will accumulate to the point where responsible elements in the leadership will in time recognize the need to act responsibly in this crisis.

But "in time" gets harder and harder to take, after 151 days! Our mood here reflects it. . . . We wonder about the utility of our own presence here and what to do about it. My colleagues, especially Mike, are much attracted by escape, and I think they genuinely feel that we have an obligation to attempt it. I find myself, perhaps wrongly, of the opposite view—skeptical that it can be done, concerned about the impact on the welfare of our 50 colleagues if we do succeed, and beset with a sense that it would be morally wrong for me, still theoretically at least in charge here, to appear in this way to "bug out." Yet there is merit to the argument that we may be able to help our 50 colleagues more by a successful escape, both in terms of the psychological impact and the contribution we might be able to make back in Washington to the continuing process of dealing with this crisis. An attempt would be difficult, which is another reason I am skeptical, because of the nature and the numbers of soldiers who have duty around the building and garden. Certainly for the moment, with the issue of transfer of the 50 to government control so much on the front burner, it would be wrong for us to attempt anything, lest this queer the prospects; the "students" would be almost sure to say then that this would be evidence that the regime is incapable of holding the hostages.

DAY 152, *April 3, 1980*—The news this morning is that Bani-Sadr has received a further message from Carter that reportedly satisfies the conditions posed relating to the transfer. White House spokesmen are quoted as saying the USG has been exercising restraint on this matter and will continue to do so. *Indeed.* God, how we've been restrained! It is galling that we should be asked to say it, but we have taken so much abuse from the authorities here that we have become immune to it.

So we will now wait to see what happens—whether, for example, the hostages are brought here or taken elsewhere; whether it can be done at all, because it requires the students' acquiescence who, when last heard from, were saying they would not agree without a specific order from the ARK.

I have written a letter to the FM this morning, taking account of the news, offering to help in whatever way feasible, and making the suggestion that coincident with the transfer the Iranians announce the total release of the two women, the two men (Keough and Plotkin) who were simply visiting the embassy at the time, and those with special medical problems like Ode. I am not optimistic, but there is no harm in reminding them where humanitarianism begins.

So our morale is a bit better this morning. It will be even better if we are joined with our colleagues, here or elsewhere. . . . I think Mike feels our isolation and lack of freedom more than any of us, among other reasons perhaps because of the frustration he feels as a security officer himself. But his sense of humor helps. The other day he quipped, "My God, if Khomeini keeps this up, he'll give terrorism a bad name!" Vic, quiet and thoughtful, is our constant source of knowledge about this country, this culture, and what makes it tick; he served four years in Iran, plus a stint in Nepal as a PCV [Peace Corps Volunteer]. Perhaps for this reason and his capacity to speak in their language, Vic has remained remarkably civil and courteous throughout with the local staff, whereas I have retreated into a pattern generally of ignoring them after a curt "Salaam" at the start of the day, and Mike's exchanges are more in the form of banter and sharp exchanges, especially when his temper, quick but not lashing, is aroused. All of us find that we need the release of talking vigorously and contemptuously among ourselves about the shortcomings we think we see in Iranian behavior and culture—particularly among the group that we sense as responsible for our plight and that of our colleagues—and about the seeming inability of this place to begin, even a year after the Revolution, to put some order and direction into things. And yet each of us remains fascinated with Iran, which is why we came here in the first place, much attracted to the many Iranians who were and, we think, remain our friends, and deeply regretful that circumstances have resulted in the situation that we, and Iran, now find ourselves.

So, as I complete five months here in the ministry, I realize that on this Iranian tour here I have by now spent more time as a prisoner than as a free man.

DAY 153, *April 4, 1980*—Good Friday. My religious experience has caused me always to associate Good Friday with gloom and darkness, the shadows of death before the promise of Easter and life. Today in Tehran, the weather is magnificent; this being an Islamic rather than a Christian country, I suppose that is appropriate enough. But for us hostages, at least those of us who are Christian, the atmosphere if not the weather is highly appropriate. The atmosphere is one of gloom, thick enough to cut with a knife. Four weeks to the day since I was summoned to the Foreign Ministry's office to be told, in the context of the UN Panel of Inquiry operation, that our 50 colleagues would join us the next day. Today we are *again* reminded of the vagaries of a system here that either cannot or will not take a step to resolve the crisis. . . . The Revolutionary Council is now asking "further clarification" from Washington on the latter's response to Bani-Sadr's demands, a response that Bani-Sadr yesterday had said publicly *met* Iran's conditions for the transfer of the hostages to government control.

What has gone wrong? Presumably Bani-Sadr has not been able to convince a majority of the Revolutionary Council that the Carter response *was* adequate. Or has the Imam posed *new* conditions? We ask ourselves, as we mull over this latest setback, whether this system is capable of making a decision, on this or any other subject. Is it a further indication that perhaps what the hard-liners seek is an impasse sufficient to defeat Carter at the polls this fall? . . . The sentiment among the three of us is increasingly that we must draw a firm line, quietly but firmly telling Bani-Sadr that we will not concede further and that unless action is taken we will have no alternative but to impose sanctions that hurt. Yesterday, in a phone call with Precht in Washington before this latest snag, I asked him to convey to the secretary and the president that we admired their response to Bani-Sadr as reflecting the regard they felt for the welfare of the hostages as the first priority, but that we also agreed strongly with Washington's expressed view that there was a limit beyond which the president could not go in acceding to Iranian demands, and that the three of us had had *very* mixed feelings about the extent to which we had already acceded to those demands.

A footnote: Yesterday's telcon (telephone conversation) conveyed to us the Washington view that the idea we had considered at times (that of escape) should be put out of our minds and that this judgment came from the secretary himself. I welcome this counsel.

DAY 154, *April 5, 1980*

Dear Bill,

A short note, written in light of the possibility we may be visited tomorrow by clergymen from the United States invited here by the "students" as a gesture for Easter. Although I am in strong disagreement with the position of these clergymen on the issues involved in the embassy takeover, I see no reason not to take advantage of their visit for mail.

And, despite my disagreement, there is also something to be said for *any* visit by Americans to our 50 colleagues, since it provides at least a change from seeing their captors all the time.

I'm not sure where things will stand by the time you get this. The last few days have seen another round of contacts, frustrations, switched signals, and political runarounds with what passes for government in this strange place. With luck, the result may be to get the hostages out of the hands of the students, and that would be progress. But we sense the American public is growing increasingly impatient, and I don't blame them. A line has got to be drawn, even if it represents risks to those of us here. We have been pushed around long enough as a nation, and the principle for which we have sat here these five months, i.e., diplomatic inviolability, is being weakened in the process.

The three of us are fine. . . . Our spirits are good; we get *mad* as can be sometimes, not at each other but at the whole ball of wax in which we're involved, and that's good for our mental well-being. We joke about it a lot too. We are in no mood to give in *on anything*.

                              Sincerely, Dad

DAY 154, *April 5, 1980*—The day is beautiful. A Persian spring day at its best, the grass rapidly greening in the garden below us, gardeners putting down yellow pansies, the forsythia bushes beginning to turn green with foliage, their yellow flowers falling to the ground, the air almost translucent with clearness—or at least it is so until the pollution of the city gets the better of it. Tomorrow is Easter, and the weather is appropriately Easter-like with its strong promise of new life. How do I feel about the fundamentals of all this after five months?

- I had placed too much reliance on the Bazargan government's assurances it would "do its best" to provide security for the embassy after the Shah's admission to the United States in October.
- The seizure of the embassy and its personnel had *no* justification on any ground whatsoever—legally, morally, or politically. The World Court has adequately spoken to the legality of it; there is no morality in holding innocent men and women hostage in retribution for the sins of someone else; there is no political basis for an action that, if political objectives are to be pursued, could far more rationally have been pursued by other acceptable means, in this society as in any other.
- The charge that the embassy was an espionage center and its personnel agents is absolutely without foundation, whatever documents the students may cite. Their charges are supported by doctored documents, and they have made no reference to my instructions, which would demonstrate the falseness of their charges.
- The personnel of that embassy were, in my experience, a remarkably cohesive and able team who had reached a high level of efficiency and effectiveness at the time of the seizure.
- Those now held hostage have, to our knowledge, demonstrated an impressive degree of resistance to brainwashing by their captors. The extent of public identification with their captors' position has been small indeed.
- No one can question the depth of feeling of many Iranians about the misdeeds of the Shah and his entourage; no one questions Iran's rights to seek redress or to pursue the Shah's extradition.
- No one questions Iran's commitment to Islam, Shi´a Islam, and its right to base its social, economic, and political life on Islamic precepts, if it chooses. But in terms of its international intercourse, it cannot expect the rest of the world to adjust its own value judgments to those of Iran.
- In this respect it must recognize that most if not all of the civilized world will and does react with revulsion to the idea of using captive diplomats to bargain with another country to achieve its national purposes.
- It must also recognize that to allow credibility or respectability, to any de-

gree, to the action by students in seizing the embassy damages the entire fabric of international diplomacy and diplomatic discourse—to the detriment of Iran as well as all countries dependent on diplomatic inviolability as a principle governing such discourse.

- And, in this respect, the USG's posture of restraint in response to this crisis has been so marked and pronounced as to earn it either respect or disdain, the latter in the sense that our degree of restraint may by now have been damaging to that very principle of diplomatic inviolability that we have sought to defend. A final reading on this can only be made when the crisis is over.
- My own regard for Iran and its people remains strong, despite a sense of bitterness about the treatment of us and my colleagues that colors my judgment in the short term. Individual Iranians remain among the most charming of the world's peoples, their culture and language remain rich and appealing, and I am confident that there is a large minority (and a majority of the educated class) who deeply regret their government's policy on this.
- Finally, while recognizing the special and historical identification in Shi´a Islam between church and state, this experience has reminded me of the great advantage our own system enjoys because of the conviction of our own founding fathers that church and state should be and must be separate.
- And yet another point. When this is all over, let us not be so preoccupied with the ephemeral strategic advantage that an Iranian relationship offers—or that we think it offers—as to forget what has happened here or to press for ties that the Iranians themselves don't want. Far better, let us avoid resumption of Iranian oil purchases, *insist* on indemnification for financial losses here, and *stand aloof* from this place for a while. That is what the leadership here says it wants; fine, let us respond in that manner, allowing political and strategic considerations here to evolve in the context of this Revolution, leaving it up to the Iranians themselves to decide what kind of link they want with us. Let them come to us, rather than the other way around. That need not mean cutting all ties; it means that the ties should evolve only as there is real advantage in them for us and a felt need on the part of the Iranians. Without being blind to strategic considerations, that policy suggests one that rests on the premise: they will need us more than we need them.

DAY 155, *April 6, 1980*—Easter Sunday. The day has been beautiful, the kind of Easter weather we long for at home and often don't get. The sun bathes the snow-covered Elburz Mountains with an almost amber glow, and outside our windows the late afternoon sun is soft and gentle on the pale green of the budding leaves of plane trees. . . . There is a gentleness about the atmosphere that momentarily makes us forget the major political trauma in which we and our colleagues are little more than pawns.

And yet what we have triggered by the trauma that began with the seizure of our embassy five months ago! Within weeks the popularity ratings of the president began to climb, the issue seen by many as having totally transformed his political prospects, and now five months later, with the crisis still chaotic and the hostages not released, the trend is in the opposite direction, and there are those who speculate that lack of progress soon could spell the president's defeat. Indeed there are those who are convinced that the ARK's objective is to achieve exactly that.

Now the effects have produced new problems, the latest being those flowing out of the flight of the former Shah from Panama to Egypt. Muslim fundamentalists in Egypt have protested in small but highly publicized demonstrations against this gesture by Sadat to his old friend and supporter. And yesterday Iran's president called on the Egyptian people to overthrow Sadat and return the Shah to Iran. Iran's Islamic Revolution, loudly proclaimed to be *not* for export but only an example for all the world's "oppressed" to emulate, seems very much an export for Cairo! . . .

One would have to assume that one of the reasons for this much-publicized action by Bani-Sadr is to strengthen his credentials among the Islamic fundamentalists here, looking toward the second stage of the elections, but also looking toward strengthening his hand in trying to bring some order and direction in the affairs of this Revolution. His inability to implement what he says in the hostage crisis is simply one manifestation of his lack of power to implement anything. He presides over an administration powerless because of the influence of the fundamentalists in the Revolutionary Council and because of the Imam's failure to back him up. In this respect, his position differs for the moment from that of Bazargan when he was PM, when his position used to be described as that of a knife without a blade. Bani-Sadr's position is the more regrettable because he is the holder of a 76 percent popular mandate from the people. . . .

Two days ago the new chief of protocol came by to say hello, obviously to see what his charges look like, having succeeded to the task of his predecessor in being our link with the outside world. He was the soul of courtesy and protocol, inquiring as to our welfare and full of confidence that all this will end soon, for which he has obviously no evidence. He is the typical Iranian diplomat—long on courtesy and Persian hospitality but shorter on matters of substance. His family? They live, he said, in Paris, where his three children attend school. In that respect, too, he is not unlike a good many of the Iranian intelligentsia and upper-level bureaucracy. It is a matter of keeping a finger to the wind, never totally confident how things will develop here and conscious of the need to preserve some options.

DAY 157, *April 8, 1980*—Today's VOA morning news carried the momentous but not unexpected news that we have severed relations with Iran, imposed a formal trade embargo, given all Iranian diplomats in the United States 24 hours to leave the United States, and canceled all outstanding visas. New ones will not be issued, except for "compelling" reasons. The president warned that further measures would be taken unless the hostages are promptly released.

All this followed rather swiftly following yesterday's announcement by the

ARK that the hostages would continue to be held in the custody of their "student" captors pending a decision on their fate by the yet to be elected Majlis, the statement noting that since the hostages were receiving "excellent treatment," there was no reason for their being transferred to government control, as the USG had demanded as a first step looking to their release.

The USG clearly had no alternative but to take the steps it has now taken. Yet again we had been promised action and we had promised to continue a posture of restraint, and yet again we were led down the garden path. There is a limit beyond which no respectable government can go in standing firm in the defense of the principle of diplomatic inviolability, so outrageously violated here. Indeed, there are critics in the United States who believe we should long since have taken these steps, and more, and that our failure to do so has made us look muddling and weak and has weakened the fabric of diplomatic practice to the detriment of *all* governments. With that I disagree. I believe the case for our action now, our credibility both at home and especially abroad is that much stronger *because* we have gone the extra mile in demonstrating restraint in the pursuit of our purposes. The mark of a great power in my view is, yes, to use force when necessary in defense of what is right but to do so only when all other options fail. And in this particular issue, when Iran has so grievously broken international law and practice, it has been especially important that we demonstrate total fidelity to that law and practice, avoiding indulgence in the crudity and callousness that have been demonstrated here. Perhaps we have paid something for the short term, but I believe we will be the stronger for the long haul because of it.

So where does that leave us? Those with more experience in international law and precedent can answer that better than I, though God knows there are few if any precedents for this problem anywhere! It dawned on me this morning that I am no longer American chargé d'affaires in Iran. I suppose my two colleagues and I technically are interned, while continuing what we were before as well, that is, in the protective custody of the Iranian government ("guests," to put the best face on it) or "hostages of the Iranian people," as the "students" would put it. . . .

We are struck by the short time granted Iranian diplomats in the United States to pack and leave. It reflects a president whose patience has been worn thin and an American public equally fed up with the way their country has been abused and its citizens mistreated. It is all very sad and tragic, especially since so many people of good will—Americans, Iranians, and others—have tried so hard in recent weeks to arrest the downward trend that has now resulted in this deepened crisis.

Men of that kind came to see us yesterday. The "students," for Easter, had invited back to Tehran three clerics from the group of 49 of their American sympathizers who were here two months ago. The government here invited the former Greek Catholic Archbishop of Jerusalem, Monsignor Capucci (imprisoned by the Israelis for gunrunning some years ago and then released in some understanding with Rome, where he now lives), and, together with the papal nuncio here, these four men held Easter services at the compound for the

hostages. We had no desire to see the three Americans, whose fawning regard
for the "students' " "idealism" has angered us. But we said we would welcome
seeing Capucci. He arrived in our quarters along with Swiss Ambassador Lang,
the papal nuncio, and two lawyers, Bourget (French) and Villalon (Argentine,
but resident in Paris and now rumored the author of the mysterious "letter"
from Carter to the ARK). We talked for more than an hour. . . . They were
clearly weary and not a little dispirited, having just themselves heard the ARK's
edict siding with the "students" and against President Bani-Sadr. . . .

It was a good meeting, especially in light of the reservations we had earlier
felt about Capucci because of some of his public statements. But we found we
like him. Impressive in bearing, he wore his full robes with a high headpiece,
carried his silver-headed bishop's staff and a large cross pendant, and was
ruggedly handsome with a strong, graying beard. He smiled warmly while
making an opening statement about the promise of Easter and the benefits to
character from suffering, and then listened gravely but carefully while I made
a statement in response, emphasizing our concern for our 50 colleagues and
decrying the way in which their purposes and character and activity had been
so grossly distorted and maligned by the "students" and others in authority
here. Mike intervened with a good statement of how the real victim in this
crisis is Iran and its people—we being capable of withstanding this setback but
Iran sure to suffer seriously.

We asked about our colleagues, and he told us what his conscience permitted
him, obviously restrained by a commitment to the "students" not to discuss
anything about the physical location inside the embassy compound, etc. We
asked especially about our two "girlfriends," Ann Swift and Kate Koob, which
required some help from Ambassador Lang in translation, Capucci's American
idiom being not that good. He responded vigorously when he understood,
bringing two fingers to his lips to connote, in the French style, perfection. His
face lit up with enthusiasm as he described their dignified, strong behavior,
with Monsignor Bugnini chiming in to tell how, when each of the hostages
apparently was allowed to speak to their families via TV, these two women had
spoken "with joy, as tears streamed down their faces." And at that point I was
very near to tears myself. . . .

Withal there was an atmosphere, as we talked, of depression that I think we
all felt. I was especially struck by Ambassador Lang's clearly exhausted state; he
had been active a long time representing our interests here in both formal and
informal ways. . . . The two lawyers, too, looked tired; they had been engaged
in the extradition aspects of the crisis as well. But through it all there was a
remarkable serenity on the faces of the two clerics—Bugnini because he is a
genuine, almost angelic-seeming Christian and Capucci perhaps also that (but
much more, as his record indicates, a man of political action) and also because
of his own experiences with prison and physical isolation (three years in a small
cell without news of the outside world, he claimed). Probably also he is conscious of the political implications for him (and his Palestinian objectives) if he
can be helpful on this crisis involving us. He spoke warmly of Carter, describing him as a "good man," and appeared to believe his policies vis-à-vis Pales-

tinian concerns were positive (tossing his hands above his head in mock despair when we mentioned the possibility of a Reagan election!).

DAY 158, *April 9, 1980*

Dear Penne,

Our 158th day, whatever that is. I'm pooped. (Reason is I've got my spring allergy again. Chief of protocol got me some pills, which I hope will help.) It's about 10:30, and we think there's to be another student spy "revelation" on the late show tonight. I don't look forward to watching it, but I guess I'd better.

This is Wednesday. On Monday, mail day, the Swiss ambassador brought in letters from you. . . . So it was a good day, after poor mail for the past several weeks. A good thing, too, in light of all the bad news on the issue here. In fact it was Monday, too, when the ARK lowered the boom again on his own president and sided, again, with our student "friends." . . . We've gotten so we don't really expect much when things begin to look promising, but it's nonetheless a letdown when things again go sour. In the main salon here, adjacent to the narrow dining room where we "live," the salon still stands starkly empty, except for the 50 steel lockers that were hurriedly moved in (and the furniture moved out) about a month ago when I was told by the foreign minister that the 50 would arrive the next day. This time again the plan fell through, and this time again we had an emotional letdown.

Our spirits soared with the news of the break in relations, simply as a reaction to the frustrations we've felt. . . .

But emotions are nothing on which to rest policy or plans. So we wonder what next. We know little, being pretty much cut off now. . . . That will probably get worse, since relations are broken and now I lack any status here whatsoever. . . . Your letters were terrific. I read them over and over, several times, to make sure I've caught every nuance. Fascinated by your references to the boys, of course. Jim sounds like a young man! Tell him not to grow up completely before I get home! . . .

What a great thing the POW (former prisoners in Vietnam) people are doing to help. No one would understand better than they do.

Your newsletter to the families sounds great, and, as always, you'll do it beautifully. . . .

I'm so very proud of *all* of you, for the way you are demonstrating to everyone the dignity of a good and active family and the pride you have in our country. I could not be more fortunate in the wife and the sons I have who back me up so beautifully.

I love you all, B

DAY 159, *April 10, 1980*—We are amused by a press report quoting the Iranian chargé in Washington as saying how much relief he felt at *leaving* Washington, having felt, he said, as if he had been a hostage himself in those 156 days manning his embassy on Massachusetts Avenue. Poor man! He must

have been troubled by all that police protection outside the chancery, and possibly he felt overworked having received, said he, some 2 million letters of protest from Americans (270,000 of which he claimed to have answered, of which 70 percent wrote back "with understanding" [sic]). Or he may have felt spied upon by the 50 to 75 loyal members of the Sunday evening candlelight vigils outside his embassy that friends of mine conduct every Sunday night! . . .

Today the "students" have, predictably, come out with a strongly worded statement threatening death to all the hostages if the United States uses military force in any way to free them and the burning of the chancery to boot. We tend to dismiss this as idle words, a bluff that can be called—though we remind ourselves, too, that these are the same people as the young "student" who reportedly strangled his own sister when he learned that she was pregnant, allegedly by one of the Marines at the embassy, an act said to have occurred before the embassy was seized.

It is also the same type of Iranian as those who last night, on a late TV show, presented one of the hostages, Joe Subic from the defense attaché's office, a young man of perhaps 22 who had appeared in a different film at the turn of the year, speaking now with apparent conviction of how the embassy had indeed been engaged in espionage. . . . Why? Someday we may know, but someday, as a result, what charges face him? What burden will he carry in his own heart and mind for the rest of his life? It was a cold and chilling performance, to see a young American so clearly *used* by his militant captors to further their cause, whatever the cost to this man's future. . . .

These "students" demonstrate in other ways their political skill, the latest being a long film shown on local TV two nights ago of the Easter services conducted at the compound for the hostages by three invited U.S. clerics (sympathetic in previous visits to the students)—Archbishop Capucci and two Iranian clerics. All but six or seven of our colleagues we eventually identified, those missing either not wishing to participate or regarded as superspies possibly and therefore deprived of such "generosity" as this. The film was clever— the atmosphere gentle and seemingly with few restraints, the clerics leading each group of two to four in hymns and prayers before communion, followed by Easter snacks at a decorated table, and the camera only occasionally focusing on the numerous anti-American posters now gracing the walls of my former office, where most if not all the services seem to have been held.

Our colleagues, said some of the Iranians here in these quarters the next day, "looked good." In a sense they did; all were clean and well, if casually, dressed, many clean-shaven, the women looking bright and cheerful. But we who knew them as colleagues could see what Iranian viewers could not—the tenseness in most of their movements, the nervousness in many, especially in their half-smiles, the way many of them have lost weight, the sadness in the expressions of most, the wariness in some, and barely concealed anger in others. One, Bob Ode, I think, pressed by the clerics on the efficacy of prayers, responded that "prayers are fine, but what we really need is action." Another, Keough, was perhaps most eloquent of all and put the whole business well and succinctly when asked how he was: "We are comfortable in the sense we are not abused; we are uncomfortable in the sense we are not free."

That's beautiful, but who in Iran *heard* it? Who among the people care? Do they see what they should in such a film, that these are men and women with families who love them who are being held like prisoners against their will by a group of "student" terrorists whose government, at every crunch, backs them up? Don't the people of Iran see the enormity of this indecency? It is madness. I have never agonized through a TV film before in the way I did that one—some of them young Marines with sadness and anger mixed in their eyes; older men speaking to their children and wives at home, their words often stumbling with emotion.

DAY 161, *April 12, 1980*—The three of us are given to much speculation these days as to where all this is going. Having moved from a posture of massive restraint as a means of encouraging the so-called moderates in the regime here to find the means to evolve a political framework in which Iran could accept some kind of arrangement where a settlement was possible, we have produced a new situation that in the short run makes a settlement impossible. The moderates here have in effect thrown in the sponge, noisily and publicly. Bani-Sadr, for example, says, "This is war," meaning that Iranians must unite in resisting American "pressures," with the Iraqi situation thrown in for good measure as an American ploy to bring pressure to bear on Iran. . . .

For our part we have now applied most if not all of the measures we can apply to bring pressures to bear here short of force, though Washington spokesmen speak of a range of other "legal" measures available to us that we can and will apply if there is not a prompt release. What those are is not clear to us. We assume we will now mark time while we wait to see what our allies and other friends will do. . . .

Bani-Sadr's conditions—(1) a pledge not to interfere in Iran's internal affairs, (2) an "apology" for our past role in Iran, (3) a pledge not to stand in the way of Iran's efforts to achieve the Shah's extradition and the return of his "ill-gotten gains"—presumably still stand, but not much has been heard of them lately. The Shah is now nonextraditable, short of a political change in Egypt. Thus some new means will be sought here to try the Shah in absentia, possibly along the lines of the international tribunal once talked of by McBride. And the hostages? What new demands for their "trial" as spies will we hear? And what can we do to counter that? Is any compromise settlement possible from a Majlis dominated by clerical elements whose decisions cannot be implemented in any event without the ARK's concurrence and blessing?

Meanwhile, there are variables that could have pronounced effects on an uncertain but evolving picture: the border tension with Iraq (who and what are behind the Iraqi actions), the Shah's health, the political situation in Egypt, the political composition of the Majlis after the second round, the political scene in the United States as the primary process continues, the ARK's health. Any one of these elements could have a major effect on what happens here, and none of them can now be predicted with certainty. Subject to that (or these) proviso, the hope will be that with the measures we have taken in place, the allies quietly adding to those pressures, and international public opinion again developing a head of steam, that enough cost, or prospective cost, will be felt here so that a majority in the Majlis can be brought to put forward a release package that is salable to the ARK and that is tolerable for us. But what is "tolerable" at this point? My colleagues argue strongly that we should promise nothing, that we should refuse to consider *any* concessions until the hostages are released, period. And that, on the surface at least, *is* the president's new policy; he has served notice on Iran publicly that every passing day that the hostages are not released will mean greater cost for Iran, and that we are prepared to take additional measures, still short of force but not excluding force, if Iran does not "promptly" release the hostages. . . .

DAY 162, *April 13, 1980*

Dear Jim,

It's 11:30 A.M., and I've just finished my morning laundry—a shirt, underwear, two pairs of socks. Now I know what it's like for Mom, having to wash for us at home every day. Only she's got a machine, and I haven't.

It takes us about this long every morning to get organized. We don't get up till 9 (after going to bed at midnight) and then wash up, eat breakfast, and listen to the Voice of America news. We also get the *Tehran Times,* a daily in English. So that's the way we use up our mornings.

Afternoons get a little longer—lunch, reading, some writing. (We each keep a daily diary now, I think.) Around 5:00 P.M. I do my 45 minutes of jogging in the stairs and landings of the reception area. Until a few days ago, we were allowed out on the balcony in the sun, but that's been stopped again since the president broke relations with Iran. We also have added guards now—whether to protect us from extremists or to ensure that we don't try to escape isn't clear. It's probably a little of both. And we've been moved to a different room. . . .

Evenings we watch the local TV news—nothing like seeing another street demonstration again! I call this kind of government that we've got here "mobocracy." That may not be in the dictionary yet, but Iran is rapidly making sure that it gets put there.

We play a lot of backgammon. If you don't know it, get a set and practice up so we can play when we get home. Mr. Tomseth is a whiz at it. And we read a lot. Kissinger's 1,500-page memoirs took me about 15 days. He's pretty heavy going, but it's magnificent history of that period. By the time you've finished, you're not sure who was president—Nixon or Kissinger. Henry's ego is no small thing. . . .

. . . This letter is getting too long, and I know how impatient you are with long letters, Jim. But I thought I should chat awhile with you, since I don't get a chance to talk with you. I hope school is going well—about all I can say on that score, Jim, is this: the harder you work in these lower grades and the better you do your homework, the easier next year will be, and the year after that. It's a matter of building a solid foundation; like building a house or anything else, the stronger the foundation, the stronger the house. The more you get your math down pat this year, the easier it's going to be next year to master what gets tougher each year. . . .

Did my 15 minutes of calisthenics when I got up this morning, including 50 push-ups. Can you beat that?

Some stinker stole the card Mom sent me once: "Happiness is knowing you've made it through one more day," a Snoopy cartoon. I had it taped in a window. We suspect that some zealous security guard decided that it showed we had too much "freedom."

Remember that word, Jim: *Freedom*, the most prized possession Americans have. But we've got to work to keep it, and sometimes sacrifice a bit to be sure we don't lose it.

Love, Dad

DAY 164, *April 15, 1980*—Income tax filing day. That's one deadline that I understand will not apply to us this year, extensions having been assured. I remember around Christmastime thinking about possible problems in getting my return filed, but then dismissing the problem by telling myself that, of course, I'd be out of here *long* before April 15! So here we are.

Yesterday was mail day, bringing welcome letters from several people, especially from Penne and sons Jim and Bill. Jim's was a card with a short message, including this: "I hope you get out soon, because it's rather lonely around the house. These people will soon realize what they've done is wrong." I like that. And Bill, writing from the Naval Academy (second year), wonders how things are at the "Tehran Hilton" and tells me that he's been to a lecture at the Cosmos Club in Washington with his grandfather to hear a former CNO [chief of naval operations] speak on "The Dangerous Decade, the 80s." Bill's comment: "It's quite frightening when you look ahead at the deteriorating world situation. I hope our next few leaders are strong-willed men."

Bill speaks from the vantage point of being one of those men who will, as a naval officer, be very much involved in that dangerous decade. For his sake, and our country's, may the decade yet prove more tranquil than now seems the case. He is right, however; we *will* need good leadership, and I am confident that Bill will provide his part of that in full measure. That was apparent in the ending of his letter when he wrote: "Remember, keep your guard up, expect anything, and above all, don't give up. Keep America's standards flying high!"

With that kind of backing from my sons, I haven't got any worries. The more so because of Penne's support, whose letter describes the incredibly active role she's playing in keeping the families of the hostages as united as possible and as constructively involved as possible—a difficult task, given the frustration that many of the families must feel after all this time and all the disappointments they have suffered. She writes of the many letters she receives from people around the country, like the fourth grader from Montana who says he's wearing his "Montana cares about you" button, and the group of ladies in Virginia Beach who have distributed 900 yards of yellow ribbon to distribute to people in that area to hang on their oak trees. It's incredible to see how this issue has captured and held the humanitarian concerns of the American people.

But here in Iran we are as much pawns in the chaotic Iranian political process as ever. For the past ten days a new (in the age-old) confrontation has developed between Iran and Iraq, and the leadership here has now added this to the emotional mix, loudly trumpeting charges that the United States is behind the Iraqis, that they are masterminding things like the expulsion of Iranian Shi´ites from Iraq, etc., not bothering to tell their people that our political relationship with Baghdad is about as bad as that with any Arab state. But again, the facts seem not to matter so long as a charge can be contrived in some fashion as "truth" to serve local political purposes.

Another example of the way certain facts are set aside is in the nature of the remarks by Chargé Ali Agha following his embassy's expulsion from Washington. He is quoted in the press as saying that Iran's "victory so far in rubbing their noses in the dirt has been unprecedented. America was never so humiliated so much, even in losing the Vietnam War, and was never made to look so small." For someone who has lived in the United States for 14 years, his reading of history leaves something to be desired. Mr. Agha conveniently ignores the contrast with the treatment of our diplomats here— seized by terrorists, blindfolded, held with their hands bound for months, without the freedom to speak to their colleagues, and today, 164 days later, still held prisoner, the government openly backing that state of affairs. Mr. Agha apparently cannot see what that means and how much it stains Iran's own image.

We read that frustrations and anger at home have extended to our able country director for Iran, Henry Precht, who, conducting Agha and a colleague to see the undersecretary of state to receive their expulsion orders, reacted with the expression "Bullshit!" to claims that the hostages were in the custody of the Revolutionary Council and being well treated. That, according to press reports, caused Agha to storm out of the department, alleging that he had been insulted in language that he would not repeat and requiring a department officer to deliver the expulsion orders to the embassy.

Well, anyone knowing Henry Precht, as patient and optimistic a man on Iran as walks the halls of that department, would have to conclude that he has reached the end of his great store of patience in listening to his Iranian visitors. We suspect that his outburst has won him virtually universal accolades among his colleagues—and probably done more for the reputation of the Foreign Service among the general public than anything in a long, long time! . . .

Dear Bill,

. . . We're in a curious state since the break of relations took place. Our security is tighter—whether to protect us or to keep us from escaping isn't clear. At the same time, our physical comfort has improved. We've been moved to the main dining room, where we rattle around in an enormous space (40 by 60 feet and 20 to 25 feet high). But the room is carefully closed off from where we were, and our exposure to the street side is ended. A Ping-Pong table has been brought in (no balls or paddles yet!), and starting yesterday we are allowed in the garden for an hour of exercise each afternoon—under careful guard. And the papal nuncio has sent in a record and cassette player and a lot of records and cassettes (even some Elton John!) for our first decent music in five months—except for the VOA breakfast show on shortwave. . . .

Good sailing, Bill! And give my regards to all your colleagues.

Dad

DAY 166, *April 17, 1980*—The day is beautiful, this 166th day. The view of sky and garden from our windows is such that momentarily we can forget all this, if we try. . . . Yesterday, the Swiss ambassador and his deputy, Kaiser, were allowed in to see us, in response to my request to the chief of protocol, the visit personally approved by the minister. We had one and a half hours of good talk, much of it on the practical problems faced by the Swiss in assuming protecting power responsibility for our interests here—a role in which the Swiss have much experience, but there being no precedents for the situation they face here, where our embassy remains occupied and its personnel held hostage. . . .

Late in the day, we were allowed to talk with our families by phone, only it turned out that only Vic and I had five minutes each, the phone cut thereafter. I had not talked to Penne in almost a month. We had only brief opportunity to talk about anything in that short time; clearly she was "down," unlike her usually buoyant spirit, which she may not always feel but which she is good at showing to me. But not this time. . . . I was reminded again of how much *she* (and Jim) and the other families are hostages as much as we, if not more so. Hostages to the whims and weaknesses and wrongdoing of the regime here, hostages to the lack of information and certainty that affects everyone, hostages to the cruelty of a fate that has resulted in their loved ones sitting here in captivity for the blackmail purpose of terrorists condoned by their government. And yet, the families' spirits appear to remain high, symbolized now by the yellow ribbons that are to be seen, we are told, everywhere in the United States. . . .

I think, to lighten the mood of what I write, I should record the jingle that I wrote on a birthday card we put together for Victor's 39th birthday on the 14th (with apologies to all poets!):

To Vic

In your 40th year that you begin today
Remember these things that we say,
Avoid Ayatollahs
They're determined to fool us
Don't give 'em the time of day.

And never be seen with chargés
Whose views of Iran are passé
They'll drag you to meetings
Where agreements are fleeting
And no chances for instant replays.

There's also a risk with SY*
They'll sell you a pie in the sky
They talk of security
With them it's a surety
But best give 'em a good jaundiced eye. . . .

You may ask what's in the ARK's kit
That he wants his people to get
It's not hard to guess
For people like this
You said it: Bullshit!

So on day one sixty and three
With the outlook still gray as can be
Remember to doubt
Advisers who tout
That Tehran's the place to be.

But whatever you think of this mess,
There's no doubt we'll get our redress.
We wish you the best
Whatever the test
And may your shadow never grow less!

(We told Vic we looked forward to celebrating his 40th birthday under better
circumstances.)

———

Dearest Penne,

   As I write this, our newly acquired record player is belting out, you know
what? You're right! "Tie a Yellow Ribbon." We've got it, by chance, in two
versions on the cassettes and records that the papal nuncio sent us. He is a
Monsignor Annibale Bugnini, a sweet and kindly, rather cherubic-looking
man, whose every act seems motivated by gentleness and love of all things.

* Security

He sends us an occasional letter, like the one that accompanied these records, ending with the words, "Once again, Mr. Laingen, retain your courage and confidence in the Lord. The whole world has you in its thoughts; we also in a special way and with unfailing remembrance in our prayers. Yours affectionately." . . .

All this love and decency contrasts so sharply with the enormity of the indecency done to our colleagues, and it buoys our spirits by reminding us that out there there are people who care, millions of people who care and want to help. For that matter, there are obviously many, many Iranians who also care, some of them among our staff who serve us and clean these rooms but who must be wary of the way they show it. . . .

Love, Bruce

DAY 169, *April 20, 1980*—Today I wrote a farewell note to Luigi Salvia, the Italian who has served as the cook at the ambassador's residence in Tehran for the past 25 years. Since November 4, he and his family have waited, hoping that perhaps this crisis would yet end and permit him to resume the job he so very much enjoyed. But, that now being clearly impossible, he is leaving, and fortunately he has a future. The Danish ambassador, who left a month ago, is hiring him to be his cook at his embassy in Rome, where the Dane is to be transferred. I wrote Luigi an affectionate note, thanking him for the magnificent support he has given us and wishing him well. . . .

Several days ago, a week possibly, we were informed that henceforth we would be allowed an hour a day in the ministry's garden, via access to the balcony. So we chose the hours 4:00 P.M. to 5:00 P.M. That promise had paid off, as of today, only once, three or four days ago. It was nonetheless welcome— the day beautiful, the garden in spring green, roses bursting into bloom. We jogged and exercised and walked round and round in the area designated (far from the outer walls), all the time carefully watched by three or four zealous civilian guards and up to 15 or 20 soldiers from the platoon assigned to the ministry. Those on regular guard duty carried their guns; those off duty simply stood and stared at us, presumably not wanting to miss this chance to see honest-to-goodness "American spies," "superspies" at that! They were not unfriendly, simply curious, possibly even friendly, though we deliberately avoided engaging them in any conversation.

Today things apparently were in order again, so Mike and I (Vic chose not to go) went out to find this time that only those soldiers on guard duty were to be seen. Within a few minutes, the reason became apparent. Suddenly a photographer was to be seen, and two gentlemen whom I assumed to be Foreign Office officials, curious to see what we were like. These gentlemen I avoided, by switching my jogging route, only to have the photographer pursue me, even after I called out that I wanted no photos, that I was not an animal. After a few more moments, we decided to leave, but before doing so, Mike, who realized that one of the two gentlemen strollers was a reporter, apparently English, walked up to them and said, "You realize that all this is a deliberate setup, don't you? And that we have only been allowed outdoors only twice in the past six months?"

Back up in our "ballroom," I asked Vic to translate for me as I read my own riot act to our chief security guard, once commended to us by the former chief of protocol as a "man with a heart" but whose principal preoccupation these days seems to be to redouble his efforts to ensure that we cannot possibly escape from this room. I told him that I was furious at being used in this way, that I may be a hostage but that I am not an animal in a zoo to be put on public display in this fashion. . . . What his role was we will never know; but clearly he and others had laid this on, undoubtedly at the foreign minister's request, so that these two journalists (reportedly from *Newsweek*) could see with their own eyes how "generously" we were being treated, all of which would be part and parcel of the current gambit here to counter USG criticism of Iranian policy on the hostage crisis by showing—here and with Red Cross visits at the embassy—that there should be no undue concern over the hostages by world public opinion. . . . I was outraged. I realize we are honest fare for journalists who can swing this, but I do not intend to cooperate with the Iranian authorities to serve their purposes. It was deception, deceit, with which I want nothing to do. If they want us to be photographed, let them ask—even then I would decline. We *are* fortunate, the three of us, in the sense we are not held by the militants and we have outside contacts that our colleagues lack. But we are hostages in the same sense they are in that we lack freedom and that our opportunities for outside contact are entirely in the hands of the regime to grant or deny. . . .

Dear Penne,

What a treat it was to talk with you and Jim last night. How that call got through, we don't know. There is little logic in all this. And you sounded a lot more cheerful, which always relieves me. I don't think I fully appreciate the burdens on you and the tedious nature of this life for you: day after day the same frustrations, the same questions, the phone ringing constantly. You must be dead tired of saying the same things to the same people a thousand times while this "cuckooland" (I like that) goes on with its madness—the latest being student (real ones) problems that have turned local universities into chaos. . . .

I'll miss Jim's confirmation. I regret that, deeply. But I'm proud of him for it, and will be thinking of you all on May 11 especially keenly.

Dinner is about to be served; the only thing that varies is the main course. Otherwise there are the same French fries, the same cold peas, the same weak and soggy asparagus. But currently there are fresh cucumbers, we get apples and oranges and, following our request, plenty of yogurt. And if we're lucky, tonight's barbecued chicken will not be half-raw, or the barbecued beef will be chewable, or we won't have what we call goatburgers.

I've just looked—it's mystery meat #22. . . .

Love to you all, B

DAY 170, *April 21, 1980*

Dear Jim,

Thanksgiving, Mom's birthday, Christmas, New Year's, Valentine's Day, Easter—all that I didn't mind missing *too* much, but your Confirmation Day, *that* I didn't want to miss. But barring an Islamic miracle (they're rare), I will miss it. And I regret that very much.

When I was young in Minnesota, that day was one of the most important in our lives. It was not simply a matter of becoming a full member of the church but also a kind of growing-up rite. It was rough going, too—endless rote learning of questions and answers from Luther's *Catechism*, the doctrinal statement of Lutheran faith in those days. Then we had to stand up in front of the congregation with our fellows and be prepared to answer, word for word, whatever question the preacher chose to ask us. Woe unto us if we failed to know the answer. It was embarrassing if we made mistakes, not least with our parents afterwards!

But it was a big day. I can remember to this day the excitement of a new suit. And there was a big dinner, with relatives and presents afterwards.

I suspect your experience will be different, though the same too in many respects. I have no doubt that you will have learned more than we did; the emphasis on word-for-word rote learning has its weaknesses. I'm sure you've had a lot more opportunity to talk things over, to talk and think about what the words really mean, what's behind all the business about doctrine.

I wonder what it's meant to you, Jim. I know you're a skeptic, or at least you used to be. That's all right. Every man has to reach his own conclusions, to come to his own understanding within himself as to what helps make your life a full and active and rewarding one. The real purpose in "reading for the Minister" (as we called it) is to give you the framework within which you decide yourself what kind of relationship you're going to have with the church, and with God as you judge that God exists.

I'll tell you how I feel, even though I think you know already how I feel. There is nothing all that sacrosanct about churches as such. Some are good, some are not much, some or perhaps most of them get overly preoccupied with the physical aspects of the church building, finances, air-conditioning, or whatever. But I have no doubt in my mind that churches in our society play a very important role in public morality, a force for good in the way our communities function. At the same time, I think we are extremely fortunate as a society that our founding fathers insisted on separation of church and state. (I have only to look at what is happening to Iran to see what happens when clerics attempt to run a government!)

Churches also provide to most of us the framework within which we practice our religion. Attendance at regular services gives us momentum as Christians, helps us understand what we mean by our religion, and—in my case at least—sends me away from a collective act of worship feeling that I am closer to God and a force of good.

But in the final analysis, it's still an individual matter, and participation in a

Sunday morning service can't substitute for the basics—and that's the kind of private religion you've got, your personal communication with a supreme being, your own feeling in your heart and mind that there's some larger purpose in life than just three meals a day and making it from day to day. Again, if I can cite my own experience, I think the heavy emphasis on church in my own growing up helped give me a kind of moral discipline that has helped me a lot. The Lutheran church—and I think the Episcopal too, but to a lesser degree—puts heavy emphasis on *faith,* which means that not everything about life and death can necessarily be logically and rationally explained. There is a lot about church doctrine that I'm skeptical about, but on the whole I rest on a personal faith that there is a God, that our lives benefit from a pervasive kind of love that He shows to us and that we are in turn obligated to show to our fellow men, that there is Someone who is listening to me when I'm in trouble and need some guidance.

So prayer to me is what religion is about most—both the collective prayers in church and, much more importantly, the private prayers—the dialogue—I have with God, who I'm convinced must be listening. If nothing else, prayer gives me confidence—not that everything will work out exactly right but that I've got some special support up there.

In fact, I think that's what religion does most for me, that dialogue through prayer gives me some assurance and confidence about life that I wouldn't have otherwise.

The big question, of course, is what happens when it's all over, what comes after life, and does religion mean anything on that score. Well, I think it does, but that's where faith really comes into the picture. Exactly what happens, none of us knows—no one has ever known. We'll all find out soon enough, so I'm not going to worry about it too much. But a faith that there is something in the afterlife—call it what you will—makes my present life a good deal more meaningful than struggling aimlessly through three meals a day.

Well, Jim, if you've hung on this long in this letter, you're a patient man. I suspect when I reread what I've written, it won't be the ultimate in religious philosophy. But it's part, at least, of the way I see things, and I hope the fact that organized religion has given your father (and millions of other people) some satisfaction in life, some order in life, will cause you at least to do what matters most about life: *Keep an open mind.*

God bless you, James Palmer Laingen, on this big day.

                           Sincerely, Dad

DAY 172, *April 23, 1980*—Evening. Some days are harder than others, and evenings are usually hardest of all. In a sense, our newly acquired music makes things more difficult to take. The majestic music of Handel, the elegance of Mozart, the power and dignity of Bach—they should be enjoyed with those you love; they remind one of concerts, the excitement of sharing good things. Then there is the poignancy of "Don't Cry for Me, Argentina," making us all very sad. And it's not been a good day in any event. The fundamentalist who's on duty today in the kitchen (we call him the "Mullah," thanks to his views and his scruffy beard) asked Mike today: "If Carter is such a Christian, why is he imposing a blockade?" To which Mike responded that it was because Americans were being held hostage, and that produced the answer, "Return the Shah!" How many million simple-minded colleagues of the "Mullah" have the same answers, clearly unreachable with any kind of logic, totally mind-set in line with the vindictive, single-minded ARK?

That incident is simply symbolic, but it has heightened our sense of frustration this evening, as has the news from Europe indicating that the European Community, rather than forthwith imposing sanctions in our support, has decided *in principle* on sanctions. It will not impose them until the end of May, meanwhile using diplomatic pressure to try to force action before then by the Majlis.

We are disappointed, emotionally, because we would welcome the feeling of support. And because sanctions, now, would begin applying the hurt that will produce action from the Majlis. The Europeans, however, are approaching it from the standpoint that the *threat* of sanctions can be effective in producing positive action from the Majlis without the dislocations for European interests that an immediate blockade would cause, presumably without the risk of pushing Iran closer to the Soviets, and without making the Majlis even more negative. . . .

Beginning with the break in diplomatic relations early in April and continuing throughout that difficult month, my journal entries reflect a deepening sense that we had been pushed around long enough and that we needed to find ways to increase the cost for Iran. In a secret message to Washington dated April 18, I wrote: "We welcome steps announced by the President this past week. They can only succeed if they in fact hurt and if the prospect for further hurt looks real to those who will seek to guide and influence the way the Majlis handles this issue. It is vital that we have the maximum support of our Allies and friends. . . ." I went on to say that we needed to convince Iran that it "can now only hope to limit the damage that is being done to its own vital interests . . . that damage will increase each additional day the hostages are held."

In President Carter's own recollection of this time (Keeping Faith, Bantam Books, 1982), he writes that my cable was one of two reports (the other a pessimistic report by Ham Jordan from a secret Iranian source) that "confirmed my resolve to proceed with the rescue [mission]."

DAY 173, *April 24, 1980*
Dear Bill,

It's almost 7:00 P.M. of a beautiful day, outside, that is. I've just finished my hour plus of exercises—ten minutes of walking, 30 minutes of jogging, ten minutes of push-ups, etc., and a few games of Ping-Pong. Exercise helps me sleep, and I do need help on that here.

Today is another holiday. The Iranians seem to average almost one a week, most of them mourning this or that imam's death or martyrdom. Today was declared a holiday and day of national mourning because of the reported execution of a prominent Shia leader in Iraq who was a close associate of the ARK. Iran needs to mourn less and work more. They also need less clerical influence, but that's a long story, isn't it? Thank God for your founding fathers, Bill, who knew the perils of a state church. . . .

We are 100 percent behind the president in his current policy on Iran, and we welcome what support we've had from the allies so far and hope for more. The Canadians, bless them, are prepared to help. And I think the Japanese have done the world a great service in telling the Iranians they're not prepared to buy Iranian oil at the highway-robbery price they're asking these days.

If I sound belligerent, it reflects the fact that my colleagues and I are all agreed we've been pushed around long enough and that application of pressure is now the right course, while we remain open to anything the Iranians might have to say to us, looking toward whatever "conditions" they put to us when the Majlis tackles this issue. And there is no doubt in my mind about the need to avoid any "conditions" that concede anything to their blackmail and threats. If we get enough allied and friendly support, we can come out of this all right. . . .

Cheers, Dad

Today is a day of national mourning to mark the death (say the Iranians) by Iraqi execution of a prominent Shi´a religious leader (and his sister). It is part and parcel of the current friction between the two countries, involving also the eviction by Iraq, say the Iranians, of up to 27,000 Iranian Shi´ites who have been living in Iraq. The two countries are long-standing antagonists, so there is nothing new about this, though there is a greater emotional intensity about it this time, at least on the Iranian side, because of the ARK's personal vendetta against Saddam Hussein and his Sunni Muslim minority leadership in Iraq. . . .

There is nothing lacking about the day. It has been one of those perfect spring days that remind old Persia hands of the great attraction Iran offers, or offered, as a country of assignment. Tonight at sunset the sky is clear, the distant mountains undimmed by dust, the new green of spring in the garden below still brilliant and clean. But the garden remains verboten to us. Since our little contretemps with our security guard over the setup involving the photographer and reporter (we learn since, from an Italian paper) and my angry abuse of our chief guard, no more has been heard of our hour-a-day outing. The chief guard, or rather a Komiteh representative who seems to have taken over all responsibility for our security, was originally described to us as "the man with the heart." Well, he seems to have heart so long as we know our place and stay there; that means staying put inside the four walls of this room, with an occasional stroll to the small bathroom and shower on the floor above ours. Locks and sliding bolts of various kinds now grace the doors from this room, reminding us as never before that we are hostages and that our "guest" status is now tenuous indeed. . . .

DAY 176, *April 27, 1980*—Little did I know, as I wrote on the late evening of April 24 about that beautiful night in Tehran as we looked out on the garden below, that at that very moment, elsewhere in Iran, American aircraft were en route on a mission of rescue, some of those aircraft supposedly to land in this very garden. What subsequently took place is now painfully clear to everyone—the mission was aborted, and eight American servicemen died.

Our minds and hearts are filled with thoughts and emotions that leave us confused and perplexed. Had there been no mechanical failure, where would we be now? On board an aircraft carrier, stranded in the desert, still here in the ministry, injured, or even dead? Who can say? And who can say, now, what might have happened to our colleagues, to their captors, and to personnel guarding us in this ministry? In a sense, we are, in the aftermath, less fortunate than our 50 colleagues, since they will not know, presumably, what happened, while we do and must now live with the emotions and frustrations that are the consequence. Our colleagues, of course, *may* know. Perhaps their captors have told them. In any event, they can conclude that such a rescue attempt was made, or perhaps is feared, because the consequence for them, announced yesterday by the "students," is that they are being dispersed around the country's major cities to preclude such an effort being made again and to "involve the entire nation" in the holding of the hostages. That is cruel for them, cruel in the sense that they can only be left in new and debilitating unease and uncertainty, seeing themselves carted off to a distant city and probably moved in a car with its windows taped over so they have no clue where they're headed, or why, and all the while without knowledge of what their government is doing for them.

So now they become even more like pawns, pawns in the chaotic political process that is revolutionary Iran these days, only now, at least for the moment, a political process given new revolutionary zeal and momentum because of the popular fervor stirred up by the unsuccessful mission. The ARK's words are symbolic of this fervor: "This stupid maneuver was defeated on the order of God, and our doctrine is jihad."

There is more from him and from every other Iranian leader, none of whom for the moment can afford in any way to sound moderate in reference to this issue. It gives the leadership here the opportunity now to claim that *we* are the aggressors, that *we* have violated international law, and that it is *Iran* that is demonstrating restraint and resisting the "predator," the "world-devouring Satan," the aggressive United States—conveniently clouding the basic issue, which is the continued illegal detention of 53 Americans for political blackmail purposes.

So we are filled with an enormous sense of sadness. Grief for those eight courageous men who volunteered and were ready to give their lives for their country and for the principle we represent here—the nation should be forever grateful to them. A sense of compassion for a president who made this difficult and lonely decision and who now suffers this bitter disappointment and must bear the full responsibility of failure. Concern for the hostage families whose worries now are deepened. Regret for our country that it should suffer this blow to its self-esteem and pride. Sorrow for the Iranian people whose future is so jeopardized by the continuation of this whole tragic affair. Anger with those who perpetuate this crisis here, when the simple act of decency of releasing the hostages would turn this whole thing around (but who *will* not because these same people cruelly choose to continue to use these hostages for political purposes). And finally pride in our country for this demonstration of resolve in our efforts to get the hostages released.

What enormous sympathy we feel for those who led this mission and who suffered such incredibly bad luck and mishap! I feel too for young Americans, whose pride in their country and its capability may have been affected by this. I think especially of my two navy sons, how bitterly disappointed they must be. I hope they are not disillusioned—they should not be.

I agree with Reagan and Kennedy and Bush, who have taken the position that this is no time for recrimination. The president needs the support and understanding of all Americans, whatever doubts there may be about timing. We need all of us to reserve our judgments until, at least, we have the facts and the assessments available to the president when he made this lonely and difficult decision.

For the three of us, the residue, however, is one of deep disappointment and gloom—not for ourselves, however much we want to leave here, but for our colleagues and for our country. Our sadness and anger have brought each of us close to tears over these past 48 hours, as we strain our ears for every bit of news we can get from BBC and VOA. The days seem longer, the nights much more difficult, as we think of what has now happened and what might have been. And yet we remain confident. Every other previous disappointment has resulted in new hope, and the same is true now. Aside from the terrible cost of losing eight Americans (adding a dimension that everyone had hoped could be avoided in this crisis), the situation has not basically changed. Iran still holds, illegally, 53 Americans in violation of all standards of law and practice. The rest of the world knows that. Justice is on our side. The allies and our other friends like the Japanese will, we believe, stick to the plans adopted last week to bring pressure to bear on Iran. The local timetable—the Majlis and its decision—still stands. It is in *that* context that the decision will be made. Our demonstration of resolve, however unsuccessful, may improve prospects of getting allied support and of forcing action here. . . .

Meanwhile, we reconcile ourselves to our daily routine. The security guards and serving staff, already instructed on nonfraternization following our break in relations, are now totally aloof, or virtually so, no doubt on renewed instructions, but also probably out of their own sense of shock, unease, and uncertainty as to what these latest happenings mean—indeed, what this may have meant for them, physically, had the thing not aborted. . . . From some of them we detect anger, from others perhaps renewed but very secret sympathy, from others puzzlement, from the committed a new sense of revolutionary zeal and fervor; security is further tightened, and there is no talk of fresh air access now, but there seems also to be no intention to move us. Even now the chief of protocol talks of our being "guests," however incongruous that status is with the doubled guard, the locks on our doors, and the all-night watch. . . .

Our confidence has been momentarily jolted, but it is coming back rapidly. We hope the same for our families and for the other hostages, though we know for them it cannot be easy.

DAY 178, *April 29, 1980*—Today's news tells us that Secretary Vance has resigned, as a matter of conscience and principle over the president's decision to attempt the April 25 rescue mission. Telling the president in advance that he could not support it, whether it failed or succeeded, he submitted his resignation prior to the attempt being made.

It is described by the media as the first resignation of a secretary of state for 65 years—who set that precedent isn't said. This is a loss—a serious one for the president—both in terms of substance and in terms of the political outlook. Among the Foreign Service's professionals, Vance was greatly admired, particularly for his integrity, again so evident in this instance. We wonder to what degree the resignation also reflects the inevitable conflict between Vance and national security adviser, "Big Z" Brzezinski. As the British ambassador put it to me today in a note, "The system you have developed makes the Secretary of State's position very difficult." That is unhappily true.

Locally, in Iran, the reaction is one of further jubilation that right is on Iran's side and that Carter is now further discredited, to Iran's advantage. One minister terms it evidence of "U.S. folly." The reaction is to be expected in the zeal and fervor of the righteousness of Islam and the special wisdom of the Imam that is now to be heard at every hand here. The rooftops of the city for a night or two were the platform for shouting thousands, perhaps tens of thousands, of Iranians giving voice to "Allah O'Akbar," the rallying cry for the masses in this Revolution.

Meanwhile, our position is essentially unchanged locally. The aloofness of the serving and security staff has become more pronounced. . . . We sense a continuing nervousness over what it might have meant for *them* had it *not* failed—and one can understand that. One wonders whether their judgment as to the blame for that—for that risk of injury or death—extends only to the Americans or whether they carry it back further in their minds to the ultimate cause—the seizure of sovereign American territory and the holding of American diplomats by Iranian citizens, encouraged by their government.

The monstrosity of that act continues to boggle one's mind. It was well expressed today in a note I received from a friendly ambassador in response to one I sent him on his country's national day. He wrote that his embassy had not celebrated its national day this year, noting that such receptions are "all of a piece with a code of civilized conduct among nations; a code which unfortunately is no longer universally honored. In the circumstances, to pretend that there has not been an enormous breach of this code, and continue to socialize as usual, would be both insensitive and indecent." I am proud of that letter and its sender, the Greek chargé, who reflects both great decency and courage in what he writes.

Another attractive note came from the papal nuncio, who sent—in response to a request I made of the chief of protocol, a request the chief sent on to the nuncio—a Bible in the King James version. (I weary of modern English idiom versions of the Bible. Why indeed tamper with the elegance of that earlier period?) The nuncio wrote that he had celebrated mass for those he calls "the victims of the desert," the eight Americans who died in the rescue attempt. Archbishop Capucci (here on Easter Monday), the Swiss ambassador, and he are involved in arrangements to return the bodies to the families via the IRC [International Rescue Committee]. . . .

9

May 1980: Dead in the Water

May marked the beginning of a period when things were essentially dead in the water, while the newly elected parliament (Majlis) slowly began to address the hostage issue, pursuant to the Ayatollah's directive of February. My own reluctant recognition of this becomes apparent in journal entries during that period, though not without evidence of intense frustration as well. A letter that arrived in mid-May from son Chip at the University of Minnesota reminded me of the need for patience: "At least the American spirit is still with you there—hope, faith, and of course a sense of humor." And on the back of his letter he wrote—this son who had never quoted Scripture to his father before—words from the 18th Psalm: "I will love thee, O Lord, my strength. . . . I will call upon the Lord, who is worthy to be praised: so shall I be saved from mine enemies."

DAY 181, *May 2, 1980*—The Iranian Embassy in London has been seized by Iranian Arab terrorists, who are holding 20 Iranian diplomats hostage and demanding the release of 91 imprisoned Iranian Arabs in Iran. We need not search long for the inspiration for this latest example of "diplonapping." And the pacesetters here, the student militants who hold our embassy and its staff, have the gall to denounce this act of "terrorism" and, even worse, to

accuse the USG of being responsible! Indeed, a Foreign Ministry spokesman
has been quoted here to the same effect. Incredible? No, routine here these
days. Particularly since the rescue attempt, we are being blamed for everything.

The days go on. We marvel at times at the extent to which this crisis has
mushroomed. Its effects have been horrendous, politically at home and externally as well. . . . A secretary of state has resigned because of it (now replaced
by Senator Muskie). Our fleet in the Indian Ocean has grown to its largest level
ever. A president's political future is in danger because of its continuing effect.
The issue remains a continuing national popular emotion to a degree that
amazes us. And the issue continues to propel millions of Iranians into the
streets in frenzied agitation against U.S. aggression, now seen as responsible for
every Iranian difficulty, bar none.

Within our "prison" (the most elegant prison I've ever been in, says Vic),
the days go on without much meaning for us anymore. We no longer stop to
count them; one day is like another. We conceal our private emotions rather
well. Mike, more gregarious than Vic or I, talks a good deal with the guard
force and the four or five men and one lady who make up the kitchen force,
although repartee with them is no longer what it was before the rescue attempt. Gradually that has eased a bit, though it varies among them. Some
make no secret, or little secret (with us), of their own reservations about the
trend here. One is downright contemptuous of the ARK. But most are careful, reserved with their own views, except for those whose Islamic credentials
are so intense that there is no question. One, whom we've labeled "Mullah,"
makes little effort to conceal his dislike for us. We sense the irritation he
clearly labors under when he has the assignment of serving our food—it no
doubt galls him that the Revolution has brought the personal result for him
that he must wait on three American "spies," who are given living conditions
that he probably feels are far too comfortable, given our sins. . . . Some of
our guard force, incidentally, intimated to us that they believe we knew of
the rescue attempt in advance. Perhaps much of the staff here believes that.
We have emphasized how impossible that would have been. Indeed I am
glad we had no clue of it.

DAY 183, *May 4, 1980*—Pigeons. They can be rather pleasant companions
when you think about them or pay some attention to them. The ministry's
garden has a good colony (or whatever batches of pigeons are called) of them—
rather nondescript gray and white and such-colored pigeons. They sit at our
windows doing a good deal of pigeon talk, until we disturb them. They seem
not yet to have accepted us as permanent occupants. But most of the time they
seem preoccupied with flights from our windows or the roof, up and down from
the handsome pool and fountain in the middle of the ministry's gardens. Indeed, they seem to waste a good deal of time in the exercise, a longer drink or
a more thorough bath at each stop would give them more time to relax, one

would think. But never mind, it's pleasant to watch them. Not frequently can one see such graceful gliding and soaring, downward, on their way to the pool, their wings outstretched and unmoving, their entire bodies moving gracefully with the air currents and then braking for a landing with a clatter of their wings. Moments later, they are off again in a rather noisy and *not* very graceful flutter of wings on their way back to the roof.

Where do pigeons roost? Apparently not in trees—they seem to avoid them. There are gaps in the brickwork on the inner courtyard walls where some seem to have nests, oblivious to the commotion in the concrete courtyard below, where ministry employees come and go during working hours and where men of the army unit assigned here seem to spend every minute after working hours kicking a soccer ball around, with much shouting and obviously much wear and tear on their shoes and, when they fall or collide, their knees. They are a very young group of soldiers who found us rather interesting to joke with and to watch before the abortive rescue mission, but who now look at us very differently—with reservations at best and with anger and hatred at worst. But the pigeons seem not to have changed; they ignore us as easily as before.

Another week has passed, another month, the sixth month starts today. We talked facetiously about marking the day with a tea party—a kind of "bring your own tea" party, inviting the minister, the chief of protocol, our guards, perhaps even dear Ali Agha of Washington fame. Wouldn't he like that! We abandoned the idea, leaving it just another day, the only good news being that at long last the second round of elections for the Majlis is next Friday, the ninth. Then the next step is for it to assemble, and maybe—well, perhaps—my date, July Fourth, might yet prove realistic.

Meanwhile, the regime does not relax in using the fervor triggered by the rescue attempt to urge more and more zeal in building the nation's revolutionary defenses at the grass roots. The "20 million–man army" is much talked about, obviously not in any conceivable way to really man any defenses but very much designed to strengthen mass support for the Revolution and to resist the Fedayeen and Mujahedeen and the other forces that the leadership sees as so corrosive to what it seeks to do. . . .

Today there is more—now a reference to a call from something called the National Mobilization Headquarters to the people to form "resistance groups" in all cities, towns, and villages "to combat all likely dangers posed by the US and its lackeys." Every resistance group is to be composed of 22 persons, with a commander and deputy commander and a "task force" of ten persons, the whole drawn from four to five local families and trained in neighborhood mosques in accordance with "Islamic tradition from the early period of Islam." It is another manifestation of the highly effective way in which the neighborhood mosque and mullah were used as a network, an apparatus, to achieve the Revolution last year—and now to preserve it against the dangers of the United States and its lackeys, that being a euphemism for the dangers *within*, i.e., the non-Islamic elements. . . .

All this does not make life within our four walls—and it is literally that now,

except for the 17 steps up to our garretlike bathroom—any easier. The room's
dusty chandeliers, rather garish draperies, and vastness pall on one very
quickly. I find myself waking in the morning and wondering how long I can take
this monotony, but by midmorning I find myself sufficiently reconciled to all
this, having looked again at the now-beautiful garden of roses below and reminding myself that there *is* beauty and decency out there in the world outside
and that it *will* yet prevail, hopefully even in the neighborhood mosques of
south Tehran.

DAY 185, *May 6, 1980*—The seige at the Iranian Embassy in London
ended yesterday, with the British SAS (Special Air Service) force storming the
place after two diplomats were shot. The British took it without further loss of
hostages, but four terrorists were killed. The Brits have done the world a great
service, demonstrating the regard their government has for its responsibility in
protecting diplomatic missions and demonstrating also that this kind of terrorism must not succeed. The Iranians have sent off a message of thanks, while
insisting all the while that this situation is totally different than what has happened here. Much pomposity from Ghotbzadeh on tonight's TV news. But the
Iranians cannot fool the rest of the world. . . . Terrorism is indivisible, . . . and
nothing that these people say can change that.

DAY 187, *May 8, 1980*—This morning, just as we were to sit down to
breakfast and before some of us were fully dressed, the chief of protocol swept
in with the Swiss ambassador in tow, accompanied this time by a Mr. Castelli,
a Swiss diplomat assigned here to help get that section of their embassy organized that is to protect U.S. interests (some seven people have so far arrived).
The ambassador had with him six cans of baked beans, a big bottle of catsup,
and a cake from Mrs. Lang's kitchen. I told him we regarded Mrs. Lang as *our*
protection service; we didn't really need the official variety, thank you, so long
as we had Mrs. Lang.

The ambassador was here on his weekly visit. Usually he comes on Mondays
with our mail, but he was delayed this week until today, Thursday, because of
his preoccupation until yesterday with the sad and difficult task of working with
the papal nuncio and Archbishop Capucci in the dispatch of the eight bodies of
U.S. servicemen killed in the rescue mission. He told us of the great difficulties
involved—the normal difficulty of getting action out of the Iranian bureaucracy,
vastly complicated in this instance by the political sensitivities over the U.S.
military intrusion. He told also of the gruesome scenes at the morgue, not so
much of these eight bodies, but of the heavy inflow of the dead from the
fighting in Kurdistan—the emotional scenes of families arriving to claim
the bodies of their loved ones, the chaotic order or disorder of the place, the
crowds, the anti-American sloganeering, etc. But the matter is now resolved,
as far as the eight are concerned. . . .

DAY 190, *May 11, 1980*—Sunday. Today is 13-year-old Jim's confirmation at All Saints Episcopal, presumably the honors being done by Bishop Walker, the Episcopal bishop of Washington. This was one event I *didn't* want to miss, so I have thought much about home today. . . . These are days when these four walls bear down awfully heavily, despite the attempted good cheer of the chief of protocol today, who pressed the line that we would look back on this period of free time—to read and relax—and regret it is over. We told him we needed only five minutes to pack. . . .

Today that good and decent man, the papal nuncio, sent me a two-page letter (written in his halting English), describing "the matter of the corpses of the Tabas raid," i.e., the disposition of the eight bodies, in which he was involved, together with Capucci and the Swiss ambassador. He writes that, in the end, the authorities here behaved "with great dignity," and one must hope that he is right, after the regrettable abuse of the bodies by Ayatollah Khalkali. He writes also that he feels Capucci is "doing a good work for the solution of entire problem." Again, he may be right—Capucci could well prove to be a person who can act as an intermediary at some stage.

The nuncio concludes his letter: "I am sorry that the hostages are dispersed, because more difficult is a friendly assistance. But God is great! And, as a writer writes, the men write crooked [wrong] but God read right." What a good man he is (however fractured his English may be)!

The nuncio's secretary, a man named Mulligan, the man who sent us the record player and who is also a priest, sent a letter, too. He too had taken part in religious services for the eight dead at the morgue. He writes: "Seeing them I thought how they did more than anyone could do . . . giving their lives for their countrymen. 'Greater love hath no man than that he lay down his life for his friends.' That was their silent testimony."

DAY 195, *May 16, 1980*—Some days are harder to start than others. Like today. It's 11:00 A.M., and we've just finished breakfast—slow in coming today, for some reason. . . . Another reason it's hard to get started is that the weather outside is so fine these days; today there's a cool breeze, the sky is clear, and it would be a fine day for almost any outing. Possibly even a ski trip—a letter yesterday from the Danish chargé spoke of the season having been "exceptionally good and only coming to an end now." And, said he, tennis is well launched. Oh dear, that's hard to take. . . .

Yet another letter from the British ambassador, who does not fail to send us newspapers and magazines (and chocolate bars). He writes that he has moved to his summer residence in Gulhak, up in the mountain foothills, the same residence that Churchill writes about in his World War II memoirs, he (Churchill) staying there "in the cool wooded glades high above the city" when he transited Tehran twice during World War II trips to Moscow. Even then, however, he wrote of the "dreadful traffic" of Tehran, where everyone seemed to have a car and everyone seemed to lean on his horn for attention. Now, says the British ambassador, the "cool wooded glades" are as attractive as ever; but he complains of an owl that hoots through the night as regular as clockwork, and when it misses a beat, he is kept awake "waiting for the other hoot to drop," like the proverbial second shoe. How's that for hardship?

DAY 196, *May 17, 1980*
Norwegian Independence Day!
Hi, Honey,

Got a card from you when the Swiss came in last week, Tuesday. It was the card you'd written on the morning of the day when you got the tragic news of the failure of the rescue mission. Did I tell you I liked what the press referred to as your telegram to the president?

It's been a rather dreary week. Well, they all are, but sometimes they seem to go better than this one did. This one dragged—these four walls seem more confining than usual. Perhaps it's the weather, now so beautiful—so near and yet so far from us. Perhaps it's also been the local news—so full now of propaganda of how we are behind all things that go wrong here, how U.S. "agents" are landing in Kurdistan, and God knows what else. Perhaps it's the news, almost daily, of the hostages being parceled out, like sheep, to yet another distant Iranian city.

Mainly it's the fact that we're approaching 200 days. I remember when we hit 100—we thought *that* was bad!

But we are philosophical about it all—confident now that the thing will be resolved in six to eight weeks. My date remains the Fourth of July!

Miss you, love you, B

DAY 197, *May 18, 1980*—Today the local press continues what appears to be a sustained effort by President Bani-Sadr to enhance his revolutionary credentials by finding new and better charges against the United States and its "evil ways." Today we read that his newspaper has come out with the news that the United States has 20(!) secret airstrips in Iran, similar to that used at Tabas in the attempted rescue mission. Some of these have not yet been "traced," some had not even been asphalted! The implication is that yet further U.S. intrigues are planned, against which the Revolution must be on redoubled guard.

It is all wearisome. And yet I suppose one could say it is also normal. This Revolution is by no means complete, and until it is, or is replaced, we will have more of this kind of thing. There is also the political power struggle that is a part of the Revolution, a struggle that has seen Bani-Sadr in recent months constantly undermined and frustrated by the clerical forces, still in the ascendancy. The assumption is that these forces will be similarly strong in the Majlis, although it is also probable that a good number of those newly elected are malleable, politically, and will go with the highest bidder, in political and ideological terms. All of which will have a bearing on our fate in the decision the

Majlis is to take to resolve the issue. In that respect, today's press also quotes our good friend, Dr. Yazdi, late of this ministry, as saying that the hostages, in the view of most members of the Majlis, must be tried . . . as a means of putting the United States on trial for its role in the restoration of the Shah in 1953, etc. For good measure, he throws in the idea that Iran should seek financial compensation for U.S. "interventions" in Iran, causing the loss of "basic rights" of 35 million Iranians.

That, too, is wearisome. As if Iranians had nothing to do with the political and economic crisis of 1953 or the scene in Iran over the next 26 years! It is also yet further indication of the historical tendency here to seek scapegoats to blame for their ills, for their own shortcomings.

But the real question is what all this means for Iran's political future—what will come of all this revolutionary zeal, this political posturing, this search for scapegoats, this turmoil? Can the Revolution produce the Islamic state and society that it professes to be capable of? Is such a thing, a theocratic state resting on the moral and political and economic precepts of the Koran, which at its writing rested on an eighth-century society, conceivably feasible near the start of the 21st century? Yesterday's press quoted the ARK in a long statement warning of the need to "purge" the radio and television network of "corrupt" people, saying that this network must become "100 percent Islamic" if the Revolution is to be furthered. "The Islamic Republic should become reality, not just talk. There are corruptions everywhere . . . most important is the news program. You have to be careful that misguided people do not have control over it. . . ."

Yes, a continuing Revolution. But to what end? How can such a system, such an approach to daily life, really last? It is easy to conclude it cannot. But it is also clear that Islam, to a greater or lesser degree, is going to be a powerfully determining political force here for a while, as it is in the Islamic world generally these days. Even those here who oppose the ARK cannot ignore that fact.

DAY 199, May 20, 1980—I woke early and couldn't sleep. I lay there and thought of the injustice of what has been done here, an injustice that was glaring and visible last November but that has inevitably been dissipated in terms of its public notice and impact by the passage of time. The result is that today the foreign minister here can go to Islamabad and tell the assembled foreign ministers there that Iran is acting with "great restraint" in the face of the "provocations" that the United States constantly forces on the noble people of Iran. Who is guilty of provocations? Who has violated international law? Who is holding 53 men and women hostage for purposes of political blackmail? Where, Mr. Minister, would the world community be if every country, angry with another and seeking redress, whatever its grievances, were free to seize that other country's diplomats and their embassy and demand redress in that fashion? What chaos the world would confront!

That, of course, is exactly what happened in London, where terrorists, quite possibly Iraqis, or at least that is what the Iranians claimed, seized Iran's embassy and demanded redress. Then it was Iran that denounced terrorism and said that Britain must fulfill its obligations. But here? Here the issue, more blatant than that anywhere in recent history because the government itself stands behind the local terrorists—here the offense is lost in the passage of time, and Iran increasingly seems able to cloud the issue with its long-established skill in blaming others, in finding scapegoats, in clothing itself in raiments of "restraint." As that young hero said in *The Far Pavilions:* "It isn't fair!"

The day was uneventful, except for a package of newspapers and a jigsaw puzzle from our good British friends. One of the newspapers has excerpts from an interview that Bani-Sadr recently gave an Italian newspaper, in which he pleaded for "help" from Europe to resolve the hostage crisis. The interviews, the bulk of which appeared to be focused on Bani-Sadr's political contest with the Beheshti group, quoted Bani-Sadr as urging Europe *not* to go the sanctions route: "Suggest to us what to do. Put forward concrete proposals. Act as mediators. Do something. Instead of just condemning us, take notice that the hostage problem is making objective difficulties not only for us but also for you."

Well, with all due credit to this man, who I think genuinely *does* want to resolve the crisis, this is a classic example again of another manifestation of the scapegoat syndrome in Iranian politics. Bani-Sadr knows full well that the obstacles to a settlement are internal, not external. It is the Iranian body politic that must sort itself out before there can be a settlement. No outsider can do much more than affect this crisis at the margins. Until the power struggle here is resolved or, since resolution is probably impossible, until some kind of modus vivendi is worked out within the parliament that will permit the opposing factions to work together on some issues, there will be no solution of the hostage crisis. When that modus vivendi is reached, the hostages will have lost their value as pawns and can be let go. Meanwhile, however, Bani-Sadr, like so many Iranians, rationalizes his failure to get the crisis resolved by, in effect, blaming Europe and the United States for not "helping"!

DAY 201, *May 22, 1980*—I stood at our window at dusk and watched swallows, not pigeons. The latter seem to disappear totally by dusk, but swallows on the other hand seem to appear only at dusk. What kind of swallows they are, I can't say. They look like the bird we called barn swallows at home. I think I had not realized before why they appear so frenetic in their flashing to and fro across the sky—and I realize now they're catching bugs! But I wonder what their radar system is that makes it possible to catch bugs at that speed, at such rapid twists and turns. And why doesn't one swallow occasionally collide with another? What if two swallows spy the same bug and say, "That's for me"? But they don't collide. Perhaps there are so many bugs there's no likelihood of colliding. And the sky is big—like space, where all those missiles, satellites, and space garbage never seem to collide either.

All of this, of course, assumes that the theory of swallows behaving like that because they're catching bugs is correct. Maybe it isn't. Maybe they're just getting their evening exercise and feel in high spirits. Amazing how little I know about swallows, when we lived with hundreds of them on the farm. We took them for granted, I suppose. Perhaps that's an advantage of being a hostage—you don't take things quite so much for granted, like freedom, for example.

DAY 202, *May 23, 1980*—We read in a *Tribune* that arrived yesterday that Mansur Farhang, Iran's UN representative (via Sacramento State), has said that it was no longer in Iran's best interests to hold the hostages, that Iran had achieved all the political and propaganda gains that were to be had from the hostage-taking, and that the standoff was putting Iran in a position of international isolation. Either in this same interview or separately, he was quoted in a local paper as saying much the same thing. The man has obviously spent too much time in the United States; he is frank. We have felt all along that the crisis would only be resolved when Iran, or when the political groups in Iran who make decisions here, concluded that there was no longer any domestic political benefit in keeping the hostages: that is, as political pawns they were no longer useful and possibly even counterproductive. But that has not been much said, *publicly*, until Farhang's statement. . . .

DAY 203, *May 24, 1980*—The Friday prayers had a new rallying cry yesterday to drum up anti-American fervor. (Not that one was really needed, mind you, the sentiment is pretty strong as it is, what with all those American agents building secret airstrips and messing around in places like Kurdistan!) But this one was too good to be ignored: the race riots in Miami. So Hojjatol-Islam Khamanei at the Friday prayers, Ayatollah Khomeini from his home, and the student militants, all expressed anger at the crime being done American blacks. Khamanei even went so far as to allege that black Muslims in Miami were supporting the Iranian Revolution because force was required to put them down! And the ARK spoke about martial law being imposed on several U.S. cities to keep the blacks down. And, said he, Islam had resolved all racial problems 1,400 years ago at the very advent of Islam!

Oh, how I wish I were free to speak out, possibly even to write a letter to the press. It would say something like this: "Americans have no claim to purity in the area of race relations. Their society is far from perfect, and they lay no claim to such. But as a government and a people, they are committed to the goal of racial equality. It ill-behooves another government, especially one that uses tanks and helicopter gunships against its own ethnic minorities, to advise Americans on the subject of racial equality."

DAY 205, *May 26, 1980*—We pursue our totally *abnormal* routines each day, trying to fill up the day's hours, knowing we are marking time until something happens, and yet developing our own routine—after 205 days—to the point where our own psyches, probably more than we realize, have become accustomed to this routine. We wonder sometimes what long-range effect it will have on us. Will we find it difficult going back to a nine-to-five office routine? Is this making us permanently lazy and indolent? Or is it going to make us nervously frenetic, anxious to make up for the time and events we've missed? So far, I think, I don't *feel* any different. And yet how do I know? We interact here only among the three of us and occasionally with the chief of protocol and the Swiss ambassador, and to a limited degree with the kitchen staff. What will we be like in the great wide world? How will we react with our families, with the daily routine of work and home? Penne tells me she has bought four new tires for the car. I'm reminded of the small but constant pressures that she faces of running a home and family. How will I react to that again? With alacrity? Or with a level of frustration that is much more easily triggered than it used to be? . . .

Meanwhile, back at the ranch, the Majlis met yesterday with the ARK; the ceremonial opening is May 28. Work presumably will begin in some earnest, at least on organization, on Saturday, May 31. Then we shall soon see what is feasible. The ARK's speech to the members was predictable—be Islamic, think Islamic, act Islamic. And if you don't, dear children, you will be seen as "deviationists" and treated accordingly. Emotions at the meeting were such that some wept, especially the women, at hearing the Imam's protestations that praise of him by the introductory speaker was not deserved. So much for that. . . .

Sometimes it is hard *not* to react, especially in reading the daily columns of the *Tehran Times* or hearing the Iranian interpretation of news and U.S. intentions as broadcast by NIRT. Today, for example, the press quotes President Bani-Sadr as saying, "Over the past two days I have received information that the Americans have sent three groups to Iran and assigned to them the mission of killing the hostages so that the United States has the pretext to intervene overtly in our affairs. But we ordered sufficient precautions to protect the lives of the captives."

I'm reminded again, in reading such, of the plaint, "It isn't fair!" It isn't fair that such should be said and that I'm not in a position to challenge it. What nonsense, especially when it comes from that level. It is of a piece with earlier nonsense of "20 secret airstrips" supposedly built here by the Americans, of "90 U.S. agents" parachuting into Kurdistan. But this is even worse—to allege that we would stoop to killing the hostages to further our larger purposes! What *is* the president's purpose in giving credence to such calumnies? Much of the same was heard in a statement issued yesterday by the "students," who claimed that because of these things, because of threats to the hostages that they claim they have already uncovered, they are taking extra precautions to ensure the hostages are safe—and those "precautions" include a strict ban on visits to them by *any* outsiders. . . .

We note with some appreciation that the ICJ [International Court of Justice] at The Hague has announced its definitive ruling on the U.S. appeal to it over the hostage issue, following up the court's interim judgment of December last. By unanimous vote, the 15 judges (including Soviet, Syrian, Polish, and Indian judges) called on Iran to release hostages and U.S. properties forthwith and to refrain from putting any of the hostages on trial in any way or form. A separate decision, calling on Iran to pay reparations, was approved 12 to either two or three—the Soviet, the Pole, and possibly the Syrian voting no. All of this the Iranians have dismissed as "meaningless" since the Iranians had previously announced that the court had no jurisdiction in the matter.

Iran may say what it wishes, but for us and the rest of world opinion it is a definitive, authoritative affirmation of respect for international law and practice that fully endorses the U.S. position. More important, it is a judgment that will stand in the annals of such law and practice as future protection against recurrence of the kind of violation that has been so blatant here. . . .

DAY 210, *May 31, 1980*—That long-anticipated Islamic body, the Majlis, has convened and, supposedly, gone to work. . . . The Majlis met in ceremonial opening session to hear a message from the ARK stressing in 11 points (manifestos should never exceed ten points!) the need to be, act, and think Islamic or be seen as "deviationist." From Bani-Sadr it heard a warning of public dissatisfaction growing and time running out. And from the Students Following the Line of the Imam, it heard a warning that to resolve the hostage crisis without getting the Shah back or, if he is not returned, putting the hostages on trial would be acting contrary to the express, earlier position of the ARK. For good measure, they reminded the Majlis that to act out of fear of the "Big Devil" would be to risk renewed "enslavement" by that "Devil" (the United States).

So far so good—or bad, depending on how one chooses to put it. The important thing is that the body is real, is meeting, and, God willing, will sooner or later face up to the issue. We are agreed, among ourselves, that this is the time for us to cool it, despite, for example, the temptation of using the ICJ decision to make another run for UNSC action to force results here. The time for that may be later, when we see what Majlis sentiment is.

One thing is clear: the Islamic Revolution has produced a clearly Islamic-oriented Majlis. The sweep of cameras reveals a veritable host of turbaned types in their parliamentary seats. To be fair to this Revolution, it can be said that it cannot be judged until its institutions of government are in being; until now, albeit 15 months into its history, the Revolution has not had the benefit of parliament or permanent government apparatus. Soon it *will* have. Then it must produce, and Bani-Sadr is exactly right: public expectations will demand results.

Results will not be easy. The economy is prostrate; oil production (for export) may be less than a million barrels a day; the government's swollen bureaucracy absorbs much of its available revenues; housing problems (and expectations) are acute; sanctions, however incomplete, hurt; Iran is isolated among much of the world diplomatically (despite its claims to the contrary). And there remains the fundamental question whether Islamic precepts can somehow be made to serve as practical guides to the whole social, political, and economic society in this decade of the 1980s.

But again, it is fair to say that the Revolution deserves a chance to try. Islam is in any event an ideology. There is no question about this Revolution being armed with an ideology, a highly pervasive one, a situation not always the case in countries undergoing revolutions, coups d'état, or whatever these days.

I do not believe it *can* work, not in the form now being touted, not in the rigid, inflexible approach now being demonstrated in the face of practical problems of governing—not least the issue of nationalities, ethnic minorities, the tribal elements that, as someone has commented, ring this country in *U*-formation, beginning with the Azari Turks, the Turkomans, Qashqais, Bakhtiaries, Arabs, Baluchis, and other smaller groups. All of these have demonstrated disaffection over the past 15 months, the Kurds massively so. . . .

Today I did what I should have done weeks ago—wrote letters to each of the families of the eight men who gave their lives for us in the Tabas rescue mission. Writing them reminded me, again and painfully, of the tragic element now forever a part of this crisis. It reminded me, too, of the courage of these men and their colleagues and the courage of their families, most with very young children. I said to each of the families that to us these men would forever be shining symbols of the courage and dedication that make us proud to be Americans. . . .

Today is Memorial Day at home, and our thoughts go naturally to those eight Americans. Our country has thousands of reasons to pause and remember today—to remember those countless numbers who have made the supreme sacrifice—but none so recent or so poignantly as those eight men, for whose families today must be an especially trying time. God bless them and the memory of those men.

———

Dear Chip,

When you get this, your first year of college will be behind you, and you will have experienced that wonderful elation, the satisfaction, that relief that we all felt in exactly your position. And pride too, pride in being on one's own, in a way, away from home and on your way to something. Most of us aren't that certain at the end of the first year where it is taking us, although you—with your navy direction—have a better idea than most freshmen. And that's a good thing. I certainly wasn't sure where things were leading me when I finished that first year. And I guess I didn't until after the war and I got back to school at the U of M. . . .

Our seventh month as of June 4. Remember that telephone call at the farm in Minnesota, almost a year ago to the day now, in which the director general told me the secretary wanted me to go to Tehran? For how long? Oh, no longer than four to six weeks!

But then something happened. . . . And I'm still here. Locked up tight and hot too these days.

It's soon midnight. I hate the nights, but we try to put in our eight hours, sometimes nine. Not much point in getting up early. (I wonder sometimes how I'm going to face getting up and meeting a schedule when I get out of here!)

Good luck, Chip—Dad

10

June 1980: Patience in Short Supply

Summers in Tehran are hot, dusty, and smog-ridden, unless one has the good fortune to live in the mountain suburbs, which was not the case for us in that fateful summer of 1980. In what probably reflected our impatience and discomfort—both physically and mentally—we wrote to the foreign minister to volunteer as "witnesses" before the parliament as a means of speeding its painfully deliberate process regarding the hostages' fate. It did not merit a response. My irritation with the course of events extended as well to former Attorney General Ramsey Clark, visiting Tehran as an American representative at something called the Crimes of America Conference. Under the circumstances it seemed unconscionable to me that any American would take part in a conference under that rubric. But my irritation was eventually eased a bit to learn that his speech to the "delegates" included this reminder to the students about their hostage gambit: "God knows it is not right."

DAY 211, *June 1, 1980*—Today we hear again, in the *Tehran Times*, from our watchdog of the foreign press corps in Iran, Mr. Abolghassim Sadegh, director general of the foreign press in that aptly named ministry, the Ministry of National Guidance. Presumably all revolutions need that kind of guidance, or at least those do who, for whatever reason, feel that perhaps their Revolution is not fully understood abroad. And Iran feels that way in great earnest, especially regarding the Western press.

Today Mr. Sadegh is quoted as saying that it is dangerous to admit American journalists because the United States was sending out spies under the guise of journalists. This was presumably based on recent public comments by CIA Director Adm. Stansfield Turner to the effect that he did not think this should be excluded, though claiming it was not now the case. Mr. Sadegh went on with the usual line about the foreign press being allowed to operate here, "provided their performance was not biased and their reports were factual." And that, of course, raises the old question about where truth lies. If a foreigner's collection of "facts" adds up to a description of problems for the Revolution, is that "bias" or is it the truth? If facts attesting to the absence of due process in judicial proceedings, for example, are rather substantial, as surely has been the case in Iran in recent times, does that mean that the reporter who reports them is "biased" against Iran? Or is he simply reporting the truth, however unwelcome that story may appear to those trying to sell Iran's Revolution abroad?

Perhaps the best one can say for such situations is that happy is the country whose society and government, however imperfect, do not fear for judgments by outsiders of its state of political and social health. For a country like Iran, 15 months into a sweeping revolution, that stage has not been reached.

All of us tonight are writing letters in some frenzy against the possibility that the Swiss may be in tomorrow. But our chief of protocol, who must escort the ambassador in, may be too busy tomorrow, being almost totally preoccupied in preparations for the "clambake" that begins here tomorrow. That is the gathering, commanded to be held by the ARK after the Tabas affair, to demonstrate to the world the enormity of U.S. "crimes" against Iran. It has been an on-again, off-again process, possibly because of getting delegations to come. For that reason it has ended up as a conference of nongovernmental bodies, mostly liberation movements of one brand or another, the delegations taking over much of the Hilton Hotel, suitably renamed for the occasion as the Freedom Hotel. (After all, how can a good revolutionary movement have the name Hilton around?)

We don't know as yet whether any Americans will be here. If they are, they will have to defy the USG ban on visas for Iran, but that has been done before, in other places and times. I told the chief of protocol today that if they needed someone, perhaps I could represent the Sioux Indians of southern Minnesota. Mike suggested the three of us could go, representing deprived and oppressed hostages! No takers, on either count. . . .

So life goes on. The Swiss brought in copies the other day of the medical reports on each of us following the doctors' visit here last January. Each of them includes the finding (among much that is numerical and technical) of "moral sadness"! In addition, mine includes "moral sadness, with some nervousness"! I like that. Moral sadness, you bet; there was a time when we showed it purposely, to every visiting Iranian. By now we've pretty much relaxed with most Iranians, except those, like our "man with the heart," who continue to merit our scorn. But "nervousness"? That too reflects what was my tactic for a time with such Iranian visitors, deliberately maintaining the most aloof posture that I possibly could. Why should I demonstrate anything but barely controlled anger?

Having recorded all that, I must record what matters most. Today is our 23d wedding anniversary, Penne and I. Who of us could have forseen that, 23 years later, we would spend it thus? . . .

I think of my sons, wondering if they too will be so fortunate in marriage as I. How does any man—or woman—know when the decision is right? How can there be any sure way? Surely it is, for most of us, a matter of fate, of luck, of happenstance. Or is there something else that works for some of us and, unhappily, doesn't work for so many in today's society? I know there is no easy answer. But I know how fortunate I have been. And in many ways, it has taken this forced separation now to remind each of us of our good fortune. From all sides I hear of Penne's support for me—and my colleagues—of her having set aside all her own interests to focus on help for all of us, including a public posture that has shown the intelligence, integrity, and good sense of a remarkably able and attractive person. To see and know this as I know it now almost make this trauma worthwhile!

DAY 212, *June 2, 1980*—Ramsey Clark? Here for the "Crimes of America" Conference? It seems a bit incredible, but the evening news tells us it is true. He is here at the head of a 40-person delegation, traveling to Iran despite the ban on such travel by our government and thus, theoretically, I suspect, liable to prosecution on his return.

Whatever else one says of it, there is vast irony. Seven months ago, almost to the day, Ramsey Clark was en route to Iran (with Bill Miller) at the president's request to try to open a dialogue with the regime that would seek release of the hostages and restoration of the compound. Given approval to come by the Revolutionary Council, his mission was thwarted en route (in Turkey) when the ARK ordered that no one would see him, an early example of the kind of undermining of authority here that the ARK and his entourage have subsequently made a matter of depressing practice.

Now Clark returns to grace a conference designed to condemn American policy toward Iran over the past 25 years. Presumably he sees it as a way of opening dialogue. Perhaps it will contribute to a sense of achievement on the part of the regime here that will finally cause it to conclude that the hostages can be released, their retention no longer necessary in light of the "universal" condemnation of them and their government. But if the price to be paid for that is to have a former U.S. cabinet officer (our chief judicial officer at that!) come to lend dignity to the charade now being played out here, I wish he had stayed at home. . . .

DAY 214, *June 4, 1980*—The seventh month anniversary.

Yesterday, Ramsey Clark spoke his piece before the Conference on U.S.

Interventions in Iran. His remarks fill me with a classic case of mixed emotions. I cannot be sure where the balance rests. Let me see if I can sort them out.

I remain troubled that a man of his stature (a former cabinet officer, however one may feel about his policies and posture in the past) has lent credibility to this conference by coming here. No one of any other delegation can claim anywhere near the status he holds; the others are virtually all representatives of far-out leftist, liberation, or fringe elements in their own countries. Thus Clark and his delegation unquestionably add class to this conference simply by being here.

I confess also to pain in hearing a prominent American speaking out here, in this setting, against my country and its policies, the latter including some that I too question. Perhaps it takes a big man, a man with a big heart, to do that. Perhaps it is I who suffers from a narrow vision. Whatever the faults of men like Kissinger, Nixon, Helms, Kermit Roosevelt, Allen Dulles—whom he cited by name in his speech—it pains me to see them denounced by an American here in Iran. It troubles me to hear him say that the United States "still clings to the idea that it can control the government and the destinies of other people."

But I must give him credit as well, and that is where my mixed emotions arise. In the first place, I must remind myself that we have said ourselves, the three of us, that, recognizing the reality of this place and its temperature, some such public "trial" and condemnation of the United States are going to be needed to permit the leadership to work itself out of its corner or, putting it differently, to get itself off the hook on the hostage issue. This conference can serve that purpose well, if the leadership is prepared to use it, though the question will remain whether it will suffice to meet the demands of the funda- mentalists and the street mobs behind them. It is in this context that one can tolerate the wild extremities now being expressed by the other partici- pants. . . .

There will be more—the conference is only half over—but it is this kind of thing that the regime can cite if it wishes as background (and reason) for a decision to terminate the hostage issue. Clark's presence here in this context can also be cited.

Then there is what Clark said in his speech about the hostage issue, and there I am prepared to give him full credit. He was forthright in calling on the regime to release the hostages, putting it in Iran's own interests to take this step if its Revolution is to succeed. . . . The *Tehran Times* gave full coverage to Clark, quoting him as saying, "It is imperative that the hostages be released now. . . ." He could, he said, understand what had motivated the students: "God knows it is understandable. But it is not right. God knows it is not right."

Moreover, he said, these are "little people." They were not the "villains"; the real culprits were the Nixons, Kissingers, etc. (see above). "If you had one of them, that would be different, but little people never matter to them. Isn't that the meaning of this whole history and course of conduct?"

Except for the latter paragraph, added probably to make his appearance more acceptable locally, this is courageous and honest, and I give him credit for it. Perhaps it is too much of a good thing for some of the local fundamentalists.

As the story in the *Times* notes, his speech "drew hums of disapproval" from some Iranians at the conference, some delegates accusing him of presenting the U.S. government's point of view, which I guess only proves we can't win for losing! . . .

The departing British ambassador, Sir John Graham, was allowed in to see us today to say good-bye. He leaves the sixth. He and his wife, Meg, have been magnificent. He wrote frequent notes of encouragement and sent in chocolate, newspapers, magazines, and puzzles, and she, too, let us know in various ways of her concern and support. He is the best of the Foreign Office style—unflappable, low-key, competent, a very human approach, good-humored, widely intelligent, spare of frame, a good tennis player, a man who clearly believes in the special relationship. We will miss him. . . .

Perhaps no group was more understanding of our plight as hostages or more supportive in every way possible than our colleagues in Tehran's diplomatic corps. Only our Soviet bloc colleagues wavered, but they, too, especially the Soviets, maintained an official, public posture of being opposed to actions in violation of diplomatic norms and convention. But it was our colleagues from Western countries who reached out to us in every practical way to let us know they cared, that there but for the grace of God go we. Regrettably, it was almost always only the three of us in the Foreign Ministry that they could reach with that message. We could only hope that our 50 colleagues knew of that support in their hearts.

DAY 216, *June 6, 1980*—Today in Tehran it's warm. Not warm—hot and unpleasant. Yesterday's temperature was 100°. Today should be even hotter. The air is thick with heat and smog pollution—thick enough to slice with a knife. I judge the quality of the air by the visibility of a mountain that lies to the far side of south Tehran. Today it's not visible at all. The room becomes stifling by midafternoon, however much we try to keep drapes drawn to keep the sun out. The dust is quickly thick on the shiny parquet floors, which the kitchen staff swabs with a thick rag occasionally. The kitchen staff tells us the room has air conditioning; we wonder how the powers-that-be will react to our asking that hostages be allowed captivity in air-conditioned comfort!

Yesterday was a holiday (as is today, Friday). Yet another holiday, yet another day of mourning, yet another day of mass street processions, yet another day of anti-American fervor. Work is not a feature of the Iranian Revolution, it seems, not when one can take to the streets and enjoy another day of mass fervor. Yesterday's events recalled the date of the Shi´a calendar in 1963 when antiregime riots were put down by force, including the alleged martyrdom of hundreds in Qom and the exile to Iraq of the Ayatollah Khomeini. These were triggered in part by Majlis action at the time giving extraterritorial judicial status to U.S. military advisers working with the Shah's armed forces.

Given that special link with Khomeini himself, the day had special significance for the fundamentalists, who produced what looked (on TV) like very large crowds indeed. We are without a newspaper today, but the TV news reports that "the people" adopted an 11-point resolution or manifesto, the tenth of which was a demand that the hostages be put on trial and sentenced if the Shah is not returned to Iran. If that is so, it does not help. It does not help us, and it does not help those here who now are trying to find some way to get the Majlis to act with moderation. It reintroduces an element of rigidity and at the level that could be most dangerous of all, the level of the street masses, the level of mobocracy, which the fundamentalists have used so skillfully ever since the start of this crisis to keep tensions high while they proceed with their political purposes, which are now to solidify their control in the new Majlis and ensure that a PM [prime minister] and cabinet malleable by them is put into place.

It is an interesting political process, this use of mass public fervor and slogans in this way. One wonders who drafts these resolutions, who is the architect of policy that is then so easily and without opposition adopted in the streets. It is the fundamentalists, but who are the prime movers? Beheshti, Hashemi Rafsanjani (yesterday's featured speaker), the ARK himself? Or does the entourage around him act largely independently of him, confident of his backing if necessary in a crunch? He, after all, has not failed them (or the students) yet when decision time comes.

This is a revolution, and revolutions depend on mass support—or look for it—where it can be found. When it can be put into the streets to silence opposition and to demonstrate the new regime's strength, that is a natural process in any revolution. But there comes a time, surely, where a regime's leadership must recognize the need for elitist leadership in terms of the substance of a revolution, rather than the revolution being preoccupied with mass fervor and agitation. It is now 16 months into the Iranian Revolution. Where are its bearings, other than the uniting force of Shi´a Islam? Bani-Sadr warns that popular expectations are at a high and dangerous level. But who listens to that? Those who control the direction of things here seem still preoccupied with keeping up mass fervor, still focusing (as yesterday) on the past, on the Shah, on martyrdom, on the United States and its "crimes." Meanwhile, the economy reflects this drift, the masses clearly have not benefited materially from their fervor in the Revolution, housing remains chaotic, and another oppressive Iranian summer faces them. The picture is depressing.

DAY 217, *June 7, 1980*—The Crimes of America Conference is over, adopting a document that predictably condemned the United States for all manner of wrongs toward Iran, said that the United States should pay reparations, and even denounced us for mistreatment of Iranian nationals in the United States, "particularly the students." Ghotbzadeh's windup speech said that the U.S. Embassy had been seized because Iran wanted to turn over a new leaf in history, but the United States "only saw this as a sign of weakness." The U.S. delegation, to its credit, tried to get the concluding document to include a reference to the hostages; this was rejected, Ghotbzadeh taking the position that the document's call for a peaceful resolution of all U.S.-Iranian difficulties included the hostage issue by implication. There were, he said, many other outstanding issues that, "as far as we are concerned, are more important than the hostage issue." . . .

DAY 220, *June 10, 1980*—Ten at night and the ten o'clock change of the guard. Our army guard force in the garden and at the main gates below has just gone on duty. The force numbers some 36, and eight or ten have just moved off to their posts. They don't notice us watching them, but frequently during the day they look up at us, some smiling, most simply curious, one or two attempting a greeting in English. We wonder what they think of us. They are young, probably in the 18- to 20-year range. Often, now in this warm weather, they relax off duty in the garden below us, lounging on the grass, practicing karate, reading, and on very warm days, with the gardeners out of sight, cavorting with hoses of water trying to douse their buddies. They remind me of our Marines at the embassy—young, fit, full of mischief, and, when they go on duty, quite trim-looking in their summer fatigues. Sometimes I find myself resentful when I look down at them, not because they're enjoying themselves but because they are our captors, our guards, and therefore participants in the wrong. But am I justified in holding it against them, simply doing their duty?

I am reminded of a comment by Penne in one of her letters that arrived yesterday, telling me that among American public opinion there is apparently a growing consensus of "no retaliation [against Iran] if the hostages are released unharmed." She wonders how I feel about that, noting her own natural reservations. The question is a good one. How should one feel about this place when this matter is resolved? The answer will depend in part, of course, on *how* the issue ends. If it is a matter of show trials, hate, and vindictiveness, followed by expulsion, there could be a national feeling of anger. But if the matter is ended with some element of compromise, where both sides see that their interests have been at least partially met, then the reaction could be calmer. Inevitably I suspect it will end in a way that leaves a sense of bitterness in our mouths, and then it will be hard to be magnanimous.

But what other policy is worthy of a great power except to demonstrate the maximum of understanding and magnanimity? It must *not* be such as to suggest in any way that we condone the act of hostage-taking, that we blithely forget the grievous act of violation of diplomatic immunity here. That would be prejudicial to the concept and harmful for the future. And it would be demeaning to the hostages who have given so much to uphold the sanctity of diplomatic immunity. So a way must be found for the record on that score to be reinforced, to say in a clear and public way, that what was done here by the militants and its being condoned by government was wrong, as the World Court has now so firmly stated.

That done, however, the future beckons to all of us, and I would think the

American posture ought to be one of in effect saying to the Iranians: We hold no basic grudge against you or your relations with us and other big powers for much of your modern history; O.K., we respect the way you feel, and, if you want, we're prepared to talk about these grievances with an open mind but with our own views, too, about the contributions we think we've made to Iran since World War II. We aren't going to crowd you. . . .

Americans generally will find a need to give expression to this in *one* area in particular, and unavoidably. That is in the area of the Iranian student community in the United States. I suspect that, so long as an Islamic regime is in place here, they will try to cut down on the Iranian student flow to the United States. That would be good. And for those they allow to come, our (and their) requirements on English language and learning capability should be greatly tightened. For the Iranians already in the United States, I would like to see the U.S. academic community, and Americans generally, make a massive effort at dialogue. Indeed, I think it should begin now. These people are the future of Iran (those who return, that is), and we have no interest in alienating them. Indeed, we have an interest in communication and in understanding them, however difficult they've been. There is *one* exception: To the extent that we can identify those who have occupied our embassy and held our hostages, with those I would be brutal—no truck with them, no visas, ever. I think I cannot forgive them. Certainly I cannot forget. But is *that* fair? What of the Islamic crowds that have backed them?

I am left with the sense that to forget is human, to forgive divine—if I have the expression right. We *are* human, and our reactions will differ. Perhaps the best maxim would be that those of us who have been closest to this tragedy have the greatest obligation to demonstrate both realism and decency—realism in recognizing our country's interests in this part of the world, and thus the need to be open to whatever relationship Iran wants; decency in recognizing that Iranians have had a difficult history and that we are big enough to be prepared to talk about that, so long as the wrong done to us is also recognized.

On a human basis, I am always reminded of what Gary Lee [fellow hostage] wrote to someone, perhaps his father, to the effect that *he* was prepared to be forgiving, citing Paul's admonitions to the Romans (12:18–21), verses that conclude with "be not overcome of evil, but overcome evil with good." If Gary Lee, after the wrong done him and his colleagues, can think that, shouldn't we all do the same?

DAY 222, *June 12, 1980*—There is continued chaos, instability, and drift, and it has brought the ARK to the point of a major public expression on the subject, and—will wonders never cease—without once mentioning the hostage issue! He actually used the term *chaos* to describe the internal scene: "This problem will not be solved unless we have order and collaboration between powers." At another point he said, "The masses produced the Revolution; the masses cannot any longer govern the nation." Amen. As if the masses ever could or should govern, as they have done in effect by their presence on the

streets. The ARK has pinpointed the problem. One wonders what he is prepared to do to resolve the problem; probably only he can bring the internal
power struggle to some resolution, by knocking a few heads together. . . .

Bani-Sadr, to his credit, has recently again expressed opposition to trials of
the hostages, warning that if that process were to begin, who knows where it
would end. If the hostages had lawyers, there would be those, said he, who
would ask why, when Iranians are tried and convicted without lawyers (a nice
way of denouncing summary judicial processes in Iran, which in the recent past
have seen almost 100 new executions after summary trials). And, said he, if
some of the hostages are found innocent of espionage, the criticism will be:
Why then, have you held them for so long? . . .

> By midsummer, my two colleagues and I, in our lengthy bull sessions, began to
> speculate about how our crisis would impact on the approaching presidential
> election campaign at home. At that point we had not even heard the term "Oc-
> tober surprise." But I doubt that it ever occurred to me, sensing the anathema the
> regime and the students pronounced on Jimmy Carter, that they would consider
> doing anything that would facilitate his reelection. "Carter can do nothing" was
> a never-ending revolutionary refrain.

DAY 224, *June 14, 1980*—Today's press did *not* carry the text of a fiercely
anti-Carter commentary on the 2:00 P.M. radio news yesterday, the kind of
commentary often carried on Fridays and often anti–United States. This one
picked up what was apparently a message of greeting from Carter to a gathering
of Islamicists at the Washington Mosque, marking the 14th century of Islam, to
tick off about a dozen alleged anti-Islamic actions by Carter in language particularly hostile and vindictive. . . .

One wonders what the source of such is—who approves such; is it cleared
with anyone in authority, or is it simply those in NIRT who are saying what they
believe the fundamentalists want said? It makes one wonder sometimes—this
type of personal attack on Carter and similar denunciations of him by the
ARK—whether the latter's real objective is not to hold the hostages through the
elections in hopes of seeing Carter defeated. You will ask, ah, yes, but surely
he realizes that Reagan would be more difficult? I don't think that matters. The
hatred of Jimmy Carter among some of the fundamentalists is *so* intense as to
regard his defeat as an end in itself, an end or objective that if it can be achieved
would be hailed as one more example of the justice of Iran's cause—Allah
O'Akbar, God is great, and He is on our side. That is not a very pleasant
prognosis as to intentions here but, among some of them, I do not exclude it at
all. . . .

DAY 225, *June 15, 1980*—Today we sent a letter to the minister offering to
meet, on a background and strictly off-the-record basis, with selected members
of the Majlis, if the minister feels that our doing so would be helpful in devel-

oping a more realistic assessment by the Majlis of the hostages and of who and what they are and did. We are skeptical that he will pick up the offer, but he may, since we assume he is interested in persuading members toward his own view that trials would be contrary to Iran's own interest. We would want to avoid any *public* meeting with members or to appear in *any* way that we were offering ourselves up to be interrogated.

Today is Jim's 14th birthday. I wonder how he's celebrating it. I remember birthdays on the farm when I was that age. They were *big* days. We knew without being told that aunts and cousins would arrive about 3:00 in the afternoon for a party and a great angel food cake. There would be presents—not a lot of them, but all the more exciting because there were few. And we felt terribly important, very much the center of attention for that one day. It was a special feeling that somehow seems missing today, possibly because by contrast we have so much, *all* the time now.

DAY 226, *June 16, 1980*—It's a long time since I felt so depressed about this trauma as I do tonight. I'm not sure why, but I can think of several possible reasons. Today was *hot*—99°, with a dry, hot, and tiresome wind whipping through our room. Nor did it help that it was the 226th day of this outrage. Nor did it help that it was Pasdaran [Revolutionary Guards] Day, with a parade of these ragtag types passing by the embassy—there, standing atop *our* compound walls, were Bani-Sadr, the Imam's son Ahmed, and various other bearded luminaries. But perhaps the most important reason for my gloom is that at dinner tonight, as we have done so often in the past, Mike and I talked about that fateful day, November 4, and what *might have been* had we done things differently. As usual, we largely concluded that that day's events were foreordained and that probably nothing we could have done would have resulted in any different end result. And yet one is left with the nagging agony that it should never have happened at all and that maybe, just maybe, we could have affected the outcome.

We find ourselves also recognizing that until we sit down with our colleagues who were in the compound that day we cannot really determine what happened, why it happened, and indeed if things might have been done differently. We know too little now.

But how it hurts! How it weighs on one! How it acts on one's confidence! How it pains one to know that, for whatever reason, 50 of our colleagues have suffered and borne the cost of that day's events for more than seven months now, *used* in the most callous way as political pawns in the pursuit of this Revolution's objectives, used indeed for much of this time simply to keep the damned Revolution afloat.

And still we wait. Still we have no alternative but to wait out the resolution of this country's problems, a country obsessed, as Vic puts it, with the devil theory of history. The devil, the "Great Satan," the convenient scapegoat is the United States. The hostages are the symbol. . . .

DAY 227, *June 17, 1980*—The department telephoned today and was put through, so that each of us had a half-hour plus talking with our families. Penne commented that she found it interesting that the three of us here have managed to remain so compatible. It *is* rather remarkable, at that. We have spent seven-plus months now, in *very* close proximity, without one instance that I know of where we have crossed swords or even raised our voices with each other. That, I suppose, is due to several things, aside from the fact that we have no alternative but to get along!

First, I suppose, there is the fact that we all feel commonly aggrieved. We all feel equally offended by what has happened; we feel a common experience where there is no basis for casting blame on any one of us or on our 50 colleagues. The blame rests with those who did us harm, and we are strongly united in our anger over that. Another reason is that the three of us are each fairly even-tempered types; Vic is introspective and thoughtful, very balanced; I am perhaps less introspective but certainly not a flaring extrovert, desperate for human contact; Mike is more gregarious than either of us, but he too is a modest, rather soft-spoken man. Each of us is therefore by nature fairly open to the views of others; we do not press ourselves or our views on others. And Vic and I are also the products of a service that takes pride in a reasoned, rational, open-minded approach to most things.

There are also physical reasons. Our "cell" is not small; we do not feel crowded. Even in the first room we shared, there was a much larger outer room where we could walk and find some solitude. Our current room is strictly four walls, but it's big enough so that there is no danger of our rubbing shoulders. We can sit in a window and at least imagine we are out there, away from all this. . . .

We also each have fairly well-established routines that do not clash and that permit us to go off and do our thing. Each of us writes a good deal, keeping diaries that we do not share but that we each recognize we keep. What these diaries are for is another matter, but I think we each recognize that we are participants in something rather unusual and that at least our families would expect us to write our reactions in as frank a way as possible. Fortunately, we are fairly assured about being able to send out mail without its being censored. Without that assurance, keeping diaries here could and would be another matter.

All this is not to say that the three of us have become inseparable! We will go our separate ways when this is over, as will *all* the hostages. But we will have shared a unique experience that will make for a common fraternity of sorts that will always cause us to want to keep in touch with each other.

Penne's comment about our compatibility appeared to have reflected the fact that among the hostage families as a group there *are* problems of compatibility, which, of course, is a very natural thing. In many ways they are hostages, too, even with their physical freedom. But they are buffeted by pressures and emotions and concerns that must be *very* difficult, especially for some of the families. We and the other hostages know our limitations, know what we can and can't do, know roughly what the future holds. Not so the families, who must be constantly pressed by friends and strangers alike as to how they feel and what they know, and who must be weary as hell of the whole thing.

They, too, have to try to go on living normal lives; we, by contrast, have very precise and known limits in what we can and cannot do. It is all very circumscribed, but nonetheless it is known. There are few unknowns, except the big one of the timing of our release. We have, in other words, put ourselves in well-worn ruts, but they are known and easy. Our families go from one uncertainty to another, with fear, anger, hope, and frustration passed from family to family, feeding on each other and often, no doubt, irritating each other. Again, we have no publicity to worry about; there is no way we can get angry or upset about comments others of our colleagues have made.

But at home the pressure to go public, to criticize, to find fault must grow as time goes on. And that is my chief concern—that there will come a time after we are released when a good many pent-up emotions and frustrations may find public expression, resulting in backbiting, faultfinding, and a search for scapegoats. . . .

DAY 228, *June 18, 1980*

Dear Penne,

. . . We're glad to hear that a group of you is talking about what you call repatriation, i.e., the mechanics of our return. As far as the three of us are concerned, the less fanfare the better. And yet we realize that too much public interest has been focused on this issue to avoid fanfare altogether. Fundamental to the way we're received on our return will be *how* we're released, i.e., if we're released in dribbles or in one big batch of 53 at once. We doubt the latter, for several reasons. And if we can come home in groups, then it seems to us that there should *not* be any big reception arrangements. Better to let us return quietly to families and then later be received as a group in the White House Rose Garden or some such thing. But much of this depends on the attitudes and conditions of our 50 colleagues, who matter most. Presumably there will be a decompression period of several days (hopefully not more) in Europe somewhere. Decisions could be made *then*, after talking within the group, as to how we are brought back.

We recognize that home communities will insist on their own welcome affairs, especially small towns that have native sons among the hostages. That's fine. It's the national arrival that troubles us. Ideally it would seem best to have a quiet, family-type return, followed by something in the Rose Garden, and possibly welcome-back things in our respective departments, State, Defense, Marines, etc. But, I don't know; if we all come back together, a big thing at Andrews [Air Force Base] is probably inevitable.

Love, B

DAY 233, *June 23, 1980*—Today the Swiss ambassador came by with mail, together with Mr. Kaufmann, the Swiss diplomat who heads the American protection section of the embassy. . . .

The Swiss seemed especially anxious today to get some impression from us as to how we felt, physically. We suspect Washington may have put them up to it. What does one say to that? Physically we are all right, aside from occasional minor problems and aside from losing a few pounds (good, anyway) on food that by now has become infinitely boring and dull. . . . We could only tell the Swiss that we are fine, but inevitably our frustrations, our occasional anger, our sense of irrelevance—these things wear on us physically as well as in a psychological sense. I said I supposed one could express it best by saying that it was not a place or a situation where we woke up each morning enthusiastic and raring to go, looking forward to new challenges or new excitements. It is pretty damned dull and wearing, and hot weather doesn't help.

Nor does word such as we heard tonight, that the Majlis didn't even bother to meet today, help our morale. It couldn't; it lacked a quorum! Which is not all that surprising. Until this power struggle between the Bani-Sadr and Beheshti circles is resolved in some fashion, we are *all* dead in the water. I cannot even say that I sense that something is about to break. Instead, there seems to be a total impasse, and about all that makes news is the continuing bloodletting in Kurdistan (which Bani-Sadr bravely announced two weeks ago would be ended in a week!) and Khalkali's continuing campaign against drug smugglers and the like, he now having summarily sent 100 or so to the firing squads in the past month. . . .

DAY 235, *June 25, 1980*—Tonight at dinner we spent a good while talking among ourselves (whom else do we have to talk with!) about the outlook for action here and found ourselves easily persuaded that things could drag on for a good long while on the basis of present indicators. The Majlis again today was without a quorum, although able in the short period that was required to make *that* decision to talk about yet another fact-finding mission to Kurdistan, where things seem to be going badly for the regime. Small wonder, there appears to be no sense of realism here yet that would permit the leadership to make some generous and dramatic offers of autonomy. Small wonder, too, that the Majlis does nothing, except fiddle with the credentials process—deciding yesterday, for example, that the *one* Zoroastrian representative was proper! Until some decision is taken on the power struggle, on the PM issue, the Majlis cannot act in any event. . . .

All of which makes gestures from some of our diplomatic corps friends seem the more warm and genuine—like the Dutch, who sent a beautiful letter the other day conveying the regards of their new queen, *and* also sent a jar of pâté, some Dutch chocolate, a bottle of catsup, and several women's fashion magazines. You may scoff at the last, until you remind yourself that we have not seen (except distantly through our windows) women in Western-style dress since the Swedish ambassador's wife visited our quarters in March! They are very colorful fashion magazines, full of all sorts of dramatically dressed (and undressed) women and all of it most un-Islamic.

Someone might suggest to the Maidenform bra people that they could do a wonderful ad of their lady appearing suddenly in a room full of diplomatic hostages. I think their current line is something like, "You never know where the lady with the Maidenform bra will turn up."

It better not be here in revolutionary Iran. Today's press tells us that, in addition to 18 counterrevolutionaries executed in Azerbaijan and four at Evin Prison (making close to 200 all told in the past month or so), four women were flogged in a town on the Caspian for appearing in public in one-piece bathing suits on a beach reserved for men!

DAY 236, *June 26, 1980*—Today we read in the press that at the start of a talk yesterday by the ARK to a group of workers who met with him at his residence, he told them: "Do not call me your leader, but call me your worker, your servant." At that, said the press, "the entire audience burst out weeping." We had heard the broadcast of this speech, his speeches being never interrupted, except with shouts of "Allah O'Akbar" or some such revolutionary phrase. We thought the unusual sounds we heard on the radio to be laughter, however unusual *that* is in anything these days in Iran. But, no, now we learn that it was weeping.

To a Westerner, it is hard to understand such fawning respect, such total reverence, such blind following. But there is no question of it here among the masses; the reverence appears to be entirely genuine. This man, however rigid and vindictive he appears to us, can do no wrong here. The talk in this instance was more of the same—a warning that counterrevolutionaries are everywhere and that behind them all stands the United States: "The United States has still not given up its desire to come here and dominate us, and that is why it is creating troubles for us."

It is all madness, but there is apparently nothing that will change *his* mind, and since he continues to say it, the masses will continue to believe it.

Today an Iranian—*not* a member of the street masses—with whom we had a brief exchange volunteered to us the analogy with the Jonestown cult in Guyana, the point being that some people, like Jones and indeed the ARK, have a mystical quality about them, a power of attraction that is difficult for the rest of us mortals to comprehend. The analogy is apt, if amusing and sad at the same time.

For the record, I should note that the press also quotes the foreign minister today as saying that the Majlis would take up the hostage issue in the next two or three weeks and that "negotiations" for their release could start "in a month and a half." Well, that's a dismal scenario, however realistic it may well be. It suggests that it will take a full six weeks after the Majlis begins to focus on the issue before it can come to a decision. Then that decision is to be "negotiated" with us. Now, one can hardly assume that the Majlis decision will be something we will snap up like a rare bargain at the store. It won't be. That means more delay. In other words, Ghotbzadeh's scenario from today's date means a good *two months* before they're even ready to start talking to us. That is cruel; it is callous; it is indecent.

And to add to the indecency, Ghotbzadeh insists that the package *must* include a "serious and profound" Watergate-style inquiry into the U.S. role in Iran. In other words, we must agree to grovel further before the hostages are released. For the regime at this point to *use* the hostages so blatantly to achieve political objectives is repulsive even by Iranian standards. We cannot and must not agree to such indignities. He forgets that the taking of the hostages was illegal from the outset. On what basis, that being a fact, can Iran now claim the right to use this illegal act to demand something from us in "negotiations"?

DAY 238, *June 28, 1980*—Another holiday—the birthday of the 12th Shi´a Imam, the one who disappeared rather than died and will some day reappear.

Yesterday, to mark the event, the ARK met with hundreds of family members of the Iran-Iraq War's "martyrs." The affair proved a great emotional experience and moved the ARK to lash out at his own Revolutionary Council and government.

Watching it on TV, I was impressed in the first instance by the man's vigor— and by his anger. As he got going in his talk, he became more animated and angrier than I had ever seen him. He looked like what an Old Testament prophet must have looked like, lashing out at the sinful! His audience, of course, stimulated him further. They were understandably emotional, many carrying photographs of family members killed. As the ARK spoke, they continued a fairly loud din of weeping, talking, and gesticulating, and in the background children were fussing and crying. Periodically, in response to something said by the ARK, the crowd would erupt with shouts of "Allah O'Akbar," arms and fists flailing the air, and shouts of the ARK's name. But the frenzy became even more pronounced when individual members of the crowd stood up and began shouting their own short speeches of praise of the ARK or denunciations of counterrevolutionaries, especially those in Kurdistan. That in turn brought more weeping and shouting from the crowd, and even the ARK's son Ahmed, sitting next to his father, broke into tears.

One cannot—should not—underestimate this. For these people it was an intense, emotional, religious experience, not unlike an emotional black audience responding in a church to a spellbinder of a preacher. Clearly this man's hold over the segment of Iran's population represented by this crowd is intense, strong, and apparently not diminished in the slightest. To them the man is a saint. . . .

DAY 239, *June 29, 1980*—A note on a rather unattractive day of developments. The press quotes Agha Shahi of Pakistan as saying that all the United States needs to do is pull out its fleet, lift its sanctions, let Iran's internal processes take their natural course, and be patient. Brilliant, meaningless advice (from one of the Pakistan bureaucracy's better-known scramblers) that ignores the fact that for the first five months of this year that is what we did. Did Iran's internal processes "produce results"? Indeed. Stalemate. He has one

Chargé d'Affaires Bruce Laingen (foreground) with Maj. Gen. Philip C. Gast, USAF, chief of the Military Assistance Advisory Group (left); Col. Thomas Schaefer, USAF, defense attaché (right); and the embassy's Marine security guard detachment, August 1979. *State Dept.*

The country team of the U.S. Embassy in Tehran, September 1979. Front row from left: the author; Lt. Col. Lee Holland, USA, assistant defense attaché; Major General Gast, USAF; Elizabeth Anne Swift, political officer and first secretary; Mark Lijek, consular officer. Back row: Tom Ahern, first secretary and political officer; Richard Morefield, consul general; Barry Rosen, press attaché; Charles Mast, political officer; Alan Golacinski, security officer; Gary Lee, assistant administrative officer. *State Dept.*

With Deputy Prime Minister Sadegh Tabatabai in Tehran on October 24, 1979—just eleven days before the embassy takeover.

The three prisoners in the Foreign Ministry: Victor Tomseth, Mike Howland, and Bruce Laingen. November 1980.

Penne Laingen, with Jim and Chip, placing the original yellow ribbon on an oak tree in front of their home. This ribbon is now in the Folklife Collection of the Library of Congress. *Bruce Hoertel*

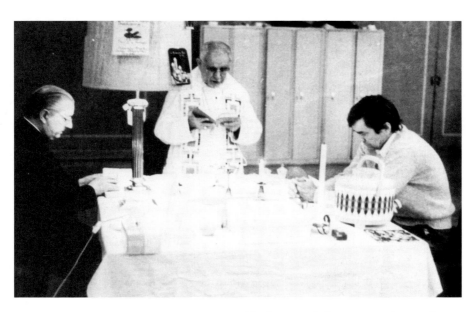

Christmas 1980 in the Foreign Ministry. Archbishop Annibale Bugnini, the papal nuncio; Archbishop Yohannan Issayi of the Assyrian-Chaldean Catholic Church in Tehran; and the author.

The author occasionally tore pages from paperback books for his journal entries, which were smuggled out from his solitary confinement.

Watercolor of view from the Foreign Ministry painted by the author while in captivity.

The Algiers airport, January 20: Hal Saunders, assistant secretary of state for Near Eastern and South Asian affairs (NEA); the author; Sheldon Krys, executive director, NEA.

The author with Jimmy Carter and Walter Mondale at the USAF hospital in Wiesbaden, West Germany, on January 22. *White House*

*To Chip —
Thanks for backing
us up! Dad

Freedom Day
Andrews AF Base
Washington
January 27, 1981*

Andrews Air Force Base, Washington, on January 27: Jim, Chip, Penne, and Bruce.
State Dept.

*Of all the days
in Office, this was
the best — Warmly,
Barbara Bush*

*To our admired friend Bruce Laingen —
with respect & high esteem —
Geo Bush*

Traveling with Vice President and Mrs. Bush from Andrews AFB to the White House.
White House

Receiving a boxed miniature flag from President Reagan on the South Lawn. *Jack Kightlinger/White House*

Home: Chip, Penne, Bruce, Bill, and Jim Laingen, Bethesda, Maryland, January 28, 1981. *Karen Keating*

Jim, Chip, Bill, and Bruce in 1985. Bruce is wearing his World War II uniform.

Bruce and Penne today.

further word: "Don't worry about the hostages. . . . They are being well treated and in good health. Everyone knows that." Well, I don't, and assuredly he doesn't. Who can honestly say what their condition is today, and who can honestly judge the psychological cost of eight months of captivity under the conditions they have had?

Such unsolicited advice from people who don't have a clue—that we don't need.

Another item in today's press triggered one more of my many appeals, this one to Bani-Sadr:

Dear Mr. President,

Today's press has reported you as deploring what you describe as a fundamental hostility on the part of the United States toward you.

With all respect, Mr. President, this can only reflect a complete misunderstanding of the American government and people.

There is *no* hostility toward Iran that one single act will not remove. That is the release of the American diplomats held hostage for the past eight months. . . . The United States has only one other interest in Iran, that is the maintenance of Iran's independence and territorial integrity by a people and government pursuing policies of their own choosing and without outside interference.

Sincerely,
L. Bruce Laingen
Chargé d'Affaires

11

July 1980:
One Less Hostage

A fascination with intrigue—a suspicion of plots and maneuvers all about him—is second nature to an Iranian. Nor is the focus always on the "foreign hand," however common that is. That was evident throughout the summer and fall of 1980, as the power struggle between President Bani-Sadr and the more radical elements in the regime intensified, reaching the point where one report noted the formation of a new body: Organization for Coordinating the Diffusion of Plots. Running simultaneously was a cultural purge campaign to deepen the outward appearances of Islamic purity, not least in women's dress. Watching all that, we found that July Fourth and the freedoms of which that festival reminds all Americans had special meaning for hostages in Tehran. The month brought those freedoms back to reality for Richard Queen, suffering with an illness that his captors could not diagnose and that moved them to at least momentary humanity.

DAY 241, *July 1, 1980*—We are halfway through 1980. That hardly seems possible. It was only yesterday that we tried to celebrate New Year's with some smuggled "cough medicine." And now it's six months later. On New Year's Eve, had someone told us we'd still be here six months later, we would have laughed him out of the room. Now we'll believe anything. The thought of six more months? No, we don't think anything *that* depressing, but neither do we exclude it from our thoughts.

I tell myself that I'm too old to give a half-year—no, eight months—of my life to a room in Iran's Foreign Ministry. I find myself measuring these eight months against the future. I find myself toting up what I've lost in terms of being with my family, watching children grow up. I tell myself, "It isn't fair!" But here I am, and nothing now visible suggests early action.

On the contrary, the power struggle apparently continues, with no one sure enough of his position to venture any resolution of the issue, and as a result the matter of naming a PM and installing a government isn't mentioned—in the press, on radio, or on TV. Silence on that subject, seven months after the constitution was approved and six months almost since 76 percent of the people gave their mandate to a president. The ARK? He apparently prefers not to become involved on this key issue, or is not yet prepared to, or doesn't want to see a government installed. Who knows, it could be the last. A government in place would leave less room for maneuvering for the fundamentalists.

Meanwhile, time is occupied—revolutionary zeal is occupied—with the current purge process, or "purification," if one prefers that word. . . .

Today one of our two security guards (who normally sit in a small room just outside our door) walked in with a soldier in tow. They said nothing to us but went to one of our windows overlooking the garden and spent several minutes studying it before leaving. We could only conclude that their concern was four large bird droppings that from the garden below may have looked to our stalwart soldiers as if we had splotched some kind of message on the windows ourselves! This relates also to the fact that on several occasions, when we *have* hung things in our windows, like small pieces of yellow ribbon sent by Penne, the guards have come in within a day or two and ordered us to take them down. (*They'll* have to clean the bird droppings!)

DAY 243, *July 3, 1980*—The process continues. Clearly the Islamic circle sees an opportunity to develop a momentum that will achieve "purification" on Islamic lines far and wide. . . . Last night's TV news included extensive guidance to women on how to dress, as well as a long spiel about how Reza Shah's order banning the veil in the mid-1930s had been inspired by the British, and how this had subsequently been taken up by both the Russians and Americans!

A non-Iranian listening to all this is appalled by the preoccupation with symbols, with antiquated customs, on the part of an entire country when so many *real* problems confront this land. But the ARK and the Islamic leadership see it differently. They see it as a healthy effort to cleanse and purify society, so that Iran can find and act on the basis of Islamic principles. As the ARK so often says, Islam provides everything society needs, if only people will practice it.

As a non-Muslim I confess never to have comprehended the focus on women's dress, while men are free to wear what they will. I guess I'm simply saying that all this is unnatural on the face of it and totally inconsistent with modern compulsions, whether in Islam or outside it. We shall see how the women of this country react; the mass, of course, will go along. It will have to be a small minority that sees things otherwise. . . .

Today's press also reports that a federal appeals court in Louisiana has thrown out a lower court's decision approving action of the Mississippi State Legislature; the upper court said it was discriminatory against Iranian students. Another story reported that the Board of Education in Atlantic City, New Jersey, has bowed to pressure from the State Civil Rights Board and agreed to apologize to an Iranian girl student denied the right to give the valedictory address to her class because a majority of the teachers had objected.

These are welcome developments, demonstrating that our system continues to function to protect basic civil and human rights of people resident in our country, however objectionable have been acts by the government of Iran and the students here to the American hostages. It would be wrong to blame Iranians *in* the United States for these acts, just as it was wrong what we did as a government to the Japanese-American community at the start of World War II. The three of us had earlier urged the department to encourage our political leadership to give expression to the basic fairness of American principles of justice, and these two events are steps in that direction. But our leadership should now act to give greater *public* expression to these principles. That matters not simply to the outcome of this hostage issue here, but more important, it matters for the legacy of justice and decency that we either honor or dishonor over the longer term. We cannot ignore human rights at home and expect to see them honored abroad. The fact that this is an election year is no excuse whatsoever for courageous leadership not acting.

DAY 244, *July 4, 1980*—The Fourth, the 204th anniversary of the Declaration of Independence, the eight-month anniversary of our being held hostage by militant Islamic Iranian "students," supported and encouraged by revolutionary authorities of the government of Iran. Fifty-three citizens of the United States, representatives of their government in the U.S. Embassy in Tehran, seized and held hostage to further the political objectives of the government of Iran, an act continued in defiance of international public and official opinion as expressed by the UN Security Council, the International Court of Justice, and governments around the world.

A most unusual way for American citizens abroad to observe their Independence Day. . . .

The news today tells us of a further reversion to Islamic dictates of the past in another area: capital punishment for moral offenses. Four persons—two men and two women—in southern Iran were sentenced to death by stoning several days ago. And today we hear that the sentences have indeed been carried out, the victims buried in the ground up to their heads and then stoned to death.

The times are different, the crime different, the circumstances different, but the effect and the purpose are the same: a society, a dominant social and political thought seeking revenge, retribution, and discipline by what must surely be one of the most awful of punishments—to be stoned until dead. One is reminded of Stephen, condemned to death for religious beliefs then regarded as both heretical and treasonous: "Yelling at the top of their voices, they all rushed at him, dragged him out of the city and began to stone him. Meanwhile the witnesses laid their clothes at the feet of a young man named Saul. While they were stoning him, Stephen prayed, 'Lord Jesus, receive my spirit.' Then he fell on his knees and cried out: 'Lord do not hold this sin against them!' When he had said this, he fell asleep."

Who is judge in this instance? Neither I nor any other non-Islamic observer, viewing what has happened here from such a vastly different perspective. And yet we are all human beings with the same physical and emotional impulses. I wonder how Iranians react to this means of ending what is God-given, the life of a human being. . . .

Dear Chip,

. . . Today is Independence Day. I wonder what you're doing. I remember other July Fourths more interesting for me than this one! Extended family picnics in Minnesota at some nearby lake, firecrackers and rockets bought with carefully saved money and set off in the middle of the farmyard at night; noncelebrations during the war in the Pacific; a parade down the main street in some town near Newport, Rhode Island, in 1946 just before leaving the service, with me carrying a flag as a lieutenant (j.g.) USNR; those parades we organized for a couple of years for youngsters living on Honeywell Lane; and that fantastic evening on the Mall in Washington, D.C., the night of the bicentennial celebration four years ago, among crowds with a friendly, united, patriotic spirit of a kind that I think I've rarely seen or experienced in our country.

And then there's Tehran, where we were wakened this morning at seven by the loudspeaker voices of police directing the crowds beginning their procession to Friday prayers, the women given pride of place this time to emphasize their wearing of the Islamic chador and their commitment to the current national frenzy organized by the fundamentalists to "purify" the society of un-Islamic tendencies and the deadening corruption of "Westoxification."

Not exactly my idea, Chip, of how to spend the Fourth of July. All right, I can live with it. I can because it simply reminds me as an American of the enormous strength we have as a society in our concepts and traditions of justice and freedom and tolerance. No society deserves that more than the people of Iran, given their complex and tortured history; no society seems so ill served in the pursuit of those aims as this one seems now. A tragedy.

Don't let all this get you down, Chip. Instead let it strengthen your own personal commitment to justice and tolerance, both so essential to human freedom, and to the sense of personal and community responsibility that is needed if a people are to live and work together with good effect. That begins at home, it involves the personal and moral standards you maintain, and it affects others in the way you live your life and do your thing—whether stopping for a moment to pick up litter in the street, demonstrating courtesy in the grocery store or gas line, or carrying that flag for NROTC Minnesota. For all of us, these big and little things add up to the kind of people we are and the kind of country we can expect to be.

And no one could be prouder than I in the way you and your brothers have shown that you know what these words mean.

Many happy returns, Chip—Dad

DAY 246, *July 6, 1980*—A hot and unpleasant day, the news is singularly unattractive as well. Especially a statement from our "students" saying that to protect the hostages and to keep them in the nation's custody until the Majlis acts, those held in three listed cities were being moved to alternative but unnamed locations. Moreover, said the statement, this will be a continuing practice.

We suspect a good many of the hostages have been moved back to the embassy, where housekeeping is easier for the "students" and where their control is subject to fewer pinpricks than may be the case in provincial cities, where local authorities may cause the "students" some problems. But, whatever the reason, there is also the advantage, as the "students" see it, of keeping the hostages' location as uncertain as possible. It is galling as hell and cruel as well. Human beings moved about as if they are chattel—one is reminded of the proposed MX missile system, with the missiles constantly shuttled about from one concrete trench to another to fool the enemy. Only these are human beings!

Carter is reported these past days as saying that the hostage issue is constantly on his mind and that new avenues and approaches are always being tried. But, as he accurately put it, there is still no one in the regime here with the courage or authority to make a decision. And this the 246th day, or thereabouts.

Meanwhile the Revolution dithers along, still preoccupied with the efforts of what is called the "Purge and Purification Committee" or, as the press put it, the "Delegation for Purging Offices." Choose your own translation. . . .

DAY 247, *July 7, 1980*—A Monday, the day we normally hope the Swiss will be in with mail, but they didn't show. The reason appears to be that tomorrow we are to have physical exams, and these, as before, are apparently being arranged by the Swiss. So we expect them in together with the doctors. We did not ask for physicals; it appears to be a Washington initiative, more specifically, a Penelope Laingen initiative, who told me in a letter that she had reacted with some heat to hearing, now, that we'd had physicals in January or whenever, and no one had ever bothered to inform the wives of the results! I think we three had assumed that Washington was informed; in any event, found to be alive, we concluded there was no need to inform our families.

The weather is *hot!* Yesterday it was 102°, and this room was unbearable during the night. Those few moments when I seem to have dropped off, I was awakened by the telephone—once at 3:00 A.M. and once at 6:00 A.M., the latter cut off by the time I staggered to the phone and the former some joker clearly bugging us, possibly one of the "students" or one of the soldiers downstairs. The phone is available to us only to take calls from the United States, such that are put through. We cannot call out, beyond an occasional ring to the Protocol Office. . . .

The Majlis staggers on. Today's news reported that it had examined the files of three more members and sent them back for further study. . . . That august body has now been in session for 40 days and has yet to get to the point of organizing itself! . . . Forty days to reach this point. Based on that record, what reason is there to hope that the system will ever be able to take up an issue as difficult as the hostage issue?

Meanwhile, the furor continues over issues that seem to matter more, including such weighty ones as the dress of women in government offices. We hear nothing more from those women who demonstrated before the president's office, their appeal having been quickly suppressed by decision of the Revolutionary Council and the revolutionary prosecutor. The issue becomes farcical at times; e.g., a domestic air flight from Zahedan to Tehran was delayed for five hours because of a Revolutionary Guard complaining about a stewardess's dress, the passengers joining in the debate pro and con, and the pilot refusing to take off, he reportedly siding with the stewardess.

Sitting supremely above it all is the ARK, prominently quoted in today's press as telling a visiting navy group (he sees at least one group a day now) that "in all periods of mankind's history, no government and no religion have been like the government and religion of Islam."

With that, as practiced in Iran, we can all agree! . . .

Recent mail included a good letter from Governor Al Quie of Minnesota, a friend from St. Olaf College. The letter apparently crossed one I'd written him, thanking him and, through him, the people of Minnesota, for the proclamation by the governor last January, expressing support for the president's efforts on behalf of the hostages. The governor is a deeply religious man, and that is reflected in his letter. After mentioning the many social and political problems facing American society, he strikes a note of optimism, commenting that he believes the 1980s will see a life-style change that will strengthen the family and build community spirit. He sees this as possible "because of a unifying spirit of God living in us."

I hope Al is right. It is an approach rarely heard these days, in the midst of all sorts of doomsday predictions of the decade ahead. There is much to be said for acting and talking like this—not to be naive, but to try in any event to accent the positive. That, it seems to me, is an obligation resting on leadership, and I credit Al for that. It is certainly possible that the problems we face—the limitations we now must live with in terms of resources—that these things *will* cause us as a people to value more dearly what we do have, including the strength of family and the satisfactions of responsible community life. We have been burning the candle at both ends in terms of our resources and the demands we place on our life-style and institutions. A new awareness of some of the limits we must live with can make life better all around. . . .

Life got marginally better here yesterday, with word from the chief of protocol that we could go out on the balcony for one hour in the afternoon, provided we all go out together. It's hot there—the balcony is concrete and stone with no shade—but by late in the afternoon it is pleasant. . . . There we can be unobserved, too, except for the soldiers in the garden below, who continue to find us worth studying. . . .

Someone has sent us copies of a three-part piece by Robert Shaplen in the *New Yorker* on David Newsom. It is a very full and highly informative piece, especially on the complex negotiations involving Iran and notably those surrounding the ill-fated UN Commission effort. The three of us learned much from it that we had not known before, although even with this background there is much that remains murky. What is clear, however, regarding that (so-called) "gentlemen's agreement" is that one important "gentleman" was overlooked, i.e., the ARK. There are several good lines in the articles, including Newsom's description of the whole painful eight months as like something from a Russian novel:

> . . . against the background of a world crisis involving hostages from a major power, the plot moves the action to a small obscure nation, and links the health of a deposed ruler, a conflict among doctors, the Chief of Staff of the American White House, and two Paris lawyers who are intermediaries in resolving the hostage situation, and the representatives of the nation holding the hostages, with that nation's deposed ruler flying off to another country a few hours before the deadline for an attempt to gain his extradition. . . . There are times when diplomacy can be an emotionally charged and trying business, and when the satisfactions, if any, can only be those of pained relief.

DAY 250, *July 10, 1980*—This morning VOA news brought us the exciting word that Richard Queen, 28-year-old vice consul in the Consular Section, has been released on "humanitarian" grounds. Tonight's TV news showed him being carried off a Swiss Air plane in Bern, looking very wan and motionless. We wonder what this means—in the first instance, of course, what his problem is. Psychiatric problems are mentioned, and he has been in a Tehran hospital for three days. Richard is young and physically strong, and he has a good spirit and sense of humor, which cause us to believe he'll be all right. But there must be something serious involved, unless the "students" or the regime here chose him to send us a signal of some sort on the larger picture. These things will become clearer as we learn more from him.

The three of us have amused ourselves today by finding ourselves with serious "medical" problems. Mike was seen at one point pulling a large red bow attached to a long string and walking from one end of the room to the other. No chance, I fear; we are disgustingly healthy.

The news of Richard's release has led VOA and BBC newscasts all day—an interesting commentary on the way this hostage issue still captures world attention. That, I suppose, is a reflection of the impact that this singularly egregious act has had on world public opinion—the first time, as our speaker before the World Court at The Hague put it, since the 16th century that a government has violated international law and practice in seizing and holding another government's diplomats. That is the stain that will remain irremovable from Iran's history and image, visible there for all the world to see from now on. Whatever Iran may say about its own grievances and however it may try to rationalize this act by pointing to the "understandable motivations" of the "students," the fact remains that the act was a crime, the regime encouraged and condoned it, and the regime is culpable for having allowed a precedent with grievous implications for international order and discourse.

DAY 253, July 13, 1980—Tonight is the eve of the beginning of the Islamic fasting month of Ramadan. Beginning tomorrow, the faithful do not eat, drink, smoke, or indulge in any vice between sunrise and sundown for the next 30 days. Not a drop of water may pass one's lips, even in this 100° heat. But with the breaking of the fast at sundown, all is free again, so that most persons probably make up for the food they've missed during the day and then some.

To mark the occasion, the watchdogs (pardon that non-Islamic expression) of Islamic purity in Iran, the Qom Theological School, announced that everyone would go to the rooftops at 10:00 P.M. this evening and, for the next 15 minutes, shout "Allah O'Akbar" at the top of their lungs. And that they did. The TV news program was interrupted, followed by recorded "Allah O'Akbars," and outside our windows there was reasonably spirited yelling in all directions. Our soldiers, not to be found wanting, marched by our windows in a body, yelling as they went, to the main gates and back. . . .

Last evening, during our hour on the balcony, the security guard accompanying us sat reading an evening newspaper (in Farsi). Suddenly he found something he wanted to share with us, and that turned out to be excerpts from letters that Mrs. Laingen and Mrs. Morefield (wife of the consul general, a hostage) had reportedly written to the platform drafting committees preparing for the Republican and Democratic national conventions. As he interpreted the report, the letters called on the two political parties to go on record as opposing any kind of U.S. "apology" to Iran for past actions in and vis-à-vis Iran by the U.S. government or its agencies. I told the guard that Iran had better be careful; if our wives get involved in this way, Iran would be in *real* trouble. That brought a wisecrack to the effect that our wives would be tired of us within two days after we got home. I said, *"Never!"*

DAY 254, July 14, 1980—"How do you spell *chaos?*" Mike yelled across the room as we all three sat writing this afternoon. (Mike's spelling leaves something to be desired, as he himself would be the first to admit.) "C-H-A-O-S," answered Vic, a better speller than either of us. "Wrong," said I. "It's spelled I-R-A-N."

One would think so, to read the daily newspaper or listen to the radio or TV news. There appear to be plots everywhere; every segment of society appears to be ripe for "purge and purification"; the very number of executions would suggest something is wrong. . . . The ARK speaks of chaos in the country; the president laments the country's lack of unity of thought and action; the border with Iraq is the scene of daily, if insignificant, firefights. Kurdistan remains agitated. The women of Iran, though accepting the veil, clearly do it grudgingly. The Majlis has spent 50 days purging *itself* of duly elected representatives of the people, and now it calls for new purges and purification, especially in the Ministries of Foreign Affairs and National Guidance. . . .

The atmosphere is heady with intrigue and uncertainty, and to cope, as is the local custom, yet another committee or commission is formed, the latest having the apt, perhaps, title Organization for Coordinating the Diffusing of Plots. Meanwhile, the Majlis members make angry noises and demands of their government, to the point where one member today suggested that some of those arrested for the latest "coup plot" be publicly executed in front of the faithful gathered for Friday prayers. . . .

We wonder what effect all this will have on attitudes toward the hostages, quite possibly negative. A lady member of the Majlis (daughter of the popular and moderate Ayatollah Taleghani, who died last fall) today proposed that we be tried before an international panel of judges, and "when their espionage crimes are proved, we ask the nation to free, imprison, or execute them." We appear to have a choice?

All of which makes one wonder what the average Iranian *does* think of us, or whether he thinks of us at all. We wonder what the security and kitchen staff *here* think, our only contact with the Iranians beyond the chief of protocol who represents a very specific and limited (in number) type of Iranian. . . . Some are zealous in their devotion to the ARK but at the same time not necessarily hostile to us. Two of the guards are clearly more zealous than others, but probably all of them have long since concluded we have no intention to attempt escape and that another rescue attempt is unlikely. The one female staff member, devotedly Islamic in dress and manner, is nonetheless genuinely friendly and clearly is deeply troubled that we are separated from our families. Very few if any of them, however, have any love for Carter, the regime's propaganda campaign against him having had very effective success among the masses. One or two of the group, or possibly even more, in varying degrees, have little time for the mullahs, however much they welcomed the Revolution, the clergy—the rank and file, that is—long regarded with some aspersion as a burden on society by a good many average Iranians. An old expression puts it this away: "There are three things I have never seen—the feet of a snake, the eye of a flea, and the charity of a mullah."

But there is no doubt that the clergy are in the saddle, and they are determined to exploit their current opportunity to entrench themselves as deeply and firmly as possible, all this out of that group's genuine conviction that Iran's problems stem from its failure to follow the precepts and practices of Shi'a Islam in all aspects of life. Hence the drive now for "purity" and for "cleansing" of the body politic of all contrary tendencies, not least the exterior manifestations of aping Western ways and the pernicious (in their view) penetration of Western cultural influences that have exposed Iran to weakness and that threaten the Islamic way of life so precious to these clergymen.

DAY 255, *July 15, 1980*—The Swiss chargé, Marcus Kaiser, was in today with the mail, not much of it but it is always a great treat to see the Swiss. As we told him today, their visit is the high point of our week; it's downhill all the way after that until they come in again. . . .

A bit of local revolutionary color: the purge and purification process proceeds apace (alliteration, that!), the focus including wholesale renaming of scores of streets in Tehran, removing names with any connection whatsoever with the ancien régime or with the hated "Big Satan," that being us. A long recital of such name changes on the radio news this afternoon included the report that Los Angeles Street, somewhere in north Tehran, has been appropriately renamed Kiabani Hejab, or "Islamic Dress Street"! Strike one up for the Revolution! . . .

In Iran yesterday, 24 more persons were executed by firing squad for offenses ranging from gambling to treason, as locally defined. The press reports Bani-Sadr as saying the same day that Iran would not be able to overcome its existing political and economic problems until the present "international isolation" was overcome. Indeed. A small wonder, such "isolation," in the face of such summary justice.

DAY 257, *July 17, 1980*—It is near midnight, still hot, and I feel lousy. I have a sinus infection of some sort, the worst possible weather to enjoy something like that. . . . I slept badly last night, one reason being the sinus but a second being a cockroach that descended, or ascended, to my pillow at one point. (We have become adept at scrunching cockroaches under our feet, the average-sized ones termed *mullahs*, the larger ones—you guess it—*ayatollahs*.). . .

DAY 259, *July 19, 1980*—We *do* tend to grasp at straws (for which no one surely can blame us!). Today we heard a rumor expressed in terms of our being released "within a month." And the person passing it on said, "I even know the date!" But that was as much as he would say. Enough, however, to excite our minds. We came quickly to the conclusion that it may be linked with Ramadan, the fasting month now under way that ends on August 11 or 12 with the great Muslim feast of Eid-ul-Fitr, the feast of sacrifice and atonement. No better time would offer itself than this for a grand gesture of Islamic mercy, no better time to declare a grand amnesty that would extend to us as well. . . .

Our grasping at straws reminds me again of the book *The Fixer* by Bernard Malamud, which the Norwegian ambassador sent us. It is a novel about a young Jew in Russia under the tsars, sent to prison after a pogrom, with the charges against him clearly framed and fraudulent, but he is left to rot in his cell for month after month and eventually years, alone in solitary confinement, grasping at straws far less sturdy than those *we* grasp! His frustration becomes such that he is eventually desperate, almost mad, to have the charges raised against him in a bill of particulars, so that he can at least challenge it before meeting a fate he knows is inevitable. I do not suggest our situation is anything so desperate, but there have been times—when we read the constant talk of trials—that we say to each other, "Try me! Give me the charges! Just don't leave me sitting here!" . . .

The *Tehran Times* of the past two days has carried excerpts from an interview with the celebrated cleric, Mousavi Khoeini, the clerical link with the "students" at the embassy since the day of the seizure and, as it now is even clearer, the link before that, too, in the planning for the seizure. Much is made in this interview over Khoeini's insistence that the ARK had not been informed *before* the seizure of the "students'" plans. Said he: "We knew it would have been incorrect for the leader of our revolution to know in advance what we were going to do." That, said he, would have been "politically unwise." Later, "we simply did not think that our action would have such grave international consequences." (Obviously not! The gentleman is obviously too shallow to have any such comprehension!)

It is old stuff, but it raises the question anew: Khoeini was the link between these "students," planning the act, and *who else?* Who else among the clerics, and in the ARK's entourage, knew about it in advance? It is too much to expect me to believe that there were not others. . . .

DAY 261, *July 21, 1980*—We have just listened, on VOA, to a half-hour press conference in the department with Richard Queen. He handled himself well, responding to some of the sillier questions that pressed him on substance by sticking to the position that was the only sensible one—i.e., he was not unlike Rip van Winkle coming out of his sleep. He "simply did not know" about Tabas, about what his release might mean for the others, or about the conditions for his other colleagues, etc. He said the only thing the "students" had told him on his departure was to "tell the truth." And he seemed to want to be fair, saying there had been "some SOBs" among the "students" but that on the whole they had treated them fairly (if one can conceivably say that being held in a windowless basement for two to four months—he seemed not sure how long—is fair treatment). He also seemed chipper enough, despite his MS [multiple sclerosis] condition. A lesser person might have collapsed by now in self-pity and gloom. He was full of appreciation for the warmth of his welcome home. This was said in response to a question whether he thought the American people had forgotten the hostages or, rather, whether he ever felt they had forgotten him. No, he said, and then went on to point out his amazement at the intensity of welcome he had received.

He also made a special point of saying how *very* much he (and probably the others) had appreciated the Christmas and Easter visits of American clerics. Clearly this had been a magnificent and warmly welcomed tonic. I think perhaps the rest of us have underestimated how welcome the sight of visiting Americans must have been to persons held hostage without contact with home all those months.

We received our medical exam reports today, and on each there is written "less nervousness than six months ago." There is also no reference this time to our "moral sadness." I suppose the best one can say for all that is that a person adjusts! It is certainly true, I think, that unlike the first couple of months we now find ourselves fighting this situation less than we did before. Sure, we remain angry about it, but we seem to focus less on the anger and that which is kept from us. We have our routine, we have resisted and sputtered and fumed about being held and to some degree gotten it out of our systems, and we have come to accept that it will be a long, tough haul. . . .

Meanwhile, life goes on in . . . "cuckooland." The Majlis, after two months, is now virtually organized and indeed will take its formal oath of office tomorrow before the president. A speaker, Hojjatol-Islam Ali Akbar Rafsanjani, has been elected, as well as two deputies, one of whom is another mullah and the ARK's liaison with the "students" of the embassy, Mousavi Khoeini. There can be no question of the extent to which the clerical forces are solidly in control. The High Judicial Council, also just elected, is entirely clerical, four of them. The Constitution Protection Council has six clerics and six secular types.

All of this, of course, is very much as the ARK would have it. Yesterday he delivered of himself yet another peroration on the all-embracing need for Islam in the Iranian body politic, one of the more demanding of his utterances, the tone didactic (or more so than usual), stern, and uncompromising. . . . That speech also called for execution of all those found guilty of having been involved in plotting the alleged coup d'état, so we can expect a rash of summary trials and midnight executions—five already from that affair, not to mention the continuing executions on other fronts.

For a non-Muslim, and especially for us caught up in all this, it is all very sad, very negative, and vindictive. Islam is called upon to meet every ill and every need, which is all very nice in theory, but it does nothing for the jobless of south Tehran. The president makes a speech at yet another seminar, this one the Seminar on the Crusade for Low Prices, and is quoted as saying that "without spiritualism prices cannot come down." What he is doing, in all sincerity, I suppose, is trying to appeal to the better side of human nature, and in Iran that is like blowing into the wind. Where are the plans, the rational approach, the get-on-with-the-job style? All we seem to get are speeches,

words, appeals to Islam—as if all that were to produce the results that this place
so desperately needs. . . .

DAY 263, *July 23, 1980*—Since we are now allowed on the balcony for an
hour a day, we must walk through the main reception hall to reach it. The hall,
to which we used to have access during the first five months of our stay here,
is now a sort of warehouse for furniture and for carpets, and today we noticed
even more carpets stacked on the floors, the place looking like nothing so much
as a traditional Persian carpet shop. Literally hundreds of carpets, some huge,
most at least 15 by 20 feet. We asked our kitchen staff-type tonight what this
meant. Oh, he said, offices in government ministries under the Islamic Republic are not allowed to have carpets, so they are being collected for disposition. . . . All of this is the product of the Islamic "purification" set in motion
several weeks back by the ARK, railing at the ministries for the inefficiency,
their Taghooti [old regime] ways, and their lack of Islamic zeal and spirit. . . .

Some of this calls to mind the conversation that Henry Precht and I had with
Ayatollah Beheshti during Henry's visit here last fall, just a week before the
seizure. I recall Beheshti saying that there would be resistance from the small,
Westernized, educated classes to what the Revolution sought to do, but "if that
1 million didn't like it, that was regrettable but they would have to go along
with the wishes of the 34 million in the country. The majority was not going to
be prevented from achieving an Islamic Republic because of the foibles of the
minority who might not like some of this."

Much the same philosophy was apparent in a press interview yesterday with
Hojjatol-Islam Rafsanjani, the prominent cleric just elected as speaker of the
Majlis. Rafsanjani told a group in Shimran that while there may be sections of
the populace who oppose the wearing of the veil by women, "millions of our
people approve the plan. That is why the government has to decide on behalf
of the majority and not the minority."

Meanwhile, there is continuing talk of purges, especially at the Foreign
Ministry, which is seen as a center of unpurged corruption, administering
embassies abroad that are alleged to be even worse. Minister Ghotbzadeh is the
target of widespread clerical criticism for not being sufficiently Islamic and
specifically now for having said in Paris that Iran dissociated itself completely
from the attempt on Bakhtiar's life. One must assume that he is not likely to be
taken into the new government when it is formed. That presumably is imminent. Yesterday Bani-Sadr made what the press describes as the "curious"
move of sending a letter to the ARK asking that his son, Ahmed, be named
prime minister. The ARK declined, saying that Ahmed should be kept free
from such responsibility so that he could serve the country better elsewhere.

We wonder what was behind this unusual move. Was it an attempted end
run by Bani-Sadr in hopes of naming someone over whom the fundamentalists
under Beheshti would not have control? If so, does its failure presage new
delays while Bani-Sadr tries to work out something with Beheshti that will save
him some degree of power? Speculation is rife tonight over the choice and what

it will mean in terms of Bani-Sadr's influence, now so seriously weakened by events, by the power of the fundamentalists, and by his own indecisiveness and fuzziness. . . .

DAY 264, *July 24, 1980*—We have watched for several nights running film strips on the TV evening news of a number of the "coup plotters" now facing trial as they speak of their motivations and their activity. Those films are not of their trial, for most of that is yet to come. It appears to be simply an effort to show the public what kind of persons these plotters are and how they had been misled. (Some 30 have already been executed.)

But what motivates *them* in agreeing to speak as they do before the camera? Most must know that the prospects for their execution are almost certain. Why then agree to speak publicly in this way? Are they somehow led to believe that by doing so they will gain credit that might spare them from execution? Or do they do it as an act of penance of sorts? It would be hard, I suppose, to *force* them to speak in this manner against their wills. They could simply refuse and assume that they will be none the worse off for refusing. If these men did, in fact, plot the kind of coup they are accused of (and they seem to confirm it in what they say), one would think that the strength of their convictions would cause them to refuse, on principle, to be used in this way on TV. Their manner varies; some seem repentant, none are lively and in good spirits, all look disheveled and careworn, but all seem to speak without being forced, albeit in a dull monotone. One or two seem proud of what they planned; most seem to give or add little credence to the constant theme in the press that the Americans were behind it. I find it all very curious.

DAY 266, *July 26, 1980*—Executions continue—some 27 in the past two days, of whom some 20 were in connection with the attempted coup of two weeks back. The numbers are staggering, the judicial process strictly special and Islamic and brief. Most of the executions are by firing squad. I wonder how *that* is managed. Are there specially designated squads of this type? Or do they use whatever soldiers or Pasdaran who may be on duty at any given time and simply says, "O.K., fella, you're on. Here's your chance to bump off a few counterrevolutionary and corrupt-on-earth types." One would assume that the practice requires a bit of training or at least a special sort of mentality. . . .

DAY 267, *July 27, 1980*—Today, late, we had a visit from Bourget, the French lawyer who's been involved in the negotiations on this issue for a long time, a shadowy figure whom I met (together with the Argentine-born Villalon) when I saw the minister in his office in March and whom we all met here at Eastertime. Today he apparently asked the minister for permission to see us, and we talked for almost two hours.

And what a treat it was, just to be able to carry on a conversation with *someone* on a serious topic. That is no reflection on the three of us, but after nine months, we don't find all *that* much inspiration to begin a spirited dialogue on some new subject!

Bourget appeared to have nothing special in mind, so most of the time was spent in our grilling him on what he could tell us. He seemed forthcoming enough. But it was clear that he sees nothing imminent, barring some political breakthrough here that will permit some readiness—or courage—to face up to the problem. . . .

The other big news today is that of the Shah's death. What does one say about that? Had his health been good, we wouldn't be here. Had he died earlier, in Iran, the monarchy might have lasted. His death now doesn't change much for us; larger issues have taken his place in the negotiations that have yet to begin. But it could have a marginal effect in softening hostility toward us. What a human tragedy the Shah was, what his life might have been had he played his cards better! What a bitter and tragic end to a rather substantial chapter in the history of this part of the world!

DAY 268, *July 28, 1980*—Today's press in Tehran focuses a bit on the death of the Shah, though in general the reaction here is low-key. No masses on the streets, only a few cars blowing their horns when the news hit yesterday. He seems a non-issue, and one can understand that. Eighteen months after he left, the average man is no better off, and many are worse off. What is there to celebrate? . . . One newspaper reports that the CIA killed the Shah! Several have picked up this theme, playing it as fact. Others are quoted as being skeptical that he is dead. A certain Reverend Brewer in the celebrated Lawrence, Kansas, group is quoted as saying, "I do believe that if the death of the Shah can be confirmed firsthand by Iranian authorities, if they actually see his body, I believe it can ease the tensions." *That* can only be called well-meaning, but *dumb*.

We continue to wonder about the future of Foreign Minister Ghotbzadeh, now under attack for running an un-Islamic ministry and tolerating a bunch of Taghooti [old regime] embassies abroad. As a newspaper put it yesterday, he has become "the underdog of the revolutionary old guard." He has been summoned to appear before the Majlis to answer questions about the "mishandling of his ministry." Rumors are that when the new government is formed, he will go abroad, possibly as an ambassador at large. He would be wise to do so. . . .

A magnificent moon fills the sky tonight; the place doesn't deserve it. The weather is hot—102° again—and our soldiers are cavorting tonight in the pool that surrounds the fountain in the garden below. It is no deeper than 18 inches, so one can't say they're swimming, but it is no doubt cool, and I don't blame them.

DAY 270, *July 30, 1980*—For the past two nights the guards (now reduced to one on this floor) have been nervous about reports/rumors that the ministry may be taken over by some revolutionary group. No one quite knows who that might be; the threat variously comes from "students," Komitehs, even "Communists." A kitchen on the floor above us has been opened as a place where we would flee or hide if that happens, though what we would do there is beyond me. In any event, we have slept the past two nights with plastic bags beside our beds containing those papers we want to be sure not to lose should something happen.

The ministry continues to function. It seems quieter, but people come and go across the courtyard below. The women employees have accepted their fate. All wear head scarves, long-sleeved and loose-fitting blouses, long skirts. It must be warm, especially in Ramadan when they can drink nothing. . . . The local press and radio is full of slanted stories and distortions about the Sunday demonstrations in Washington by Iranian students and others who supposedly were seized upon "by the oppressive police." Rafsanjani, the Majlis speaker, said how this contrasts so vividly with the "humane" and "Islamic" way in which the hostages are treated here and especially with the Khomeini action releasing Queen as soon as he heard he was sick. Good grief—as if there was any justice or right in holding the hostages in the first place. Said the worthy Ayatollah: "When students with God's aid went to defend their rights, the police attack our youth. This shows America's nature once again."

What distorted thought processes this suggests! There seems no willingness or capacity to concede that there might be a root cause for all this that could be dealt with by compassion and reason *here*. But it is lacking, and in the heady and Islamic orthodox atmosphere of that Majlis, distortion becomes dogma and lies become truth.

12

August 1980:
Belated Valentines

By its end, 300 days into the crisis, August was probably our nadir. The summer's heat seemed unending, boredom with our routine weighed heavily, the regime's propagandists were at the height of their invective about alleged mistreatment of Iranian students in America, and the parliament seemed no closer to action of any kind, whether on the hostages or on the deepening power struggle within the regime. My journal found me so frequently expressing my frustration as to accuse myself of sounding like a broken record.

Our spirits got a powerful if momentary boost, however, when a day in August became our Valentine's Day. For reasons known only to God, the three of us suddenly found ourselves recipients of two mail bags full of hundreds of valentines from the schoolchildren of southern California. Their uninhibited expressions of affection—and, yes, advice too—reminded us that there was a lot of good in the world out there that still beckoned to us. Of the probably millions of cards and letters addressed simply "To the Hostages in Tehran" by the American public, these were the only ones ever to reach us. To my knowledge, our colleagues in the compound across town fared no better.

DAY 272, *August 1, 1980*—Another miserable, absolutely deplorable day—the breeze feels as if it came straight from the Dasht-i-Kabir Desert. With windows closed, the room serves the purpose of an oven, the sun heating the roof and two sides. With windows open, the heat and dust of the Dasht-i-Kabir blow in unrelentingly. Evenings bring little relief. . . .

Today being Friday, we've had our stint of Friday prayers, with the good Friday preacher of Tehran, Khamanei, giving forth at great and impassioned length about—you guessed it—police oppression in the United States. That has become the new hobbyhorse of the hate-makers locally, with Iranian students in the United States busily reporting their "oppression," their Islamic piety, even claiming that those now held by the police have been "taken hostage" in response to the hostage situation here.

So we have Khamanei telling his audience today to ask the American Congress (which has sent a letter to the Majlis urging priority focus on the hostage issue) to look to the scene on the streets of Washington where "dear Iranian students are being harassed by the fascist police of the United States." The issue has the potential for endless distortion and embroidery by the local propagandists. Meanwhile the masses lap it up, like those who listened in ignorance today to Khamanei while he, who ought to know better, engages in this outrageous demagoguery. Why? Because they can agree on *nothing* internally so that again the focus of all energy and abuse is the Great Satan, the United States. . . .

DAY **274,** *August 3, 1980*—It is Sunday morning, a quiet morning. It is also a Shi´a Muslim holiday, the anniversary of the martyrdom of Hazrat Ali, the first Imam in Shi´a Islam—a day of deep mourning, or perhaps I should say a day of *unusually* deep mourning, because most of Shi´a Iran's holidays seem to be mourning days, for one reason or another.

So, unlike most mornings, one can hear the sounds of nature outside our windows. The roar of the city is stilled; traffic is probably very light, and the air-conditioning motors on the roof of the next-door building are silent. One is reminded of nature elsewhere—of sitting on the back terrace of our home on a quiet Sunday morning, with a good breakfast perhaps, the Sunday paper, and the sounds of birds. Or an early morning walk on the beach. It is not hard, in any event, for the mind to take one elsewhere than here. . . .

During the month of Ramadan here, by 5:30 A.M. it is already late. The faithful (and it is hard to be anything but that here now, except very secretly) are up at 3:30 A.M. and busying themselves with breakfast and other means of fortifying themselves for the long day of fasting ahead that does not end until about 8:30 P.M. So there is a great deal of bustle among our soldier guard force in the courtyard below, accompanied by the amplified call of the mullahs from mosques in the neighborhood. By 5:00 A.M. it is quiet again until the city begins its din and commotion by 6:00 A.M. or so.

And today is also the eve of our ninth month of captivity, an anniversary that never in our darkest moments did we expect to see here. It is marked by news of Iranian students in the United States fostering a protest against alleged "police brutality" and, we are told, by the Iranian UN representative at New York lodging a protest with the secretary general about the deprivation of the human rights of Iranians in the United States. What does one say to that, after the Iranian government's complicity, over nine months, in the holding of diplomats for political ransom? Obscene is one possible description. What twisted purposes they seek to serve by their obscurantist approach to human affairs! . . .

God knows that this country has problems that are large, real, and serious. Yet the newscasts today have been roughly 50 percent focused on this affair in Washington, as if nothing else mattered. Why? Why? Is there a deliberate campaign to add flame and fire to the hostage issue, so that those in power here, unable even to form a government, can avoid coming to grips with the hostages? Does it suggest that they have no interest at all in resolving the issue, keeping it instead as the political football that it has become?

Just now the Ayatollah is on with a statement responding to one from the Pope, the statement apparently damning the Vatican for its sins and reminding the Pope of the venality of the Great Satan, the United States. As the statement ends, as is the custom, the TV carries the Khomeini hymn, an obsequious paean of praise of the worst personality cult type; the words being simply "Khomeini the Imam, Khomeini the Imam," repeated for several minutes' duration. It is worse than anything in the Shah's regime, as indeed is the absence of a rule of law governing the revolutionary courts, where executions continue apace. The country has cut itself off from the civilized world.

I feel defeated. Since the start of this tragedy last fall I have preached restraint at home, not simply because I felt that that was the only way to get the issue resolved here, but because it seemed to me that a posture of restraint in the face of the total lack of it by the Iranians was right and appropriate for a strong and mature power. I felt that the record should show that in contrast to the total violation and abuse of law here, our record at home toward Iranians in the United States should be scrupulously just and legal, with those Iranians benefiting from every aspect of our laws and regulations.

To my knowledge, our record in that respect *has* been good. But I fear we are now risking defeat on this point, including the need for dignity and restraint on the part of the American public, not because of what they have done on their own initiative but because of what Iranians in the United States and Iranian authorities here, egging them on, are causing Americans to do. Thus we hear reports of Georgetown University students throwing dog food at Iranian students on a hunger strike in front of the White House and of others taunting them with verbal abuse. Perhaps some of the police, in the July 27 demonstrations, *did* apply force in excess in the face of those Iranian students' determination to achieve "martyrdom."

And here? How can any American, justifiably aggrieved by the continuing fact of 52 Americans held hostage for political purposes for now nine months, be anything but angered by what is happening? A campaign of hate, based on skillful distortion of the facts, that would surely rival anything achieved by Goebbels is the result here. The official radio and TV pour forth endlessly a stream of abuse, joined by cables of endorsement from political, religious, and economic groups in all directions, fanned, of course, by the students holding our embassy, where last night at midnight a quarter-million people were whipped into a frenzy of rage that seemed to exceed even that of last November. The speaker, Iran's leading vote-getter among deputies elected to the Majlis, a man with unique skills in demagoguery, got them going. And at the very top, there was the president of the country calling on the students in the United States to "resist the Americans. If they want to deport you, force them to pull you along the ground to make you board the plane. The Iranian people approve of your struggle."

That from the president of a country who presumably knows, or should know, the facts—i.e., that almost 200 Iranians, arrested for disobeying our laws but now freed of all such charges as a result of the State Department's intervention, are totally free to return to their universities if they give their names to INS authorities and if their visa status is found to be in order. Those whose visa status is not in order, and therefore in violation of our laws, have two options: either to leave for Iran immediately at our expense or to remain in detention if they wish and use legal means to fight their deportation.

Those are the facts. They indicate that every effort is being made that these men and women have every benefit of our laws and judicial procedures. But does that matter here? Apparently not, even in the face of the total deprivation of access to laws and judicial procedures for 52 American *diplomats*. They, of course, the answer goes, are "different" because they are "spies." But even so, one mullah is reported in the press as saying: "We treated them very well. But our students are tortured." For that accusation, of course, there is no basis in fact, but never mind. That can be created. . . .

So a quarter of a million Iranians turn out in the midnight orgy of hate. Our kitchen staff reflects it, one of them bearding Vic Tomseth and saying, "How can you treat our students like that when we have treated you so well?" (That so infuriated Vic, a gentle man who has bent over backwards to be decent and understanding with these people, that he exploded in a response that caused him to be unable to eat his lunch.)

But it is not these simple people, the masses on the streets, who are basically at fault. It is those who lead them in this deliberate exercise of invective. Like the president, whose statement above surely qualifies as one of the more unseemly expressions from that quarter and level that could be imagined. . . .

The initiative by 180 U.S. congressmen on the hostage issue, appealing to the Majlis to give that issue top priority, is also the victim of this emotional hate—the United States accused of lies and therefore "What is behind this unbecoming haste in calling for release of the hostages?"

What is behind our "haste" is obvious—simple humanity and justice—but those qualities seem not to apply in the Iranian Muslim mind. What is behind the delay here, of course, is the continuing power struggle, still unresolved and possibly growing worse: the president, operating from a presumed power base of a 76 percent voter mandate last January, frustrated at every turn by a Majlis dominated by clerical forces strongly opposed to him and led by a decisive,

Machiavellian cleric (Rafsanjani), who seems to know how to use power; the president a victim of his own indecisive, fuzzy flailing about and seemingly capable only of endless speech-making about the need for "unity" and "Islamic spiritualism," whatever that means. And above it all sits the Ayatollah, surrounded by his own special entourage, watching it all with perhaps more amusement than the occasional stern lecture suggests. . . .

Yesterday, by some miracle, we got a telex message from the department, the second in six months, allowed by the ministry by some fluke, giving us the U.S. factual position on the issue of the demonstrators. I have sent copies to the foreign minister, together with letters and copies to Dr. Beheshti and Minister of National Guidance Minachi, emphasizing in my letter the facts of the matter and suggesting how Iranians in the United States are the beneficiaries of our laws. But I doubt that the foreign minister will forward the letters and, even if he did, whether they would do any good. . . .

DAY 277, *August 6, 1980*—This is not the day to focus on the dark side of things. On one's birthday, one ought to think positive thoughts about something, if for no other reason to divert one's mind from the fact that one is 58, going into 59! That's getting along, isn't it? Especially, for example, when I think that I'm almost twice as old as Mike or three times as old as two of my sons and four times as old as Jim!

Ah, but 58 isn't that bad, especially if one doesn't feel that old, and even in my present circumstances I *don't*, except perhaps about midafternoon when the temperature outside hits 104° and the inside of this room must be several degrees hotter!

Mike and Vic reminded me of my birthday today by presenting me with a large card, the front having a copy painted by Mike (exceedingly well, too) of the American eagle with a tear in his eye and a yellow ribbon in his beak that appeared on the cover of the department's *Newsletter* recently. (The British ambassador has sent us his used set of watercolor paints.) Inside the card is a long poem in Vic's particular style, describing our incarceration since November and concluding: "So happy fifty-eighth, and we hope that next year, when you mark the occasion, you won't still be here!"

I told them I was deeply grateful, but did they really have to put the "hope" in the context of a whole *year?*

DAY 280, *August 9, 1980*—Today is my mother's birthday and my older brother Ken's, both gone now. . . . My mother, my older brother—few persons can ever be quite so important to anyone; few could have played such an important role in my life. But now, how interesting it is to think how they have moved into the back of my mind, into a distant memory only occasionally at the surface of my thoughts. That is natural, obviously, and to be otherwise could be something forever corrosive and hurtful to my life and those of others in our family. It must be God's way of helping ensure that life goes on, that there are others to whom one can transfer one's thoughts and affections and with whom one can interact and, in the process, forget the sadness of loss.

But on their birthdays, I wonder sometimes whether and how their spirit exists. At a minimum it does exist in one place, and that is in the minds and hearts of those who remember and were close to them. Who is to say, for example, that a mother's spirit does not live on in the heart and mind of a son, or daughter, and thus have some bearing on what that person does every day of his life? Or that Ken's influence on me during many years of growing up together does not continue to play some role, subconsciously, in things that I do and say? I believe that and, believing that, I remember today with a special affection the kind of people they were. . . .

. . . Tonight we have a prime minister, at least one that's been designated. He is Education Minister Mohammed Ali Rajai, much rumored in recent days. Whether this is the product of a definite consensus between Bani-Sadr and Beheshti is unclear, but presumably it is. Perhaps Bani-Sadr has recognized as final yet another defeat—his one-day nomination of Mir Salim, who immediately ran into the IRP buzzsaw and saw his career as a prime minister collapse within a day or so. If this is the product of an agreement, perhaps we will see Rajai approved by the Majlis promptly, and a cabinet too, so that at long last something might begin to happen. . . .

The scene on this floor, our corner, of the ministry here in itself says something about the state of affairs. . . . In the next room, the main salon to which we had access when this affair first began, the scene is especially revealing. Against the wall and the main windows are the 50 metal lockers hurriedly brought there in early March when, the very next day, our hostages were to have been brought there when the government hoped (and failed) to take custody of the hostages. The lockers still stand there, mute symbols of the regime's failure on that issue. The rest of the room—and the adjacent narrow dining room where we spent four months—is now a carpet and furniture warehouse. . . . Hundreds of dining room chairs are stacked atop each other, as are a pair of elegant Shah and Empress dining chairs (their high backs ripped and torn to remove the hated crests), and various odds and ends of handsome side pieces and lamps. Overhead are the massive chandeliers, more dusty than ever. . . . On the floor in great heaps are Persian carpets, taken from offices all over the ministry and from its public rooms and brought to this room for ultimate disposition as unnecessarily Taghooti in the ministry. . . .

Everywhere there is drift and disrepair, dust and limited maintenance. The ministry is purged (said the minister in a defensive statement to the Majlis yesterday) of 30 percent of its professional staff and headed by a minister closely linked to the ARK from Paris days. But he is considered now by the Islamic hard-liners as having been delinquent in purifying his ministry and allowing Iranian embassies abroad to go in their ancien régime fashion, spending money foolishly, accomplishing nothing, and—say some—serving as "centers of prostitution."

Little wonder nothing gets done.

DAY 282, *August 11, 1980*

Dear Bill,

. . . We've been angered by the nonsense about "tortured" Iranian student demonstrators in the United States, and now the radio here is full of reports of Iranian students demonstrating in London, Manila, Stockholm, Karachi, Kuwait, Rome—and God knows where else—all of them, of course, persecuted by "fascist police." One would think that they are not the most popular people in the world these days, whether good Muslims or not! But it is vital that angry Americans *not* take the law into their own hands and attack these demonstrators. That *won't* help, and it is degrading to *our* traditions.

Can't give you any predictions on us, Bill. We've given up setting any dates. It is hard *not* to conclude that they will hold on to us until after November 4. Then, if Carter loses, the rooftops here will be crowded with the mobs yelling "Allah O'Akbar"—God is great. Another victory for the Ayatollah! That's not a pleasant thought, and we hope it is not going to be fact. But we are realistic enough to see it as quite possible. . . .

                                        Dad

DAY 283, *August 12, 1980*—Yesterday will remain a day long to remember. The Swiss brought mail—for the first time in many weeks—and it included something like 165 reminders in cards and letters that I am now 58! More important, it brought that many reminders from relatives, friends, and total strangers that the American people remain remarkably obsessed with the wrongness of this entire hostage issue and that they care.

I'm overwhelmed. It has taken me 24 hours to open and read them all, since most include letters, or at least notes, as well. They come from all over Minnesota, though most from Odin, Butterfield, and St. James, some from Wisconsin and Iowa, and from scattered places elsewhere. Some are from shops and restaurants, where many people signed, some from church groups, two from old people's homes (in St. James and Mountain Lake), one from a factory in St. James, a card which all the workers signed.

There is a religious theme in virtually all of them. I think fewer than five are the humorous, frivolous variety of birthday card, now so popular. That theme is written, or underlined, in printed words on the cards, summed up by expressions like "Never despair, God's always there" or "I will lift up my eyes unto the Lord." One comes from a former neighbor farmer, now 86 and in a retirement home, saying, "I think of you often and pray of your safety." . . .

I remind myself that all this sentiment expressed toward me should really be directed toward those who have suffered so much more—my 49 colleagues. And in a sense that's where it *is* directed, using me as the vehicle. Yet it is also for me a reflection of the remarkable cohesion and togetherness of these small Midwestern communities—mine and so many others—standing together, in good times and bad, strongly conscious of a sense of family and community responsibility. A simple note on one of the cards puts it well: "A trouble shared is but half the trouble; a joy that's shared is a joy made double." People in small-town America still mean and believe that, I think. Seeing it expressed in this way has given me enormous reassurance of the health of our society.

DAY 285, *August 14, 1980*—Yesterday, yet another demonstration of how the American people have seized on the human aspects of this issue to show their support. Midmorning the guard walks into the room carrying two large plastic bags—the one carrying another batch of paperback books from the ever-friendly Swedish Embassy; the other, larger, containing hundreds and hundreds of valentines! They are all laboriously handmade, ranging from the bright and primitive colors of first-graders to the more sophisticated efforts of fifth- and sixth-graders, all from a group of schools in southern California—Mission Viejo, El Toro, etc. All date from late January, where the bag has been since then is anyone's guess. All the guard could tell us was that both bags came "from Sweden." Well, that's unlikely but curious nonetheless. We can only assume it is typical of the projects of literally hundreds of schools across the country at Thanksgiving, Christmas, Valentine's Day, Easter, and who knows what else. Many mail sacks arrived at the compound at Christmastime, but we wonder how many hundreds did not.

We have enjoyed going through this bag, prior to making an effort with the ministry to have it sent over to the compound. Youthful enthusiasm runs through all of them. Uninhibited concern, friendship, patriotism, anger, puzzlement—but *confidence* above all. Don't worry, they tell us, like one who wrote: "Believe in the Lord and soon you will come out." Another: "Help is on the way." Another: "Don't worry; if they don't let you go, we'll come and get you out, even if we have to fight." Quite a few have some ideas of their own on how that might be done. One suggests: "I hope you can sneak out of Iran when the people go to bed. Then you can go back hom[e]."

A young girl writes: "Hi Dream Boat, I wish you a lot of luck. I am going to give you a plan to get out. Number one: Cry for food, then hit them in the face and run out. If this isn't a good plan, hear [*sic*] is another one. If there is a key by there, all of you should get each a sock and try to throw the sock and get the key. Try your own [idea] if it doesn't work."

Another frequent expression: "It's just not America without you." There is anger with the Iranians, like this: "Iatolah, if you were over here we would hit you in the face with a pieatolah."

And one reflected another recent episode in American adventures overseas: "Dear friend, I hope you can come to America soon. I also hope my cousin Tommy and my Grandma can come here too. They are stuck in Viet Nam. Love, Anthony Tran."

How wonderful it all is—and how sad, too. We wonder what these youngsters are thinking now, six months later—more anger? Irritation with their own country for not *doing* something? Or do they really think much of this at all? Certainly one impression must have been indelibly registered in their minds—a dislike of all things Iranian, a dislike that will not be easily forgotten.

Another one: "Everybody is pulling for you hoping you'll get out soon, but what do I know about Iran. I'm just an 11-year-old kid born in Lake Tahoe now living in Mission Viejo. I hope you people will get back in time for the World Series, and there will be a warm welcome for you. Fellow American, Beau Cole."

DAY 286, *August 15, 1980*—I get up some mornings—or try to get up— and think to myself, what a stupid way to spend nine-plus months of one's life! Another day of waiting, waiting while these egocentric and ethnocentric people pull themselves together with their Islamic experiment—the ultimate in political philosophy, we are to believe. While they squabble and fight—in a classic power struggle that has nothing whatsoever that is redeeming about it—52 men and women supposedly protected by all laws and norms of civilized international discourse are held hostage in an unprecedented act of political blackmail. It is all so wrong—and so bloody unnatural and indecent. The lives of 52 families (and related families beyond these) are upset by this heinous act, while the local apologists claim that it is justified because we are different, we are *spies!* . . .

To wake up in the morning and think of this is demoralizing—and if I feel that way, how much more angry and depressed must be my 49 colleagues, kept from almost all contact with family and friends and their own government. I sound like a broken record.

DEC 287, *August 16, 1980*—A current *Newsweek* has a feature on the novelist V. S. Naipaul. He is completing a book on Islam and was asked a question about the rise of Islamic fundamentalism. His answer: "Islamic fundamentalism has no intellectual substance to it; therefore it must collapse. . . . It will be replaced by an advance toward rationalism, though the process will be slow."

How right he is! There *is* no substance in it. In Iran it is only the notions of a vindictive recluse, full of visions of unity and spiritialism but based on what? Bani-Sadr professes to have developed an economic philosophy resting on Islam, but it too appears to have little more than fuzzy notions of unity and cooperation, which themselves are goals made impossible in Iran by the ruthlessness of the fundamentalists in having their way. Their concern is with the mosque, the nature of Friday prayers, the purging of Iranian society of all influences, East and West. . . . What is left here by cutting themselves off from the rest of the world? Archaic social forms and practices, the veiling of women, the proper form of prayers, masses in the streets—but these are all form rather than substance. It cannot endure. . . .

DAY 289, *August 18, 1980*—Today for the very first time since this all began I seem to have succumbed to what we called, when I lived here in the

1950s, the TTs (the "Tehran trots," pardon the expression). Then the water was unsafe to drink without boiling. Today the water is excellent. Where I have picked up this bug, I don't know. But I am reminded how fortunate we've been. Hopefully it will pass and is not a reawakening of long-dormant amoebas that last had their fling some years ago in Afghanistan.

DAY 291, *August 20, 1980*—I have had today an example of the application of the one-dimensional humanitarian concern for hostages. My dysentery problem finally caused me yesterday to ask the Protocol Office for some medicine. That caused the acting chief to see me, who promised to get the medicine. Then this morning I mentioned to a kitchen staffer that I wasn't feeing tops. Word spread to the guard, who—as a consequence of a communications gap—alerted Protocol again, and this time the house doctor appeared. Again a promise to get the medicine. But, late afternoon, the protocol chief walked in again, this time with yet another doctor, from the Red Crescent. I explained I felt better, but he asked to check my heart and general condition. O.K., he would send medicine, and indeed it arrived within the hour.

From Protocol we learned that the minister had ordered the doctor to see me. The doctor is one of those who have seen the other hostages, three times, he said. I told him I wished he would go again. Obviously not wanting to pursue the subject, he said he'd not been asked. I replied that was because the "students" wouldn't permit it.

The exercise suggests, clearly, that the minister has instructed Protocol to let him know whenever we have the slightest complaint on health grounds. They clearly don't want any sick hostages. And, so long as they're not, they are being "well treated." We should not worry. One-dimensional. Physical health alone is not "good treatment."

DAY 292, *August 21, 1980*
Dear Jim,

Tomorrow is the day I promised you I'd be at the airport to welcome you back from camp. I won't be there, Jim. And I'm more sorry about that than perhaps you'll ever know. No, that's not true. Some day you will—when you have children of your own and, for some reason, can't be there to share in something your children have experienced and enjoyed. . . . Dads are pretty good to have around too, don't you agree? I used to think so, about my own dad, even though he was pretty austere, and there were times, lots of times, when I didn't understand him. I understand him better now.

That's the way life is. You'd like to be able to benefit from hindsight all the time. But that's not possible, so we all have to learn from experience.

You have concluded—if you've read this far (!)—that I'm preaching again. I hope you don't think that. The point is that I miss you, and I miss sharing in your life as you grow up. These are pretty important years, and I should be there to help (when you need help) and stay out of your way when you don't want parents around.

But I suspect that when I get home I'll find that you've done very well indeed. All I can say is, don't conclude after this that dads are dispensable. Like paper plates. We're not really, and I look forward to proving that to you and your brothers when I get home. . . .

You are about to start school again. This is a tough year, Jim, but a very important one. I wish you all the best. Remember, a teacher can only do so much; *you* have to do the rest. Remember too that you're carrying the Laingen colors now, Jim, and we will all look to you to carry them proudly. Stand tall for what is right and decent—don't let the crowd tell you what to do. That will take a lot of courage once in a while, but people will respect you for it—even those who try to abuse you. Let your conscience be your guide. That's as good a rule as any. Love to Mom—and to Doug and your friends—and another pat on the bottom for Duchess.

I would sure like a letter from you, son—Dad

DAY 293, *August 22, 1980*—I'm fine again. It must have been food poisoning. No ill effects for the long term. . . .

The Majlis, after some debate, has decided to answer the letter from the 187 congressmen. We wonder why more didn't sign. The Foreign Affairs Committee recommended a response, observing that "the United States was waging a full-scale war against Iran." In the debate, one member said that it should be stressed that the reply was to the American people "because we don't regard the Congressmen as true representatives of the American people." The *gall* of these people, ignorant clerics that they are, almost none of whom has ever set foot outside Iran! They persist with the notion that somehow the people of the United States understand Iran's Revolution, in contrast to the government. And they are so wrong!

Meanwhile, we continue to search for clues as to when (or if) progress is possible. Beheshti is quoted as saying that the hostage issue will have to be put aside because of other priority issues facing the Majlis. (He is right in the sense that the Majlis surely has things to do—some six months after the elections and still not started on its work!) But another prominent mullah, Bahonar, is quoted as saying he hopes the hostage issue can be resolved "close upon a month after a cabinet is formed."

Bahonar was brutally frank on one point, saying, "We will *use* the hostages as an issue in this cause (the anti-American campaign) to the fullest extent possible." Indeed they will. And *have* been using them all along, in a historic demonstration of a government stooping to international blackmail, using captive humans as leverage. Bahonar, incidentally, is the cleric, member of the Revolutionary Council, who I was told by Foreign Minister Yazdi on that fateful November 4 day was being sent by the council to resolve the situation at the compound "tonight, or at the latest by tomorrow." And here we are, nine-plus months later, with Bahonar talking about "using" us and Yazdi now the editor of *Kayhan* (a leading paper) and calling for our trials.

DAY 296, *August 25, 1980*—"Iran is the only country in the world that does not recognize that holding these hostages is damaging to Iran." In roughly those words, in Farsi, spoke Foreign Minister Ghotbzadeh in a long interview on last night's TV broadcast.

He is a fascinating man—tough, clever, intelligent, articulate, suave, rather handsome, poised, and self-assured. The last is a basic trait, no doubt, but strengthened in the local context by the fact of his long association with the ARK, in Paris, which relationship is apparently still in a good state of health, despite the increasing criticism directed at the minister by the fundamentalists in the past month and the total lack of amity between him and the "students" following the line of the Imam.

He is also courageous, or perhaps *gutsy* would be a better word. He has taken on the "students" in public before, and he has been tough in some of his public remarks recently, including a long defense of his tenure here in front of critical Majlis members the other day. He is a born politician, totally at ease, much given to hand gestures, good with quips. And skilled at double meanings where necessary—witness the quote above. What does it say? He can be accused of saying that hostage-holding is wrong. But, he can also say that what he meant was that while the rest of the world may be critical, Iran is on its own revolutionary course and doesn't give a damn *what* the rest of the world thinks. I think I know what he really means—and that is that Iran's interests are not served by this. We have watched, over these many months, a considerable metamorphosis in his attitudes. One can quote him from last summer, while head of NIRT and in his first month as foreign minister, in ways that suggest the most extreme of revolutionary leanings. But with the responsibility of this job, that has changed, and we three have come to respect him for what he has tried to do. We wonder where he will go next, and who will replace him here, and what that will mean for us. . . .

DAY 298, *August 27, 1980*—Islamic justice continues in the Iranian Revolution, including the zeal of the Revolutionary Guards. Yesterday's press reported that a former justice and interior minister under the Shah (apparently one of those who continued quietly to remain in Iran) had been arrested at his home by Revolutionary Guards and sent to Evin Prison. It was said that "quantities of gold, clothing, belts and handbags" had been confiscated at his house, such articles presumably reflecting corruption. Today's press reports yet a further example of corruption by this hapless fellow: the guards had found "156 bottles of alcohol in his doghouse" and, before carting him off to Evin, had given him 50 lashes on the spot. Summary justice, Islamic style. Big doghouse!

Meanwhile the campaign against the Anglican Church continues; some five English missionaries are still held incommunicado, including the secretary to the now-exiled bishop. Yesterday the Revolutionary Guards revealed what they claimed was evidence of a link between these Anglicans and the coup plotters, the Anglicans branded as an "assembly of international and experienced spies." Reportedly the United States—the CIA—had sent $500 million(!) to the Anglican bishopric in Isfahan "to be distributed among army personnel, Baha'i leaders, and counterrevolutionaries." And according to last night's TV news, Britain's former ambassador, Sir John Graham, "is charged with sending 650 pounds of TNT to the Isfahan Anglicans." An earlier report had alleged that Graham's predecessor here had been similarly implicated.

The whole of it is so insane as to boggle one's imagination—even after a year in revolutionary Iran. A half-billion dollars! Routinely sent off by a casual CIA to finance counterrevolutionary activities in Iran! And who was to dispense this tidy sum? Why, none other than those "experienced" espionage types, the Anglicans of Isfahan, cloaking their activities in the work of their hospitals, schools, and clinics. The whole thing is such a patent fraud and forgery that even Iranians must find this kind of nonsense little more than a joke. Unhappily, it is *not* a joke for those now held, incommunicado, in prison, both English and Iranian nationals. Nor is it a joke for Bishop Tehghani-Tafti, who fled earlier and who saw his son murdered here by unknown assailants.

All this is somehow seen as justice and a worthy pursuit of the Revolution. Much of all this is the work of the zealots, those with Islamic zeal but little else, little more than street clods now given power, which they exercise in their own stupid and misguided and callous ways. And no one seems able to control them, because, in part, they are protected by equally ignorant and bigoted men in places of high authority. Yet there are others—many more than dare raise their heads—who must be repelled by all this, while also conceding that in a Revolution excesses are sometimes necessary or unavoidable to achieve revolutionary objectives. But for how long, at what cost? Almost two years into the Revolution and the result is little more than slogans, and more slogans, and appeals for unity that fall on empty air and empty heads. . . .

Perhaps if the Revolution could offer circuses, that would be something, but it achieves not even that, unless one thinks that street demonstrations still offer that release. Neither circuses nor bread, only Islam.

DAY 300, *August 29, 1980*—It is 300 days today. What does one say to that? Not much. What is there to say? Perhaps I should compare it with what I said on the 100th day or the 200th day, but what I said then is not available to me here, it having been sent home. I suspect I said what I could say now: It is virtually unbelievable. And it is something that I did not envisage as happening, even in my worst fears, during those first few days last November. Better, surely, *not* to have known it then, since being told that we would still be here 300 days later would probably have driven us into a state of gloom and despair that would have been hard to live with. As it is, we have gone from day to day, not assuming much but not assuming the worst either. So we have lived with it, thinking ahead to the day when, we know, we *will* be released but without the burden, psychologically, of thinking of it in terms of *x* number of days. Today, the 300th day, we can envisage a full 365 days, a full year, although I think I cannot bring myself to envisage 400! Another 65 days will take us almost through our November 4 elections and, in all reality, it is hard to see this regime going along with a scenario that would see us welcomed home by Carter before that election day. The regime here would probably see that as a political bonus to Carter (however much he might have conceded to get our release) that they cannot bring themselves to give. Rather, probably, they will spin this thing out long enough to extend it beyond that date; then, if Carter should lose, they can point to that fact as yet another gift from God to the Islamic Republic. Never mind that Reagan could prove to be tougher toward Iran than Carter—they will tell themselves that they will cross that bridge when they come to it. . . .

DAY 302, *August 31, 1980*—Well, perhaps there is a bandwagon psychosis developing. Bani-Sadr is now quoted in two interviews, two days running, as criticizing the hostage-holding. In the first he said that the holding of hostages has in effect made Iran a hostage of the United States, "preventing Iran from gaining its real independence from the United States." He agreed with Ghotbzadeh's call for release, adding that he wished Ghotbzadeh had done it from the beginning "and not now, after we have suffered so much damage." The latter is an interesting and accurate reference to the fact that Ghotbzadeh was among the hard-liners early on talking about trials and generally hanging tough about holding us unless the Shah were extradited.

In the second interview, with a French paper, Bani-Sadr again warns against putting us on trial since that would simply give the United States "a pretext for intervention." Bani-Sadr said that it would also play into U.S. hands in the sense that "it is the United States that has created the hostage problem and which is still preventing a solution." That, of course, is garbage, but in terms of putting pressure on the Majlis to act, it is not a bad line to take publicly here. . . .

Well, all of these things are interesting and possibly suggestive of something. But as Mike said at breakfast this morning, he would be prepared to concede that there is change here "only if and when some of the 'ragheads' are quoted as saying these things." I agree with that. . . .

13

September 1980:
The Ayatollah's
Conditions

On September 12, in a speech to the faithful about to depart on pilgrimage to Mecca, Khomeini spelled out four conditions for the United States that he said would determine the resolution of the hostage crisis and that in effect dictated to the Majlis how that body should proceed.

- *Return the late Shah's properties in the United States*
- *Cancel any claims against Iran*
- *Unblock Iran's frozen assets in the United States*
- *Promise not to intervene, politically or militarily, in Iran's affairs*

We in the ministry thought we had heard it all before. Granted it did not include the ritual insistence on an American apology or mention the hostages being placed on trail; but it had a tone of bitter defiance, including talk of being "officially at war" with the United States.

Our colleagues in Washington sensed something new and found ways to say as much to us. Soon they had further reason to think so. Unknown to us, an emissary of the Ayatollah appeared in Bonn within a few days to talk with the

German ambassador to Tehran and other West German officials. They used the same language as in the Ayatollah's public speech to convey the regime's readiness to begin talks toward our release.

The emissary was Sadegh Tabatabai, a German-educated deputy prime minister before the embassy was seized and a man with a link through marriage with the Ayatollah's family. Within days thereafter, Deputy Secretary of State Warren Christopher would arrive in Bonn to meet secretly twice with Tabatabai. Thus began the four-month process that would see us released. That process began with complications enough, and it risked foundering completely with the outbreak of the Iran-Iraq War. By now, however, Iran's leadership had concluded it was time to end the crisis. The utility of the hostages as pawns in putting the Revolution back on course—the real reason for the embassy's seizure—had ended, the new constitution was in place, an ideologically correct Majlis had been elected, the secular moderates were politically isolated, and the United States, in the leadership's view, was proven helpless.

By now, moreover, the Carter administration's efforts to isolate Iran were beginning to hurt. Economic and commercial sanctions were never complete, and in themselves did not prove decisive; but they did add to Iran's fiscal and economic pain. Japan's boycott of Iranian oil was especially important. Iran's oil-pricing policies had already adversely affected Iranian oil sales. Its credit rating among European banks was under increasing question. Its internal economic infrastructure was already badly disrupted, and soon the drain of military spending for the war with Iraq would make the pain even sharper.

So a deal was necessary, but a deal required negotiations, including intermediaries other than the West Germans, too closely linked with the Americans in the Iranian view. Enter the Algerians, a nonaligned Islamic state with impeccable revolutionary credentials of its own, a reasonable if not warm relationship with the United States, and as time would demonstrate, a country with officials of remarkable diplomatic skill and dedication.

The process would now begin, albeit slowly. It gained a new target date after Ronald Reagan's election; the Iranians had no desire to risk dealing with this new administration by allowing the crisis to run beyond January 20, 1981. For the three of us in the ministry, reasonably informed of events in the outside world, that date now loomed increasingly large. The complexity of the issues involved, not to mention the difficulty of getting agreement within the revolutionary leadership, could easily frustrate agreement before January 20, and then many more months could go by while a new American administration took form. Furthermore, we could not exclude (nor, happily, could the Iranians) that Reagan's tough rhetoric on Iran might mean resorting to force, which the Carter administration had abjured. My two colleagues and I were not without mixed feelings about the days ahead.

DAY 305, *September 3, 1980*—The latest impasse in the Revolution's penchant for impasses continues apace—this one between Bani-Sadr and PM Rajai. The issue is the usual one—Bani-Sadr's last-ditch effort to hold onto some shred of power in the evolving arrangement, against the fundamentalists' determination to cut the president down to size so that they can continue their drive to totally Islamize this place. It appears to have boiled down to Bani-Sadr's effort to have his own way on the choices of ministers of defense and interior, but perhaps there is more. It is not clear. In any event it can only be contrary to our interests, since it delays things further. . . . But evidence continues gradually to accumulate that the Iranians are beginning to see that the issue is hurting *them* more than it hurts us, and that realization is crucial to anything happening here. . . .

So here we are, on the eve of the anniversary of our tenth month in captivity, to which a footnote or two: We are reliably informed that the new Iranian chargé in Beirut will be none other than one of our "student" friends at the "spy nest," i.e., the occupied U.S. Embassy. We know nothing more beyond that and the fact that he wears a beard and rides a moped. We suspect this is not the last such assignment. As Vic said, why not? Perhaps that's one way to cope with that crowd: Give them diplomatic assignments of their own. After all, they've presumably been well trained in diplomacy, having occupied our embassy for ten months! I can see our ambassador in Beirut, John Gunther Dean, a man quite capable of cutting this fellow down to size!

Our guards seem relaxed these days—call it perhaps a reverse of the so-called Stockholm syndrome (where hostages begin to identify with their captors). Perhaps they are simply tiring of the whole affair. They are clearly troubled by one aspect—that is the long separation from families. (Iranians are strongly family oriented.) Their relaxation is evident in frequent naps, indeed I had the devil of a time waking one the other night so that I could get the key to go to the bathroom. Also, they now come in occasionally to borrow our soap so they can take a shower; what they do with their guns while they do that—or with their concern about our intentions—is not clear. But they seem to have accepted the fact that we do not propose to attempt to escape.

DAY 307, *September 5, 1980*—An amusing letter came this week from a young girl, perhaps 11 years old, in Hastings, Minnesota, whose earlier letter this summer I had answered, saying among other things that we were not allowed outdoors except onto an adjacent balcony. She writes: "All my friends say 'Hi!' When they heard you didn't get outside they said, 'I'd go nuts!' Well at least you get out on the balcony an hour a day." She also wrote: "Hey did you hear about Billy Carter? He's making front-page news (but he always has). Just in case you didn't know."

Well, Cindi (that's her name), we *have* heard about Billy Carter—indeed we've heard more than we care to know. And, after ten months, it takes more than a denial of the outdoors to drive us "nuts," though I can well understand how a lively youngster of your age would find it intolerable. After ten months, we have adjusted reasonably well to the denial of a good many things—our basic freedom of movement above all. And one of the reasons, I think, that we've been able to make that adjustment is the realization that we've got support and friendship from people like Cindi, our families, and countless other people, both in our country and around the world. . . .

That applies especially to the support I've got from my family, without which I would find all of this very hopeless indeed. An example: When Penne and Chip were on vacation in Maine, the deadline for registration for the draft came along. Chip, together with his friend Tom Jellison, went down to register at the post office in Bangor, Chip wearing his "U.S. Marine Security Guards, Tehran" T-shirt, of which he is a proud owner. There the press noticed him, interviewed him, and quoted him as saying, "It probably sounds like pretty corny patriotism, but that's what we need. I think it's about time we had a draft. We have to be prepared. I don't know what all the anti-draft fuss is about." . . .

A footnote on today's attitude: I lay in bed for a time this morning before I could find the conviction to get up and face yet another day. I found myself looking at one of the dusty chandeliers and thinking to myself: The day will surely come when I will be unable to stop myself from flinging a glass or some other available object and watching crystal from that useless piece of decor in this dreary place go flying in all directions.

DAY 309, *September 7, 1980*—I have just finished reading—or perhaps skimming is a better word—a two-volume history of Persia by an Englishman named Sir Percy Sykes . . . printed in 1930, but the writing ended with World War I and the advent of the Pahlavi dynasty in Iran in the early 20s. As in the case of that much earlier book, also by an Englishman, Morier's *The Adventures of Hajji Baba,* there is much about Persian character that would suggest how a nation's character is rooted deep in its past and in its historical experience.

In this case, I cite the following passage, written to describe some of the problems surrounding the constitutional period of 1905:

> Persians have not learned to work together. Internal discord, personal advantage, pecuniary or other, and personal animosities, influenced the Assembly and prevented its cooperation with any Cabinet. Moreover, many of the leaders were unpractical extremists or mere visionaries, filled with anarchical ideas, which they had not digested, and yet ready to preach to their listeners on any subject. Persians are easily swayed by eloquence, and thus the views of the extremists gained the upper hand in the Assembly and ruined its chances of success.

One could easily apply that description of the times to the situation in Iran today. . . .

DAY 310, *September 8, 1980*—It is Monday evening. The ministry has been closed today because of a holiday commemorating the so-called Jolleh Square Massacre of two years ago, when the Shah's forces fired on a large number of demonstrators, killing a number that will never be known but that has grown from a figure of 58 (government figures at the time) to one of several thousand today. The affair grows in size and meaning with the telling, embroidered in countless details that probably rest on a core of truth but now are well into the domain of hyperbole. As one of the more celebrated local mullahs put it the other day, "The gathering was completely encircled by army troops who, for hours on end, made the Islamic fighters the target of their roaring tanks and guns."

I mention this not to denigrate the fact that a lot of people were tragically killed but to cite this as an example of how the truth tends to get lost in the implementation of a Revolution. Truth and facts are acceptable, so long as they serve a revolutionary objective. . . . As Hajji Baba put it in a different context: "Truth is an excellent thing when it suits one's purpose but very inconvenient otherwise."

Last year on this Jolleh Square occasion, the chiefs of mission here were all bussed down to the square to hear a speech, watch a film, have tea, and then view an exhibition of photographs taken during the massacre. I was a free man then, and it is ironic to look back on it now, especially since one of the things that marked the affair for me was a long and very friendly chat I had (over tea) with a mullah. . . .

DAY 312, *September 10, 1980*—The guards have just brought in a package of magazines and jigsaw puzzles from the British Embassy, together with a hurried note from the chargé telling us what is now in the public news, that his embassy was being closed. Only four officers had remained for the past several weeks as the court battles continued in England over the 50-plus Iranian students arrested following a violent demonstration in front of our London embassy supporting the arrested demonstrators in Washington. But, as these court actions now begin to see some of the students deported from England, the Brits decided to reduce the risk here and simply close down, without breaking relations and keeping one officer on the staff of the Swedish Embassy. That means that Britain's two vast compounds here, one in the center of the city and one in the mountain suburbs, stand ghostly empty. Yet another consequence of the incredible series of bizarre events that began with the seizure of our embassy now a year ago. One wonders where it will end.

There is a trace of a good sign, perhaps, in the public response yesterday by the PM here, Rajai, to the [Secretary of State] Muskie letter of two weeks ago. Rajai is quoted as saying that Iran is prepared to talk with the United States if it "repents" its past role in Iran and if it agrees in principle to Iran's demand for compensation for the "damages" to Iran that resulted from that USG role. That doesn't sound positive perhaps, but in the Iranian context, there may be something there to which we can respond. Maybe. It will depend on the atmosphere in the Majlis, where hard-liners abound, including the former foreign minister, Yazdi, who has been a principal public advocate of trials. Whether that is really meant or is simply his way of atoning for his long residence in the United States is open to question. Personally, I have often wondered whether he ever thinks about the fact that I sit here as a hostage in the ministry he used to head, in the building where he and I had many conversations, some of them difficult but all of them on a reasonably friendly basis. Does he ever reflect on the illegality of the fact that that U.S. chargé sits here as an instrument of political blackmail? . . .

DAY 313, *September 11, 1980*—The unique reality of our life here intrudes occasionally. Like yesterday. I decided I couldn't put off any longer the onerous task of washing my sheets. So it was done, and I find I'm becoming reasonably adept at it. There is a technique—in this and in everything else. Soak them in a kitchen basin for an hour, then pummel them to the extent that soap and muscles permit, then take a shower with sheets draped over your shoulders—there is no better way to get the soap out. Try it sometime when your automatic washer doesn't work. . . .

We have, the three of us, received a fine letter of encouragement from Secretary Muskie, delivered via the Swiss. It expresses his and the president's admiration for our role here and his appreciation for the substantive contributions we have tried to make. As he puts it, "A principal focus of our present efforts is to persuade the new leadership that there are acceptable ways of dealing with the crisis which will meet both Iranian needs and our fundamental requirements for the early and safe release of our people."

The gentleman we affectionately refer to as "the old fart" (Khomeini) is droning on the TV in the next room, counseling his new prime minister's two-thirds cabinet (one-third rejected by the president) as they sit on their haunches on the carpet around him—he, this time, seated in an armchair. Vic is listening, and we will get a briefing from him shortly. We don't expect any surprises: the government must be Islamic, work together in Islam, Islam has everything we need, neither East nor West, support the world's oppressed who are looking to Iran for leadership. That sort of thing. Thank God it's not my country. . . .

DAY 316, *September 14, 1980*

It seems fair to conclude, in any situation, that if there is still a sense of humor abroad, then things can't be all that bad. Yesterday one of our regular visitors told us of a story going around town during these past few days of ceremonies commemorating the first anniversary of Ayatollah Taleghani's death. It seems Taleghani sent the following message from his heavenly abode to Khomeini: "The Shah arrived safely; no word from the martyrs."

One has to have lived here the past few months to appreciate that joke. To die in the cause of the Revolution is a glorious thing, an assurance of martyrdom and an assured welcome in heaven. But here is Taleghani, assured of his heavenly rest and finding the Shah arriving there as well, advising the ARK that apparently none of the glorious martyrs has arrived! Something is wrong!

Dear Bill,

By the time you get this—mail being what it is—you will be 21. That will make you a man, in law as well as in body.

So I congratulate you, Bill, however much I rather hate to face up to the fact that you *are* 21. Parents, you will find, rather instinctively don't want to face up to the fact that their children are becoming adults. The reasons for that are several—not least that parents are reluctant to admit that they themselves are growing older! . . .

These 21 years have gone fast, a lot faster for me than for you, no doubt. Perhaps they've not gone fast *enough* for you. That's the way young people see things—always have. . . .

So, Bill, we're proud of you on your 21st birthday and wish you many, many more going long into the future. Keep up that sense of responsibility that you have demonstrated toward everything and everybody, and all will be well. And if I may give you one prescription from the Bible to live by, it's this—from Paul's Letter to the Philippians (a town in Greece in those days).

> Finally, brethren, whatsoever things are *true,* whatsoever things are *honest,* whatsoever things are *just,* whatsoever things are *pure,* whatsoever things are *lovely,* whatsoever things are of *good report;* if there be any virtue, and if there be any praise, think of these things . . . and the God of peace shall be with you.

I think that's a pretty good set of rules to live by for anyone. And there are few words in literature with that kind of timeless eloquence. . . .

Happy Birthday—Dad

DAY 317, *September 15, 1980*—Things are stirring, one wonders what the brew will be like. The Majlis is to debate the issue tomorrow, for the first time formally, looking toward the establishment of a study commission to come up with subsequent recommendations. The debate will possibly give us some sense of the timing we can expect. Today's press has what is said to be the full text of Ghotbzadeh's letter to the Majlis on the issue. The letter is, in the first instance, clearly designed to affirm Ghotbzadeh's revolutionary zeal, his acceptance of the utility of the hostage-taking, his awareness of American perfidy. But it is also an effort to tell the Majlis how the continuation of the affair can only hurt the Revolution, while furthering the U.S. interest. . . .

The letter is an interesting reflection of a man whose own views on all of this have been interesting to watch over the months. His distrust of the United States, dating from his student days in the United States, remains strong. But his appreciation of the Soviet threat appears to have grown. And there is no doubt that he genuinely now believes that continued holding of the hostages hurts Iran. His letter, to the extent that what we read is in fact the full text, makes no specific proposals for resolving the issue. But it is strong in rejecting some of the ideas floating about—notably trials. Perhaps his voice will carry greater weight than we think. The fact that he puts his case in such fervently revolutionary, Islamic, and anti-American terms may make his points on specifics, such as trials, more credible to the hard-liners. He has now left office, as of September 13. So we have gone through three foreign ministers while we have sat here: three days of Yazdi, a month of Bani-Sadr, a long stretch by Ghotbzadeh. We wonder what we will see next.

DAY 319, *September 17, 1980*—I have a letter from Robert Neumann, for whom I served as deputy chief of mission when he was ambassador to Kabul. He spent some time as a youth in a concentration camp in Austria before World War II and before emigrating to the United States. His story makes a strong case for the capacity of the human spirit to survive such situations . . . and in some respects to be strengthened in the process. As he puts it, ". . . Life with its amazing revitalizing force takes one immediately under the arm and propels us into the normal activities and preoccupations which are indigenous to the human condition. Truly, human beings are far more resilient than everybody, and especially many so-called experts, think."

I am prepared to agree with that. And while our condition is not in any way so adverse as that suffered by our 49 colleagues, it seems to me that Richard Queen's experience and his behavior on his release would very much corroborate what Neumann writes.

As Vic said today as we discussed this matter, he is inclined to think that a good many psychiatrists and medical types have a vested interest of sorts in taking the opposite approach, i.e., of highlighting all the risks and dangers to the human psyche and condition that go with a hostage situation. . . .

One of the kitchen staff came in yesterday and, as is his wont, proceeded to assure us—for the thousandth time—that Inshallah (God willing) we would soon be released to join our families at home. I told him this time that if it were dependent on God alone, I would have no doubt on that score. . . .

Not that the outlook is all that bad, now that the Majlis has actually begun to focus on the issue. In debate yesterday it agreed to set up a special committee to study the issue and presumably come up with recommendations. Its membership and possibly some thought of guidelines are to be considered further in a Majlis session tomorrow. Yesterday's debate provided some glimpses of attitudes, none very favorable, although trials did not seem to be a preferred course. Nonetheless, at one point there seemed to be acceptance of the thesis expressed by one member that it should not be forgotten that some of the hostages are "hardened criminals and spies" and that a trial, which would be a trial of U.S. policy in Iran, might well be in order.

That report left me in a foul mood for the balance of the day. Hardened criminals and spies indeed! Not *one* of that gallant band is a criminal—hard or soft—and not one is a spy. If there are criminals on the scene, it is exactly those people in the Majlis and elsewhere in the leadership of this place who have condoned the hostage-taking on behalf of this regime and who now are blatantly engaged in political blackmail, using these hostages to achieve their purposes.

Again I am tempted to throw a bottle at that chandelier. It really would be a beautiful explosion of dust and glass and crystal!

———

Dear Penne,

Congratulations on your ABC interview! Henry Precht mentioned in a letter to me how impressed he was with what you said and the way you said it. I couldn't agree more with the line you took. Nor could I do anything other than warmly concur in your point in one letter about not overlooking the principle that has been violated here. As you say, that would be weakness. It would also not serve anyone's long-term interest to appear to tolerate the violation of diplomatic inviolability that has been so gross here; it would be a disservice to the hostages themselves, and it would risk encouraging other extremists, here or elsewhere, to try something like that again. Indeed I hope our best legal minds at State are focusing on what can be done in light of this experience to devise some strengthening of multilateral machinery for the future that would help prevent—or at least punish and thus deter—such acts in the future. . . .

I agree with your comment that we are at the start of a long bargaining process like a carpet-buying exercise. It is important that we not be "had," however long it takes. Not that I look forward to even another *hour* in this place, but after putting in all this time in defense of a principle, I don't want to see it sold short now either.

What a crazy state of affairs all this is! A whole year now since I've seen you, a whole year deprived of seeing my family evolve. For the 49, ten-plus months of not even being able to talk with family, by phone or letter. And we are to be assured, like that nitwit at the Iranian UN mission, that, never fear, the hostages are well! As if he knew anything in any event! He hasn't a clue. I hope we walk out, ostentatiously, of every session at this fall's UNGA [UN General Assembly] session where these gentlemen speak. It is frankly galling to see Iranian reps abroad continuing a business-as-usual kind of stance in diplomatic discourse, benefiting from the very practices and laws that they have shunned here.

Love, Bruce

DAY 321, *September 19, 1980*—I reviewed the other day just what our objectives are—and have been—in this crisis. It seems to me there are three: the preservation of American national interests in Iran and in the region, the protection of the principle of diplomatic inviolability, and the return of the hostages unharmed. I put them in that order of priority because it seems to me that is the only way our leadership *can* order them. There will be some blurring of that order in any event, of course, as we get into discussions. Some would have us turn the ranking around and put #3 at the top. The fact is that all three are important to us and, to the degree possible, all must be achieved.

It seems to me, however, that as we now get into direct bargaining with these rug dealers locally, and as we cope with what is an understandable humanitarian concern over the return of the hostages unharmed, we must keep very much in mind those other two objectives.

In the process, I think we need worry less about the first than the second (of the three listed above). In terms of U.S. national interests, there is no likelihood in any event of bringing the current leadership here around to the point where they will want *any* kind of relationship with us. We, as a system and in historical terms, are anathema to those who now control the destiny of Iran. Therefore, the most we can hope for in any hostage settlement, in terms of furthering our national interests here, is simply the removal of the special irritant that the hostage issue represents. That is all right, in my view; we can live with that kind of arm's-length relationship with Iran for the present, given too the equal disapprobation that they hold for the Soviets.

As I see it, there is indeed an advantage for us, over the longer term, in this kind of situation if it means that we continue to deny ourselves as much as a barrel of Iranian oil. That, especially if we could bring ourselves to reduce our crude imports permanently in absolute terms by the amount we once got from here, would serve our most important national interest in the region—oil.

But I *do* worry about the second of our objectives listed above, i.e., the protection of the principle of diplomatic inviolability. It is vital that that objective not be lost sight of in the weeks ahead. It must be kept constantly in the forefront, on the public record, and not forgotten. Whatever settlement is worked out for the hostages' release, it should at all costs not be one that dilutes or obscures that principle and the way in which it has been violated here. To do that would be a disservice to the hostages and their ordeal, would invite other nuts elsewhere to try the same thing, and would weaken international resolve to act to strengthen multilateral mechanisms designed to cope with future violations of the principle. . . .

In this and other respects, we should not forget that it is our hand that is strong, not Iran's. It is Iran that stands condemned at the bar of world public opinion. It is Iran that is now feeling the consequent costs—material and political—of the holding of hostages for political ransom.

DAY 324, *September 22, 1980*—Three hostages with a window on a war. On the afternoon of Monday, September 22, we hear through our open windows to the south and west the sound of heavy explosions, followed by the thump-thump of what can only be antiaircraft fire. Within what seems like minutes, the kitchen force is alive with rumors that the Iraqis have attacked. The celebrated Iranian grapevine is alive and well.

In this case the rumors are correct. In a series of simultaneous strikes against Tehran's Mehrabad Airport and air force facilities in six other cities, Iraq has suddenly escalated what has been for several weeks a low-level border conflict into a full-scale invasion. Saddam Hussein's purpose appears to be to demonstrate, by a quick and successful military assault, that Iraq is now the dominant military power in the Persian Gulf region—taking advantage of Iran's weakened military strength and its self-imposed political isolation intentionally to accomplish that purpose.

Iraq's action follows quickly on its public abrogation a few days before of the 1975 Iran-Iraq border accord, reached under Algerian auspices, by which Iraq agreed to a demarcation of its border with Iran in the Shatt-al-Arab estuary along the middle of the channel (Halweg), rather than along the Persian bank of the estuary, as had been the case since the British period. Iraq had also agreed to minor border rectifications elsewhere along its eastern border, generally favorable to Iran, in return for the Shah's commitment to cease support for Kurdish insurgents fighting for greater autonomy on the Iraq side of the cross-border Kurdish minority areas.

What larger objectives the Iraqis may have are not clear as the war begins—whether, for example, they seek actual territorial gains in Iran's oil-rich Khuzistan ("Arabistan") province, populated by a substantial Arab minority. They may even have in mind the overthrow of the Islamic Revolutionary regime in Tehran—a regime that for its part has made no secret of its hostility toward Saddam Hussein's regime in Baghdad, variously described as a "bloodsucking, imperialist puppet," acting according to the dictates of the Great Satan—the United States—and of international Zionism, and brutally suppressing the people of Iraq, including the large Shi´a minority. . . .

Whatever may be the facts at the front, the mood in Tehran at the outset is one of confidence, excitement, patriotic and Islamic fervor, and rallying 'round the regime. There is also shock and some incredulity, with the inevitable questions concerning the pass to which Iran appears to have come, where a smaller neighbor such as Iraq would dare to attack a larger and supposedly stronger neighbor such as Iran. Not a few Iranians, we suspect, recall that during the Shah's period, whatever his faults, such an attack by Iraq would have been out of the question, given the sheer preponderance of Iran's military power, real or imagined (in any event, untested).

But for the moment these doubts and questions are swept aside in a wave of patriotic and Islamic fervor, buoyed by the traditional sense of Persian cultural and indeed racial superiority over the Arabs and particularly those from neighboring Iraq, with a people that had assaulted and converted to Islam the kingdoms of the high Persian plateaus in the eighth century. From the Ayatollah Khomeini comes a series of calls to the nation to defend its Revolution "even to the point where each one of our militants is martyred. . . . Everything we are doing is for Islam. What matter if we die? We shall go to Paradise." But the Ayatollah's messages also invoke Persian nationalism, a sentiment heretofore decried as inconsistent with the dogma that Iran's Revolution rests on Islam, which knows no national borders. This time the Ayatollah declares that "our beloved Motherland is prepared to send every one of its children to struggle against the falsehood." . . .

For a people like the Iranians, not celebrated for a sense of discipline in their history, their immediate response to the challenge of war on this scale deserves recognition. It is reminiscent of a similar record of discipline in the chaotic weeks of the Revolution in early 1979, when street masses seemed to appear and disband on cue and when instances of miscreants taking advantage of the collapse of public order to loot or pillage were rare indeed. Yet this is also to be expected in the early days of the war, when patriotic fervor would be naturally at a high level. The greater test will come as the war goes from days to weeks and possibly months and the economic dislocation and shortages have their impact on the general public, not to mention the capacity of the armed forces to carry on the effort. . . .

Meanwhile, there remains the issue of the American hostages, now beginning their 11th month of captivity. The three of us in the Foreign Ministry are aware that this tragic affair can be said to have contributed to the hostilities, at least indirectly, and thus a still further consequence of the fateful events of November 4, 1979. To what degree did Iran's international isolation, itself certainly a consequence of the hostage affair together with the other internationally perceived excesses of the Revolution, figure in the timing and degree of the Iraq attack? As a speaker at this week's Friday prayers in Tehran reportedly said, "Oh Blind World! There is not a single country which defends us. It is a veritable crime." Indeed, it is; but it is self-imposed. . . .

For the three of us, in our corner of the ministry, there is an escape mechanism available—the news from VOA and BBC (and the somewhat contradictory news from Radio Peace and Progress in Baku), magnificent music on the cassette and record player sent to us by the papal nuncio, and there is Radio Monte Carlo late at night, reminding us in its modern rock and the sultry Arabic of its female announcer that there is another world out there.

As the French would say, *"sauve qui peut"* (every man for himself).

DAY 325, *September 23, 1980*—Caught in an air raid on Tehran, followed by an evening blackout of the city! What else can develop to complicate our lives? And what does this deepening fighting between Iran and Iraq mean for the Majlis consideration of the hostage issue?

Yesterday was not what I would describe as my best day in Tehran. Down with a bacillary infection of some kind, a sore throat, and generally tired. The day was another marked by severe dust storms that filled the sky with billowing dust clouds and covered the floor and furniture of our room (and us) with a heavy coating of Iran's limited topsoil.

Then at about 2:15 P.M. we heard explosives in the direction of Tehran's airport, followed by the thump-thump sound of what seemed to be (and probably was) some kind of antiaircraft firing. And over the next hour there were jet fighters (Iranian) actively heard (but less seen) over the city. Indeed the Iraqis *had* attacked, here as well as in half a dozen or so other "bases" around the country, in what one must assume is a deliberate power demonstration designed to deter the Iranians from whatever they may really be up to on the borders. Or, perhaps one should say, what either of these two countries is up to in this strange war or near-war between countries that, one is tempted to say, so richly deserve each other.

The evening TV brought the expected tone and content in the newscasts.

Preceded by patriotic slogans, music, and the usual te deums for the ARK, there were long statements from him, the president, and the prime minister. All seemed carefully designed to calm public opinion, to reassure everyone that Iran had nothing to fear from the criminal, anti-Islamic, bloodsucking Baathists of Iraq. Saddam Hussein was described as a power-mad lackey of—you guessed it—the United States, who had no genuine support from the Iraqi people. The people of Iran could rest assured that Iran would soon deliver a decisive blow against Iraq and that in the meantime the people should stay calm and be confident in their armed forces.

Meanwhile, it had been announced that the city would be under a total blackout, and the newscasts were frequently interrupted with warnings that the order was a serious one and that, failing better implementation in the city, electric power would be cut. Our room has exceedingly heavy drapes so that while we were required to keep overhead lights off we could read and write by table lamps. Outside the blackout was indeed spotty at first, but by 11:00 P.M. the city was in eerie darkness from our windows, accompanied by an eerie silence as well. Automobiles, at least in the ministry area, apparently were literally banned from the streets, and not a sound could be heard of traffic. . . .

Today there were massive street parades and demonstrations marking the opening of schools tomorrow (not the universities, still subject to some sort of undefined cultural revolution). At this moment a large column is moving past the ministry, the air full of slogans shouted in unison, no doubt denunciations of that rascal in Baghdad who, as the ARK says, is a false Muslim, warring on Islam, his evil deeds the consequence of Washington's machinations.

What next, one must ask. And what of the hostages? In the short run, this can only hurt our cause, given what will now become a total preoccupation with Iraq. . . .

DAY 326, *September 24, 1980*—I feel like hell warmed over. A week into a bout with dysentery of an as-yet-undetermined type, I am only now beginning slowly to come out of it. And the weakened condition has produced a sore throat and now a dreary head cold that further exacerbates my mental state. . . . The important thing is that I am coming out of it. Today the low-grade fever of the past few days seems ended, I have some appetite back, and, praise God, things are tightening up where it matters.

All this has required time, but presumably it would not have ended without the medicines and vitamins that our doctor has prescribed. He is more lavish than the American medical practice in handing out antibiotics and pills of all sorts. For that matter, he learned it in the United States, where he studied medicine and did his internship.

Regrettably our food situation hasn't helped, and I have recently found eating more a burden than a pleasure, our menu being unchanged these past 320-plus days. So my weight was down and presumably my resistance as well. And, with dysentery, I was of course advised to stick to rice, mast (yogurt), tea, and toast. . . . Toast doesn't exist, so we have taken to fabricating it of Iranian nan (bread) in the imperial food warmer in the kitchen. Worse, for some reason, rice seems to have gone into short supply. But today, when the doctor was in again, we appealed to him, he spoke to Protocol, and there is now improvement. . . .

All of this reached the point yesterday where the Swiss ambassador, in on his weekly visit, suggested the idea of my checking into a hospital for a few days to get some good lab work done and put me back on my feet. So last night (we learned today), the acting protocol chief spoke to Mansur Farhang (now in Bani-Sadr's office, formerly at the UN) about the possibility of some kind of arrangement that would get me to some hospital and guarantee security while I was there. The Swiss ambassador even talked of one of his officers being in the room with me at all times!

Today, fortunately, I felt a good deal better, and hopefully the difficult task—logistically and security-wise—of getting me to a hospital has been set aside.

———

Later—It is night, the third in the ?-day war, the Iran-Iraq War, the war of the Shatt-al-Arab, or whatever. There is again a blackout, as there no doubt will be for the duration, although hopefully the air attacks on the respective capitals will not be repeated. Tonight the guard brings in a kerosene lantern for our use while we are en route to the bathroom and back, which is up and down one of the darkest flights of stairs in the building. Within our room the curtains suffice, although we are again told to turn out our overhead lights.

The guards and kitchen staff are reacting cautiously. Among the zealous, Islamic types, there was immediate élan, new zeal. But today one sensed more apprehension about where this might lead. None of them has much knowledge of the real situation. But then who does? . . .

We, the United States, of course, are the villain in the piece, as usual. Tonight's TV news showed clips of destruction of houses in border areas, the announcer telling us that this showed the work of Saddam Hussein "as directed by the USA." The masses believe this, of course, but who else? And who is fooled, but the masses, by such statements as that by Bani-Sadr yesterday that Iran's problem was that its U.S.-supplied military equipment was inferior to that supplied by the Soviets to Iraq! The whole of it is cuckoo, but that does not deter the Soviets from their current line that "it is the United States that is behind the crisis"! What poppycock *that* is! It has been a long time since a serious world crisis has developed where our influence, our leverage with either party, is so minimal as it is in this case!

DAY 327, *September 25, 1980*—The next morning. My physical condition continues to improve, though my cold has settled in my head, leaving me in a foul mood. Having served in this part of the world long enough to accept that the subject of one's stools can be almost a normal subject of conversation, I still find the whole business less than bearable. But, *c'est la vie*. After much negotiation involving the Swiss, the doctor, and Protocol, arrangements have finally been made for us to send out stool specimens. So today, for the second "run," our former driver arrived and dutifully waited in the guard room while we produced the required item, carefully taped the cup together, wrapped the whole in a plastic bag, and with some apology handed it over. Life goes on.

But life is not very pleasant, given the latest developments on the war front—not very pleasant for the Iranians, not very pleasant in terms of the outlook for the hostages. Currently reading Shakespeare's *Richard III*, I came on this quote, which perhaps applies: "The world is grown so bad that wrens make prey where eagles dare not perch."

One wonders if the Iranian leaders are awakening to the reality of the predicament they have created for themselves. Here this country is, subjected to what is a frontal power play by Iraq, a development nothing less than a clear invasion across an international frontier, and what options are available to Iran?

A military response of its own? Perhaps, and presumably it has some capacity to hurt Iraq, by sea and to some degree in air power, but if press reports are correct, they are being bested by the Iraqis on most fronts. Such is the condition they have reached militarily, two years into their Revolution. The military is largely discredited, its leadership having gone through numerous purges and executions, the rank and file disorganized, its equipment probably deteriorated, training inadequate, spare parts unavailable—all of which is reflected in the comment by Bani-Sadr that its U.S.-supplied equipment is inferior to that supplied by others to Iraq. That statement is clearly a cover-up for Iran's poor performance now on the front. And how galling it must be for this proud people to be bested in battle, so far, by their detested neighbors, the Iraqis (and Arabs at that!).

Or an appeal by Iran to friends for help? Where are Iran's friends? Its source of spares for its military inventory is now the hated Great Satan, the United States. Its immediate neighbors? The Soviet Union is linked to Iraq by a friendship treaty and by a military equipment supply line. Turkey and Pakistan? They have been alienated by the ARK's denunciations of their governments as un-Islamic. Iran's Arab neighbors? Who among them has any regard for the Revolution here? Most will support Iraq or seek to avoid involvement.

Or an appeal to the Security Council? If there ever was an issue where one of the two states involved, Iran, would appear to have a case immediately to appeal to that body for action to stop "aggression," this would be it. But the UN has been consistently denounced by the regime as an instrument of the United States and the West, and Iran's record in response to UNSC appeals on the hostage issue would make the leaders appear as real hypocrites should they now appeal for help from that quarter. And who on the broader world scene, however unenthusiastic most are about the Saddam Hussein regime in Iraq, have regard for the regime here, given its conduct, internally and externally, over the past 18 months?

It is all very sad. One is tempted to gloat over this country's situation—God knows their regime has brought it on themselves. But there is no satisfaction in that, other than the momentary pleasure in seeing a regime that has so abused us now given its comeuppance by a neighboring Islamic regime. American interests will inevitably lie more, over the longer term, with a country and a people like Iran and the Iranians than with Iraq, especially an Iraq led by a regime like that of Saddam Hussein. And more fundamentally it is tragic that a country such as Iran, with its rich traditions and its inherent strength, should be humiliated by a small and hostile neighbor. Our interests, over the longer term, lie with Iran—both in terms of historical and cultural contacts and in sheer power terms—it is Iran that dominates, or can dominate, the Persian Gulf.

It is all very sad on one other important count, and that is the hostage issue. Further delay is now inevitable, simply because of what will be a total preoccupation with the war. When that ends, hopefully within days or weeks at most, the outlook will depend on the nature of the outcome. A humiliated Iran will have little interest then in making concessions to the United States, even though logic would suggest that the need to dispose of the issue should then be even clearer and more urgent than now. The thought of further delay is not pleasant to contemplate. But what troubles me most on that front is the now-renewed anxiety that must be felt by the families at home. Before hostilities between Iran and Iraq erupted, there seemed at least the prospect of movement on the issue, and that must have buoyed expectations at home. Now those hopes have been dashed, amid what is probably concern on the part of many families that some of the hostages might even be in physical danger should the war continue. And on that score, we three have not failed to make some contingency planning regarding cover should bombs begin falling here. . . .

A *footnote*—As Mike observed this morning, surely Murphy's Law has applied to the hostage issue: if anything can go wrong, it will. There seems no end to the obstacles and further complications that manage to delay progress on the issue, this war being but the latest.

It is night, 8:30 P.M., and Tehran is blacked out under a magnificent full moon. . . . We hear aircraft overhead and the sound of antiaircraft guns in the distance. From the windows we see the bursts of the guns all around the city—though at a considerable distance—but there is no plane visible or to be heard anywhere. Visibility, because of the moon, is nearly perfect. What the gunners are firing at is totally unclear. After five minutes or so it is quiet again. But by now the power is cut, and we move about and write by candlelight and with the help of a kerosene lantern provided by the guard. He is as nervous as a cat, as is the kitchen man on night duty. For us, watching from the windows, it is something akin to fun, a word one is loath to use with reference to anything as cruel and senseless as war. But an adventure it surely is, and our third-floor windows give us a kind of ringside seat on what is going on. . . .

What madness it all is! Two countries that need a war like a hole in the head! And we sit here, the three of us, and our 49 colleagues, hapless captives of a regime that seems capable of little beyond hatred of the United States and a blind adherence to its own precepts of Islam.

The Tehran radio announcer pleads: "Heroic people of Tehran, especially those living in the vicinity of Mehrabad Airport: Please allow the aircraft to land. The aircraft is one of ours. Stop shooting at it."

It is comic and yet sad. . . .

DAY 328, *September 26, 1980*—Today is son Bill's 21st birthday. Twenty-one years since that memorable day at George Washington University Hospital in Washington when Penne introduced this strapping nine-pound, five-ounce baby boy into the world. I well remember my first look at him—apprehensive that he might have three legs or 12 fingers and relieved to find him completely normal. Well, almost. To me his face seemed scrunched into the strangest shape and color, and I recall asking the nurse if that was normal, which she laughingly assured me it was, because "all babies look like that" at birth. Penne and I were both on cloud nine for days thereafter, and I am proud to say that in terms of Bill's subsequent years we have never been off it as far as he is concerned. Today for him will be another day facing demanding studies at the Naval Academy. Today he is, in legal terms, a man, an adult, but the maturity that goes with that number of years in his case has already been there a long time.

I went from the hospital to a nearby church that day 21 years ago and said some heartfelt prayers of thanksgiving for what had happened and of hope for the future. I repeat them today, for Bill and the future that lies ahead of him.

DAY 329, *September 27, 1980*—This morning, a beautiful and sunny day, the air outside our windows is alive with John Philip Sousa marches and other patriotic music and recordings of "Allah O'Akbar" to boost the fighting morale of the people. Streets are greatly reduced in traffic because of a total ban on private cars on the streets and highways of Iran during daylight hours. The purpose is to save fuel, obviously, and necessary, given the demands of the military and the fact that the refinery at Abadan, which supplies Iran with half its refined products, is in flames and probably destroyed. That, if true, is a very serious development. It apparently has not yet been conceded by the regime, and there is little public awareness of the loss, but when the public *does* become aware of it, there will be a very profound psychological impact. . . .

Facts, of course, are never clear in war—and less so to us sitting where we do. Today the Iranian press claims massive Iraqi materiel losses, e.g., "72 MiGs, 114 tanks destroyed" in contrast to only modest losses by Iran, only 8 aircraft and 16 tanks. The truth is somewhere in between, but where? Truth does not apply to the Great Satan. We are the real villain in the piece. . . .

Hence it is difficult to see how this war can have anything but a deleterious effect on the prospects for our release. No one here, emotionally and psychologically, is going to want to be seen as negotiating a deal with the Great Satan, the country behind the hated Saddam Hussein. Over the longer term, however, things may be different. This war will have dramatically demonstrated Iran's lack of friends and the costs of holding hostages. That appreciation will help; the question will be how long it will take to see it translated into movement. . . .

14

October 1980: Window on a War

Nearing 11 months as hostages, suddenly we had become witnesses to war. On one occasion we watched almost at eye level as Iraqi jets streaked low across the ministry's gardens; at other times we stood at blacked-out windows and watched the fireworks of apparently futile AA [antiaircraft] fire directed at anything that moved. And within earshot during the day we could hear martial music blaring from loudspeakers along distant city streets, music designed to stir up popular fervor, much of it from John Philip Sousa, including "The Stars and Stripes Forever."

That was, no doubt, an unintended recognition of an American contribution. More important, there were strident accusations that the United States was involved with Iraq in coordinating strategy for the war. We feared this would divert the parliament from focusing on the hostage issue. The real reason for continued delay, however, appeared to lie more in time-consuming differences within the regime on the conditions to be demanded of the United States rather than on possible maneuvering with the Reagan campaign to preclude our freedom in an "October surprise."

DAY 334, *October 2, 1980*—How the war is going becomes increasingly obscure, with claims from the two sides virtually canceling each other out.

197

Iran's official list of tanks and other wheeled vehicles destroyed over the past several days, if true, would mean that a substantial part of Iraq's inventory is gone. So we must dismiss such claims as largely rhetoric. . . .

It is difficult for anyone, above all, us . . . to know what the real situation is at the front. But it seems clear that Iraq's hopes of quickly capturing the Shatt-al-Arab cities, Ahwaz and Dezful, have not succeeded and that Iranian resistance has been stiffer than expected. I also have the feeling that the Iranian Air Force has performed rather better than that of Iraq. Today we learned that the Iranian Air Force has been strengthened by the release from prison of some 80 to 90 air force pilots charged with involvement in the alleged coup plot of early July. The report would have it that Bani-Sadr went to the prison himself, offered them freedom if they would join in Iran's defense, and, when they agreed, kissed them on both cheeks to seal the contract.

All of which contributes to a notion I have that Iran, as the aggrieved party in this war, is demonstrating a rather strong surge of patriotism and nationalism that may yet serve them rather well at the front. That assumes, of course, that they can pull themselves together in some sort of organized defense and also have the resources, the reserves, to make a strong defense and ultimately an offense possible. Their record on that score since the Revolution would have to make one skeptical that they are capable of that.

DAY 335, *October 3, 1980*—I feel at loose ends, lacking any enthusiasm for much of anything. I weary of what I write. There is no mail, and little prospect for any in the coming weeks. Our reading material is at a low point; we have read through most of our last batch of books from sympathetic embassies. . . . I am bored. There is nothing we can do to affect the war, and the war, despite some movement in the Majlis, has effectively put any decision from that body on the hostage issue on ice until the war ends or winds down. We have few ideas left to pass to our colleagues working on the issue at home. We receive a message from that quarter assuring us that we are being "thought of often, during this period when you presumably hear the air raid sirens daily, an additional burden you did not need."

That person is right, we didn't need the war. But he is wrong on the air raid sirens. Hearing them is at least a change, a diversion, something different in the dreary routine of our lives. . . . My boredom and depression are not unrelated to the fact that tomorrow marks our 11th month of captivity. Eleven long months inside a building, a prison, deprived of freedom and, worse than a common prisoner, deprived of seeing our families. Eleven months are forever lost in experiencing the love and laughter, and problems too, of family life— that remains the heaviest burden of this whole tragic affair.

Later—I have just watched the evening TV news coverage of today's Friday prayers at the Tehran University grounds. As usual, the numbers were probably in the hundreds of thousands. But perhaps even more than usual, the atmosphere was one of particular frenzy. The prayers begin with a cheerleader of sorts, standing on a stage and leading the crowd in slogans, both religious and political in nature. . . . Today the preliminaries ended with the Tehran Friday preacher, Hojjatol-Islam Khamanei, striding on stage, being handed the bayonet-tipped rifle that such preachers always brandish in their right hand as they speak, and reveling in the shouts of the crowd. Khamanei is a black-bearded, bespectacled mullah who looks the part of a Rasputin and who no doubt plays exactly that kind of role along with the other mullahs in the entourage that surrounds the ARK.

DAY 336, *October 4, 1980*

Hi, Jim, Chip, Bill,

I write this by my trusty candle—keeping my eye occasionally on the TV screen here in the guard's room as we watch the evening news. There is a lot of film on the war—shots of captured tanks, burned-out trucks, and men in various places being called up for service and, for the camera, busy shouting all sorts of slogans about Khomeini, Islam, and beating the Iraqis and marching on Baghdad. I will remember Iran as a place where everyone shouts—at Friday prayers, in demonstrations, for the TV cameras. And they can't shout without flailing the air with their arms and fists at the same time. It's a national pastime. They thrive on it. If they put as much energy into work as they do into their demonstrations, this country would *move*. . . .

I hope all is well with each of you. I think of you a great deal—imagining to myself what each of you is doing at any given moment. By now it must be cool in Minnesota—good football weather for Chip, who, I assume, is again playing for the navy team. And Jim—I can hear his trumpet now—probably driving Duchess wild. Bill—I wrote to the superintendent to thank him for that great Navy Band salute to the hostages. The academy has been superb in its support for us. . . .

Not a day passes that I do not thank my God that I live (or *did* live) in a country like ours in which three young men like you can have the opportunities and hope for the future that you do.

Good luck, Dad

DAY 337, *October 5, 1980*

Dearest Penne,

I'll write a short note, against the possibility that the Swiss may be in tomorrow. They may not, since they will again have no mail, but we are encouraging them to continue coming in nonetheless. We fear that if the practice is interrupted, it may be difficult to restart. . . .

We are a bit down these days. As the war drags on, the hostage issue drags with it. Day after day we wait, while we and our colleagues sit. Forgotten by most Iranians. As if the hard-liners ever cared about the human aspects! Most of the time I think we each try to put the issue out of our minds—and focus on a book, news of the war (it's at least a diversion), and dabbling with paints. I spend about one and a half to two hours on that most afternoons, Mike does more. We can lose ourselves completely in that, however slow we may be or bad the product is. We spend some minutes each day leaning out our windows, sometimes watching people come and go in the ministry's inner courtyard. The employees look at us—some nervously, others with curiosity, some who seem to try to tell us by their looks that they are sympathetic. Occasionally one will wave. To each—whatever the look—I respond with a cold stare. But I am correct and will not offend. Sometimes two or three will gather and stare, at which I withdraw. I don't want to make myself an object of curiosity.

Whoops, news interrupted. Another air raid alert. They've been going on all day, since Iran rejected Iraq's offer of a cease-fire this morning. . . .

How depressing it all is. Here we sit, there you wait. Our elections approach. Our full year is only a month away! I can remember how we said early on that, unlike the guys on that ship (*Pueblo?*) in North Korea, we'd *never* be here a year. God, how tragic it all is. Meanwhile, the news suggests that Reagan will win—I find that hard to believe.

Love, B

DAY 338, *October 6, 1980*—The boredom seems heavy these days as we wait out this war; . . . so long as it lasts, there will be no real movement on the hostage issue. In a sense, however, the war at least relieves some of the boredom. We have a renewed interest in news developments and the diversion that occasional air raid alerts offer.

Like yesterday. At midafternoon there was the sound of explosions from the direction of the airport, followed a few minutes later by the wail of air raid sirens. Iranian radar defenses were obviously not up to speed. The Iraqis claim the destruction of two 747 aircraft on the ground; the Iranians admit no losses and assert that one Iraqi plane was shot down. As usual the facts are hard to come by. . . .

In the midst of one alert, one of our kitchen workers volunteered that "all this mess is Khomeini's fault." Following which, when Vic commented, "Yes, and someday the people will recognize that," this person brusquely responded as he walked away, "Ha! The people—they are cows!"

Such comments, which we hear occasionally, cause us to wonder how much dissatisfaction may in fact exist beneath the now high-riding crest of patriotism and Islamic fervor being assiduously cultivated by the regime's propaganda organs. There cannot be much expression of it, and yet it is surely there, to some degree. How much will not be clear for some time, and what conse-quences it may have will be heavily dependent on how the hostilities end. . . .

Well! I've come as close to a pair of MiG-23s as I ever care to come! At about five this afternoon, out of a beautiful clear blue sky, we heard the sound of explosions to the west and south of us. I was sitting close by an open window, painting, and got up quickly to look out. And there, within spitting distance, was a pair of Iraqi MiGs leisurely crossing overhead, certainly no more than 750 feet almost directly over the ministry's gardens. I was so startled that I froze on the spot, although it occurred to me that perhaps they're going to drop a bomb or two on the government buildings in our immediate area.

I think I have never seen a MiG before, and I was startled to see how large they seemed. But what really struck me was their leisurely speed as they passed virtually in front of us at what seemed like almost eye level. One of them had its drag chute trailing behind, presumably as a consequence of the bombing run. And their speed was obviously a deliberate flaunting of their ability to fly into and directly over Tehran without being detected. After they crossed over us, they swung to the west slightly and then gunned their speed as we watched their afterburners. . . .

I can imagine the excitement of my three sons were I able to describe directly to them what happened. I've been on edge ever since!

DAY 340, *October 8, 1980*—Looking out our carefully blacked-out windows last night, I think I had not seen such total darkness or experienced such total quietness since I lived on the farm in Minnesota and stood in the middle of a quiet barnyard on a moonless, cloudy night. It is remarkable how effective the blackout is and how absolutely the streets are deserted. Probably it is hazardous in any event to be on the streets. Auto lights are not allowed, and driving without lights on Tehran's streets would be taking one's life in one's hands, what with open jubes along the sides of the street and all manner of obstructions at one place or another in the streets. And to walk in the darkness would probably invite challenges by gun-toting revolutionaries, busy enforcing the blackout. . . . Earlier this evening the AA guns were relatively busy, obviously shooting at shadows—but nonetheless zealous. We joke among ourselves that when the alert is sounded, we can relax; by that time the Iraqis, if they've been here at all, are already back in Baghdad. . . .

Today we hear that the Majlis commission on the hostages "took some decisions" and continued work on others. We wonder what that means. Yesterday's *Tehran Times* carried an interesting interview with Mansur Farhang, the Iranian ex-professor at Sacramento State (I think) in California, who, for a time, was Iran's UN representative and is now here on Bani-Sadr's staff. The interview was a candid reminder to the newspaper's readers of the mistakes the regime had made on the hostage issue, especially in frustrating the work of the UN Commission of Inquiry last spring. Prolonging the issue now was not in Iran's interest. He termed those people who said they were not interested in international opinion on the hostage issue as "not realistic." Iran had to take account of the "realities of international politics." Iran's refusal to accept these realities had given Iraq a "clear field," and "for the first time in the history of the UN, a Security Council resolution calling on two contending parties, Iran and Iraq, to end the fighting had not condemned the aggressor, who in this case was clearly Iraq."

How right he is. Iran is losing the diplomatic and public relations war with Iraq, however the military struggle ends. The same point was made by Bani-Sadr in an interview on October 6: "This is the first time in history that a country comes under aggression with no one in the world supporting it. . . . Iran is isolated." . . .

Such indeed is the product of the ARK's rhetoric and rigidity of the past 18 months that he has alienated all the Arab states by his call for the overthrow of the governments of many of them. And he has antagonized the rest of the world by his stance on the hostage issue. . . .

For that matter, however the war ends, even if Iran *is* able to pull itself together militarily and pushes the Iraqis back across their borders, the cost will have been frightful for Iran's economic potential. An economy already crippled will now be saddled with much of its oil refinery plants destroyed or damaged, with its oil fields and pipelines disabled, with its major port at Khorramshahr demolished, railroads cut, and its military reserves heavily drawn down—not to mention the countless ancillary costs of war, the disruption of what productive capacity existed, and the death and injury to people.

DAY 343, *October 11, 1980*—Today, this morning, the acting chief of protocol walked in, unannounced, with the Spanish ambassador. The chief left us, and we talked for well over an hour. It was a most pleasant diversion. And unexpected. . . .

The ambassador was genuinely concerned about our situation, asking repeatedly what he could do to help . . . send books? He offered to try to get us a videocassette player. We said, "By all means!" He also saw no reason why he shouldn't press the Foreign Ministry that we should be allowed access to a tennis court! We said by all means to that, too, but we all laughed that that was about as likely as being freed tomorrow. . . .

At one point in our conversation he commented that he had heard I had taken the position that I would not leave myself until all of my colleagues were freed . . . and said that he felt this was an honorable position to take. I simply acknowledged what he said, while adding that, of course, if we were offered freedom, I was sure the department would expect me to act on that basis.

That brief exchange—and a subsequent conversation on the subject initiated by Mike tonight—triggered for me another agonizing reappraisal of that whole issue in my mind. What *is* my responsibility in that area? Where does my obligation to the service end—if it ever can end—and my personal obligation to myself and family begin? What is involved in the question of escape, a large question indeed? If I were offered freedom by the regime, I have no doubt that the department would order me, and my two colleagues, to leave, however much even then I would be pained at the thought of leaving behind my 49 colleagues. And I would obey that order.

But short of that, does the option of escape exist for us? Whether it does, in fact, or not, that option must be seen on two grounds: the practical one of feasibility and the second one of the rightness or wrongness of exercising the option, assuming it is feasible.

My own sense of honor, of service, and of responsibility precludes escape, unless I can be persuaded that I could do more for my colleagues in Washington than here. I doubt that I could. Here I cannot do much, either, but I am at least available, in Tehran, as a point of contact for the department. It may yet be demonstrated that, as this thing evolves, I—we—can play a role in the release process. I also feel that by staying here, by patiently sitting it out with pride and dignity, that we demonstrate in this additional way to the Iranians the wrongness of what they have done and the strength of our country.

There is, of course, also the question that would have to be considered of what impact any attempted escape on our part would have on the welfare or future of our 49 colleagues. Indeed, that question has to be said to be *all* important. We can all agree that we should do nothing that in any way complicates the outlook for freedom for those men and women.

There remains the question whether there is a prospect for our release. If we were to conclude at some point that we are putting ourselves in danger by remaining—or that the prospects for action to release us are nil—then the option of escape would have to be considered. And should be, both in terms of logic and morality. We would do no one any good by remaining then. On that point, I have been, since the first day, 100 percent convinced in my own mind that we will be released and that we will be unharmed, all of us. I have never had any doubt on that score. That rests both on a strong faith and also in my reading of the Iranian scene. That being the case, I have not felt the personal compulsion to even consider the escape option.

Having said all that, I must concede that others may feel differently. I think my two colleagues themselves do. They must come to their own conclusions, their own role is different from mine as chargé, but they too are members of a disciplined service and also responsible to their compatriots.

Finally there is the family equation, the personal responsibility that I have to them. That, too, is strong, but I think they would understand why I feel that in these circumstances my first responsibility must be to my colleagues here. And I can live with that conclusion because of the confidence we will be released. If that confidence were lacking, then would my responsibility to my family not be greater? Perhaps. But *with* that confidence—and feeling that my family shares in that confidence—I can live with the conclusion that I must sit tight, keeping my patience and dignity intact against the day when my simply being here may be helpful, or at least reassuring, to my 49 colleagues, who I hope will credit the three of us with having done the right thing by staying on board this drifting, but still not sunk, ship.

DAY 344, *October 12, 1980*—Rereading what I wrote last night, I have no problem with it. It does not speak to the point of the department's role. What I have written rests on my assumption that at no point could I—we—even consider an escape without the department authorizing it. That is because we would, assuming we could get beyond this building, be dependent on someone to move beyond that point. Another embassy? Iranians? Other neighboring governments? And, of course, the implications for our 49 colleagues of any such attempt. The latter is now—and I think will remain—decisive in my own judgment, because anything, in my view, that would jeopardize or complicate their situation and the prospects for their release, would be wrong. . . . I also remain skeptical of the odds of getting beyond this building without detection. For all these reasons I find myself convinced, at least for now, that we have no real alternative but to sit tight. . . .

The war is nearing the end of its third week. There appears no end in sight. In several respects, the fighting deepens and intensifies. Popular emotions grow on both sides, feeding on the distrust and dislike that has traditionally characterized relations between Persians and Iraqis. Third-party positions, until now marked by a strong preference for noninvolvement, are beginning to reflect a willingness to choose sides, raising the risk of broadening conflict. For us, and probably for much of the outside world but including the populace of both combatants, the facts of the matter on the ground remain as unclear as ever, although the Iraqis appear to be committing additional forces. Moreover, despite some Iranian resistance, the bulk of Khorramshahr appears to be in Iraqi hands, and their forces have crossed the Karun River and have the city of Abadan as their next objective.

The leadership in Tehran continues to talk of heroic resistance by its forces that has blunted and humiliated the attacking Iraqis. They also speak of an imminent Iranian counteroffensive. But this seems not to materialize easily, and the fact remains that Iraqi forces appear well entrenched in several areas. If the Iranians have the advantage in any area, it is possibly in the air, where their aircraft and pilots seem to continue to demonstrate a degree of both tactical and strategic superiority. And, of course, at sea, where the Iranian Navy has had the upper hand from the beginning, effectively controlling the Persian Gulf and totally denying Iraq any use of Basra or other access to the sea by way of the gulf. Hence the growing importance of the Jordanian connection for Iraq, King Hussein now outspokenly open in support of Baghdad, offering it full use of the sea access via Aqaba. Saudia Arabia remains avowedly neutral, but of its identification with and support for Baghdad there can be no doubt.

In the face of this situation, the regime here in Tehran appears to find assurance in its habitual reliance on self-created political mythology and the ultimate assurance of God and Islam. . . .

The myth of American backing and direction of its alleged agent, the "godless and bloodsucking Saddam Hussein," has by now become virtual dogma in the Iranian media and in government statements. The speaker of the Majlis, Rafsanjani, a real cleric, professes, however, to see a much more Machiavellian plot. In a speech at this week's Friday prayer gathering in Tehran, he describes a clever scheme on the part of the Americans, Russians, and the British to push Iraq into aggression against Iran so that, in the fighting that would then ensue, both countries would so expand their arms that they would need later to *increase* oil production and sales abroad (to the benefit of the three schemers) to obtain the necessary funds to make arms purchases. . . .

There is clearly intense public pride in the air force that remains, TV films now to be seen every evening of Iran's military hardware in action. But most of the films appear to be prewar and some are even prerevolutionary, especially those of impressive flypast demonstrations of both Phantoms and the F-14s. Among our guards are those who watch these films and exclaim with bitterness that "they," the clerical leadership, "have ruined our air force. They thought they could defend Iran with prayer beads and 'Allah O'Akbars'!" Among the kitchen force are those who, speaking of the destruction at the Abadan refinery, lament that slogans and "Allah O'Akbars" are not gong to rebuild that installation so vital to Iran's economic future. These persons are not unpatriotic. On the contrary, their patriotism is real, and their anger at the Iraqis is intense. But their anger at the hard-line clerical elements is also discernibly mounting, simultaneously with their pride in and regard for the now long-maligned military leadership.

The president's image is also enhanced, at least for the present. The war's implications for his longer-term political strength in the continuing political power struggle is dependent on the outcome of the fighting, with which as commander in chief he is now heavily identified, as well as his own capacity to *use* the opportunities that the war and accompanying public patriotic fervor give to him.

But the clerical elements do not fail to recognize that their political future is also in the balance. They, too, are actively engaged in keeping in the forefront, both in the media and on the fighting front itself. For several days so many of the Majlis members are in the war zones that a quorum is unavailable. Every evening's TV newscast includes films of mullahs en route to the front or standing with groups of soldiers and Pasdaran at the front. The practice of Friday prayer mullahs giving their sermons with a G-3 rifle in one hand and their notes in the other is now more evident than ever. Khomeini's personal defense adviser, the Hojjatol-Islam Khamanei, is frequently reported as just back from the war zones and reporting to the Ayatollah. Never do the groups of soldiers filmed describing their exploits against the Iraqis fail to end their presentation without the ritual three "Allah O'Akbars," followed by the equally ritual "Khomeini is our leader. . . ."

The cost of all this, however much volunteerism may be involved, is obviously enormous. And the costs to Iran and to its economic future can only increase. The massive oil refinery at Abadan, supplying Iran with roughly half of its refined oil products, must now be assumed to be virtually a total loss. Many of the remaining refineries elsewhere in the country are also heavily damaged. Port installations at the major commercial port of Khorramshahr, whether in Iraqi hands or not, are undoubtedly destroyed. Iran's already heavily weakened military inventory is being further and probably dangerously drawn down. The economy as a whole, so weakened as a consequence of revolutionary excesses and the abrupt departure of foreign technicians, now faces further disruptions. Iraqi aircraft continue to try to knock out the almost-completed petrochemical facility at Bandar Abbas, so important for Iran's longer-range plans for its oil sector. Thus, even though superficially in Tehran life in the streets and bazaars is not yet seriously altered, time will see new and massive economic problems, regardless of the military outcome of the war. And with that will come sociopolitical fallout that will be heavily circumstantial in the political power struggle that has not ceased and has yet to be resolved. . . .

As yet there is absolutely no evidence locally that a cease-fire is being considered. On the contrary, the emphasis in public statements is entirely one of confidence in Iran's capacity to succeed militarily. Hence, too much cannot be read into the fact that Iran has sent a delegation to the UNGA and that the prime minister intends to take part in resumed UNSC discussion of the war. This move, however, is at the very least a nod to reality—a recognition that revolutionary rhetoric and a disregard for the UN cannot alone serve Iran's purposes in the real world. It is also a recognition that in boycotting the UN, Iran has given Iraq an open field there, contributing to the "isolation" of Iran that Bani-Sadr now publicly laments. . . .

It is a strange mix, reflecting the political cross-currents of the Arab world, the conflicting forces of pan-Arabism, nationalism, and resurgent Islam; the oil factor; the Arab-Israeli issue; the role of the Soviets and the United States; the force of nonalignment (almost totally neutralized in this conflict by the nature of the two combatants); and the inability of neighbors such as Turkey, India, and Pakistan to play any role at all.

Among the Islamic leadership in Tehran, still totally motivated by Khomeini and the rhetoric and doctrine of the Revolution, the emphasis is on Islam—both as the force that will ensure Iran's success on the battlefield and the force that will see the toppling of such "godless" regimes as that in Baghdad. . . .

We see this theme in almost every statement by the regime's leaders and by its news agencies, in the media, and especially in the heavy exposure of mullahs, so prominent in every newscast, every public relief or clothing drive, and on the floor of the Majlis. Iran's success in the war is ensured not only because of the unity of the Iranian people and their identification with Islam but also because of the shallow nationalism of Saddam Hussein and what the regime's propagandists claim to be growing internal dissension within Iraq over a war forced on them and contrary to their interests as Muslims.

I complete this as the war ends its third week, longer than any pundit, including the three of us, prognosticated at its beginning. Several things seem clear: Iraqi strategic planning and/or the quality and skill of its military seem deficient. Three weeks of fighting, presumably preceded on the Iraqi side by some amount of prior strategic planning and placement of forces, have yet to see Iraq in undisputed possession of any of the cities that it must have set out to capture. And some of these, like Khorramshahr and Abadan, lie only a few miles from the Iraqi border across flat terrain now in good condition for tank advances in the dry season. Second, Iranian resistance seems to have been greater and more determined than anyone, the Iraqis among them, anticipated. Third, however, this capacity to resist seems not to include a capacity to counterattack. A much-talked-of Iranian counteroffensive does not materialize. Fourth, Iran has control of the sea on the gulf (although not on the narrow Shatt), and its air force is generally considered to have outperformed that of Iraq. Fifth, there is evidence in news reports that the Kurdish rebellion in Iran has not receded and may be more serious than is conceded. Sixth, both countries have suffered serious damage to their principal industrial sector—oil. And seventh, Iran's isolation diplomatically remains pronounced, even with Syria and Libya having announced their support. However the war ends, it would seem, therefore, that Iran will have greater difficulty finding the material resources to rebuild than will Iraq—the latter able to count on financial support from Saudi Arabia to help in reconstruction. . . .

Meanwhile, what of the Soviets? Already having a special relationship with Iraq, they have hoped ever since the Revolution to achieve something similar with Iran—at least a relationship profiting from the expulsion of the United States. The Ayatollah's "neither East nor West" philosophy and dictum put basic limits in what the Soviets can achieve, and their invasion of Afghanistan is now a fundamental obstacle to promotion of their interests here. . . .

For the three of us in our room in the Foreign Ministry, the war by now is almost routine—a normal part of our lives. We continue to be glued to every source of news we can find—the local media, VOA, BBC, Radio Israel, Deutsche Welle, Radio Moscow, and the grass-roots information and rumor available to our guard and kitchen staff. For the past ten days, the air raid sirens have virtually ceased to be heard. The nightly blackouts continue, but there is less nervousness over the slightest sliver of light through our drapes.

DAY 346, *October 14, 1980*—A nice thing happened today. The Swiss came in, and although the airport is still closed and hence no mail, they brought telex messages for each of us from our families. Mine I include below:

> Message de Madame Laingen à Monsieur Laingen
> Citation
> Jim and I going to USNA [U.S. Naval Academy] for parade and reception and Oktoberfest at All Saints. My folks celebrate fifty-fifth October 19. House painted, hedge clipped, furnace on, Duchess spayed. Absentee ballot will be late. Gladys coming to help type and edit letters for future. Chip happy with school, job, work, and girlfriend. Bill is XO of Liberty and working hard. Jim still having back problems but plays soccer anyway. Planning to get big butter-ball even though there is a scarcity of turkeys on this side of the world. Expect you home to paint ceiling with cold duck. Almost two years since we were a family; our flags may be fading but our spirits are not flagging. Please stay out of the window. We love you.
> Penne and boys.
> Fin de citation
> Teheran, le 12 octobre 1980

What could be nicer than that? Well, that's a silly question. One thing obviously would be nicer and that would be to be there with them. But how wonderful it will be when it does happen!

The reference to turkeys is a good Penneism; "turkeys" being a good current idiom to denote clods, misfits, and rude, crude, and unattractive types. In other words, we know where the "turkeys" are these days. She is right. . . .

The reference to Bill is to his role on the Annapolis sailing team and to his promotion to become executive officer of his eight-man racing yawl, *Liberty*. That's great. Duchess? That's the dog, the Duchess of Apap Bologna. . . .

Last night a guard on duty came in to ask Mike to show him how to repair his pistol! Where else would prisoners be asked to help the guard keep his guns in working order? It is not the first time or the first of our guards who have sought help from Mike on that score. We have our favorites among the kitchen staff, including one who has recently joined us who works harder than anyone else at keeping our room clean and who delights us with his expressive way of speaking Farsi. Like an Italian, he is all arms and gestures as he talks. And although extremely unprepossessing in appearance, he is sharp, alert, and keeps up-to-date on as much news as he can find to read or listen to. He is a born skeptic, and his reaction to the regime's claims of war successes is marked indeed. There is no fooling him. When he is on duty, he is always coming in to ask Vic what he has heard of note on various news broadcasts. Last night, coming in after we had listened to VOA's 7:30 P.M. news, Vic began by saying: "President Bani-Sadr said. . . ," only to be quickly interrupted by our friend saying, "He's gong to launch a counteroffensive!" That had to be a reference to the constant theme we hear on local media about a counteroffensive that never seems to materialize. He is a worn-looking man, with hardly a tooth in his mouth, but a man who believes in hard work and who has little time for the sloth and indolence he sees around him.

DAY 350, *October 18, 1980*—This morning's news confirms our expectations. The prime minister's speech at the Security Council was totally uncompromising on a cease-fire, calling instead for the total defeat and punishment of Saddam Hussein. He refused to answer questions on the hostage issue at his news conference, but apparently he has promised to say something on the subject before leaving for Algeria later today.

I find myself modestly encouraged by the venture on the part of the regime's PM into the previously despised councils of the UN. It may suggest something about the future. . . . So let us talk of happier things—of a change in our daily lives here at the ministry that reflects the fact that there is decency in the world. That change, a small thing perhaps but large for us, is that we now have a videotape TV set in our room! And for that we can thank the Spanish ambassador. . . .

So our lives are changed. Blackouts are far more tolerable. We have promise of four movies a week, on a rental basis, and the ambassador made his purchase and the film arrangements through an Iranian friend of Mike's, who is in the business and who was more than happy to help. In the first two days we have watched all four, and Mike and Vic have watched them more than once. After watching a Clint Eastwood cowboy film and a Peter Sellers detective spoof (Inspector Clouseau), I felt completely removed from the room. I could have been in a theater at home (though we lacked popcorn!). I actually found myself rubbing my eyes and looking rather absently around me for several minutes before I brought myself back to my hostage status in Iran's Foreign Ministry. There is another world out there, and it looks worth waiting for!

And there are magnificent, decent people like Spain's ambassador to the Islamic Republic of Iran!

DAY 351, *October 19, 1980*—Today the telephone rang; it was Washington, and it was my turn to talk to Penne. We had a half hour—"the luck of the draw," as Mike said. Recently the calls have been cut after five minutes. We have grumbled, and perhaps it was heard. Or perhaps we were simply the beneficiaries of a friendly telephone operator. Who knows? Penne filled me in on her life and the activities of the boys. Bill, in his third year at Annapolis, is hard-pressed academically in aerodynamics, executive officer on his racing yawl *Liberty*, and a company training officer. Chip is enjoying his second year at the University of Minnesota, polishing his first car (a red Ford Pinto) down through the paint, and polkaing every weekend with his Polish-American girlfriend. Jim is goalie on his soccer team, bothered with a muscle spasm in his back, and not very enthusiastic about school. . . .

Today our church, Penne told me, was having a special service in honor of the hostages, and several of its members remain the prime movers in the Sunday night candlelight vigils across the street from the now-closed Iranian Embassy. Those vigils, now almost a year in duration, continue with 15 or 20 stalwarts present each Sunday night, and on November 2, a large turnout of several hundred is expected to mark the one-year anniversary.

What marvelous people! What real dedication, friendship, and concern! How much we are indebted to these people, who have given so much of their time and energy to demonstrate this support for us and their message to Iran that what it has done is wrong, both in human and political terms. We will forever be in their debt.

Today is also the 55th wedding anniversary of Penne's parents, Margaret ("Mother B.") and Fred ("Papoo") Babcock—two people still active and independent in their eighties and a fine example to their friends, their church, and indeed their entire neighborhood. My family, and especially my sons, are extremely fortunate to have had such active and supportive grandparents as neighbors for the many years we have been able to live in Washington. . . . How many home leaves did we camp out at their house? Indeed, I have often said to young, unmarried Foreign Service officers: marry someone from Washington. It greatly simplifies your home leave arrangements, and in time you have available a built-in baby-sitter!

DAY 352, *October 20, 1980*—Today was Eid-ul-Ahza, or Eid-e-Ghorban, the Eid that commemorates Abraham's willingness to sacrifice his son, Isaac, in a test by God of Abraham's faith—an event recalled by both Muslims and Christians, a reminder of the things that these two great religions have in common, a fact obscured in Iran by the ARK's abuse of Islam for his political purposes.

This morning a large white Mercedes bus was in the garden below us, ready to take the ambassadors from Islamic countries to an *Eid Salaam* (audience) with the ARK. And tonight's television carried the text and the show, the ARK sitting on his elevated balcony against a rough brick wall and looking down on the faithful squatting on the floor below him. Cries of "Allah O'Akbar" and "Khomeini is our leader" and the text of his speech followed on the TV newscast, with the Khomeini hymn of praise, a te deum of sorts. One wonders what some of the Islamic ambassadors think in their hearts about this. One wonders how the dean of the group, the Somali ambassador, is regarded by the ARK— whether the latter is reminded that in Tehran, by coincidence, the spokesman for these good Islamic types is this representative of a regime that has recently agreed to a base use agreement by the American Navy! Sacrilege. The Great Satan's clutches are everywhere!

The speech was classic Khomeini. Islam provides everything we need, if we will only read the Koran and abide by it; they say we are "isolated," but we are not isolated; the governments of these states may be against us, but the people support us, in South Asia, in the Near East, in Africa, in the Far East, and "other places"; we will not lay down our arms until the Iraqi mercenaries are driven from our soil and the American puppet Saddam Hussein is overthrown. That and more. It is a further reflection of the closed world in which this man lives and his rejection of reality, deliberately apparently, out of a rigid conviction that Islam has triumphed before, that the Revolution succeeded, and that faith will see the Revolution triumphant again.

But reality is cruel at the moment for Iran: its oil province in danger of total Iraqi occupation, soldiers and civilians dying in larger numbers than is conceded, heating oil rationed, gasoline for private cars rationed at one liter a day, and at least half and perhaps more of its refinery plant in ruins. And there is no evidence yet that beyond heroic resistance, the Iranian armed forces are capable of putting together any kind of force capable of pushing the Iraqis back. The result is reality that sees the Iraqis increasingly dug in and thus inclined to stay. Yet the ARK, receiving the secretary general of the 40-state Islamic Conference, tells him that there is no reason why Iran should agree to receive a special commission from the conference appointed to try to achieve a cease-fire. Iraq is the aggressor, says the ARK, so why should the commission need to come here?

All of this is reminiscent of our own experience last November. Why should Iran receive the Clark-Miller mission? It is the United States that stands condemned. Why should the UN secretary general come—or be received by the ARK—when the embassy seizure was the act of an oppressed people against a "spies' nest" that masterminded American interference in Iran for 37 years?

Unreality. Worse, rigidity. Intellectual rigidity, an arrogance born of a closed mind that has saddled this country with a regime that has destroyed the best in a Revolution that once promised so much. How long can such a state of affairs go on?

DAY 354, *October 22, 1980*—A year to the day since a flash telegram from Washington instructed me to seek an appointment with the prime minister and inform him that we had granted permission to the Shah to enter the United States for emergency medical treatment in a New York hospital. He arrived the next day.

A year later and the Shah is virtually a forgotten man, lying dead in a tomb in Cairo. But the events that his entry into the United States brought about continue, culminating in Iran's war with Iraq now in its fifth week. Once imperial Iran, predicted by the Shah to become the fifth or sixth most industrialized state in the world by the end of this century, now invaded by Arab Iraq, ancient foe of the Persians, its oil fields of Khuzistan partially occupied and otherwise threatened, the cities of Abadan and Khorramshahr beleagured by Iraqi forces, Iraq threatening to retain its hold on captured Iranian territory until Iran accepts its terms on border rectification.

If dead men do in fact turn over in their graves, surely the Shah is restless. His son, the crown prince, coming of age on October 31, is said to plan a message to the Iranian people on the occasion of that formal accession to his throne in exile. The Shah's last prime minister, Shahpour Bakhtiar, announces from Paris that he is ready to work with the Iraqis to achieve the overthrow of the Islamic regime in Tehran. The president of that regime announces that he intends to remain in the field with his troops until the Iraqis have been repulsed. And the Ayatollah Khomeini flings doctrine from his Islamic heights that Iran will not rest until Saddam Hussein's supposedly un-Islamic regime is destroyed. . . .

"Young men fight old men's wars." In the garden below our windows, a group of 60 to 70 new soldiers are drilled each morning. Calisthenics: "Yek, doh, seh, char! Yek, doh, seh, char!" (One, two, three, four!) Bayonet and gun butt drill. Hand-to-hand combat. With their G-3 rifles they slither along the blacktop driveways learning stealth tactics. They assemble on the steps of the entrance to the diplomatic reception rooms for lectures by a phalanx of officers who earn snappy salutes from stragglers. Training in the use of backpacks and helmets. Groups are sent off running around the garden's circular drive. The rawness of the recruits is obvious. Their backpacks flip and flop and slow them down. Their helmets refuse to stay in place. Rifles are held in any and all directions. Jogging is hard work. Some drop out, or they slow to a walk, especially on the far side of the drive where they hope not to be noticed; but they are noticed, and a noncom upbraids them and sends them on. What began as a running patrol of 12 in neat formation ends up with four or five slogging their way with more determination than order, the remainder straggling along in disorder to the rear.

And there is close-order drill. Marching, with the clump, clump, clump of the goose step at a quick command. Again, more determination than precision. But they seem proud of what they are learning, and there are spirited "Allah O'Akbars" to wind up the morning's performance. Young men, learning to fight old men's wars. . . . What grievous seeds of bitterness are being sown for the future. The two countries' historical hostility deepens with each passing day of war. That psychological cost looms larger for the future than even the severe economic costs. And that cost promises to complicate the future of the entire region, the product of the political-military ambitions of a rigid, autocratic, ruthless regime in Baghdad and an equally rigid, narrow-minded, pan-Islamic, and clerical regime in revolutionary Tehran.

DAY 355, *October 23, 1980*—Today the news reports are crowded with rumor and speculation about our imminent release, with one Iranian source suggesting that it could come as early as Monday next. All of this is the product of a number of developments, statements, time, and the imminence of the November 4 elections. We are skeptical.

On the campaign trail both the president and the secretary of state are quoted as expressing the view that although the United States is neutral in the war between Iran and Iraq, that is not to be interpreted as a lack of interest or concern. The United States regards the continued territorial integrity of Iran as in the interest of the entire region; we would be opposed to any attempt at dismemberment of Iranian territory. The president tells an audience that, with the release of the hostages, we would be ready to lift the sanctions, unfreeze the assets, and resume a normal trading relationship with Iran. In Tehran, the prime minister, back from New York and brief stops in Algiers and Tripoli, tells a press conference that he believes the United States has in effect agreed to the ARK's stated conditions for the hostages' release, but that "it is all up to the Majlis. . . ." From the Majlis there are reports that the commission on the hostage issue is completing its recommendations and that the full body will debate the issue on Sunday.

But news reports from official Washington suggest strong caution there, noting that nothing has yet been received from Tehran through official chan- nels, and no one, say press reports, is making any predictions. One reporter notes that an unnamed department source observes that the department's record of making predictions on the course of events in revolutionary Iran "has not been one blemished by accuracy."

Reagan is quoted as saying that he believes the Carter administration's for- eign and defense policies are to blame for having contributed to a situation where the taking of hostages was possible. The administration, says he, "owes an apology to the families of the hostages" for their being held for almost a year. We wonder here whether Reagan is fearful of the effect on voters of a release in the ten days remaining in the campaign. I think he well might—should release come in the week before the elections, the criticism and concern that may exist as to how and why this all happened will be temporarily set aside in what will no doubt be a great national excitement and satisfaction that we are free. I would assume Carter would benefit from that politically.

But we are not packing, though we have information from a source that offers much corroboration to the optimism in the press. We sense that whether release comes before the elections, something is in motion that may well not stop, leading to release sooner than we anticipated a week ago. . . .

Yesterday the Dutch ambassador was allowed in to see us—a distinguished gentleman named Willy Campagne, who is departing on transfer to The Hague. . . . He brought us more books and canned items, and another glossy fashion magazine from the United States—the latter full of magnificent photos and ads of beautifully dressed women. It has not been our practice—any of us—to read fashion magazines in the past. Having met and talked with only one woman here in the past year, a magazine of this sort has a certain appeal!

Today, the German ambassador—Gerhard Ritzel, whom we have not seen for six months and more—came in. Gerhard is about to transfer to Copenhagen—allowed in to see us, as was the Dutch ambassador, for that reason. He is an extremely able, friendly, and highly efficient man—actively engaged behind the scenes on the hostage issue in ways that hopefully will soon manifest themselves. . . . So, we have had a good week, . . . and, however skeptical and cautious we have become from experience, we are not without hope that we are close on to something big, very big indeed. . . .

DAY 356, *October 24, 1980*—Today, a Friday, has been quiet for us. In New York, the Security Council has again met on the Iran-Iraq War. From VOA we learn that [Ambassador to the UN] McHenry spoke out against any territorial dismemberment of Iran, urging a cease-fire and withdrawal of forces. By implication he also criticized Iran, noting that it was unacceptable for any government to call for the overthrow of other governments—in other words, criticizing the ARK's calls for the overthrow of Saddam Hussein. . . . News from Washington continues to quote senior officials, including the vice president, counseling against undue optimism about an early hostage release and noting that we are not yet in direct negotiation on any release proposal. . . . Iraq has announced during the day that its forces have now occupied the entire city of Khorramshahr, referring to it by its Arabic name and speaking of its now having been "returned forever" to Arab sovereignty. Meanwhile, its forces are said to be crossing the Karun River in strength for a full-scale assault on the much-beleagured city of Abadan.

Surely the authorities here, unless they have yet to reveal a military counteroffensive capacity not evident after five weeks of war, must now see the urgent necessity of cooperating in a cease-fire/withdrawal process before the Iraqis become so entrenched in Khuzistan that their withdrawal becomes almost impossible. Should that happen, we will have seen the introduction into the crucial area of the Persian Gulf an irredentist issue of serious consequence for the years ahead.

DAY 358, *October 26, 1980*—"I will miss you very much"—the words of the acting chief of protocol yesterday as he turned and left us, near tears, after telling us good-bye. He came in, very briefly, in midafternoon to say that he was leaving his position immediately. The reason is his failure to seek permission from the front office of this ministry for the visit to us earlier in the week by the German ambassador. He had apparently felt that permission should not be necessary, the German ambassador scheduled to depart Tehran soon and for that reason, as had been the case with the Dutch ambassador, a farewell visit with us might be considered permissible, if unusual. But for reasons known only to the gentlemen occupying the front office, the acting chief in this case had gone too far.

I was emotional myself—we have grown greatly to respect this man—and expressed my irritation at this "madness," this "sickness" in this building. We thanked him for his kindness to us, and I patted him on the back and wished him luck as he turned hurriedly to leave. . . .

It is a tragedy for him and for his country's interests. It needs such men; in this case a man superbly trained in the affairs of protocol—respectful of others, proud of his own country, committed to stay and work with the new regime, and yet summarily bounced. Yet another casualty of this tragic hostage affair.

Tonight, Sunday, we wonder if it is our last Sunday here. The Majlis met in open and closed sessions and will continue its discussion tomorrow. Reportedly it turned down a motion to defer any further consideration of the hostage issue until after the war ends. That's encouraging. . . . Our own optimism has not diminished, even though it is guarded. Mike and I are the optimists on this round, each of us busy cleaning out our gear and getting ourselves ready to leave at a moment's notice, with books sorted and ready to be returned to friendly embassies, undated letters of thanks written to friendly and helpful ambassadors, clothes washed. Vic tells us, "You're gonna put a hex on it if you keep this up! You're gumming up the works." To ward off that hex, he spreads out another jigsaw puzzle—one of the toughest we've got. That should help!

A press report quotes an Iranian source as saying that all of our colleagues have now been moved back to the compound in Tehran. Another hopeful sign. . . . Certainly too much is in motion now to see this apple cart upset. . . . If it comes at *any* time this week, the release will almost certainly strengthen Carter's prospects. And yet, I see no evidence whatsoever this time that the administration has sought to achieve this timing for political purposes. It has evolved in this way, so far as we can see. We wonder, however, whether the Iranians are trying to see a solution before the elections. Does it mean they fear Reagan more than they hate Carter?

There was a time last fall when Carter's standing in the polls climbed sharply as a consequence of the hostage seizure. Then it fell, in part again because of the hostage issue, suggesting for a time that this tragic affair might cause the defeat of a president. Now, should release come this week and the resulting popular euphoria serve to strengthen Carter's standing, perhaps the issue may yet cause his reelection!

What repercussions have ebbed and flowed over the past year over this affair!

I am unnerved at times when I contemplate the role that the strengths and weaknesses of 72 American citizens have played in all of this.

DAY 359, *October 27, 1980*—Another day closer to freedom. God willing, Inshallah. Or, as the Iranian expression puts it, "Baleh, baleh, Inshallah; Cheshm, cheshm, pasferdah." (Yes, yes, God willing; O.K., O.K., day after tomorrow.)

The Majlis has now met on our "fate" for two days running. Still no decisions, so far as we know. And Washington continues to tell the press to quiet down; we are still not in negotiations with the Iranians, etc. . . . It must be a cliff-hanger in the United States, where the whole country seems to be on the edge of its chair, and where our families must be finding it very nerve-wracking indeed, although by this time most of the families are probably pretty immune to euphoria. But the press can't subside, and one can imagine the pressure the families are under from them.

The kitchen staff and guards are convinced we will leave soon. One prediction had it today within 48 hours. The guard offered to buy us small handbags in the bazaar, but I think I will ask the Swiss. The latter sent in some supplies we had asked for today, causing us to wonder whether the contretemps over the acting chief of protocol and the German ambassador means that the Swiss are locked out too. Not yet clear. They had planned to bring in a barber on this week's visit. We are in serious need of haircuts. Perhaps we'll look more like real hostages if we go home looking the way we do. . . .

DAY 360, *October 28, 1980*—The day passes quietly; news this morning had it that the ARK would speak on the hostage issue when he met today, as scheduled, with members of the Majlis. But that was pure press speculation. His sermon dealt mainly with Islam and the meaning of today's religious holiday and with the sins of the "godless" regime in Baghdad. The United States got off without much abuse. . . . The sermon had its usual high state of religious fervor and Khomeini adulation. The cult of personality has set in here with a vengeance, and he seems to welcome it. His appearance at these sessions brings the crowd to its feet, waving its fists and shouting "Allah O'Akbars" and "Khomeini is our leader"—he looking down at them in his totally unsmiling and almost expressionless face, his right hand raised in a kind of blessing, palm down and stiff. Then he lowers himself into a low armchair, the mikes are arranged in front of him, he looks impassively out at the upturned and adulatory faces, pronounces the customary "in the name of God, the Merciful, the Compassionate," and he is off. For an hour or more, his monologue, his preaching, is interrupted only by more "Allah O'Akbars" at appropriate moments.

DAY 361, *October 29, 1980*—It was up at six this morning to listen to the Carter-Reagan debates via VOA. I think one could only make a judgment on their respective performances if one could also see them, visually, since their style and poise, or lack of it, must inevitably be a major factor in how the viewer reacts. Without that, I would have to conclude that Reagan seemed to have outperformed Carter. He sounded poised, more so than Carter; Carter's tactic of putting him on the defensive was sound, but it meant that Carter sounded abrasive, aggressive, at times peevish, and occasionally extreme. Reagan was able to take a highroad position, avoiding specifics where he is normally outclassed by Carter. And yet I thought Reagan this time had considerable command of specifics and substance. News reports suggest that sample pools would call it essentially a draw. But that's an early judgment; I should think it could be fairly decisive among the undecided.

Barbara Walters asked a question about how each would act to try to prevent a repetition of what happened here to our embassy. Neither answered with anything specific, Carter focusing on the need to keep nuclear weapons out of terrorists' hands and Reagan saying that what happened was a product of Carter's inadequate defense and foreign policies. Moreover, the administration, knowing the risks here, should have pulled people out of our embassy and strengthened security. That is a simplistic judgment. And on Barbara's larger question, the two candidates failed miserably. An answer will be difficult, but it needs to be faced up to.

DAY 362, *October 30, 1980*—According to the BBC this morning the scheduled public session of the Majlis has been canceled—due to a lack of quorum. Another attempt will reportedly be made on Sunday, which happens to be the 365th day. . . .

The absence of a quorum may suggest a real problem, especially in light of the speaker's announcement yesterday that attendance at today's session was "compulsory"—whatever that may mean in practice. I conclude that the Majlis leadership recognizes that although the majority may by now have agreed on a set of conditions for our release, there is at least a minority, made up of individuals and factions, who disagrees with the conditions and seeks to frustrate action by the Majlis. . . . Even more likely, I suspect, is a relationship to our elections on Tuesday next. Surely there must be many in the Majlis anxious that nothing be done that would in any way strengthen Carter's chances for reelection, which could happen if a release arrangement were to be worked out this weekend. Those individuals or groups may therefore be doing everything they can—including preventing a quorum—to ensure that no action occurs in time to permit a release before Tuesday. . . .

All of which leaves us where we've been for these 362 days—stuck, dead in the water. After 362 days, perhaps three more should not matter. But in time they add up painfully. I am reminded of another quote from that book *The Fixer*, by Bernard Malamud, the story of that hapless Jew in a tsarist prison whose trial was endlessly deferred: "A day was a bad enough burden of time, but within the day even minutes could do damage as they piled up. When one had nothing to do, the worst thing to have was an endless supply of minutes. It was like pouring nothing into a million little bottles."

That hopeless we've not. But the days seem to be now in endless supply.

DAY 363, *October 31, 1980*—Trick or treat. Halloween. One is tempted to make a comparison with our situation. Happily the practice is foreign to Islam, at least to Islam as practiced in revolutionary Iran.

Yesterday, for the first time since the war began in earnest on September 22, the three of us, and presumably our colleagues as well, received mail, via the Swiss. . . . How fortunate we are to have this Swiss connection. But for out 49 colleagues the connection exists but is virtually unutilized, thanks to the Islamic "humanity" of our militant "student" friends. We are told by Washington, for example, that the families of six of our colleagues have heard nothing from them in more than six months. Mike Metrinko's parents have had one brief note from him in the entire year—that note possible only because of the Red Cross visit to the compound at Easter. The inhumanity of their captors is incredible. It is small, petty, demeaning to themselves and to their country. One wonders what they seek to achieve by this—what security they think they enhance by denying their captives even the chance to write occasionally to their loved ones.

Such inhumanity I can neither forgive nor forget. I hold no basic ill will for the people of Iran, but for those who have done this to them and a year later continue to treat them like common criminals—for those I have nothing but loathing and contempt.

We learn, too, that the fathers of two of the Marines, Kirtley and Lewis, are in the hospital—how ill we do not know. And yesterday, during the Swiss ambassador's visit, he brought word to Vic that his father had died the day before. A cable had arrived an hour or so earlier from the department directly to the chief of protocol, who gave it to the ambassador. . . .

Mike and I have told Vic that we think he should press to be released so that he can attend the funeral; one assumes that if there is "humanity" here it would be difficult for the regime to deny such a request. Vic prefers first to speak by telephone with his mother. So I asked the chief of protocol for permission for Vic to place a call immediately. The answer came back indirectly that the ministry would not permit a call to be placed from here but would allow an incoming call. That the Swiss have since been trying to arrange, but as of 36 hours later with no success.

It is a further example of the obscenity of this whole affair. An American diplomat, held hostage in total defiance of international law, unable to attend the funeral of his own father! As my 19-year-old son, Chip, says in a letter, "There are signs of some greater flexibility on the part of the Iranians, but it's still blackmail." Chip, you are right. Tragically right.

15

November 1980:
No October Surprise

One of our preoccupations, not surprisingly, from day one was to wager with each other over possible dates for our release. An exercise in fantasy invariably, but it did something for our morale and possibly our mental agility. A birthday, an anniversary of some kind relating to either Iran or the United States, an upcoming event, a significant election, and above all the possibilities surrounding our presidential elections on November 4. Naiveté, yes—in retrospect it seems fatuous that any of us could have conceived of our hosts, as contemptuous of Carter as they were, doing anything to help in his hopes for reelection. But hope remained a powerful stimulant one full year into the crisis, enough sometimes to inflate our view of reality. . . .

DAY 364, *November 1, 1980*—Tonight there is hope again, and I believe it better founded than ever before. I am prepared to believe that we could be en route home in a matter of days.

The signals are good and stronger than ever before in that they come this time from the hard-liners. Majlis members have been told that it is their national and Islamic duty to be present at tomorrow's session. Whatever, whoever, is the equivalent of whips in this Islamic parliament is reportedly actively at work. Yesterday on national radio, the keepers of the pure in terms of propaganda said in a commentary that it was in Iran's interest to release the hostages. Tonight we heard that the newspaper of the hard-line IRP, *Jumhouri Islami* (Islamic Republican Party), has editorialized along the same line, adding that it was in Iran's interest to conclude the conditions before the American elections, because the atmosphere for settlement could be worse thereafter, adding apparently that by acting before the elections Iran would demonstrate that it could influence the American electorate.

It is all twisted reasoning, but the important thing is the fact that all the hard-liner leadership is pressing for a settlement *now*. Why? Because they genuinely believe they can influence the election? (It boggles the mind to think that the regime would wish to do anything *for* Carter!) Because they really believe that Reagan would be tougher? Because they are that anxious to get the military spares that Carter has now indicated would move? Because the war situation is serious? Because their financial reserves are desperately low? Is it simply—or in part—a tactic, to get the really hard-liners aboard?

It is probably all of this. Time will tell. Time—tomorrow—will also tell whether the conditions posed to us are acceptable. And whether all this has been pretty much worked out in private exchanges already. If it has, then it is conceivable we could leave by tomorrow night.

Should that happen, I doubt that it will materially influence the elections. A week ago, perhaps. But now it seems too late to have much impact one way or another, though it may cause some of those who have held off on Carter because of the hostage issue to decide to support him. But this could be balanced by those who will suspect that it is a last-minute maneuver by Carter for political purposes and will vote against him for that added reason.

Much of all this will be a bit clearer—soon. Meanwhile, our trauma is soon over. How do I feel, how will I feel? Having not had the experience before, I can't predict exactly. Glad, of course. Excited, relieved, anxious to see our colleagues—to see their physical condition but even more to know how they feel about their experiences. How they feel about us, about our government, and about Iran.

How do *I* feel about Iran? It has gone on so long that I think I have overcome most of the anger and bitterness I felt earlier. It is behind us now; we are alive and well and physically no worse for the wear—only a year older! I could not feel good toward the leadership, certainly not the hard-liners, certainly not the clerics and the "student" militants. I think I feel scorn for them but not hate. They will suffer—are suffering—for what they did. The have brought Iran to the point of collapse, to a war that they encouraged in the sense that they weakened Iran to the point where Hussein felt he could attack—or felt angry enough to attack because of the ARK and his constant call for Hussein's over-throw. I think if I were to be asked, publicly, how I feel about leaving, I could honestly say that I came to Iran as a friend of the people of Iran and I leave still feeling that way. I would like to believe that my colleagues will feel the same way, granted that all of us will have *some* hurt and bitterness in our hearts after a year of forcible separation from our families. But one cannot live with bitterness, and one can feel sympathetic with the people of this country who have not much benefited from the course of their country's history.

And there is the hard reality of our country's interest. It is not in our interest to see Iran defeated or dismembered by war, or to see it weakened so that extremist political elements of another persuasion take over. On balance, our long-range interests are in Iran, not Iraq. As a people we have an infinitely greater range of shared experiences and, to some degree, values than we do with the Iraqis. Not that we can expect any warmth in our relationship with Iran under the present leadership, at least not for now. But we should act, as a government and as a people, in every way that dignity permits so that the basis for a future relationship is not irretrievably lost.

We don't know yet what the conditions for our release are that we have accepted or will accept. But if they are anything akin to what the ARK spoke of last month, they will not be such as to suggest that we have conceded on the principles involved in this illegal seizure of diplomats. That is vital; even now—or especially now—it is vital that we not be seen to have succumbed to blackmail to achieve our release. That does and will matter. Not the bitterness we may feel toward individual Iranians involved in this effort at blackmail—that is transitory; that is human; that will fade—but what must not fade is the appreciation, the awareness, of the grievous violation of diplomatic principles that took place here.

That being said, I am also prepared to say that what should not fade from *our* consciousness is an enhanced appreciation of the fact that Iran's history has not been an easy one. That, yes, the Iranian people have suffered from the interference of outsiders in Iran's internal affairs, from being overrun many times in their history by more powerful outside states—Russians, the British, us, and other European powers to a lesser extent. That encroachment—and it long predates the events of 1953—*has* affected the consciousness of the Iranian people, *has* been a factor in causing the Iranians to indulge so constantly and irritatingly in the conspiracy theory of history. And it causes Iranians—certainly the present leadership—to perceive the behavior and purposes of *us*, for example, very differently from the way *we* see and saw ourselves, our purposes, and behavior in Iran. . . .

Certainly I understand that point better myself now than I did before. I think it would not have substantially changed what I tried to do here myself in the months I had charge of this mission, but a better understanding or appreciation of it now is one of the reasons why I leave here with a determination to try to put the bitterness out of my mind and to try instead to focus on ways we can, in time, establish some sort of understanding with whoever, after this war, is left to lead these people.

DAY 365, *November 2, 1980*—Today, on the 365th day, the Majlis made its decision. And the "conditions" are essentially those expressed by the ARK in early September in his hajj message, i.e., the return of the Shah's wealth, unfreezing Iran's assets in the United States, canceling all financial claims or suits against Iran, and a pledge not to interfere, politically or militarily, in Iran's affairs. These are expressed in language that would seem to indicate a recognition that in some respects we could not immediately and forthwith do what is demanded—e.g., the language seems to indicate an awareness that the Shah's assets are a judicial matter and cannot be simply served up on a silver platter. The process is now turned over to the executive branch of Iran's government, and it is said that if all the conditions cannot be met in one fell swoop, the hostages can be released gradually as conditions are met. Should we refuse to accept these conditions, the hostages are to be turned over to the Iranian courts and tried, with regard for "due process," whatever the latter means in revolutionary Iran!

So far as I'm concerned, these are manageable, depending on whatever indirect discussions have taken place privately on the procedure by which they will be implemented. The Iranians speak of conditions that *we* must meet. I prefer to say that *they* have met *our* conditions—i.e., we have refused to concede to their blackmail. None of these "conditions" is new, all could have been had long since, well before the embassy takeover. Noninterference? That we had said privately and publicly last year. Return of the assets? Fine, we let them have what we froze as penalty for their act. The Shah's assets? They are no further along on this than before the seizure; it must remain a matter for litigation in the courts. Forswearing of claims? That, too, can be said, but it too must remain subject to judicial proceedings.

The point is that they have achieved nothing that they could not have achieved before, and they are getting back (unfreezing assets and lifting sanctions) only what we took to penalize them. And we have not conceded anything in terms of the principle involved. I am reassured; I am proud of our government; I am prouder still of my colleagues who have sat this out as hostages without loss of dignity or principle.

What have the Iranians gotten from all this? International opprobrium and isolation, a disrupted economy, and now a war brought on them by their own isolation and weakness. Briefly, at the outset of the affair, they got, by using the hostages, the internal political passion that solidified clerical control of their Revolution. But in holding onto the hostages the clerics have by now endangered their own Revolution because of the political and economic stress of war.

How much better off Iran and its Revolution would be today had the seizure never occurred! That act being perhaps inevitable, given the revolutionary zeal of the hard-liners, how much better off their Revolution and Iran would be today had they released the hostages months ago, at the time of the UN Panel of Inquiry in February! Or even in early September, in the context of the ARK's hajj speech! After all this talk of the Majlis making the decision, it is still the ARK who has in fact made it; *he* laid down the "conditions," now only slightly embroidered by the Majlis debate. *He* could as easily have applied the same conditions in February. Instead, there have been almost eight months of fuss and feathers about "the people" making the decision. Nonsense. The ARK made it, and the ARK and his entourage acted to bring the minority in line after the agitation of Thursday.

DAY 366, *November 3, 1980*—This morning the press carries the text of the four "conditions" adopted by the Majlis. In one important respect, as I see them, they are more difficult than anticipated, i.e., in the elaboration of the ARK's demand that "the claims of America against Iran . . . be made null and void." As spelled out in the Majlis statement, this demand appears to require the USG to arrange the "cancellation and annulment of all economic and financial actions and measures against Iran," whether by "an official or unofficial U.S. citizen, an American company, or the American Government."

It is difficult for us to judge whether there is any flexibility in interpretation as regards the implementation of this demand. But it would appear one that is simply impossible for our government to arrange, unless it chooses to assume responsibility for the lawful claims of as many as 200 U.S. firms for losses and damages in Iran. And that would seem impossible. That would amount to succumbing to Iranian blackmail. . . .

And so our increasing optimism of yesterday has at least slowed down in its tempo. Release before tomorrow's elections now seems clearly out of the question, the Carter spokesmen continuing to emphasize in the strongest possible terms that political considerations had never entered into the administration's decisions and actions on the hostage issue. Whatever may have been the case at times in the past, I am prepared to believe that. The president yesterday broke off his campaign schedule to return to Washington to deal with the Majlis action, but that was certainly to be expected. Reagan announces that the issue is too sensitive for him to make a statement now. If anyone is manipulating the issue for political and other purposes, it appears to be the Iranians.

DAY 367, *November 4, 1980*—One year in these rooms in this ministry. In some ways it seems only yesterday that we were escorted down to these rooms, then formal and reasonably elegant in the traditions of diplomacy. Today they are dusty and neglected, furniture stacked in heaps and covered with cloth to keep off some of the dust, the chandeliers grayer than ever, the windows dirty, the elegant Persian carpets gone. But we are here still—a year older but possibly not otherwise worse for wear. Both the rooms and our presence speak volumes for the state of Iran and its Revolution.

A year, like only yesterday, and yet in other respects like a lifetime ago. A year of growth and change in our families—our sons, our wives, Vic's daughter. A year of constant revolutionary upheaval in Iran, of the Soviet occupation of Afghanistan, of an American naval buildup in the Indian Ocean, a year of repeated frustrations in seeking our release, and a year of constantly changing presidential political fortunes, in large part a consequence of the madness of revolutionary Iran. A year later and Reza Shah Pahlavi dead, the deposed emperor who figures so largely in this tragedy.

Tonight, a year later, as we sit here, the American electorate is electing its president for the next four years, the votes not unaffected by the trauma of Iran and the hostages. And still the trauma continues: the Iranian prime minister today called on our government to "act promptly" in response to the Majlis "conditions" for our release, conditions that reached us only yesterday. After a year of Iranian shilly-shallying, *we* are told to act promptly in response to their continued effort at political blackmail!

For me, this anniversary could not have been better marked than by the news via VOA this morning that Penne had been quoted as urging Americans to respond calmly and deliberately to the Iranian demands of us. She apparently emphasized also that in responding to them we keep in mind the impact on American honor and national interests, especially in view of the fact that the hostages had given an entire year of their lives in defense of those interests. To undermine them now would be unworthy of the hostages themselves.

That appears to have been the gist of what she told the press. I am proud of her and of my sons, who I have no doubt would support her completely. We wonder how much support she has from the other families for that position. Probably a good deal at this early stage, although that could wane if there is now an extended period of further delay in resolution of the crisis.

This morning—a beautiful fall day unlike the rains of a year ago—we heard the shouting of slogans by groups of schoolchildren passing the ministry in procession. A year ago we drove from the embassy to the Foreign Ministry past many identical processions, only then they were en route to Tehran University. . . . This time these schoolchildren had yet another reason for celebration—the anniversary of the seizure of the "spy nest" and all the "culprits" therein.

If only shouts were bullets! If that were so, this country would be militarily self-sufficient for years! Today, in and around the American Embassy compound, schoolchildren (and presumably would-be university students as well, the universities still closed for their "cultural revolution") shouted their defiance of Iraq and the "imperialists," carried papier-mâché effigies of Carter, burned American flags, and paraded, with the girls all carefully done up in Islamic chadors or veils and some with rifles. Inside the compound on our football field the prime minister mounted a speakers' platform and, true to his singular capacity to pander to the emotions of the masses, said, "I clearly announce that America is the enemy of this Revolution . . . and will never take its hands off us." But, said he, if it tried to do so, "we will make Iran its graveyard."

Not to be outdone, the "spiritual adviser" of the students who seized the embassy, Hojjatol-Islam Mousavi Khoeini, told the crowd that "the final and definite fate of America is its defeat and destruction. . . . As long as there is Iran and Islam, America will always be our enemy."

Hate and vindictiveness. A year after the embassy seizure and almost two years since the Revolution, intellectually limited and politically rigid leaders such as these still preach hate and indulge in their fantasies of history. Among themselves and their own ilk, all that is one thing. But here are the leaders of this country still unable to give the young people of this country anything but this deliberately distorted view of the world in order to further their own short-term political purposes. These are the leaders who today denounce Iraq for its alleged "violations of international law and all international codes of conduct" as they stand on American soil and property stolen and plundered, their hostage victims hidden away somewhere in that very compound as they speak. One wonders whether any of the young listeners think of the irony of it all.

DAY 368, *November 5, 1980*—We are up early to listen to VOA coverage of the presidential election results, but we learn that the president has already conceded defeat, only three hours after the first polls had closed on the East Coast. Far from the close race, the cliff-hanger results, predicted by most observers, the election appears to be a virtual landslide for Governor Reagan— certainly it seems to be such in terms of electoral votes, Reagan already by midmorning our time holding well over 400, compared to only 32 for the president.

What a bitter disappointment it must be for Jimmy Carter! The first elected president to serve only one term since Hoover and to be defeated so decisively as well. A man genuinely convinced of the scope and scale of his accomplishments, now rejected by the voters and largely rejected by his own party as well. A man who narrowly avoided losing his party's nomination to Senator Kennedy because of Kennedy's appeal to the liberal wing of the Democratic party. Now that party's spokesman for its more conservative elements has gone down to a decisive defeat to an even more conservative Republican and with many other Democratic liberals in Senate and House defeated as well. . . .

Only Vice President–elect George Bush referred to the hostages in his post-election statement, saying that he looked forward to the "celebration in freedom" that everyone would experience with our return. Political experts much better informed than the three of us here will have to judge to what extent the hostage issue figured in this election. I would venture that the most recent developments probably had only a marginal effect at best. But I fear that the issue in its larger sense—the United States unable after an entire year to obtain the freedom of this group of its citizens illegally held hostage by a hostile but small country on the other side of the world—probably contributed considerably to the electorate's apparent disillusionment with Jimmy Carter's capacity to cope with the affairs of the republic.

And, if so, that is a tragedy, certainly for the president himself. Certainly no one felt more strongly than did he about the wrongness of the act of seizure and hostage-taking; no leader that we could have had in the Oval Office has felt the burden, personally, of this long year of captivity more than this immensely decent man; no man has devoted more effort, within his own means and his own view of what was feasible, to obtaining our release. In that respect this political rejection by the voters must be a particularly poignant part of the disappointment he feels as he wakes in the White House this morning.

We now have a copy of the official text (in English) of the four conditions demanded of us for release of the hostages. The document is horrendous in style, its sentence structure lengthy and confusing, reflecting an Iranian lawyer's legal vocabulary to further complicate the document for a layman. . . . Beyond that is the larger, substantive problem, especially as regards the third condition—that relating to cancellation of any and all claims, by any and all American individuals or entities, against Iran. No matter how one reads it, it appears to us to be totally unacceptable both in a political sense and in legal terms. The USG simply has no authority to do what is asked. Even one of the guards on duty this morning commented to that effect, saying, "Your government simply can't *do* that, can it? . . . These mullahs have screwed everything up!"

Where does that leave us? Sitting here, we cannot say. . . . At a minimum the Carter administration will need to bring the Reagan group into the picture by informing them of where we stand and what we propose to do. The Reagan group would wish not to get directly involved for the moment, I should think, but it cannot avoid involvement in the sense that what is done now to resolve it will impact on the Iran-U.S. relationship that Reagan will have to live with after January 20. . . .

DAY 369, *November 6, 1980*—A lovely quote today from our candidate for the cleric who has profiteered politically the most from the business of kidnapping American diplomats for blackmail purposes, the Hojjatol-Islam Mousavi Khoeini (the students' "spiritual adviser"): "A yellow dog is the brother of the jackal." This, according to local radio, was his response when asked for his comment on the election of Reagan and the defeat of Carter.

DAY 371, *November 8, 1980*—"Iran is governed by a group of fascist extremists who are driving this country to disaster." My words? No, indeed. They are the words of Sadegh Ghotbzadeh, close follower of the ARK, a longtime revolutionary, and former minister of foreign affairs. And today he sits in Evin Prison, arrested on charges of having slandered the Revolution. The statement above and other allegations directed particularly at clerical control over the Voice and Vision of Iran (TV and radio) were reportedly made by Ghotbzadeh in a TV panel interview featuring him and a man named Islami, who has been serving as director of Channel Two of the TV branch of Voice and Vision. The latter gentleman is currently being sought, having gone into hiding, Ghotbzadeh was apparently arrested yesterday. Perhaps he courted arrest. . . .

Revolutions are often said to end up devouring those who began them.

Certainly that was never more true than in the case of Ghotbzadeh; no one was more involved in the effort against the Shah than he: few have been closer to the ARK, a candidate for president in January, the revolution's first director of the regime's propaganda organs, and foreign minister for almost a year.

But he was disliked by the hard-line clerics and fundamentalists for a long time. And now they have him behind the walls of Evin. On whose orders? And for how long? And will the ARK or anyone else intercede? They may not; he has touched very raw nerves with his accusations, in the context of economic drift, political infighting, and impasse on the military front. The hard-liners will portray his behavior as treasonable.

One is tempted to say he had it coming. He is reaping the whirlwind in the sense that he has been one of the principal activists in this Revolution, especially in the propaganda and foreign affairs fields. But it is a disaster for the now more moderate/secular elements on the political scene. Rumors suggest that the real war front in this country is not on the battlefield with Iraq but here in Tehran, between the Beheshti-led fundamentalists and the Bani-Sadr elements. Decisions are not easily reached in the Supreme Defense Council; Bani-Sadr is at the front, except for occasional trips to brief the ARK. The two sides carry on a continuing battle of words in their respective newspapers.

DAY 372, *November 9, 1980*—All regimes in a war situation must necessarily involve themselves in propaganda and information activities that do some damage to truth. This is not the first regime to do that. But recalling especially Bani-Sadr's statement when the war began about never concealing the "truth" from the public, one must by now, six weeks later, question whether the regime's treatment of the facts has not raised serious doubts among Iran's public about the regime's credibility. Montazeri, for example, is quoted as saying that the Shah had been thrown out of the country "with only the bare hands of the people," and he could not understand "why now, when by God's grace, the country had the necessary equipment and forces at its command it finds itself tarrying in winning the war." As Mike suggested, as we read this report, perhaps the reason is that, unlike the Shah's forces, the Iraqis fire back!

DAY 374, *November 11, 1980*—Today we learn from the news that Deputy Secretary of State Warren Christopher is in Algiers, heading a high-powered U.S. delegation that has brought the official USG response to the Iranian "conditions" for delivery to Iran via Algeria. We know nothing of its content; press speculation is to the effect that the response meets the spirit if not the letter of the Iranian conditions. We are encouraged by the level and expertise of the delegation; they obviously are not simply messenger boys. Their stay in Algiers is described as "open-ended," which is encouraging, as is the fact that it is still quiet here in Tehran. The regime presumably has our response by now and is choosing, so far, to say nothing publicly. We three remain guardedly hopeful. . . .

Later—I have a haircut! That may not sound unusual, but it is when it's the first one since July! The barber? None other than Victor Tomseth, Foreign Service officer and obviously a man of many parts. . . . Mike concludes that he did well by me. In any event I feel better and perhaps look a bit less like a hostage. I am probably the first chargé in the history of our service to get a haircut from his acting DCM! . . .

DAY 375, *November 12, 1980*—This morning, before I was dressed, the telephone rang and a man asked for me. It turned out to be the producer (named Sean) of a radio talk show on station KAYO in Seattle, Washington. Would I answer a few questions? To collect my thoughts, I accidentally broke the connection, frankly hoping the call would not be replaced. But in a minute the phone rang again. I decided it was silly to appear so elusive. I said, "Go ahead," although I was in no position to speak to the substance of our situation. Nonetheless, that was the first question—from a lady named Laura—to which I responded that at this particularly crucial and sensitive point, I did not wish to make any comment on that matter. Was I aware of where things stood? Yes, I was generally aware, within our limitations. Did I have any further comment? To which I replied that I did want to express my appreciation for the tremendous support we had had from the American people throughout this crisis, support that I was confident that my 49 colleagues also knew and appreciated in their hearts. I said that this was a time for calm, for patience, but with confidence that the matter can soon be resolved.

Tonight, on VOA's evening English-language news, I am quoted! The only part cited, however, was my declining to comment on the matter of the conditions and of our response to the four conditions. I commented that VOA must be desperate for news. My two colleagues guffawed and said that it was obviously not *what* I said, but the fact that I had been reached at all that was news in the hostage-focused local atmosphere at home.

We suspect that the call was a fluke. The operator probably heard the U.S. operator say she had a call from Seattle, Washington, and the local operator, not that knowledgeable about U.S. geography, simply assumed that it was our periodic telephone call from Washington, D.C.

DAY 377, *November 14, 1980*—VOA the next morning carried a further and more detailed account of the interview, and the *Tehran Times* carried a rather full AP report on it. I am frankly surprised by the attention it has aroused; had I known that, I would have been even more reluctant than I was to allow the inquiry to begin. The guards here tell us that senior levels of the ministry have inquired of them who was on duty when the call came through and why it was allowed. That is a silly question, since the telephone rang in this room (as is the case with calls from Washington, D.C.), and the guards do not have control over it at that point. . . . My colleagues and I hope the incident does not cause us to lose the opportunity we've had to talk periodically with our families. . . .

Meanwhile, the Algerians have sent a team to Tehran from Algiers carrying the official USG response to the four "conditions." That response has not yet been published, or leaked, or even talked about locally, which gives one some reason for optimism of the cautious variety. So long as that does not happen, one can conclude that there is reasonably serious thought or examination being given to our response. The fact that the Algerians' team includes their ambassador to Washington and the governor of their central bank is also encouraging, suggesting that the Algerians attach real significance to our response to the importance of the Iranians giving it careful attention.

DAY 378, *November 15, 1980*—The fact that November now, too, is half over is a fact not to be avoided, but we will not dwell on it, lest it agitate these pages unnecessarily. . . .

I'm reading something called *Dear Me*, which is Peter Ustinov's autobiography. It's rather good, with many interesting anecdotes regarding celebrated people. And there is a good deal of what I would characterize as common sense, on both substantive political issues and personal relationships: e.g., "I have never ceased learning, and I am convinced that it is of primordial importance to learn more every year than the year before. After all, what is education but a process by which a person begins to learn how to learn . . . and, perhaps, a process by which a person begins the long journey of discovery of himself?"

That latter might well apply to me and my fellow hostages. Perhaps we have learned more in the past year than we can ever appreciate; certainly we have had time and occasion to learn something about ourselves, to discover ourselves.

DAY 379, *November 16, 1980*—Well, that did it. Or I did it to myself, however one wants to put it. We discovered this morning that the phone in this room is dead—cut. And on inquiry of Protocol I am given to understand that it is a consequence of "the publicity" given my talk with the radio station. . . . I rather wish now that I'd said more than I did. . . .

DAY 381, *November 18, 1980*—A beautiful late fall day, the sun shining, the sky clear and bright, the grass in the garden below showered with new-fallen leaves from the plane trees along the edges of the garden. A police helicopter lands on the helipad at the far end of the garden, presumably to pick up the director of the National Police, whose headquarters is across the street and who uses this helipad along with the foreign minister (when there is one).

The police chief is en route, no doubt, to the focal point of today's first day of the mourning demonstrations of Muharram—the day called Tasua in Arabic, the first day of the two-day battle at Karbala, in present-day Iraq, where in A.D. 661 the Prophet's grandson Husain and his small band were slaughtered by Yazid and his followers, who had claimed the caliphate—wrongly so, say the Shi´ites. Today and tomorrow (Ashura) are thus in Shi´a Islam the occasion for a kind of passion play on the streets, when demonstrations and processions of the faithful see men beating their chests with their fists and flailing their backs with small chains in mourning for the dead heroes of Karbala. The fact that Karbala lies within Iraq makes this year's processions especially important, as a means of further emphasizing the Iranian view that Iraq today is ruled by ruthless and godless deviationists who have also launched an aggressive war against Iran and, in the process, indulged in all manner of inhumane acts of war—the bombing of mosques, hospitals, and schools—as well.

So there will be, no doubt, millions of the faithful on the streets—the kind of occasion where this mullah-led regime can publicly demonstrate its political power and influence by bringing out the simple, religious masses of this country to shout their fervor and their loyalty to Ayatollah Khomeini. All of which comes at an appropriate time in the continuing political power struggle, since it will be a further means of warning the secular moderates in the revolutionary leadership that the clerics, the fundamentalists, have not lost their ultimate clout in the form of their hold over the masses. . . .

The Swiss were in to see us yesterday, indicating that the fracas over the telephone interview has at least not affected that privilege—a privilege that means more than our occasional access to the telephone. . . .

The Swiss brought in mail, but none from our wives, who probably are not aware that some mail does reach us via overland routes and Swiss couriers. The mail included my absentee ballot—a bit late but I appreciate the effort behind it!

DAY 383, *November 20, 1980*—The faithful will again conclude that God is on the side of the Islamic Revolution. The two days of Shi´a religious mourning, with their mass street processions and speeches, have ended, with two days of glorious fall weather. Today, the processions complete, it is raining and cold. . . .

I find myself repelled by this kind of mass religious fanaticism, some of it approaching hysteria. I am reminded of the man who said that religious passion brings out the worst in us; there are many examples, Northern Ireland among them. Religious pageantry as symbolism to demonstrate religious beliefs and to reenact historical events in the evolution of religion is one thing. But mass passion, mouthing slogans and expressions endlessly, strikes me as both productive of religious extremism and intolerance and wasteful of human energies. And too often the intolerance becomes political intolerance and rigidity—here, for example, the inevitable result of this passionate reenactment of the events of 13 centuries ago that are at the root of the Sunni-Shi´a split in Islam perpetuates that split, deepening the factionalism that exists on so many levels of society in this country. In the context of the current war with Iraq, Sunni-led Iraq, the passions of war are also further inflamed.

But it is the visual impression that troubles me most. The people as a form-less mass, shouting and chanting in endless unison, their fists flailing the air, responding like robots to the leads of mullahs' voices crackling over loudspeak-ers, masses of women totally devoid of individuality in their black chadors—a mass of sheep.

DAY 386, *November 23, 1980*—Another month has gone by since the euphoric days of late October, and we are still here—a further reminder of the need for the utmost in caution in reading the tea leaves in Tehran.

During the past week we have had modest signs of realism, especially in the fact that the Iranians have chosen to say relatively little, and to avoid entirely going public, on the specifics of our formal response to their four "conditions." That would at least suggest that they are currently serious about seeking a settlement. Rafsanjani, the Majlis speaker, currently spreading the word about the Iranian Revolution in Libya, Algeria, and Syria, said in Algiers that we had accepted the Iranian "conditions" in principle. That was confirmed a day later by Muskie, who emphasized, however, that we had not yet received the Iran-ians' response and that implementation was a different matter. So far, so good.

Subsequently we have had noises from Rajai's office that could suggest prob-lems, could be simply an effort to put pressure on us, or could be political bombast for local purposes. I suspect all three, with emphasis on the latter. The noises include an expression of regret that the USG persists in "politicizing" the issue. . . . Yesterday we learn that Rajai's office has described the United States as "presumptuous" in declining to give a yes or no answer and indeed has been "neither explicit nor clear" in responding to the Iranian "conditions," even posing new conditions of its own.

Presumptuous, are we? That's beautiful. That kind of accusation after a year of hostage-holding for blackmail purposes is so outrageous as to be ridiculous. And funny.

There is more outrageous irony today. That great humanitarian, the Ayatol-lah (self-promoted) Khalkali, the "hanging judge" who has presided over the summary execution of countless Iranians in the past 18 months (and the ghoul-ish display of charred American bodies at Tabas), is today quoted as accusing us of using the hostages as "a business property or financial capital"—this appar-ently in reference to the position we have taken on not being able to hand back "the Shah's wealth" on a silver platter or to blithely set aside legally instituted claims by American individuals and corporate entities. It is his "wish from the bottom of my heart," says this sweet man, that the hostages be freed as soon as possible. "After all, they have families, and humanitarian feelings would dictate they should be freed as soon as possible."

One is moved almost to tears by such expressions of tenderness from that source.

DAY 390, *November 23, 1980*—Thanksgiving Day. What does one say on such a day? We are thankful that we have our health, that so far as we know all of our 49 colleagues are still alive and presumably physically all right, and—most of all—thankful that our families are well. So there is something to be thankful for, even in our "second year of captivity." (The latter is the expression now used by VOA and other news organizations. Somehow putting it in terms of days seemed a good deal more tolerable than our "second year.")

I remember a year ago the hope in the first week of this crisis that surely we would all be home to give thanks by Thanksgiving time. And then, when it didn't happen, the great national expression of hope that it would, nonetheless, soon be over—the bell-ringing that began then as a symbol of hope and even of reconciliation with Iran.

A year later and there is no freedom, no reconciliation. Those bells are still ringing. One wonders how many and what the sound of those bells means—if anyone stops to hear them and to think a moment why they're ringing. On this first anniversary of that act there will be a renewal and a new sense of hope. For that we can be thankful, that at long last there is dialogue looking toward a solution, however indirect and however difficult and slow. . . .

In that respect we heard on today's morning VOA news that an Algerian delegation is now in Washington bearing the requests of the Iranians for additional details on our response to the four "conditions" set by the Majlis. That news reporting, noting that no information is yet publicly available on what the Algerians are conveying, went on to say—and with some enthusiasm—that the Algerians *did*, however, bring "good news" for the families of the hostages, namely, that they had been assured by the Iranians that the hostages were well and in "good condition."

Nothing irritates me more than such "assurances"! They are based on *no* evidence of any kind. The Algerians, of course, have not seen our colleagues. Neither is there any evidence that anyone in the government here has seen them, certainly not on any continuing basis. The chief of protocol confirmed to us yesterday that the government still has not assumed custody of the hostages from the students—more than three weeks since such a transfer was authorized by the ARK. . . .

Aside from all that there is the more fundamental question that underlies such "assurances": what constitutes "good condition" for men and women held captive for more than a year, totally without contact with their government, and allowed only the rarest of opportunity for letter contact with loved ones? However well they may have been fed or kept, no one can assure me or anyone else that on that basis they are now in "good condition."

What troubled us most was the enthusiasm that VOA seemed to feel over such assurances—questionable at best and only serving the propaganda interests in this regime. Had the Swiss been in today I would have asked them to send the department a snappish dissent from me.

The Swiss yesterday brought us a tangible reminder of the friendship and understanding we've had from the American people and from people elsewhere who appreciate what has been at stake in this crisis. That reminder was a "chest expander band," an exercise device manufactured by AMF for physical exercise purposes in close physical surroundings. This came together with a form letter from something called the American Alliance for Health, Physical Education, Recreation, and Dance headquartered in Reston, Virginia (an "alliance" one could certainly endorse!). That group, said the letter, had been working on this project since February, had wished to send a full set of exercise equipment, but had finally been able to arrange this smaller gift (some 45 others of the same kind are being turned over to the Foreign Ministry in hopes of their reaching our colleagues) with the cooperation of the Scandinavian Airlines System. The latter apparently arranged their transport and sent copies of an exercise booklet, demonstrating exercises that can be done in confined quarters, even in one's airline seat!

DAY 392, *November 29, 1980*—It is all so damned sanctimonious. *Newsweek* magazine once termed this the "Joyless Revolution"; that's good too. But even more, at least judged by what one reads of what these people's claim about their Revolution, it is so tiresomely sanctimonious! They can do no wrong. It is the Islamic Revolution leading the entire world, with the world gone wrong and Iran setting it right. All revolutions are probably like that, in the sense that their leaders believe they have come upon something unique that will electrify the world and be a beacon for generations to come. But this one! It outdoes them all.

There are examples of it daily, but it's perhaps heard in its purest form in the Friday prayer sermons. Yesterday, for example, we read that the Friday prayer leader for Tehran, Hojjatol-Islam Khamanei, had these things to say:

- "Islam sets men free from differences of blood, geography and race."
- "Islam helps men to free themselves from the universal imperialists, the Superpowers. It is not freedom of the kind known in Western countries and termed liberalism. Freedom in that liberal sense is license to follow any sort of desire, passion, or corruption. Freedom under Islam lies within the framework of Islamic principles."
- "Our newspapers are experiencing a freedom never experienced elsewhere in the world."

There is much more, and these are not the best examples. We read too much of it and take it for granted. There is also the vaunted emphasis on "truth," which again, of course, is but the natural product of a revolutionary society like Iran. And yet the "truth" is so totally ignored in the official communiqué from the battlefront as to have long since caused any Iranian who can read to turn desperately to almost any other source to see if something truer to the facts can be found.

Worst of all for me is the way "truth" is violated in presenting here a picture of the police in the United States as nothing but fascist thugs. Today, for example, both English-language papers captioned a story "U.S. police kill another Iranian student"—the story based on the death of an Iranian student in Oklahoma City, allegedly because the police "repeatedly beat and tortured him all night." . . . It is part of the scapegoat syndrome again, so powerful in Iran—and in this instance also part of the regime's defense mechanism in trying to divest itself of wrongdoing in the case of the hostages. As the line goes, the fascist police in America kill and brutalize Iranians there, whereas here the hostages have been treated with the utmost in Islamic humanity. As Henry Precht put it in another context: Bullshit!

The same theme was apparent in recent reporting of a visit by the Austrian ambassador to Deputy Majlis Speaker Mousavi Khoeini. The latter, after hearing the ambassador's expression of disapproval of the holding of 52 diplomats hostage, was quoted as asking: "Have you, as the ambassador of Austria, asked the U.S. government why its police's behavior toward Iranian students in that country is so savage?" (My question: Well, if conditions are indeed so bad in the United States, why are so many thousands of Iranian students so determined to stay there?)

I can only conclude that for men as doctrinaire and limited as Khoeini, there is no hope. They are ideologically blind. . . .

DAY 393, *November 30, 1980*

Dear Penne,

. . . Good Lord, tomorrow's your birthday! And I'm here and you're there. It isn't fair. Big bomb went bang only a block or so away today. Rattled our windows. First excitement we've had in a long while. But the real excitement today was in the reports of anticlerical demonstrations in, of all places, Qom and Meshed! That, if true, would be the best news since we've been here. They, the clerics, will get their just reward. I just hope it's soon. I guess there are few things that turn me off more than clerics meddling in politics—anywhere!—but especially mullahs, who, I regret to say, somehow have always to me personified the utmost in obscurantists. That is unfair, I know, to label them thus as a class, but the many who are have regrettably tainted the whole barrel of them. And despite the crest the clerics are riding now in Iran, I think history will affirm that there is a strong anticlerical streak in Iranians that periodically surfaces. It seems to me it is inevitable in Iran, though its main impact will not be felt so long as Khomenei lives. . . .

Love, Bruce

16

December 1980:
A Promising Christmas

Our knowledge of the Carter administration's contacts with the Iranians that had begun via the Germans in September and then continued with the Algerians was always partial at best. But by December we had learned enough of the discussions then under way, and of the seriousness of the Algerian commitment, to assume that the end was somewhere in sight. Inshallah, God willing. Our telephone was by now permanently dead; the Foreign Ministry's moderates could no longer ignore the "students" on that score. But the Swiss still saw us occasionally, and we continued to have access to our radio and to Iranian TV. We involved ourselves in the ongoing negotiations mentally, if not in reality. And yet it was at best a partial picture, with enough gaps on occasion to leave us worried that Washington might make concessions that would undermine the sanctity of diplomatic immunity, to which we felt the hostages had made by this time a considerable contribution.

Throughout, it was a rare moment that we did not find ourselves marveling at the role that 52 American diplomats were playing in the exceedingly complex diplomatic chess game. And we watched with continuing fascination, mixed with our seemingly unending store of frustration, the public manifestation of an unfinished Revolution inside Iran.

DAY 394, *December 1, 1980*—I neglected to make note of another event that made yesterday unique. We had a visit from two ladies! Yes, ladies—the

234

first ladies who have ever been in this room with us, save our resident seamstress and the wife of the Swedish ambassador last March.

It wasn't a long visit, but the fact of it matters. We were eating breakfast and reading the morning papers when in walked in two Iranian ladies, employees of the ministry as cleaners. Neither spoke English; both were dressed in long skirts, white working smocks, and chadors held loosely over that. At that age with Iranian working women, when the number of years is hard to determine and when whatever figure there may once have been has suffered the effect of too much rice, nan, and tea, they rather waddled in, but yet quite sure of themselves and full of smiles and curiosity. We assume they must have talked the kitchen staff into allowing them entry. They chatted a few minutes, via Vic's Farsi, spoke with enthusiasm about our "vast" room and its warmth, asked how we were, assured us that, Inshallah, we would soon be able to join our families, and took special note of the fact that two of us were "young." Then they waddled out again, prepared, no doubt, to gossip the rest of the day with their coworkers around the building about their visit to the three superspies.

DAY 399, *December 6, 1980*—Today the press quotes a government spokesman as saying what we have assumed, i.e., that the Iranian government has indeed *not* yet assumed physical custody of the hostages, now more than a month since the transfer was authorized by the ARK. The reason, said the spokesman, was to be found in "security and logistic considerations." That, as the saying goes, covers a multitude of sins.

We wonder what it *does* mean. Presumably the continuing political power struggle here, currently intensified around much agitation over anticlericalism expressions that have caused the fundamentalists to stage massive rallies in support of the militant clergy, has complicated the matter. Perhaps the "students," who mouthed much talk of wanting to go to the front, are demanding government positions in various ministries in recognition of their role. No doubt it reflects the usual problem of getting anything done quickly here.

Reflecting some of the problems involved was a bit of a contretemps that we have had over the packages sent by Richard Queen for some of his friends among the hostages and the exercise equipment sent by AMF and MacGregor Companies. The Swiss delivered the former weeks ago to the Protocol Office of the ministry, the latter more than a week ago. Late last week the entire lot suddenly arrived here in our room; nothing had obviously been done to get the packages to the hostages. Whereupon I sent a testy letter to the chief of protocol, expressing my inability to understand the delay, especially in light of what had so often been said about the "humanitarian treatment" given to the hostages. That letter produced almost immediate results, in that the Protocol Office came up to collect the boxes and promised to act.

But it also produced the inevitable, it seems, frustration. By midafternoon the boxes were back in our room, the guards telling us that the "students" at the embassy compound had refused to accept the boxes! *Plus ça change!*

An Algerian delegation is back in the city, carrying the "clarifications" sought by the Iranians regarding our response to their four "conditions." There are also renewed reminders to the Iranians from us via the media that Iran should not expect an easier posture on the hostage issue from the incoming Reagan administration.

Christmas is now less than three weeks away; one wonders what effect that is having on either side, Tehran or Washington. One assumes that Washington feels even more urgency to expedite the process. Here it may not have much bearing, although I would not be surprised to see the Iranians release a number of the hostages prior to Christmas, both as a gesture in evidence of "humanitarian Islam" and as a means of putting some pressure on us to be more forthcoming on the four "conditions." . . .

The press here carries a small item describing Penne being hoisted by crane to the top of the National Christmas Tree in Washington to top off the last of the decorations at its peak. She is quoted as asking humorously, "What am I doing here? I don't even like to go up in airplanes!" Louisa Kennedy is quoted as expressing her personal view that this year, unlike last year, the tree's colored lights should be turned on. I would agree, life has to go on, whatever happens here.

Plots! Conspiracies! And yet more plots! It is a rare day that is not marked by someone warning of yet another plot or conspiracy designed to subvert the Revolution—a well-established aspect of revolutionary tactics in the Islamic Republic. Where there is difficulty, disunity, we are reminded that counter-revolutionaries are at work with yet more plots. Not unlike other revolutions, perhaps, but the theme seems to flourish especially well in Iran, given the scapegoat syndrome so much a pattern of Iran's modern history. This in turn is reflective of the long history of foreign involvement and intervention in Iran. . . . It has been a constant feature of this Islamic Revolution. Currently there is particular focus on it, triggered apparently by concern among the clerical leadership over growing anticlerical sentiment of the kind that produced, last week, the scene in Meshed of demonstrators denouncing "the three devils": Beheshti, Khamanei, and Rafsanjani. If there is such sentiment, say the clerics, there must be a foreign hand, because "if the Ulema are separated from the people, the people will be separated from them, and then the Superpowers will celebrate."

DAY 400, *December 7, 1980*—Pearl Harbor Day, the second Sunday in Advent, and our 400th day. The days seem to grow longer, our routines more monotonous, what we do—boring. Except for the relief provided now by four video TV films each week, the days weigh heavily, especially when we take note of their number, which we don't anymore; but it is hard to avoid taking note of a good round number like 400. Four hundred days! That rings badly. Man's days on earth are numbered in any event, and to be reminded that 400 of ours have been invested in this trauma makes one wonder what it has been worth. Time alone will tell—time will tell us under what terms we are finally released and how we as individuals react to a return to our normal lives. Yesterday saw one modestly encouraging sign: even one of the last revolutionary diehards of our kitchen staff brought himself to concede that the seizure of the embassy was not good for Iran and that the behavior of the "students" had "not been Islamic."

But on the same day we read that the Ayatollah Beheshti, that prime example of mullahtocracy, of the arrogance of the Ulema, had told his Friday prayer audience in Bushehr, "You Americans cannot comprehend the depth of the Islamic Revolution and the tactics and the innovating methods of our revolutionary nation. . . . The materialistic Western mind cannot understand the standards of God-loving, martyrdom-loving, and sacrifice-loving people."

Beheshti is right in the sense that there is a virtual abyss between us in terms of understanding. But he is wrong in suggesting that it is one-sided. He and his ilk also fail grievously to understand, or even to *attempt* to understand, what it is about the clerical fundamentalists that so totally alienates the American people. And he is wrong in that his statement reflects also that classic failing on the part of his and previous generations of Iranians; i.e., they fail to understand *themselves* and their own shortcomings. . . . Statements like that from Beheshti make this 400th day even harder to take, as did another contribution from yet another Friday prayer sermon, this one by Ayatollah Montazeri in Qom. "The United States," said he, "is hatching a new plot against the Revolution every day. Don't forget that the United States is your worst enemy. *Don't forget to chant 'Death to the U.S.'* as well as *'Death to Saddam Hussein'* " (emphasis added).

They don't fear *us*, these narrow but determined clerics; they fear *themselves*, they fear their own people, they fear for the future of their mullahtocracy and the privileged place of the Ulema, in that Revolution. They are running scared. For Iran it is tragic. For a Revolution that once gave great promise, it is tragic.

Perhaps I am wrong. Perhaps Iran *is* able to sustain a theocracy as envisaged by these mullahs. But I doubt it. Islam, yes; whatever regime is to rule here for the foreseeable future, barring the unlikely one dominated by the Tudeh (communists), will need to respect and look to Islam as a powerful motivating and ideological force. But the extremes of the current crowd are jeopardizing that.

So . . . we have almost forgotten how Sunday differed from other days in the week. It becomes only another day of seven, all exactly like. I marvel sometimes how pleased I am to have something beyond the routine to do—sheets to wash, a button to get sewed back on something, periodic sorting out of papers on the table that has become "my desk," and the pretense of something occasionally bordering on substance, like yesterday's writing of a letter to the Portuguese chargé in the city to express regret over the death of Prime Minister Sa Carneiro, with whom I once met and talked about the future course of Portugal's revolution.

But there is hope too, and we haven't lost it. The Algerians are back in the city with our five-page "clarification," and so far the Iranians continue their silence on the subject, which is good. "Don't lose your confidence," the biblical verse reads. "It carries a rich reward." Like getting home for Christmas perhaps.

DAY 404, *December 11, 1980*—Christmas is only two weeks away—not much time within which to see this thing wrapped up and all of us (or some of us?) home with our families. But it is enough time, if there's a will. And I detect that there *is* that will, and I predict we *will* be home, or at least en route. The Algerian delegation is still in the city, local officials are keeping helpfully quiet on the subject, and so is Washington. All that's been said locally is the comment by Majlis Speaker Rafsanjani that "only a few obscure points" remain to be worked out and that the American "clarifications" have made things a great deal clearer. And I suspect that the leadership here is not totally unmoved by the adverse impact, internationally, of Iran being seen holding the hostages through a second Christmas. . . .

We read in the press that an American journalist has been in the country and that it is the well-known CBS man, Mike Wallace. Mike is a freewheeling, hardheaded, independent-minded journalist who doesn't take nonsense from anyone, and it is already clear that that kind of approach is difficult for the local "free press" advocates in the regime to tolerate. Today's *Kayhan*, for example, reports, under a caption "CBS Reports: Distortive as Usual," that among the group of foreign journalists recently taken on a tour of "war-stricken regions," there were some "trying to prepare reports on the basis of prejudiced and biased criteria." Such a person, said the story, was Mike Wallace, "who has obviously and calculatingly sought to analyze the subject with an irrelevant, impertinent approach revealing that while his body may be near the war fronts, his attention is on other matters altogether different."

The story then cites several examples of his "biased" reporting, including his question in a press conference as to which country had the better armaments, Iran or Iraq. The story notes that the army official had given him "the right answer," pointing out that Westerners always fail to understand that it is not the type of equipment that wins battles but rather faith and belief. . . .

Poor Wallace, he just doesn't understand. It's the old problem. The regime has something to sell and expects the press to buy it—to focus on what *it* wants, without challenge, almost without question. . . .

One can understand the Iranians. Any government prefers the press and other observers to focus on its achievements and not on the blemishes. But that government cannot legitimately cry foul if the press asks about the blemishes as well and gets official handouts or pap in response, without the right of the press to see for itself. Balance in reporting *is* essential; this and other governments are right in asking that of the press. From Iran's point of view it is *not* getting that from the American press and, further, it believes the Revolution never *has* gotten that balanced picture from the way the American press reports on Iran. Clearly the expectations of the revolutionaries never could have been achieved, given the Iranian view of American wrongdoings in the past and their view as to how this motivation was involved in the embassy seizure. Nor could American reporters ever report totally "objectively," given the American view of the hostage-taking.

But, quite aside from the fact that the embassy seizure was seen through the world as intrinsically wrong, the Iranians have been their own worst enemies in selling their Revolution. They have, in effect, trumpeted their excesses and downplayed their achievements. They have shut themselves off from the rest of the world, certainly the West. They have flaunted what almost everyone outside Iran has seen as strange, if not downright wild. They have never found a way to "sell" such achievements as exist, e.g., the popular, Islamic nature of the Revolution itself, the enthusiasm of youth, the work of the Construction Crusade, the pride and esprit of the Revolutionary Guards. . . .

Another example of Iran's *own* contribution to the problem, this in the judicial field, is the "Hanging Judge," Ayatollah Khalkali, who is again in the limelight because of charges in Iran that torture and bribery have accompanied his antinarcotics campaign and, more generally, have again become commonplace in Iran's prisons. In this context he is quoted as pointing out, apparently with pride, that so far in the Revolution some 1,000 "antirevolutionaries" have been executed and 400 others for narcotics pushing (conservative figures, by other accounts). Said the ayatollah, "We have done things in three months what the judiciary could not do in six years."

That kind of publicity, *by* Iranians and *in* Iran, is not the kind that sells this Revolution abroad, especially not when that Revolution professes to have succeeded in good part because it has stood so strongly against what it says were such blatant excesses against human rights under the Shah's regime.

DAY **405,** *December 12, 1980*—I find from a variety of newspaper clippings that arrived this week that my family has been rather actively quoted in the public press, along with families from many others of the hostages, the press having an unquenchable thirst, it seems, for anything on the hostages. . . .

Among the clippings is one from the *NYT* reporting that I had been "seriously ill" with dysentery. This report is from Penne, who is apparently quoting from letters about me from my two colleagues to their wives. Another quotes Penne as saying that my hair "has turned white and is falling out in gobs. . . . But they caught it in time, and pumped him full of antibiotics."

Well, at this distance, things tend to get exaggerated, not surprisingly. My illness wasn't quite that severe, nor has my hair turned all that white. People may be disappointed, when we walk off that plane, to see how fit we actually are—well, perhaps not fit, but not in bad shape either.

Penne also is quoted in the same press interview as drawing an analogy between the discussion now going on via the Algerians and Middle East rug-bargaining in a carpet bazaar. The trick, she says, is to remember that the first price quoted is only the beginning of the process and that we ought to have the courage to walk out of the dealer's store if necessary, since "there's a good deal more riding on this carpet than 52 lives. We don't want the fringe, we don't want pieces. We want the whole beautiful thing, but with honor."

That's not a bad analogy. But the question is, are these people really going to behave like rug merchants, this time? The question concerns who's in charge of the store and how hard-pressed they feel. I think she's right: the Iranians know, this time, that their cash ledger is pretty low and needs replenishing if the carpet shop is to survive. So they'll sell, but only after tough bargaining, and it is important that we show as much persistence as they, and more.

Son Chip at the University of Minnesota is also quoted; he was questioned just before election day. . . . "This is going to be my first election, and look what my choices are! . . . The hostage situation," he said, "will have an effect on my vote." On the issue of the hostages: "I'm not in favor of war at all, but I can't help but think that maybe the United States should have taken a strategic position toward Iran right away. Maybe that would have made all the difference. Maybe then this wouldn't have been such a very long year." On the taking of hostages, Chip says, "I see anyone remotely connected with the taking of hostages as an enemy."

Well, Chip, that's calling a spade a spade. So is your statement about the obligations of citizens to do something for their country: "I think anyone living here has an obligation to in some way protect what we have, our way of life." Chip can speak with substance. He is a second-year NROTC midshipman at the university and flag bearer in the color guard: "That makes me feel like I'm doing something. It makes me proud as hell, hearing the American anthem and holding the flag."

And that makes me proud of Chip. Chip is also quoted as saying, "When I see someone who looks Persian, I don't hate them right away, but something does bother me." There is evidence of one of the long-term costs of this thing, especially for the Iranians. The distaste now felt by so many Americans, especially the young, even younger than Chip, for anything having to do with Iranians is tragic, but not surprising. . . .

DAY 407, *December 14, 1980*

Dear sons, Bill, Jim, and Chip,

It's soon Christmas again, the second time around for us, and tonight I have reconciled myself to *not* making it home in time to celebrate with all of you and Mom and Duchess and the grandparents and the whole lot. The news quotes an official in the prime minister's office as saying he does not *exclude* the possibility of our being released before Christmas, provided, said he, the United States moved promptly to indicate its acceptance of Iran's conditions.

Well, as Mom has expressed it so well in her public statements, there is such a thing as our national honor, which cannot be sold short, however important it is to the American people to see the hostages home as soon as possible. I know each of you agrees with that, too. Iranian threats are meaningless. They have nothing to gain by continuing to hold us and a great deal to lose. And they cannot hurt us; they dare not. The world would turn its back on them then, with good reason. . . .

Last year I wrote each of you at Christmastime and tried to say how I felt about this experience. I suspect I would not write anything different this year. My anger and bitterness has subsided; time and patience have had that effect. I feel no less deeply about the wrong that was committed here, but perhaps I'm more conscious that life has to go on, regardless. Iran has already been punished, in the sense that the action has brought incalculable damage to the country's social, economic, and political framework, and the Iranians have brought it on themselves. Iran's leadership knows that better than anyone, despite the bombast we now hear. I am even prepared to be reasonably patient with the leaders as they sort this thing out; they have their own national honor to defend and are having a bit of a problem finding means to do that. And, in time, this leadership will pass from the scene. It cannot endure.

In that sense, I regard it as an aberration, and we can look, I am sure, to the time when there will again be an American-Iranian relationship, though there is no need for us to press for it now. It will come, but it should come naturally, when Iran realizes that *it* needs *us*, not the opposite. . . .

I've just read a long biography of Lord Palmerston, who was foreign secretary and prime minister in Britain for many years in the first half of the 19th century. His philosophy was that Britain had no permanent friends and no permanent enemies; it had permanent *interests*. That strikes me as a pretty sensible and hardheaded policy that would serve us well in this part of the world.

For this Christmas, even here in Tehran, I have the special gift from each of you of knowing that you are well, that you are being purposeful about working and planning for your own future lives, that you are having fun, and that you are developing a strong sense of responsibility toward those around you and toward your country. Every batch of mail that I get says something about one or more of you and about the respect you've got for the kind of lives you lead. Just today a letter came, via this ministry, from a fellow named Damon Pope in North Carolina who is a senior counselor at Sea Gull and who wrote about Jim: "He is really a fine and promising young man and one of our best kids." That's the kind of Christmas gift that matters to a father, wherever he is.

Merry Christmas and God's blessing to each of you for 1981.

Sincerely, Dad

DAY 408, *December 15, 1980*—Tonight Bani-Sadr is quoted, responding to a question why the hostage issue has taken so long to resolve, as saying that the question should be directed at American politicians who are playing politics with the issue. What nonsense! It is further effort to rationalize Iran's own failures and setting conditions that no self-respecting government has any business agreeing to (to the letter). For that matter, of course, what Bani-Sadr says

on the subject is academic. He and his group here are effectively frozen out of
the issue by the hard-liners. . . .

DAY 410, *December 17, 1980*—Yesterday Prime Minister Rajai, following
a cabinet meeting and a call on the ARK, told the press, "We only require a
financial guarantee from the United States to be given to the Algerian government and then they can take the spies. Anytime they wish, either on the feast
or the birthday, whatever they want to call it." The latter is apparently a
reference to Christmas, this singularly uncultured gentleman finding it hard to
give any particular credibility even to the birthday of Jesus Christ. Never mind,
the development appears to be a climactic one as far as the regime is concerned, given the fact that this "final answer" has been taken to the ARK
himself and approved by him. This would suggest a degree of modification in
the original four conditions, reflecting some flexibility in their implementation
at least, and responsive to U.S. government clarifications, since this would
surely require approval from that august presence to be feasible here. . . .

DAY 412, *December 19, 1980*—There have been times, in our frustration
over the past months, when we have jokingly said to each other: All we need
is an earthquake! Last night we had one, happily not serious, but enough to
wake us from our sleep and, we understand from the kitchen force, enough to
cause Iranian families in their houses in south Tehran to rush into the streets
as a precaution. The tremor was the strongest I've ever experienced, shaking
the bed enough to wake us and rattling the crystal in the chandeliers overhead.
As we got up this morning, each of us commented on the experience, causing
Mike to say: "Then it wasn't a dream after all!"
    Wonders seem never to cease. This week the Swiss brought in a large bundle
of mail, including some 200 birthday cards for me, the balance, apparently, of
that birthday card campaign in Minnesota last summer, sparked by radio station
WCCO in Minneapolis. Who can say where these cards have been all this time,
possibly lost in the paperwork of the Department of State. No matter, it has
given me in effect a second birthday, even though I long since have canceled
this 58th year from my record. . . . The preponderant theme in all of them,
expressed colloquially, is "Hang in there," but much more frequently the case,
it is also one of prayer, faith, and confidence in the ultimate outcome. There is
also much expression of puzzlement—what can Iran possibly hope to achieve
by continuing to hold the hostages?—but many of these also express the strong
hope that in time the Iranian and American people can again become friends.
From only a few is there real anger, like one man, a stranger to me, who writes:
"A lot of Americans, like myself, are going to get Reagan elected, and he will
stand for your circumstances for about 24 hours." That was in July; Reagan is
now elected; he may yet have the opportunity to see him apply himself to this
crisis. But, I doubt it. . . .
    Footnote to the day's events—The press carries the following item, verbatim:

"Tehran—The Imam has declared the game of chess 'haram' (forbidden), reported the governor of Tehran, who met with Imam Khomeini yesterday to consult about the chess issue."

Now there is a serious development! At long last we appear to be getting at the real vices in society.

DAY 413, *December 20, 1980*—Today's press carries the text of a long speech by the ARK to a group of theological students from Qom and Islamic Society students from Tehran. His theme was the need for university education combined with the teaching of Islamic thought and ethics. Theological centers and the universities must work together; until and unless they do, university education will simply "corrupt" the young and thus society as a whole and lead to Iran being again dependent on the West. That, said he, was what the current "cultural revolution" in Iran was all about, and the universities, now closed, would remain closed until that new concept was achieved. . . .

It was an interesting speech and not a new thesis among revolutionaries, although one wonders whether the ARK ever considers the singular lack of success of something not entirely dissimilar in China of recent vintage. The speech was also interesting in the way it reflects the remarkable intellectual vigor of the man: a long, philosophical speech, reasonably ordered in structure, and spoken—as are all his speeches—entirely without notes. Not only showing intellectual but also physical vigor, he is now again receiving sometimes three or four groups of a morning and giving speeches to each of them. . . .

Universities, said the ARK, "have two alternatives: the road to hell or the road to Heaven. . . . We have had universities for 50 years and all corruption has been created by graduates of these universities." Nor, for that matter, said he, had they developed any real competence: "Do you want a university which, after 50 years, sends its patients to England for medical treatment?"

But his sharpest attack is directed against science, science that is not combined with Islamic ethics:

Science by itself is useless, even harmful. After a glance at the world's universities, we see that they have been the root cause of all human suffering. All the instruments of human destruction . . . have originated from graduates of the universities lacking ethics and edification. . . . Universities can either corrupt or reform the world. If universities . . . can combine human ethics and nature with teaching and education, they will illuminate the world.

All very interesting and, theoretically, sound. But in the real world? What can come of scientific instruction and research, for example, in institutions where the Koran is the last word? Or is that doing injustice to what the Imam has in mind? It boils down in the final analysis to academic freedom, so essential to any process of learning. Iran's universities are now closed because its new leaders fear the influence from them of free and open political debate and discussion and the pervasive influence of the West's now massive lead in technology and scientific research. But what is the cost of cutting oneself off from all that and of trying to put ethics and student conduct in the straitjacket of the Koran? Perhaps, if the Ayatollah wants to try to "purify" the Iranian ethic, even to the point of declaring chess as forbidden, he can do so, providing the clerics retain their political power. But how long can Iran afford to cut itself off from the rest of the world in scientific research and from the technological interdependence that is now the mark of our time? . . .

DAY 415, *December 22, 1980*—Last night, the 21st day of December, was statistically the longest night of the year. And in a sense it was equally long in terms of the depression on our spirits caused by the news yesterday of Iran's latest interpretation of its four conditions. . . .

The text of this Iranian communication has been sent by the Algerians to Washington and was published in today's Iranian media. It is a long and complex document, but the gist—and the sticking point for us—is that it requires the U.S. government to set aside $24 billion in Algerian custody before the hostages can be released. Included in that is $10 billion, in a cash guarantee, covering the Shah's alleged cash and property holdings in the United States. There are concessions, in the sense for example that the Iranians agree that $1 billion shall be set aside to cover Iranian obligations to American banks and another $1 billion to cover the possible obligations falling on Iran of the results of investigation and (possible) arbitration into the question of suits and counter (Iranian) suits involving contracts of American companies doing business in Iran prior to November 4, 1979. But the problem is the demand for the transfer of the $24 billion, reflecting Iranian distrust of the United States. Transfer of certain portions of this sum is clearly beyond the legal power of the president, a point made clear by Secretary Muskie in an NBC interview yesterday.

News reports indicate that an unnamed department officer characterized this latest Iranian communication as "simple blackmail." That's one way of putting it, and I wouldn't disagree. Another way, expressed by Muskie, is that it is "unreasonable." I agree with that, too. Muskie, who was quoted the other day as saying that he had dropped the word *hopeful* from his Iranian lexicon, also took pains in the NBC interview to put the term *negotiations* in context. This was unlike a normal process of negotiations between governments, he said, in the sense that we are dealing with a situation where 52 diplomatic personnel were seized illegally and continue to be held illegally despite calls for their release by the World Court, the Security Council, and virtually all governments on the face of the globe. That said, he noted, we intend to continue a process of trying to come to an understanding with Iran that will see the hostages' early release—which, he now doubted, could come before the advent of the Reagan administration on January 20.

All of this is depressing, and it must have come with great distress to the hostage families on this eve of Christmas. But Muskie is absolutely right in what he has said. He—the president—has an obligation to history, to the fundamental principles involved and to larger U.S. interests that go well beyond 52

American men and women, however important it also is that they be returned home, safe and well, and at the earliest possible time. The important thing is that we continue to be firm in rejecting what is not feasible or legal or in any other way compromises the principle involved, but that at the same time we keep a process of discussions going, however indirect and difficult, via the Algerians. The three of us have considerable confidence that this can be done, given the very serious financial straits facing the Iranian regime and their now clear and almost desperate anxiety to get their hands on their funds in the United States. So we discount all this talk of the Iranian position being the final answer; there will have to be room for further adjustment in it, and I think it will come. It remains to be seen how much their concern about the advent of the Reagan administration will speed the process.

The talk—the threats that the hostages will be put on trial as a last resort—is idle chatter. The regime would gain nothing but further international opprobrium if they did and gain nothing . . . and possibly even lose a lot of the funds they so desperately need.

We had yet another earthquake tremor this afternoon, possibly even stronger than the one the other night. . . . We joked with the guard and servant staff that God is unhappy with the Revolution.

Christmas 1980—A second Christmas as hostages was unimaginable a year before; now it was real. But not before another exercise in wishful thinking in the weeks preceding this second Christmas—each of us had a glimmer of hope that the Iranians might see some merit in the kind of gesture to world public opinion that a Christmas release would represent. However, the complexity of the Algerian-led negotiations, at times seemingly hopelessly beyond resolution by the scale and rhetoric of the latest Iranian demands, made any Christmas timetable increasingly unlikely. Our own observance of the season had gained an unexpected air of tension by events on the 23d. . . .

DAY 416, *December 23, 1980*—An angry, spur-of-the-moment, neatly placed kick by Mike, unwilling to be pushed around by a "student" militant, may prove to have had a decisive impact on our continued status as involuntary "guests" of this ministry. His act in any event has made him our hero. The incident occurred at a climactic point in a highly unexpected and curious chain of events that began early this evening, when a security guard walked in with information that we were to be transferred from this building to join our 49 colleagues and that we should be ready to leave that evening and on short notice.

Our first reaction was to look at each other in stunned disbelief. . . . I asked to speak to the chief of protocol, who told me the decision was the product of a meeting in the prime minister's office, that we were to "join" our friends "for Christmas," and that we were not to return to the ministry. We were to be ready to leave within two hours. I asked to meet with or at least telephone the Swiss ambassador, the latter request causing him obvious difficulty.

By 11:00 P.M. there was still no sign of the chief of protocol or of whoever was to escort us to wherever we were to go. Through all of this frantic scurrying about, the guard and kitchen force staff on duty watched with some incredulity, as much or more surprised than we that our fourteen-month association was suddenly to be terminated in this fashion and on the eve of Christmas. . . . Our immediate conclusion was that the move had to do with the Christmas services planned for the 49 hostages. The government possibly concluded that this gave it the opportunity to at long last consolidate us with them. We speculated also that the move might be a product of local irritation with the recent surge of public criticism coming out of Washington, beginning with Muskie's statement about the "unreasonableness" of the Iranian demands on financial guarantees and transfers and including as well the statements from both hostage families and officials critical of the "supposed humanitarian" treatment being enjoyed by the hostages. . . . Throughout the evening we assumed that the government and not the "students" were principally involved and that we would be in the government's custody.

That this was an inaccurate assumption became obvious when, at almost midnight, the chief of protocol arrived, accompanied by some 15 to 20 others. These included a man he described as the deputy foreign minister (and a son-in-law of the ARK) who did not once speak to us, the ministry's administrative head, a number of other unidentified persons, and some five to ten young men in revolutionary dress who proved to be the militant "students"— our first direct contact with those who had seized our embassy. Only the chief of protocol spoke to us, he of very sober mien and obviously troubled by what was going on.

At about 1:00 A.M., the word was given that we were to leave, each of us picking up a flight bag in one hand and a plastic bag or box in the other and insisting, despite the efforts of the "students" to take them, that we intended to carry them ourselves. . . . Their insistence that we turn over the bags continued as we walked down the stairs. In the darkened courtyard below, a carryall (once owned by the embassy) stood with its doors opened and windows painted over, and in the shadows stood several of the ministry's army guard, all armed with G-3 rifles.

At this point the unexpected happened. Mike, in the lead, had already stepped into the carryall when he was ordered to get out and told to turn over his bags. (By this time, the "students" also had ready ropes to tie our hands.) He resisted, and a "student," who turned out to be the leader of the pack, attempted force. Mike reacted with sudden and unpremeditated anger, giving the "student" a sharp push. The "student" grabbed Mike's arm and ripped his sweater, and Mike landed a kick that, hopefully, struck a sensitive lower area. I attempted to separate the two men, yelling that we were diplomats and not hostages and did not propose to be pressured with force. There then ensued several rather brief minutes of confused silence, followed by the aggrieved "student" suddenly announcing that we were to return upstairs to our room. The last one to go up the stairs, I turned at the steps and attempted to reason with the angry "student," pointing out again that we were diplomats, "guests" of his government, and that I was still the president's personal representative in Iran. What difference I thought the latter would make I have no idea, and it made no impression whatsoever. Instead the "student," a man of about 25 and very macho indeed in his revolutionary dress, whipped out a .45 and, pointing at my head, said angrily I should tell my "friend" that if he were again to refuse to accede, he would find the .45 used against him. I said something about "guns, for God's sake, not needed," but was then given a good shove up the stairs.

Through all of this, the chief of protocol and other ministry types stood silently and uncomfortably to the side. Back in our room, the three of us paced the floor, assuming that this was but a momentary release and that the "students" would shortly be back with a vengeance. By this time, too, we had been thoroughly jolted into the clear realization that we were about to come under complete "student" control, with all its adverse ramifications. Shortly one of the ministry officials walked in, ashen and shaken, sitting down and saying over and over, "This is *not* Iran, this is *not* Iran. What has happened to us?" I commented sourly that this had been the first time in my diplomatic career that I had had a .45 pointed at my head. He then asked how we would feel about leaving separately, either singly, or with Mike leaving alone and Vic and I separately—this reflecting obviously the wish of the "students" to deal separately with Mike. I replied that we had strong views about leaving at all, that unless and until we could be assured that we would remain in government hands at the new location we felt that we should remain in the ministry. . . . We had been under the impression from the outset of the crisis that his government regarded us as "guests" and not as hostages, and it would be taken very much amiss by our government if that situation now were to change, 14 months after the seizure of our embassy and with our two governments engaged in a dialogue to resolve the issue.

The official then left, all of us by now thoroughly exhausted and depressed. Mike was angry with himself for having lost his temper and possibly aggravating our outlook seriously. But events were to prove that his temper had served us well indeed. Almost two hours later the same official called, telling us that nothing further would happen until the next day and that he was marginally hopeful that we would not be moved then either. It was now 3:00 A.M. We tried to sleep, but in my case not before I had gone through my papers once again to be certain that they contained nothing that the "students" could use against us.

DAY 417, *December 24, 1980*—Christmas Eve 1980.

Not the Christmas Eve we had hoped for. Instead, we understand, the American people will stand on their front lawns at an agreed hour tonight and for 417 seconds, one for each of the hostage days, will hold aloft a lighted candle or lamp. On the Ellipse in Washington, the president will light the still darkened Christmas tree for the same number of seconds. . . .

For our colleagues and for us, Christmas Eve in Tehran in 1980 is blacked out, as is every night in wartime Iran. And tonight, at dinner time, we had an air raid alert and much AA firing in our neighborhood, the first alert of much consequence for some time. The alert was noisy but short-lived. We assume no Iraqi aircraft were sighted, despite the confidence to the contrary suggested by the noisy barrage.

The alert made candlelight for our Christmas Eve dinner all the more natural and necessary. The cook's fare to us tonight was a meat patty—that we term *goatburgers*—plus the usual soggy French fries, peas, and carrots. Happily, with all the largesse from our diplomatic friends, we could largely ignore the cook. Instead we came up with a dinner of oyster stew, rice, tuna fish and cucumber salad, Danish salami, German cheese, *and* caviar—black-market caviar but nonetheless caviar. Good and special friends had sent in several half-kilo containers. And *with* the caviar, English crackers and fresh onions. So we feel a bit spoiled, but not for long, reminding ourselves that a little luxury once in a while is not all that bad for hostages.

It has been a hard day, nonetheless, and the three of us are still uncertain about our continued stay in this ministry. Christmas is love, family, and all things bright and beautiful. And 52 Americans spend their second year in captivity in Iran. Fifty-two families, in this great family festival of Christmas, spend this Christmas in a mixture of sorrow, bitterness, and anger as the result of yet further delays in the discussions, triggered by the nature of the financial demands in the latest Iranian communication. I found myself in a mood of great depression as I walked for some time on the balcony this afternoon—a depression set off by the events of last evening and deepened today by the appreciation that my colleagues sit unknowing and waiting yet a second Christmas. I felt tears of bitterness in asking myself aloud, Why? Why did it have to happen in the first place? Why is a resolution of the crisis so difficult and slow? And more fundamentally, why, dear God, must there be so much bitterness and hate here toward us that make the current discussions so difficult? We know the answer in the sense that it is an article of faith here that all of Iran's ills are a consequence of American interference in Iran's affairs. But knowing that does not provide an adequate answer, especially given the hyperbole that accompanies these claims. . . .

I think tonight as I sit here of my own family and how intensely I miss them. I tell myself that I am in good spirits knowing that my family is all together for Christmas, but telling myself does not seem adequately to make it so as the magical hours and atmosphere of Christmas Eve arrive. I think of how much more difficult it must be for my 49 colleagues, burdened in ways we have not experienced and even more separated from family than we because of the limitations on their mail and the absence of any contact with outsiders.

On such a day as this I find myself taking some satisfaction that although this crisis has frustrated and angered the American people, it has also seemingly given them a human and emotional issue on which to build a refurbished sense of unity. It has given them a cause, of human dimensions, that in a very special way has reminded our people of the need to share with others their concerns, fears, and hopes—a concern for fellow humans in distress, a concern that nurtured and deepened may well persist beyond this crisis to help build a new sense of both national unity and social awareness. If this tragedy does indeed do some of that, some of the bitterness and sadness I feel today would be less heavy. . . .

DAY 418, *December 25, 1980*—It is Christmas Day. At breakfast the chief of protocol telephones to say that the prime minister's office has just called to inquire whether we wished to be visited by the same group of Iranian clergymen who last night held religious services for our 49 colleagues. I respond that we would very much like to see them. . . .

Meanwhile, our seamstress lady from the kitchen force walks into our room, shy and modest as always in her devoted Islamic manner, carrying a water pitcher stuffed with late autumn roses and snapdragons. They are her Christmas gift to us, and she accompanies it with a little speech in Farsi full of hope that we will soon rejoin our families. The speech is familiar from this lady who is both devoutly revolutionary but also deeply troubled, as a mother and grandmother herself, that we are forcibly kept from our families. Her gesture this morning is so clearly genuine that we felt like embracing her, but that would have embarrassed her to death. . . .

Midday the chief of protocol telephones back to say that the clerics will be in to see us at five in the afternoon and will be accompanied by the Algerian ambassador and by a good number of representatives from the official state media, the Voice and Vision of Iran, to record the occasion for later public consumption. My first reaction to the latter is anger—irritation that we, like our 49 colleagues, are to be used in some sort of show-and-tell to demonstrate to the world what humanitarian treatment we benefit from. But we conclude that it would be better to try to use the event to *our* advantage and that in any event there was a limit to what we could demand and still expect to have the event occur. Victor suggests that he be prepared with a statement in Farsi that he would make to the Iranian audience, prefacing it with the insistence that if used by the V&V [Voice and Vision] of Iran it not be censored. The statement would emphasize that while we and our colleagues feel very deeply about the unjustness of our being held from our own families for 14 months, we had no ill will toward the people of Iran, for whom we wished, especially at Christmastime, a time of love and brotherhood, nothing but peace and prosperity. . . .

At 5:15 P.M., the delegation arrives, though the media corps not until almost an hour later, setting up their lights and cameras midway through the religious service. The delegation is larger than we expected, including our good friend, the papal nuncio, who had seen our colleagues last night after at first being told he could not do so. With him is Yohannan Issayi, the archbishop of the Assyrian Chaldean Catholic Church in Tehran, and two Iranian Pentacostalist preachers from the Assembly of God Church—the same two men who took part in the Easter services for our colleagues. The Algerian ambassador is accompanied by another Algerian diplomat, both having arrived just today from Algiers and scheduled to depart in another 48 hours for Washington to resume discussions with the Department of State team on the conditions bearing on our release. The chief of protocol, the ministry administrative head, and Mr. Azizi from the prime minister's office complete the delegation plus several men of our regular guard force, all curious to see what a Christmas ceremony is all about.

But before we begin, there is time to embrace the good papal nuncio, who tells us that those of our 49 colleagues whom he saw the previous evening were in good spirits but "fatigued"—it has been so long and "they are tired, so tired." He had not seen all of them, but he and the other clerics together, he feels, saw most of them. The nuncio, as had been his experience at Easter, was full of praise for the courage of "my Katerina and Elizabeth" (Kate Koob and Ann Swift)—the two of them laughing and crying, he said, at one and the same time. But strong. Some of the men looked physically better than others; the older ones seemed to be under greater stress than the younger ones. All, however, looked thinner and, by contrast with Eastertime, were now showing the strain of their long captivity. Several had, he said, objected strongly to the excessive filming of last night's services, and there had been one instance where several hostages were in a near altercation with their "student" captors (a joy for us to hear, because it suggests that they have not lost their will to stand up to the "students").

The nuncio and their colleagues cannot tell us where they had seen our colleagues; they were sworn to secrecy but in any event had been blindfolded, coming and going. But we get the impression that the services, conducted separately for groups of from one to five of the hostages and continuing until 4:00 A.M. on Christmas morning, were somewhere in Tehran, rather than in a distant city. Most moving of all for us is the news the nuncio tells us that several of them, two women and Richard Morefield, are aware that we three are still in Tehran, and they send their regards. Until now we have assumed that they had no idea what ever happened to us after November 4. Knowing this tonight somehow makes us feel closer to them, and we hope they get some sort of encouragement in knowing we are still here. But, how desperately curious they must be to know what has happened these 14 long months! What must it be like to exist, against the background of those traumatic events of 14 months ago, with almost no idea of what has happened since?

With the two Algerians, I take the opportunity, out of earshot of the Iranians, to fill them in on the curious events of 48 hours earlier, urging that they brief the department of it when they reach Washington. I also tell the Algerians that, while we understood the need felt by Washington to satisfy American public opinion with strong talk about the extremity of the current Iranian demands, that it was now time for a return to quiet diplomacy. . . .

By this time the clerics are trying to round us up for the services, so we sit in a circle, the Algerians and Iranians included, for a service of prayers, Bible readings, a short sermon, and carol singing—the last suffering from our rusty vocal cords but more than balanced by our enthusiasm. "What Child Is This" presses our talents beyond their limits, but we do well on other carols. Meanwhile, the media have arrived and are now busy filming us from every angle, with the cameramen equally curious about our surroundings.

These services are then interrupted, and I, alone in taking communion, go to a table at the far end of the room for a service conducted by the nuncio and the archbishop, the two of them seconding each other in what seemed some lack of familiarity with the English-language litany. The archbishop, done up now in a splendid cassock and richly embroidered stole, is the main celebrant and offers the bread and wine. We embrace at the end, one of many embraces during this evening's events with these good men and good friends.

With that, we resume the main service, but with the three of us now the main participants. I make a little speech, taking off from St. Paul's definition of *faith* (the substance of things hoped for; the evidence of things unseen) to say that that was the kind of faith we had in the hope of seeing our colleagues again, as free men. I said that what I had to say was in the form of a prayer—a prayer to the God that all of us shared, whether Iranians, Americans, Algerians, or Italians (the nuncio)—that the special promise of hope and love of Christmas would build the understanding needed that would see the end of the unjust deprivation of our colleagues' freedom, the strengthening of peace, especially for Iran, and the beginnings of a restoration of the traditionally close relationships between Iran and the United States. I then introduced Victor, who I said would want to give expression to some of these sentiments in Farsi. He did so, and with an Iranian style and emphasis that, said Mike and I to him later, suggested that he had perhaps been in Iran too long! Mike added his own expression of thanks to the clergy for coming, and I wound it up with a greeting to the American people, whose support and love for us throughout this crisis had been something we would never forget.

Two hours later, we are frankly all a bit reluctant, I think, to see it end. But the Algerians and the clerics seemed pressed by commitments, and the Iranians appear to feel the affair had gone on as long as desirable. Before they leave, however, the nuncio surprises each of us with a tiny Christmas tree ornament made of tinfoil, gifts from Ann and Kate. The ornaments were in the shape of animals, mine the lamb of God carrying a shield marked with a cross—surely the work of Kate Koob. This in turn sees the Pentacostalist preachers presenting us with small gold crosses for our lapels.

So it is Christmas night, and we are left again with the room to ourselves, each of us full of emotions triggered by this most unusual of Christmases. Each of us with our thoughts on our 49 colleagues, looking with wonder and tears in our eyes (how often that has been so today!) at these tiny tinfoil tree ornaments Ann and Kate gave to the nuncio from their decorated tree. We feel for the first time a direct link with these two women whose courage and spirit have seemed so immense throughout this ordeal. . . .

As we ate our dinner, cold and uninteresting by now, we tripped over each other in sharing our impressions, each of us full of new spirit and confidence— confidence, I think, that there is still a lot of decency and goodness around. . . . We sat in a darkened corner of the room for a good hour after dinner, having said everything we possibly could to give expression to our emotions and, with Christmas music as a background, getting equal satisfaction in simply sitting quietly with our thoughts—thoughts of family, of 49 colleagues, of friends—all made more real and dear to us by the uniquely emotional experience of this Christmas Day's events. I feel better tonight than I have in many months.

If there was any of the Stockholm syndrome in the hostage situation present this night, it was more the reverse of that syndrome, of the kind that we have sensed increasingly among our contacts in this building in recent months. Our guard force, augmented to three for the evening's event, clearly identified totally with us, delighted in what went on, pleased that Iran was showing itself in ways truer to the traditions of Persian hospitality. Perhaps their feelings were reflected best in their coming into the room after all had left, carefully checking behind drapes and under tables to ensure that no bombs or hostile devices had been secreted anywhere, then describing the young cameramen of the Voice and Vision of Teheran as "nothing but thugs" who should not be trusted. Then they sat down to enjoy a James Bond spectacular on our video TV!

DAY 420, *December 27, 1980*—We are still in the ministry. Although our situation is still apparently tenuous, each passing day seems to make less likely our transfer to student control. . . . So we are reassured, but not entirely so, things never being that assured in revolutionary Iran. . . .

I find myself in the minority vis-à-vis my two colleagues the past few days— which I have been not infrequently here, that being perhaps a natural state of affairs among three people, where one is between 20 and 25 years older than the other two and in a position of leadership. It is perhaps the natural state of things that the younger two would frequently be in accord and I with another view.

Currently we seem to differ rather substantially on the matter of Washington's public posture on the hostage discussions. Beginning with Secretary Muskie's statement terming the Iranian financial conditions as "unreasonable," we have had a series of such utterances by the department's spokesman, Secretary Brown, Governor Reagan, and others. Contributing to the impression of an angry Washington were comments by hostage families sharply critical of the conditions (lack of mail especially) in which the hostages have been held.

My two colleagues reacted adversely to Muskie's and other subsequent statements, their concern being that while such feelings are understandable, their expression now is counterproductive to the negotiating atmosphere and may give the extremists here a handle with which to counsel against any further concessions in the Iranian stand. There is merit to that, and certainly there is a point beyond which I, too, would conclude that critical comments from Washington, on the public record, should be muted. I do not, however, think we have reached that point; Iran's need for a settlement, its need for hard cash, is now so great that it would take a good deal more than what has been said to date for the negotiating atmosphere to be adversely affected.

Indeed it is my view, with January 20 coming down the pike, that tough talk from Washington (particularly from Reagan himself) right now is *helpful* rather than harmful. . . . There is some evidence, as a matter of fact, in a statement yesterday by the Iranian minister handling the talks via the Algerians, that the tactic may be working. Minister Nabavi is quoted as saying that Iran is open to any other ideas the United States may have to offer on ways to meet its financial demands. . . .

As for the critical statements from the hostages' families, those in my view also keep the Iranians where they belong—on the defensive. Indeed, the fairly good arrangements for the Christmas services, including the last-minute addition of the papal nuncio and the separate visit by the Algerian ambassador, who picked up presumably uncensored mail, may have been at least partially the result of this family criticism.

More fundamentally, it seems to me, there are times when a spade has to be called a spade at whatever the cost. Our leadership at home has its obligation to the American people and to history, as well as to the 52 of us. The principle is too important not to be given frequent expression.

DAY 422, *December 29, 1980*—Today's press (VOA) quotes President-elect Reagan as responding to a question to the following effect: No, we should not and cannot pay ransom to "barbarians" who are guilty of "kidnapping" diplomats. Bravo! That kind of background music from the man the Iranians will have to deal with after January 20 is welcome. Yes, there is a risk of an irrational response by the local fundamentalists, but that—in my view—is a risk worth taking in circumstances when Iran's need for a settlement is now painfully obvious to even the Iranian in the street.

DAY 424, *December 31, 1980*—The stroke of midnight and a new year begins, signaling the end of a decade and of a year the likes of which none of the three of us expected to experience. Nor did we imagine, one year ago, that we would still be here today. What more does one say than that? The Algerian delegation has now again left Washington and is en route to Algiers to discuss—this time with the Algerian foreign minister in the first instance—the latest American communication to Iran, said to be a "reformulation" of the previous U.S. position. Meanwhile, there is progress—speculation of a new gimmick involving an escrow account into which those Iranian assets immediately releasable would be deposited—and may be what now causes the Algerians first to discuss the matter in Algiers before proceeding on to Tehran.

Meanwhile, we and the Iranians are heard in public statements. Departing Secretary Christopher used an old navy expression to recall that the "tragic event" of the seizure of the hostages occurred on the Carter administration's watch; he preferred to see it resolved on its watch as well, i.e., before January 20. If that were not possible, however, the administration wished to see it turned over to the new team in a way that would be consistent with U.S. national interests and honor. Other statements coming out of Washington seem deliberately to be highlighting the likelihood that the time remaining before January 20 is too short a time to permit the issue's resolution.

Here in Tehran there is a mixture of noises. Some, coming from Nabavi, the head of the Iranian team dealing with the Algerians, include a suggestion of flexibility, saying that if the United States has other ideas as to how Iran's conditions can be met, and if they are acceptable to the Algerians, then Iran will be open to them as well. . . . Earlier Majlis Speaker Hashemi Rafsanjani has been quoted as angrily rejecting Reagan's description of the students as "barbarians" and the regime's demands as "ransom." Speaking in the Majlis, with cries of "Allah O'Akbar" from the members, the speaker accused the United States of trying to "swindle" Iran of its rightful assets and pointing to the United States as the real barbarian: "Every day somewhere in the world the blood of militant people runs from the claws and teeth of the United States. . . . They are civilized, and *we* are savage? . . . There is no one in human history more savage than you, especially the Republican leaders." Having said that, however, the speaker again indicated that he at least prefers to see the issue handled by the government, without further Majlis involvement. A mixed bag, and one cannot ignore the effect of the tough noises on the government's capacity to show flexibility. But, that said, one is still left with the conclusion that there *is* a strong wish here to see this issue settled and that there *is* a concern to see this done before the Reagan team comes in—notwithstanding dismissal of Reagan's tough talk by Nabavi as "not to be taken seriously. He thinks he is still acting in a western movie." The questions as always are, who has the power to make the tough decision? Who is capable and who is prepared to go again to the ARK, especially in the context of the tough noises, to get *his* concurrence in an arrangement that steps back from insistence on total acceptance of Iran's demands? . . .

Happy New Year! It can only be an improvement over the year just finished.

17

January 1981:
Solitary Confinement

By now, Reagan's inauguration loomed large, and we hoped it loomed large in the minds of the Iranians as well. We suspected it did, for we sensed a readiness to end the crisis. The Revolution's government was in place; the utility of the hostages as political pawns had largely ended. Iran needed its frozen assets. European trade sanctions and credit limitations, however inadequate, were nonetheless adding to the hurt. And international reaction to the Iran-Iraq War had dramatically dramatized Iran's diplomatic isolation.

We assumed our hosts hardly needed reminding that if the crisis dragged on into a Reagan administration, at best it would mean that the new crowd in Washington would need some months to develop its own policy focus on the Iranian scene, further prolonging Iran's hurt and isolation. And, at worst for Iran, delay beyond January 20 might see the new Reagan administration giving substance to its tough rhetoric about the scene in Iran, not excluding the application of force.

But all that speculation on our part was momentarily shattered the evening of January 3, when a protocol officer suddenly appeared to tell us that we were to be ready to leave in 20 minutes, not to freedom but "to join your colleagues." Before the night was over, we had indeed left the ministry but found ourselves in solitary confinement in prison cells, with none of our colleagues in sight (not, however, before I had found ways to shred and flush down the toilet several *sensitive papers, including the draft of a "future policy on Iran" telegram to the secretary of state, that only days before I had found a way to spirit out and send to Washington).*

Our hosts were now the militant "students," who at long last had custody of the three "superspies." This time, too, Foreign Ministry officials, including the deputy foreign minister himself, assured us that in "joining your colleagues" our status would not change; we would, he said, remain "guests" of the government; we would join our colleagues; and, yes, the Swiss ambassador would be allowed to see us. These assurances would prove hollow as soon as we were ordered into vans in the courtyard of the ministry, our army guards and kitchen force watching with only slightly concealed anger themselves as their three longtime charges were bundled off into the night. At Mike's whispered behest, one member of that kitchen force later that night would surreptitiously find a way to telephone the Swiss Embassy and convey the information that we had been taken away.

DAY 427, *January 3, 1981*—It is an eerie thing, a strange feeling, to be moving about the streets of Tehran once again, but this time in the midst of wartime blackouts, the streets apparently deserted with little traffic. We are enormously curious what is about to happen. But now I feel no fear or apprehension, only an intense curiosity and a hope refusing to die that we might indeed be taken to "join our colleagues" as promised. Sitting on the floor of a closed van is uncomfortable, but there are foam rubber pads, which help a bit. Perhaps freedom is nearer than we thought.

Presently we stop. There are muffled voices to be heard, as if we are on some kind of secret mission. It is cold, and I am grateful to be wearing both a sweater and suit coat. Still, I shiver. Vic wears only a polo shirt, and I wonder how uncomfortable he is. The van doors are opened, and we are told to step out into a courtyard, around which rises a building of perhaps three floors but seemingly of various levels. Quickly, however, we are blindfolded, my reminder of assurances to the contrary simply ignored. Then I am led off, up a flight or two of steps, down a long hall, and finally told to sit down on a folding chair that is pushed under me.

I sense that someone is in the room with me and attempt a conversation. Was the person a student? No. Was he with the military? No. What then? Something in between; I would see. Was I the chargé? Yes. A few other desultory exchanges. Then I am pressed to stand up and moved to a wall and spread-eagled against it. I bridle at attempts to remove my loafers, and they do not persist. I am frisked and an attempt made to take some papers from my coat pocket, but my protest again prevails, surprisingly. Then I am told to sit down. Minutes pass before the blindfold is suddenly removed, and the guard disappears quickly through a steel door that clangs shut behind me.

Alone. There is no one—nothing—to be seen. Nothing but the walls of a cell lighted by a bare bulb hanging from the ceiling. I realize I am in a prison cell—an irregularly shaped room, perhaps 12 by 15 feet, with heavily barred windows high on one side and a steel door on the other. On one wall is hung an old and dirty chenille bedspread, on the other a brown blanket. A few nails are pounded here and there in the wall, presumably for clothing. The floor is covered by a thin brown carpeting. The only furniture is the folding chair on which I sit. Scattered on the floor around me are perhaps 35 or 40 toothpicks. Toothpicks? Why toothpicks?

I realize now that we are in solitary confinement, and I find myself more depressed than I have felt for months. Contact with the outside world is totally ended; my usefulness is nil. I think of the several times that Mike has suggested that we consider an escape plan and wonder if perhaps he has not been right from the start. Yet I think too that surely we are going to see the end of this before Inauguration Day. But why have we been brought here? Why solitary confinement now? Is it punishment? Did the acting foreign minister or the protocol officer have *any* idea where we were to be taken? I suspect they had absolutely no control over the situation. Puppets.

It is cold, unpleasantly so, even with my sweater and coat, and I see no evidence of a source of heat. So I get up and pace around the room, noticing now that someone has written on the walls here and there—all entries referring to "Angela"—"Angela, my love, my life, my wife." I wonder who of my colleagues has occupied this cell and has a wife named Angela, but no amount of study of the graffiti brings memory to bear. (Later I will learn that Angela is the wife of Bill Belk, a communicator.) Occasionally I sit down on my chair and wring my hands with frustration. I count the toothpicks, arranging them in a variety of designs, amusing myself to think that perhaps they were part of a torture device but not believing that.

An hour or so later a young man enters with a foam rubber pad. I remind him that I am cold and will need a blanket. Shortly that too arrives. The light, despite my request that it be shut off so that I can sleep, glares in my eyes. I try to sleep, with little success. Pounding on the door produces a "student" guard, who agrees to my request to go to the bathroom, provided I use a blindfold. Why not? There's no alternative. The guard holds me firmly at the elbow to guide my steps about 100 feet down the hall. I am so cold by now that I shake almost convulsively, and the guard feels it, asking if I'm cold. The bathroom is prison sparseness and dirty—dirtier than any bathroom I've known. Along one side is a large steel sink, where I wash my hands in ice-cold water. Then I am again blindfolded and led back up the hall. I try again to sleep, wearing both my sweater and suit and burying myself under the blanket. I toss and turn, wondering where my two colleagues, Mike and Vic, might be. I wonder too if any of our 49 colleagues are nearby; there is no sound of anyone else, other than the occasional voices of guards and the heavy clang of steel doors. I am thoroughly depressed and angry. I pray that something *will* come of this, despite my own total uselessness at this point.

By morning I find that I must have slept for a time. In any event I am wakened by a guard who walks in and leaves a plate of Iranian bread and cheese on my chair and shortly thereafter brings in a glass of hot tea. I am more tired than hungry but eat all that I'm given. That done I am back pacing my room, still intrigued by the "Angela" reference, still cold, and even more frustrated than before. Intrigued with the identity of the graffiti writer, I decide to add my own—only mine, "Penelope—I love you," is written with my ballpoint pen; the "Angela" graffiti is done with a nail. A request of another guard for my toilet gear brings a toothbrush and dental cream—neither of which is mine, so I decline to use it. In any event, the glass is soon removed, presumably on security grounds; perhaps they fear I will slash my wrists. Am I cold, the guard asks? Obviously, I answer. I decide that the best way to stay warm and to pass the time is to crawl under the blanket and try to sleep.

Later in the day the guard returns, this time with another, somewhat older man, who introduces himself as Ahmad in reasonably good English. He does not stay long on this visit but arranges for me to be moved down the hall to a larger cell: two doors and perhaps 10 by 18 feet. There a small table is added, plus an electric heater and a card table—all these items marked with a U.S. Embassy inventory number. . . .

Except for its size, this cell is no different from the earlier one. The barred windows, high and out of reach up one side, seem even dirtier than in the earlier one, with most of the glass broken and the opening covered with steel mesh and heavy plastic, making the sky even more difficult to see. As the days pass, the cell becomes almost comfortable, at least in the sense I have the basics I need—above all, the electric heater, which keeps me fairly comfortable, providing I sit close to it. The heater is also my drying place for laundry—my shirt, my undershirt, socks that I wash in the toilet. . . . My use of the toilet facilities, however, irritates one of my guards. After I knock on my door the fourth time in the course of one day, he opens the door and snaps that "three times a day is enough for you to pee pee." I respond angrily that I am 58 years old and need to use the toilet more than three times a day. And how old was he? He growls a bit but gives me no answer as he leads me blindfolded down the hall.

My "student" guards—or at least I assume they are students; the age is right—conduct themselves as if the whole affair is a burden to them, a burden that they just barely tolerate. I detect no particular zeal of any kind, whether in terms of hostility toward me and my two colleagues (by now I assume we three are alone in the prison) or in terms of zeal toward the Revolution. They appear simply to be putting in their time, working in shifts. Some I tolerate better than others, especially one or two who are a bit zealous in terms of security. I ask one of them one day why they bother to blindfold us in our trek back and forth to the toilet, reminding him that it hasn't taken me long to measure out the distance by the number of steps I take and that it is fairly clear to me in which cells my two colleagues are located. (I can hear their knocks on their steel doors too.) The answer: "Regulations." Regulations! An indication that revolutionary ardor has settled into some set patterns approaching boredom. One of the guards, watching me voice my disgust at the filth of the toilet, growls that I should consider myself "fortunate." I look at him with disdain and go on with washing my plate, spoon (no forks are allowed), and glass—a regular diversion after each meal, something to do. And further confirmation that my two colleagues are around: they use the same garbage can for food they don't tolerate.

The guards' manner, I tell myself, must be further evidence that this thing is winding down toward some kind of finale. This prison—and it was obviously built for that purpose—must have been a good deal more lively and "purposeful" as far as these young men (I see no women) are concerned when a large number of our colleagues were held here earlier. I conclude that it had been so used earlier, not only from the scrawled "Angela" in my first cell, but also from the names written on the walls of this cell by those who had been held here earlier. They include Al Golacinski, Duane Gillette, Jerry Plotkin, Rodney Sickman, Dick Morefield, and Billy Gallegos. Their stay began in June 1980 and continued until December 18, when the last of them, the date indicates, had departed.

So six of our colleagues had lived in this cell for months at a time, with—say the guards—occasional visits to a "game room." I am uncrowded, alone in it, but it could not have been comfortable with six mats along the wall for sleeping. Room for calisthenics? Not much. There *is* room for me, and I religiously keep up my ministry routine: 15 minutes before breakfast and 45 to 60 minutes in the late afternoon. Jogging is even more boring than otherwise in a space only 18 feet long, but it can be managed. It occupies time. Regularly, every hour or two, I also pace the floor, back and forth, up and down, to stretch my muscles and relieve the monotony.

It is hard to get my mind off the fact that six of my colleagues had spent so many months here. I ask myself what *they* did to escape total boredom. I tell myself that I'm *glad* to be held here, since it gives me the chance to see how my colleagues have been treated.

One day I resort to poetry, to try to express how I feel.

> I wonder what these walls could tell
>   Of others who have known this cell,
>   And who like me
>   Would rather be
> Where freedom lives instead.
>
> What say these walls about my friends
> Who put their names thereon with pens,
>   to tell the world
>   that they survived,
> Long months without defeat?
>
> Six months and more these walls knew then,
> The strength and pride of six good men,
>   Who never lost
>   What matters most,
> The freedom in their hearts.

That freedom walls can never take
It rests on how one feels,
    Of liberty
    And dignity
Of what is right and wrong.

It rests as well on countrymen,
Prepared themselves to take a stand,
    For principles
    We cannot lose
If freedom is to live.

But most of all it rests on that
Which comes from deep within one's heart
    Of family love
    And God above
Of trust in what this means.

Of this these walls may never tell,
But Iranian men who guard them will,
    Of six held here
    Who knew no fear
Because their cause was right.

I chuckle to myself that I am hardly a poet laureate, but resolve anyway to smuggle out my "poem," written on a sheet torn from a paperback and stuffed into my billfold. . . . One day my guard unceremoniously dumps a vacuum cleaner in the center of the cell, telling me that a weekly cleanup is a requirement. So I use as much time as possible in the process, discovering that I have not been as "solitary" as I had thought in occupancy of the cell. Under an electric fan in one corner is a dead mouse, its life scrunched out when someone, one of the guards possibly, had suddenly moved the fan. I conclude that my mouse friend is the body that I detected in my first night in the cell scurrying briskly across my face but which I had had no luck in locating then. Another excuse to knock on my door; this time to confront my guard with my mouse held carefully by its tail. He grunts and goes off with it.

DAY 430, *January 6, 1981*—Today is my father's birthday. . . . He's been gone since early in 1962, dying of injuries from an auto accident while I was in Pakistan on assignment at the embassy there. How *he* would shake his head at my predicament: A staunchly conservative man in all things (although as a farmer he did not stand pat on old ways of farming if he could be shown better), it was a good many years before he fully adjusted to my going so far from home to find a niche in life. But when he did, late in life, he was satisfied and indeed pleased. I wish I could live my growing-up years with him over again; I would appreciate him more than I did then. Perhaps that's the way most sons see their fathers. I remember him as preoccupied with his farm work and the church, and as a result I stood aloof too; the fault lies with both of us, I suppose. But never did I lack respect for what he stood for, and that respect has grown steadily since he's been gone.

My lamp has not been returned (removed as punishment for reading too late), but I'm assured it will be. I have not seen my two colleagues, but they are in nearby cells along this same hall. Indeed I think Mike is just across from me, judging from a voice I've heard and especially from heavy breathing I overheard this afternoon, which is surely Mike doing his exercises with the exercise belt. . . .

Today I again asked to see Ahmad and again reiterated my request to see the Swiss ambassador. I asked if the Algerians are still here. Yes. Ahmad is hopeful, noting 12 more days remain before the new administration takes over in Washington. . . . He says we were brought here for "protection." Against whom isn't clear. I reminded him we'd been 14 months in the Ministry of Foreign Affairs, to the whole city's knowledge, and no harm had come to us. Are he and his colleagues "students"? No, "something in between" that and government, whatever that means, but he has been at the embassy and knows most of our colleagues, speaking of several of them, including those who were in this room before. He claimed they had had all sorts of comforts—video, games, game room, etc. I said that could not compensate for seven months in this small cell.

Dinner has just been brought in: a large piece of Iranian bread and a slice of what looks like a spinach loaf, ice-cold. That's it, but happily I have some butter left from breakfast, which will make things go down better. I asked for fruit today; I had an apple day before yesterday. I plan to ask for mast (yogurt) tomorrow. Just now a young man (they are all in their late teens or early twenties) brought in an orange parka and sweat pants. New. I wonder if they're from the embassy's co-op store. I wonder what I look like, not having shaved for four days; we are not allowed to shave for some reason. . . .

I wonder, too, what the Ministry of Foreign Affairs' officials who gave us such strong assurances the other night know of our conditions. Presumably nothing. What are they saying now to the Swiss ambassador? That we have joined our colleagues? That we are living in "the best hotel conditions"? Why *are* the three of us being held separately in this way in any event, now after 14 months elsewhere and with discussions so actively under way? It makes little sense. Had we joined our colleagues, that could be understood. But this? Held as hostages in the earlier sense, almost as common prisoners? It is hard to comprehend. What part of the government is masterminding this?

DAY 431, *January 7, 1981*—Today for lunch the guards brought in a can of asparagus (Jolly Green Giant—Minnesota) and a box containing a tin of Carnation sandwich spread and asked if that would be all right. What can one say? I saw no other item on the menu, though they also had a can of mussels, one of clams, and one of sardines with them. . . . All these "goodies" come from the box of Christmas gifts from embassies that was still at the Ministry of Foreign Affairs. . . . Today's lunch also included Iranian bread and a wizened, but tasty, apple. Certainly we did not draw heavily on the Iranian state budget today.

Exchanges with my guards—*They:* "You are frightened of our Revolution. That is why you encouraged the Iraqis to attack. Look at Vietnam and Chile!"*I:* "But your economy is being devastated. The war is disastrous for both countries, especially for your oil industry. You need that, desperately." "The oil?" he responds. "No, we can do without that. You will see."

DAY 432, *January 8, 1981*—The power went off for much of last evening and again for most of this morning. The problem seems to be in good part here within these buildings. A guard brought in a candle, but when the power goes and with almost no natural light coming through the so-called windows, there is little that one can do except to pace the floor, which rapidly becomes boring, or get in under the blankets on the mat on the floor. . . .

Whether because of the power problem or to save money in the state budget, our lunch and dinner today (and breakfast) were again cold dishes—and all from cans from our co-op or from the Christmas box that we left at the ministry. For lunch it was what looked like canned ham, some kind of pâté, and more of a Carnation sandwich spread. For dinner, a large pile of tinned mussels (which I could not eat), a bit of smoked oysters, and canned asparagus. Fortunately there was bread and a bit of cheese left over from breakfast. As I said one evening to one of the guards who asked how I felt about the food, "It's not Paris!" Oh yes, we did have a pomegranate today, and for once I managed to squeeze its juice without putting it all over my clothing, spending almost an hour in the process. Time well spent.

I'm not sure whether today's food was meant to be seen by us as a favor, but I recall that the first night we were brought here one of the guards said something to the effect that if we behaved properly there would be "privileges." While I may not see them as "privileges," things have gradually moved in that direction. On the first day I was not even allowed to keep a glass in this cell; toothpaste was brought and then taken away. There was only one chair. A white rag was tied around my head as a blindfold when I went to the bathroom. Now I am simply requested to hold my small face towel over my eyes as I am led down the hall. . . . The ceiling lights are now turned off at night, unlike the first few nights when they continued to glare all night and I was told to pull the blanket over my head "like everyone else." A razor is now available in the bathroom for shaving. And today my watercolor set was brought in, and I was told I could paint if I wished. There being no paper and no appropriate subject, I am hardly inspired.

This "privilege" process is something that I suppose our colleagues went through, I having been given to understand that the six to eight young men who

take turns manning this place are "experienced" in guarding hostages. I facetiously asked the one who told me this, "Oh really? And what do they expect
to do with this experience in the future, after we've left—seize another embassy?" . . . The food improves a bit each day; now there is an apple or orange
and a slab of butter each morning, which I harbor during the day. The cheese
seems to improve. Some of the new things obviously come from our co-op store
at the embassy—like this morning's cheese, a half-package of sliced Kraft
cheese, and the vanilla pudding tin at lunch, the kind Penne used to put in the
boys' school lunches. . . . Earlier a guard brought in an aspirin bottle, filled
with what I assume are vitamin pills; indeed the label includes a handwritten
note: "Vitamins for one weak [sic]." I decide not to use them, uncertain of what
variety of vitamins they might be. . . .

DAY 433, *January 9, 1981*—The seventh day in my cell. Another anniversary—36 years since the landing (I on an LSM [landing ship medium]) at
Lingayen Gulf in the Philippines, at that time the largest naval armada ever
assembled. Perhaps the record still stands. It was to be our closest call in terms
of danger—shrapnel but no direct hits. Much tension; a seaman, a radioman,
had a nervous collapse and had to be evacuated. Several men were killed on the
ship next to us as we unloaded on the beach, but we got off without serious
danger. . . .

Today is Friday. I can see through the small space in one window that it is
sunny, clear skies. I have finished Dickens's *Great Expectations*—a marvelous
story—but the other books that have been brought in don't promise much. Just
now I've been given a novel based on the life of St. Luke. It may be interesting.
Included in the carton brought in yesterday containing some 20 books to choose
from was a green hardback volume of the new (1978) *Lutheran Book of Worship*. It has no markings, but I suspect it may have been sent for Kate Koob, an
Iowa Lutheran. It is an interesting volume to scan. It includes the entire Book
of Psalms and various orders of services, all of it reflecting the compulsion that
churches seem to feel these days to modernize the old King James Version's
English; to me it is usually a mistake. Something of the old beauty of the
language is lost, as well as the mysticism that plays a part in any religion. Even
the 23d Psalm is fiddled with and with deleterious effect. . . .

No change today, except that the food was spartan indeed: bread, butter, and
tea for breakfast; rice and lentils—with a trace of meat if you looked hard—and
tea for lunch; bread and cold fish for dinner, tasting like sardines but a bigger
fish than that. That was it. . . . But I had another shower, shave, and hair
wash—and that made me feel better.

I asked for paper today to write a letter and surprisingly it was produced,
along with a separate sheet on which I was told to write Penne's address. It
offends me to write anything of a personal nature that others will read, but I did
this as a test, to see what the reaction might be. So far it has not been returned,
for rewriting or as rejected. My prayer is that I will be home long before the

letter arrives, but the days pass with no change—totally cut off as we now are, with absolutely no news. One guard, when I asked him today, said the Algerians were still active, though "presently in Algiers again."

It should not be long, said he. But whether his saying that means anything more than what he thinks I might like to hear is anyone's guess. How strange it is—and unpleasant—to be totally cut off from the outside world, my only contact being the muffled sound of the radio and TV in the distance down the hall. And, if I stretch, that small patch of blue sky scarcely visible through what passes for a window but is offended by double rows of steel bars and two layers of steel mesh outside the clear plastic lining on the inside of the window. That at least helps obscure the heavy layer of dirt on the broken panes of glass that partially fill the middle of all that obstruction.

Out in the hallway, where the guards sit, there is often the sound of dice being rolled, sometimes until well after midnight. It is obviously the guards playing backgammon, probably using the set given us by the papal nuncio and brought along by Mike and Vic in hopes of their being able to play here. For me, for that reason, the sound is grating on the ears. Should any of the fundamentalist clergy see or hear it, it would presumably be grating as well, Khomeini reportedly having pronounced such games as objectionable to Islamic purity.

DAY 434, *January 10, 1981*—Dinner tonight was another heap of smoked oysters, . . . a large piece of Iranian bread, and sliced Kraft cheese. Also tea. . . . Last night someone brought in a pack of graham crackers, and today there was coffee in a jar. Oh yes, the guard tonight offered me some Worcestershire sauce with my oysters. I declined.

I could hear heavy rain today on the other side of the thick walls. One hears virtually nothing from out there, not only because of the thickness of the walls but also because of the noise of the fan out in the hall somewhere that seems to be part of the heating system—a little bit like the constant hum of blowers on a ship. Once in a great while they stop, apparently because of a blown fuse, and then the silence is a remarkable thing. . . .

Another guard told me that the letter I'd written to Penne has been sent to the government, whatever that means. I wrote another letter today, to Minister of State Nabavi, reminding him of the assurances I'd been given before we left the Ministry of Foreign Affairs and asking to see the Swiss ambassador. I am not optimistic. I gather from the guard that the Algerians are still active. Again I am told "it should not be long." I tell this guard that I thought hostage-taking was not compatible with Islam, at least not what I knew of Islam's emphasis on peace, love, compassion, and brotherhood. To that I was told that in Islam not all men are brothers. What does one say to that?

I have spent some more time looking through the new *Lutheran Book of Worship*. . . . The book has a good collection of hymns, including "The Battle Hymn of the Republic," all the verses of which I put to memory the other night. . . . I use the book to sing, especially Christmas carols—to the irritation of the guards who pound the cell door occasionally telling me to keep my voice down.

DAY 435, *January 11, 1981*—There's an expression, I think, from where I forget, that says that walls do not a prison make. Well, I must say they do a reasonably good job at it.

The point is presumably that walls cannot confine the spirit, the freedom of one's own mind to think and feel beyond the confines of a cell. But I find that it is easier talked about than experienced. These walls *can* be confining to one's spirit too, especially when one feels the total injustice of being held here, the solitary nature of our confinement, the effect of being blindfolded to walk to the bathroom, the almost total absence of natural light, the sky a very distant patch of light through iron bars and screens and dirty panes of glass.

A sense of anger and bitterness lies close to the surface of one's thoughts, easily dominant unless suppressed. With no one to speak to, that means of letting off steam is absent. So I read. But the books available leave much to be desired. I assume I have no authorization to write as I do now. . . . Happily I have several pens with me that have not been taken. And I have blank pages torn from paperback books on which I can write now. I write in as small a script as possible, to smuggle this out if at all possible later. Whether I can manage that remains to be seen.

A total stranger—a man named Simon from Port Washington, New York— wrote me a letter that arrived while we were still in the ministry. He reminded me that freedom cannot be totally taken from anyone, in the sense that freedom is also a state of mind. Freedom is also my right to think, to know where justice is in this situation, to know that justice *will* prevail in the long term, to know that I cannot be held indefinitely, to know that in time I will again know the freedom of movement and expression that is so much my right in my own country. Indeed, in a sense I can take angry satisfaction in looking forward to the freedom I will again know in my country in contrast to the restrictions on it, certainly regarding freedom of worship and expression, that prevail in revolutionary Iran. In that sense I can look with disdain on these young and bearded revolutionaries who now lead me up and down these halls blindfolded. And yet I know that in their minds they feel a new sense of freedom too, though I fear it is more a feeling of power, of enjoying power, especially power over *us*, symbols as we are of the hated Great Satan, a thought so much drilled into their young minds.

I cannot say that I could indefinitely endure enforced solitude of this kind. I cannot say that I have that kind of strength. Perhaps I do, but I don't know. Perhaps, because other men have done it before. Perhaps, because the human body and mind have a remarkable capacity to adjust. What of a reliance on a spiritual being? What of God? What does that offer in such a situation? The answer will vary among individuals, but I find it hard to believe that imprisonment, especially solitary confinement, does not remind everyone that there must be a God of some kind. The three of us, these past 14 months, have often commented among ourselves that "God must be sitting this one out," or else He would long since have done something to bring this unjust burden on a hapless group of men and women to an end. Perhaps He is "sitting it out" in respect to the issue itself. But in terms of His being available to us, helpful to us, I am not prepared to say He's sitting this one out. I can only assume from my own experience that most of us have found reason to think more of what God means, of the assurance that we do have Him in our own minds and hearts—and thus in our capacity to live through this, in believing that there *is* some such Being.

For me, prayers have always been a kind of dialogue with God, an opportunity to express quietly my concerns, hopes, and fears—and in doing so, believing that God is listening, to gain confidence in living with those concerns, even if I do not see that all my concerns have been met. So now, in this state of total isolation that I live with, I have that kind of dialogue to give me a confidence that I am *not* alone and that God is with me and with my colleagues. What He's doing about the crisis is another matter. I suppose there I would conclude that He is at work motivating everyone involved in ways that, I believe, *will* see a solution and soon.

Nor has a sense of family ever meant more to me than it does now. What immense reassurance I have in knowing that in that respect I am not at all alone and that in that sense these walls do not a prison make. My family is constantly on my mind, to be talked about in a dialogue with God, to be remembered for the shared experiences of years past, to be seen in my mind's eye as often thinking of me. Surely all of us held here are stronger men and women because we know that in that respect we are not alone. I know my wife, my sons, my larger family are all thinking of me, praying for me, believing in me. Indeed, I am so conscious of that sometimes that I ask myself whether I as an individual can possibly be worthy of it, whether when I am free I will be able to prove myself worthy of all that magnificent support. God give me the strength to remember the respect and support they have shown me and to act and live in a way that shows it to them.

DAY 436, *January 12, 1981*—I think I have never felt quite the sense of isolation bordering on despair that I felt last night when the power was cut for some 10 or 15 minutes in this part of the city. The isolation was physical and mental. In the physical sense the darkness was as total as can be imagined— inside a room whose walls are two feet thick, the only windows 10 to 12 feet up one side, with iron bars on the inside and out, two layers of steel mesh in addition to that, and dirty cracked or broken glass panes in between. When the power was cut, the guards—presumably responding to standing instructions in case of such situations—double-locked my steel doors, the clanking of steel on steel and the flash of flashlights adding to the sense of being totally isolated.

Mental isolation came in the sense I think I have never felt so totally cut off from the outside world, in a cell somewhere in this city but without a clue as to what is happening beyond these thick walls. And the sense of forced isolation was heightened in last night's power cut because it coincided with one of the Revolution's periodic exercises in bringing the faithful out on the rooftops and streets at a given hour (9:00 P.M.) to shout "Allah O'Akbar" for 15 minutes.

So in the total darkness, deep inside this prison, the only sounds were the clatter of steel chains and locks on our doors, the hurried moving about of the guards, and the distant shouting of the "Allah O'Akbars." The reason, I learned incidentally today, was to celebrate a "major victory" somewhere on the Iraqi front.

For those few minutes last night I felt totally drained emotionally, totally alone physically, and—more than ever in this crisis—a momentary sense of total defeat. I know better now what feelings my colleagues must often have had, especially those held in solitary confinement in those long months of captivity and especially those early months when street demonstrations were constant around the compound. I wondered, as I groped around this cell last night, what my two colleagues in their cells here were thinking. Presumably we feel the isolation even more, because of our having been together, reinforcing each other's spirits for all of the 14 months until now. And perhaps a special sense of defeat because of the assurances given us the other night when we left the ministry about the conditions in which we would be held here, assurances that proved totally worthless.

But the despair and defeat were and are temporary. I am confident we are close to a settlement and that we will be free within the next few weeks. Our colleagues having weathered this treatment all these long months, we can the more easily do so now.

DAY 443, *January 19, 1981*—It is Monday, January 19, and we have been at this "luxury hotel" complex or whatever it is since the night of the 15th, when we were unceremoniously told that we had 15 minutes to pack up and get ready to move to another location. Were we, I asked the guards, en route to the airport? No, I was told; you are going somewhere else. Whereupon we were blindfolded, put on the floor in the back of a van, and driven perhaps 20 minutes to a location that remains uncertain to us—except that it is in Tehran and close up against the mountains in the northern suburbs of the city.

Arriving at this new location, we were led up a long flight of stairs, spread-eagled against a wall where my billfold was taken from me, and then taken to a room and told to sit on a chair—whereupon my blindfold was removed and I found myself in a small room together with Vic Tomseth. . . .

The room is luxurious, certainly by contrast with our prison cell, but what it once was is difficult to say. . . . There are heavy and handsome drapes at the windows, but the windows themselves are heavily painted over, and steel bars, crisscrossed, have been welded on the inside. If we stand on the window ledge we can see, through a tiny crack in one area of the paint, that there are mountains and that this is a residential area. A mosque appears to be nearby.

There is heat, and we have foam rubber pads for sleeping on the floor. But if one suffers from claustrophobia, it is no place to be—the heavy drapes, carpets, windows through which nothing is to be seen give one the feeling of being in a carpeted tomb. I find it less pleasant in that sense than the prison cell, where at least a patch of blue sky was visible through what passed as windows.

But hostages are in no position to complain, and assuredly this is more comfortable than elsewhere, and assuming that our 49 colleagues are some-where here too—which we do, though we cannot hear or see anyone else—assuredly *they* are better off than they have been in the past. And *that* matters.

Occasionally the power fails, and we are provided with candles—the candles clearly taken from our embassy store, as is the food we eat, or most of it at least. That was apparent in our first breakfast—our plate having not only the cus-tomary Iranian bread and jelly but also a chunk of butter, still wrapped with its Land O'Lakes label. And for our first dinner we are given chili! Obviously, canned American chili, but wonderful; however much a jolt it is to our systems, we enjoy it. But we have our duties too. On the second night a guard appears after supper with half-a-dozen cooking pots and pans, telling us that "it is the custom" for the hostages to take turns at cleaning the cooking gear, and it is our turn. So Vic and I go to work in the bathroom, determined to show that when we do a job we do it well.

On the morning of the 19th, breakfast seems never to come, so by 9:30 A.M. we pound on the door to ask why. We are told that blood tests are to be taken before breakfast, and medics should be around shortly. Finally they arrive—white-smocked men, with reasonably modern equipment—and they check all our vital signs. All of this suggests that something is afoot. Later in the day we are told that we will be given full medical examinations that evening. And at about 9:00 that evening Vic and I are taken, blindfolded, down the stairs and across what seems to be a garden, frozen now underfoot, to a separate building. Then we wait. . . .

Vic is summoned first, and he goes off somewhere. Then I am taken, across a large vestibule area, to a room where I am greeted by Ahmad, the senior guard whom I had known in the prison and who tells me now that I will be interviewed on Iranian TV before my medical exam. I express surprise and ask if we are about to be released. He nods his head, adding that it could be as soon as later that evening. A few minutes later I go to yet another room, this one fairly large, with several walls heavily draped with floor-to-ceiling curtains and with several plastic Christmas trees still in appearance. This is clearly the room where our colleagues have had their Christmas "party" with the visiting clerics.

I am shown to a chair behind a low table, on which is a microphone and a small plastic Christmas tree. My "interviewer" is none other than the cele-brated "Mary," the woman militant who has so often appeared on Iranian TV interviewing my colleagues. She is in her usual Iranian dress, heavy scarves over her head, and with a trace of a smile. She tells me that she will ask me questions about my treatment and asks if I am prepared to respond. I answer that I assume I am. Sitting and standing around the room are perhaps 20 or 25 young Iranians, men and women; what their purpose is is not clear, but all of them seem by their manner to feel they have a right to be present. I assume they are the veterans of the embassy seizure and are present tonight because they, too, sense that the climax of their operation is about to be reached, whether they like it or not.

Their manner is not hostile or friendly. We—I—seem to be regarded, as we always have been, as mere pawns in their larger purposes. Some look quizzically at me; most seem to ignore me. I make a determined effort to ignore them, and I am determined not to smile. I am angry, reflecting my frustration and anger over all these long months—now to see these "students" assembled for this final act in the drama arouses all my irritation from that long stretch of time. One wonders what is in their minds, how they really feel now, and how they regard the settlement that is presumably near.

Mary begins her questioning; the exercise lasting only five minutes at most. The questions are about our treatment in the Foreign Ministry; my answers are as factual as I can make them, as terse as I can be without being rude. I am determined to keep my dignity and to make sure they understand that I haven't lost it and don't intend to do so now. The gist of my answers is that my treatment at the ministry had been reasonably fair, but that, like all my colleagues, I had suffered from the deprivation of my most fundamental human right, freedom. Answering questions about my experience in prison, I note that life there had been Spartan at best and cold. But I add that I had been glad in a sense to have been taken there, since it gave me a chance to see what my colleagues had suffered.

Mary does not persist with her questions. There is no attempt to sermonize or to try to get me to acknowledge any Iranian grievances. She seems to conclude that I am not very interesting or useful, and so she coldly thanks me and terminates the conversation.

From there I am shown to another series of rooms where I am given an EKG and various other routine medical checks. I go from room to room to be examined by young women in very conservative Islamic dress and by a number of young doctors. I assume them to be Iranian, not learning until later that most of them are Algerian. Again, I am deliberately curt and aloof, trying to show all of them that my distaste for what they have done to my colleagues remains deep and intense. They obviously sensed my attitude; one of the Algerian doctors appearing on the airplane taking us to Algiers the following night commented that I obviously had been "very angry." . . .

DAY 444, *January 20, 1981*—There are no clues until late in the day that anything very decisive is to happen. But we wash our underwear and socks and pull together in our SwissAir tote bags what we want to take with us. The senior guard, Ahmad, told us the night before that we will be allowed to take a small bag with us when we leave.

At about 4:00 P.M., a guard arrives with copies of one of Tehran's English-language dailies, *Kayhan*, for the past three days—the most recent one head-lining the news that a deal via Algeria had been struck, the caption reading "The Great Satan accepts all our Conditions." It is now clear that departure is imminent, and Vic and I are literally on the edge of our chairs, calm but commenting with some awe and wonder to each other about the significance of what seems about to happen and how incredible the entire experience now seems. Suddenly the door opens, it is about 6:15 P.M., and we are told we will leave in ten minutes. It is a good half hour later when guards arrive, this time saying we are to leave but that our bags are much too big. In any event, they say we will not be able to take them physically with us to the airport, but we can be assured we will have them with us on the aircraft. We are told to don our blindfolds—mine at that point reduced to an old shirt, which suffices. I insist that I am not leaving until my billfold is returned to me, as promised; Vic insists that he wants his shoes back, mine never having been taken from me. Grumbling, one of the guards goes off to look, returning with my billfold but without the $50 in it. . . . Vic's shoes are nowhere to be found; I give him my running shoes to wear. We empty our bags of some of our gear—clothes, a parka, etc.—to get them down to a size that may pass the test. Meanwhile, I persist with my argument that Ahmad had assured me I could carry my bag with me, refusing to give it up as we move down the stairs, despite one or another of our escorts pulling and tugging to divest me of it.

Finally, in what I assume was a courtyard and before I enter a waiting van, I get into a heated argument over the bag—mouthing words about the lack of respect being shown me, my rights to my bag, my diplomatic status, the assurances Ahmad had given me, my doubts that I would ever see the bag again if I turned it over, etc. The affair by this point has obviously become a matter of some importance to my captor-escorts, and I begin to sense that persistence might complicate my larger interests, i.e., freedom. So when one of my escorts finally asks, "Don't you trust us?" I laugh with some scorn, indicate my doubts, but nonetheless turn over the bag and am thereupon put aboard a van, seated —I assume—on some sort of narrow jump seat. Whether others of my colleagues are in the van with me, I cannot say. . . .

But by this point . . . there can be no doubt of our destination—the airport. I find myself trying to judge the distance by the time taken to drive; we are under way for perhaps 25 minutes, which I judge would take us to Mehrabad Airport from the northern part of Tehran. I recall little passing through my mind—only a strange feeling of emptiness and aloneness, a feeling of being a tiny cog in a vastly larger operation about which I have little immediate knowledge, a feeling of being used, of being transported about as if I am a commodity or an animal of sorts. I tell myself it is important to avoid at all costs upsetting the applecart at this crucial juncture. So I sit tight, doing exactly as I am told, my hands in my lap, even cautious in my use of them to balance myself as the van turns corners or stops at intervals. I wonder what kind of convoy we represent, what kind of armed escort we might have, or whether we are moving surreptitiously to the airport to avoid possibly hostile crowds. I remember a conviction often expressed by Mike Howland that our point of greatest danger would be the last trip to the airport, when those opposed to our release or wanting to embarrass those in power might attempt a hijacking, a shooting, or what have you.

So I sit, numb and motionless, hearing very few sounds around me, but convinced that freedom is now very near indeed. The van stops, but nothing happens for perhaps 10 to 15 minutes. Then suddenly the door is opened, and I am forcibly pushed up and out onto tarmac underfoot and at the same time my shirt-blindfold is jerked off. I see nothing around me but hear and feel the taunts and shoves of a number of people. I am pushed in some fashion toward a ramp beside an aircraft, visible in the darkness from its lights and the light from the ramp—a ramp that is covered, giving me a feeling of refuge as soon as I start up the stairs.

Toward the top of the ramp I recognize the figure of a person we had met at the Foreign Ministry during our Christmas ceremony—that of Azizi from the prime minister's office—a youngish, perhaps 35-year-old, bearded Iranian, wearing an open shirt and jeans, a man who had told Tomseth on that evening that he had spent three years in school in northern Virginia. I tell him, as we pass each other on the ramp, that despite what I had just experienced from his countrymen at the foot of the ramp, that I hold no malice toward his country and that I wish him well. . . .

So I am free—or about to be in any case. I have a sense of uncertainty as to what kind of aircraft, or whose aircraft, I am on—quickly becoming aware, however, that it is Algerian. Starting up the aisle I see John Limbert, the first of my colleagues whom I see again for the first time in 444 days. He looks completely unchanged, smiling and outgoing as always. We embrace and laugh uproariously. Then I notice the lights of a TV camera crew and a group of men, seated and poring over papers, which I learn later to be rosters of all of us, our names being carefully checked as we board the aircraft. There are Swiss Ambassador Lang and his deputy, Meroni; both look tired and harassed, Meroni unshaven, and both men tense. The Algerian ambassador to Tehran is there. We are introduced, and he embraces me, as does Ambassador Malik, the Algerian ambassador to Washington. I also meet the governor of the Algerian Central Bank, the Algerian Foreign Office representative who had visited us at Christmas, and other Algerian officials. The pilot of the aircraft is introduced.

All this takes place in the midst of what matters more—meeting those of my colleagues already aboard and others as they come up the aisle from the rear of the aircraft. The scene is bedlam—all of us moving up and down the aisle, some sitting in their seats but as quickly up again to meet someone newly aboard. The two women, Kate Koob and Ann Swift, arrive bedecked with yellow ribbons in their hair, smiling broadly and enthusiastically welcomed. The Marines are already seated in a block, well into stories of their experiences and giving me a warm and enthusiastic welcome. One, I am told, is wearing a pair of my slacks from a closet in the residence. They look less like the neat Marines they were when I last saw them than like young hippies—their hair long, some with beards, all in a variety of clothing having no connection with a Marine's uniform, except for one or two wearing jungle fatigue pants.

Indeed, none of us, in our dress, reflects anything of our traditional service dress—with the marked exception of Bob Bluker, who comes aboard in a three-piece conservative suit, button-down shirt, and tie. He has held on to them, he says, throughout his captivity. Tom Ahern comes up the aisle, and I ask him where he had gotten his shirt—obviously one of mine, again from the residence closet. (Later, in Wiesbaden, he has it cleaned and carefully returned to me!)

During all this commotion, a steward and one or two Algerian stewardesses do their best to get us to take our seats and remain in them, to little avail with most of us, until their tone becomes insistent and it is clear that we are about to take off. I say good-bye, with great reluctance, to our tried-and-true friends, the Swiss, after accepting Ambassador Lang's counsel that I should not volunteer a statement to the Iranian TV team that is aboard. . . .

I sit with John Graves (public affairs counselor at the embassy), who is heavily bearded and thinner. He is quiet and subdued, as if a bit uncertain how to take it all. I sense a new and different reserve about him, a kind of sadness if not bitterness. His back troubles him because of an injury suffered when the van he was in while being transported to some distant city had overturned. But he feels lucky to be alive. One of the first things that happens as we talk is that a piece of paper is passed to us, on which someone has written figures of the compensation we should demand for our experiences—a figure going up to $1,000 a day in the opinion of one of my colleagues, unnamed. I put the whole thing out of mind, feeling that this is not the time to trouble myself with that issue.

We stay in our seats only long enough to reach our cruising altitude but not before a loud cheer as soon as our wheels leave the ground. We are free of Iran at last; our feelings mix with laughter and tears and great relief, more than we can actually sense at that moment. We are numb, tired but exhilarated, and weary with the tension and uncertainty of the past few days; many are angry and reflect it in their manner. Close associates like Mike Howland and Al Golacinski are already deep in conversation to exchange memories of the day we were seized, when those two security officers were in separate parts of the city. Someone appears with a dozen or so copies of the newspaper *Stars and Stripes* that has all our photographs on the front page. One of my colleagues suggests that each of us sign them, as a souvenir gift for members of the crew. Meanwhile the aisle is full as we ask each other about our conditions, where we've been. We find that few of our 49 colleagues are aware of what happened to the three of us—some believing we had left Iran, others having heard rumors we had found refuge in another embassy, still others convinced they had heard our voices as hostages held in other areas of the chancery. Occasionally the pilot and others of the crew make an effort to get us to take our seats, the pilot reportedly having some difficulty keeping the aircraft steady with everyone milling about.

As we cross the Iranian border and head into Turkey, there is another loud cheer when the crew breaks out champagne. We ask where we are headed and are first told Ankara for a fueling stop; this was later changed to Athens, the switch preplanned as a security measure. Beyond Athens it is difficult to pin down the crew as to our flight plan, and it is only with some probing that it finally becomes clear we are to go to Algiers and from there to Germany. I move about the cabin, trying to greet and talk to as many of my colleagues as possible. All are respectful and friendly, and I sense no apparent bitterness directed at me for my responsibility in the policy evolution that preceded the embassy's seizure or for my role in the decisions of November 4 that saw the embassy surrendered. But perhaps their feelings—or the feelings of some of them—are only momentarily hidden out of respect for my role as chief of mission. I cannot be sure, but for the present I am reassured.

I talk to Jerry Miele, the hostage who was taken by the militants the second day and paraded blindfolded before the chanting masses in the streets outside the embassy—an act so repulsive (and dangerous) that I cringe at the thought of it. His quiet courage had impressed me at the time, as I watched the scene on Iranian TV. Now he seems well, if even quieter than is normally his style. Steve Lauterbach, one of a group of four who took part in a celebrated "show-and-tell" on Iranian TV the first Christmas, talks to me about that affair— anxious to hear my reaction to that experience. I try to tell him to put it out of his mind, that I thought everyone understood what he felt he had had to do under the circumstances. Joe Subic, the MC of that "show-and-tell" event, tells me, in response to my query "Why, Joe?" that he did it to try to help get better living conditions for all his colleagues and that he really had had no alternative. I talk also to Tom Ahern, who seems tense and unsmiling; he has suffered as long a time of solitary confinement as anyone, and his manner seems to reflect the pain of that experience. He has little to say, but again I do not detect bitterness at me. It was "inevitable," says he, that his captors would in time determine his associations.

While our plane is being refueled at Athens I take the aircraft's PA (public address) system mike and speak to my colleagues. I try to give them some advance indication of the kind of welcome I think they can expect on their return home, they having much less idea, I assume, than I do of the way in which the American public has backed us, prayed for us, and identified with us. I tell them that as a group we have a kind of mystique about us, an image of strength and fortitude that had won the admiration of Americans, and that I am sure they would agree it was important that we try to maintain this on our return. . . . I urge that in saying or doing what they chose, they consider carefully in their own hearts and minds what effect their words or actions might have on the image we now had as able government servants who had tried to do our duty. . . .

Airborne from Athens, and responding to a suggestion from one of my colleagues, I speak to the governor of the Algerian Central Bank about food. I say that I am sure he would agree it would hardly be appropriate if, on arrival at Algiers, we were to come down the ramp in a state of some alcoholic imbalance. He apologizes that regrettably there is little to eat aboard; most of the food on the aircraft spoiled during the two to three days the aircraft had waited on the tarmac while the final agreement on our release had been reached. But, said the bank governor, there are cheese sandwiches and fruit, and he hopes my colleagues will understand. We do; respect and gratitude for our new Algerian friends is at a high pitch, and no sandwiches ever tasted better.

At Algiers there is another loud and raucous cheer as our wheels touch down—a cheer to be repeated and grow in volume at every takeoff and landing as our flight to freedom continues over the next week. We agree that the two women, Ann and Kate, will be the first to go down the ramp. For a good length of time (a time that I learn later seemed like an eternity to the American public watching on TV that open door to see us emerge), we sit impatiently in our seats as our Algerian hosts explain the procedures ahead of us.   Without passports and without visas, we are, after all, a rather unusual group of late-night American visitors! As we exit, we say a warm good-bye to our Algerian pilot and his crew, standing at the top of the ramp. Then we go down the steps in a gentle rain to be greeted by Warren Christopher, the outgoing deputy secretary of state and the principal American negotiator in the exceedingly long and complex exchange that has finally achieved our release. There too are Ambassador and Mrs. Ulric Haynes, a handsome pair of diplomats indeed, and representatives of our respective services—the State Department represented by Assistant Secretary of State for Near East and South Asian Affairs Harold Saunders, and Sheldon Krys, executive director of that bureau. Someone offers me an umbrella, and I respond that after 444 days it is sheer delight to walk bareheaded in the rain, especially with the feel of free soil underfoot. I walk arm in arm with Saunders and Krys, the three of us—or at least I—too exhilarated to talk very coherently, they probably as exhausted as I by that point. My feeling of respect is unbounded for these two who had played such central roles in the long drama now behind us, and I do my best to tell them so.

We hostages are probably the most unusual group ever to walk across that rain-swept tarmac—52 Americans in all manner of dress, long haired, many bearded, tired, a bit wobbly on our feet, and still just a little incredulous that our freedom was now becoming very real. We are directed to the airport's VIP lounge and to a double semicircle of seats, forming an audience together with a variety of Algerian officials and airport employees for a short but formal ceremony. Algerian Foreign Minister Benyahia reads a statement of his country's satisfaction at having played its intermediary role in achieving our release, in what would become known as the Algiers Accord. Secretary Christopher responds with an eloquent expression of the gratitude of the American government and people and presents the minister a letter, formally accepting custody of the 52 of us, the Algerians having asked for a "receipt" of this kind for this special human cargo, now safely delivered from Tehran. The entire proceedings last less than 30 minutes, and there is little flair and no hype. It is as if all concerned appreciate that there is plenty of that ahead of us.

On the tarmac, two beautiful U.S. Air Force medical evacuation (med-evac) aircraft are ready to leave, and on the fuselages are our first sights of the Stars and Stripes. It is a very special moment indeed. Walking to the first plane with Secretary Christopher, I find it difficult to put into adequate words the grati-tude I feel for this man who had led the enormously complex negotiating process that had won our freedom, a process involving agreement on disposition of billions of dollars of frozen Iranian assets and completed only in the final minutes of the outgoing Carter administration. No one could appreciate better than he the historic significance of the short ceremony just completed inside that VIP lounge.

It is now past midnight, the start of our first full day of freedom. Aboard those aircraft, air force personnel wait with open arms, a special turkey dinner, and unlimited hospitality. And on board as well is a team of psychiatrists, understandably immensely curious about this group of fellow passengers.

18

Day One of Freedom

It is shortly before 7:00 A.M. on January 21 when we land at Rhein-Main, where we file off the plane in our arctic-wear jackets, courtesy of the U.S. Air Force. Former Secretary of State Vance is at the foot of the ramp, along with Ambassador Walter Stoessel, several American military officers, and a delegation of German government officials. Facing us is the control tower, bedecked with a huge yellow ribbon, and massed on bleachers behind restraining ropes are thousands from the American community in the area, waving flags and shouting a welcome.

The ceremony is brief and regrettably efficient. We feel a strong desire to plunge into the welcoming crowd, but instead we are shepherded by escort officers in the direction of buses and urged to get aboard. Early-morning traffic stops to watch our motorcade and to wave and salute. Germans and Americans get out of their cars to shout additional welcome messages. We are surprised but jubilant, too, to see this kind of interest and support. Until now I think most of us were uncertain exactly what kind of reception we might get, but it is clear that we are regarded well and not looked upon somewhat askance as having messed up our assignment.

Then we arrive at the USAF Hospital, in Wiesbaden, and there lining every foot of space on the hospital balconies and entrance area are hundreds of staff members—nurses, doctors, air force personnel in uniform, German employees—all of them waving, some of them singing, with banners and flags everywhere. Across from the entrance a great assembly of reporters and photographers record our arrival at this first "home" en route home. We walk to the third floor through corridors alive with posters and banners of welcome prepared by American schoolchildren in the area. We name that floor "Freedom Hall," and for the next several days it is our home, a place of seemingly endless conversation, good will, meetings, and—not least, that being our major purpose—medical exams, security debriefings, and psychiatric counseling. I find myself breaking into silent tears in relating some of my impressions, particularly when asked to describe my feelings about what had happened to my staff and how I had thought about my family at home. I apologize, but Dr. Esther Roberts, my assigned psychiatrist, sees nothing unusual in tears.

A TV screen runs constantly, showing a five-hour cassette compilation of major network newscasts throughout the time we have been held—an effort to help bring us up-to-date on the traumatic events in which we were major players but about which most of my colleagues have known little or nothing. There are banks of telephones in a room set aside for us to use round-the-clock and with lines open to any part of the world. My first telephone conversation with Penne since early November seems almost routine, despite the novelty and excitement, perhaps because I sense a normal life so fast returning and because of the contrast with the tension and uncertainty that had surrounded those calls to our Foreign Ministry room. But I have much to talk about. I tell Penne how much I love her for her strength and courage throughout the crisis and for her leadership with the other families.

We are kept from the press. The official position is that until we have had a chance to collect our thoughts, talk with our families, get our medical situation in order, it is best that our privacy be respected. That is unwelcome to the press corps, vast numbers of which have descended on Wiesbaden and berate the department's spokesman at his daily session with them for feeding them pap and excessively coddling the returned hostages. To get around the restrictions, many maintain a vigil at the hospital gates. All want our reactions: how do we feel, were we mistreated, what about Carter, how did we regard the Iranians? One of my colleagues gains the headlines with his quip that he would return to Iran only in a B-52. We are serenaded from the front lawn of the hospital grounds by schoolchildren from American and German schools in the area; we watch from balconies, boggle-eyed at the intensity of their efforts to reach out and figuratively if not physically embrace us. The young Marines, virile and handsome in newly acquired T-shirts, are especially popular.

My roommate is Col. Tom Schaefer, defense attaché of the embassy, a proud member of the U.S. Air Force. In Tehran he had been a frequent partner on the tennis courts and a dignified and highly cooperative team player in embassy business. As a hostage he had suffered long periods of solitary confinement, grown a beard, and lost a great deal of weight, but he had not lost his dignity or the Christian faith from a strong family background. Our only excursion beyond the hospital's walls is to a post exchange—at the incredible shopping hour of 5:30 in the morning, so arranged because of our already crowded schedule but also to avoid the curiosity of other shoppers. But there is no lack of curiosity on the part of the PX staff, prepared without dissent to inconvenience themselves at such an hour. We are suddenly with money again—the first time in a year and a quarter—and anxious to make ourselves a bit more presentable at home.

Meals in the hospital's cafeteria become virtual banquets. We are doted upon at every hand, watched with intense curiosity. For our last evening in the hospital, lobsters are flown in as a gift from a seafood restaurant in New Jersey, Italian ice cream from Naples, and champagne from Germany's best wine cellars. The Marines, meanwhile, have begun to catch up with lost time, somewhat constrained in their romantic pursuits by the limitations on our movement but resourceful nonetheless. They miss some of our evening sessions with Washington briefers, and I note their absence at one of them by acknowledging that there is after all a matter of setting priorities and I can understand theirs. These late-afternoon and evening sessions are a means for senior Washington officials—in particular, Harold Saunders and Cyrus Vance, secretary of state until the ill-fated rescue mission—to bring us up-to-date. They seem to hold back nothing, Vance especially, whose frankness and enormous integrity in explaining his reasons for opposing the rescue mission win him a strong round of spontaneous applause. He appears close to tears at several points, particularly when he tells us that it was his understanding that planning assumptions for the mission included the probability of 10 or 15 of us not returning. I find myself incredulous at that information and more convinced than ever that the mission was ill considered as well as ill timed.

But nothing is more emotional for us than the visit of Jimmy Carter, president until the hour of our release and now dispatched by the new president, Ronald Reagan, to welcome us. Below our third-floor windows we watch as the Carter motorcade sweeps up, Secret Service agents jumping from cars as they pull to a stop, the press behind restraining ropes excited by the promised trauma of this meeting but frustrated at not directly observing it. Only a few of the more enterprising find ways to photograph us with telescopic lens through closed hospital windows. I wait for the president at the top of the stairs on the third floor; he is trailed by a large entourage including outgoing Vice President Mondale, Secretaries Muskie and Miller of State and Treasury, Jodie Powell, Ham Jordan, and an assorted collection of those senior officers in State who have worked so long to make our freedom possible, not least Henry Precht, that veteran of so much crisis in American relations with Iran over the past several years.

Carter recognizes me as he comes up the stairs, embracing me and asking about my health. Fellow Minnesotan Mondale does the same as we walk into the room where my colleagues stand in two large circles. Carter seems, and probably is, a bit apprehensive and uncertain about the reception this group of fellow citizens will give him, their president and commander in chief until only hours before; the man who gave the go-ahead on the Shah's admission after having asked his advisers what would happen if that produced another seizure of the embassy; the man who as president must take responsibility for what befalls those citizens caught up in the consequences of government policies abroad; the man scorned by our "student" captors as the man who could do nothing; the man who many of my colleagues felt had pursued policies directly responsible for prolonging the crisis at their expense, and yet their president during all that time and still surrounded by the images of power and prestige that go with an office that commands the awe of all Americans.

If he is apprehensive walking into that room, it is largely dispersed by the ovation that greets him—a welcome reflecting perhaps more respect than regard but nonetheless real. I move with him about the room, introducing each of my colleagues, their names quickly familiar to him. Many embrace him; the Marines give him respectful salutes. He is close to tears, as I am; quick conversations with each of the men and two women, Carter occasionally mentions names of family members, and the atmosphere relaxes as we move around the room. Then he stands in the middle of our two circles, speaking softly but in a clear and confident tone, describing to us with obvious pride the enormous focus on us of public interest at home and his own great sense of relief that we are all alive and well and free. He pulls from his coat pocket a newspaper for January 21 from Atlanta, pointing to large headlines describing our return to freedom and then, with obvious glee, noting that another item of news, the inauguration of the new president, got secondary treatment at the bottom of the page. He speaks for perhaps 15 minutes, explaining without apology the policy he had followed to achieve our release and acknowledging his regret that that release had been so slow in coming. He asks for questions and gets several, each of them reflecting the critical view of the questioner, posed in cold but respectful tones. Why had the Shah been admitted without better security assurances from the Iranian regime? What had motivated the rescue mission and why at that time? Why had the release agreement included a denial of the hostages' right to bring suit against Iran? Carter answers each in straightforward policy terms, again without apology.

The session ends earlier than I would have expected, Carter seeming to feel that he is imposing on us. At the end he tells us that we will be warmly received when we reach home, evidence of the intense and sympathetic concern of the American people. Before leaving, he poses for individual photographs, promising to autograph one for each of us. He seems especially pleased and proud to be in a group picture with the Marines. Then he is en route back down the stairs, probably no more than an hour having elapsed.

We spend what remains of the evening sharing our impressions of a very poignant and emotional event, one among the countless moments of high drama that this experience has brought us but one with a special trauma about it. A president who has fought for a second term denied him by voters—who rightly or wrongly had sensed in his handling of the hostage crisis a quality of indecisiveness—Carter's last year in office had been almost totally dominated by our misfortune. Very few of us, I suspect, could help but feel as we looked at him in our midst that we had been players in a drama of historic and unexpected consequences. I found myself asking again, for the thousandth time, the question whether there were not things I should have done differently prior to the embassy seizure and that might have spared this man, my colleagues, and our country the enormous consequences of the events of that fourth day of Novem-

ber 1979. How, I wonder, does Jimmy Carter in his heart of hearts feel about
this Foreign Service officer who had presided in Tehran over events that had so
massively affected his own political future and the course of my country? It was
a recurrence of a sense of guilt, whether appropriate or not, that I have never
been completely able to put from my mind.

Four days at Wiesbaden, a stop that we had all questioned and about which
some had been rebellious, delaying our reunions with family. But a time that
most of us come to find was hardly long enough to pull together our thoughts,
to share with doctors concerns—real or imagined—that we had kept to ourselves too long, and to begin a gradual process of reunion with the outside
world. We will remember those four days of hospitality from a German and
American hospital staff as without parallel in any of our experiences, a love affair
in the warmest sense of the word. Each of us leaves a little bit of ourselves in
that building, a place prosaic in appearance but whose occupants have gotten
us well launched on the road to a restored sense of physical and mental health.

Our flight to freedom resumes the morning of January 25, en route to reunion with families, a reunion long and painstakingly prepared by Washington
officials at West Point—West Point selected for its seclusion, its security, a
place that officials conclude after talking with our families will give us the
privacy that our long-delayed reunion deserves. En route we refuel at Shannon
Airport in Ireland, where the airport tarmac and terminal are sealed off for our
arrival. Prime Minister Charles Haughey and virtually his entire cabinet are on
hand to receive us. The prime minister asks to board the aircraft personally,
where he gives Ann Swift and Kate Koob a kiss and embrace and where he gets
an enthusiastic endorsement to his invitation to join him in the terminal for a
reception. The prime minister makes a moving speech of welcome, centered
around a gesture in which he pulls from his pocket a folded piece of weathered
paper. It proves to be the letter I had sent on St. Patrick's Day almost a year
before in Tehran to the Irish chargé, a diplomatic colleague. That handwritten
message, saluting all Irish, including the many in America, was one of the many
I had written from the Foreign Ministry to embassies of friendly countries. I
had sent such messages via the kitchen staff to the Office of Protocol, never
certain of their delivery, but here was the Irish prime minister confirming in
this gesture that at least this one had been received.

That brief stop, which ends with the prime minister's gifts of Waterford
crystal freedom bells and bottles of Irish Mist, makes further apparent to us the
wide dimensions of public interest in our adventure and in our welfare—
dimensions that would not become really apparent, however, until we had
reached American soil. Over Canada we send via the aircraft's radio a salute to
the prime minister and people of Canada for their gift of freedom earlier to six
of our colleagues in the "Canadian caper." Landing at Stewart Airfield near
Newburgh, New York, we are on an emotional high. At touchdown there is the
biggest roar of applause yet. We are finally on American soil. Freedom One has
landed. This control tower, too, is wrapped in a yellow ribbon. There are flags
everywhere. Coming down the ramp, I search the crowd for Penne, not immediately visible, but she is there, and we wrap each other in an embrace all

these many months in the making. She is beautiful, radiant with excitement. We are too excited to say much of anything, the emotion too great to make talk easy. But then I turn to three strapping sons. Bill and Chip are in navy mid-shipman uniforms. They look tremendous, they look proud, they are proud. I suppose fathers and sons at that age rarely embrace. We do this time, but not before I stare in amazement at the physical change in number three son, Jim. A year and a half earlier he had been a boy; now he is a teenager, almost as tall as his brothers, spruced up in trench coat and tie. He is as excited as I, delighted with the surprise he has given me.

Reunited with family, I am reminded again of what family had meant for me in that long crisis. My wife—strong advocate of my character and leadership role, a sensitive and thoughtful leader of the hostage families, organizer of FLAG, close friend and counsel to many family members, a firm but soft-spoken spokesperson on many occasions with the media—now rejoices with me, bubbling over with the conversation that always comes so easily for her, smiling, and waving with enthusiasm toward other reunited families.

And my three sons—proud and patriotic, the two oldest taking special delight in wearing their uniforms at an event full of such meaning for national unity and purpose. I recall to myself how often during those long months I had asked God in nightly prayers to watch over them, how often I had thanked Him as well that in them I (and Penne) had such stout support at home. How much strength they had given me, how much I owed them, how much all that really mattered was centered in their good health and good fortune. How proud I am, standing there on the tarmac, to look at them and to introduce them to fellow hostages, especially to Vic and Mike, who finally meet for the first time that family that in the room in Tehran I had told them about ad nauseam. More introductions to other families, all of us encouraged to move along a long yellow carpet into a small terminal building, there to hear a speech of welcome, mercifully short at five minutes, from an old friend, Gen. Andy Goodpaster, superintendent of West Point and, in my time at the National War College, its commandant. Dignified and thoughtful gentleman that he is, he is brief and eloquent, and we are enthusiastic in response. He announces that we are to board buses to begin our trip to the Military Academy and its cadets, our hosts for the next 48 hours.

Newburgh, New York, is small-town America. Eighteen miles distant is another town, Highland Falls—home of West Point and the United States Military Academy, our next stopping place. In between are more small New York towns and country homes, scattered along a winding, rolling road that the local folks would later christen "Freedom Road" to commemorate our tumultuous journey. Flags and signs—signs on billboards, posters, banners—proclaim a welcome everywhere. At intersections and crossroads our buses slow to a crawl because of crowds of people, their cars pulled up to curbs and on lawns, everyone cheering, waving, crying; fire trucks with ladders aloft and sirens wailing; young men and boys sprawled on rooftops to see better and seemingly competing with each other in waving their flags in our direction.

And yellow ribbons! There is a virtual blizzard of them, hanging from and around trees and lamp posts, radio aerials, and front doors of every house in sight. Dogs and cats and horses with yellow ribbons. We are incredulous, boggle-eyed—a term we will all find ourselves using over the next few weeks, unable to shake our surprise at the extent and intensity of this welcome, this almost frantic effort on the part of these thousands of people along this road to tell us that we had not been forgotten, that we were loved, that we were their heroes whether we felt that way or not. On a televised newscast later that evening, we watch a young boy among many being interviewed about their reactions to the events and asked whether he hadn't been disappointed because of the smoked-glass bus windows, which made visibility into the buses difficult. His answer: "It didn't matter if I saw them; what was important was that they saw me!"

That comment described that crowd, determined to be a part of a historic event, caring most about that and about letting us see how enthusiastic they were that we were back, and proud that their towns and countryside were the first to welcome us home. It is unashamed patriotism of the kind we had all known in our own small towns in an earlier time—the kind of patriotism and flag-waving that went so much into its shell in the reaction to Vietnam and that had seemed gone forever. But here was everyone, including young men of that age that had seemed most determined of all to avoid being seen as patriotic, now unabashedly joining in a frenzy of red, white, blue, and, yes, yellow—a color that in this crisis had become synonymous with caring.

Well, we tell ourselves, this *is* small-town America, where all this is still possible, however boggle-eyed we remain. But, we say to each other, it will be different in Washington, blasé place that it is. Our families, better aware than we of how this human drama had captured the hearts and minds of the American people, tell us we will be surprised in Washington, too.

Highland Falls, New York, with West Point at the end of its main street, has known much of American history and has seen many heroes come and go. But its people, too, tell us in their numbers and enthusiasm that this day is something special. Main Street is a sea of people, a forest of flags, a crescendo of enthusiasm seemingly bent on forcing our buses to a virtual halt and refusing to see us disappear into the protected grounds of the Point and its storied fields and great gray buildings. But it is late in the afternoon, our trip taking almost two hours to cover a scant 18 miles, and our police escorts move us along through the academy's main entrance and up the entrance to the venerable Thayer Hotel on the edge of the Point. Long the stopping place of families, friends, and the "drags" of cadets, the hotel has more welcome signs, more West Point officers and staff to welcome us, more yellow ribbons, and banks of telephones in a side ballroom, with lines open anywhere.

The academy's personnel respect our privacy. The military knows the importance of family, the pain of separation, the good feeling of reunion. But proud in their role as our host, they want to show us their welcome too. So the next morning we are invited to a special service of thanksgiving at the academy's soaring Gothic chapel, its walls lined with stained-glass windows memorializing generations of officers who as cadets sat in its pews. Now we and our families sit in these pews, our emotions plumbed deep by the eloquence of the prayers, our hearts filled with the love we sense all about us, our minds recalling the pain and frustration of our experience. We hear the words of a homily, but our thoughts are elsewhere, wondering where all this will lead each of us, what it means for our family ties, our marriages, our children. The magnificence of this vaulted nave and the beauty of the service bring us back to the moment—especially when the cadets of the choir lead all of us in "The Battle Hymn of the Republic." For those of our families who live in Washington, that powerful hymn had become a kind of theme song, always sung at the Sunday night candlelight vigils on the sidewalk across from the Iranian Embassy on Massachusetts Avenue in Washington. "Mine eyes have seen the glory. . . . His truth is marching on." There are few if any dry eyes in this chapel as that hymn thunders to a close.

That evening the cadets, all 4,000 plus of them, invite us to the mess hall to share their evening meal. The hall is a vast place, reaching out in four wings from a crossing in the center. As we walk down one of these wings, there is an avalanche of sound, the cadets standing in their places clapping and cheering and waving—no sound was ever more beautiful or more genuine in its purpose. Each family is seated with a different table of cadets. They are full of questions, delighted in the role they are playing as hosts, quick to respond to our every question and request. I think I have rarely enjoyed a dinner more, proud of a country whose future defense will rest on the shoulders of men and women such as these. The evening is special to son Bill, a third-year midshipman at Annapolis, and thus busy comparing his counterpart cadets' experience and circumstances with his.

The next morning, January 27, we are packed and ready to board buses by 9:30, ready to resume our freedom flight to Washington and home. But there is first a press conference, where for the first time the returned hostages are presented as a group to the media and the American public, the press up to now having seen us only at a distance and having posed their questions to only those few who have ventured near those reporters and photographers poised behind restraining lines at the academy gates. On a walk with my son Bill I had done that, the photograph of the two of us front-paged in much of the nation's press the next morning. But I will remember that walk not for that photograph but for the sheer joy of it—the satisfaction I felt as a father walking with this tall and disciplined midshipman, this handsome son so deeply committed to the naval service, proud of his country and its purposes. He had told me that afternoon of his reaction and that of his fellow midshipmen to the many frustrations of the hostage crisis and of his effort to get the navy's acquiescence during Christmas leave in 1979, shortly after the crisis had begun, to his spending his leave on an aircraft carrier in the Indian Ocean Task Force and thus making his own personal contribution to the strength poised as a warning to Tehran. The navy had thought better of that request, as eventually did Bill himself, concerned as he was as well with his mother's sensitivities at home.

A sea of journalists face us in Eisenhower Hall, all of us sitting behind nameplates in three ascending rows on the stage, looking for all the world, one reporter quips, like a large group of "Hollywood Squares" on nationwide TV.

I make an opening statement "proud to present to you 52 equally proud, free, and happy Americans" and describe our welcome home "as evidence that the spirit of America is strong and that America has heart. Never," I said, "has so small a group owed so much to so many."

Then I field questions from the floor, trying to assign them to whichever colleague seems most appropriate to respond—all of us conscious as never before of how we are in fact on the nation's center stage, watched with the closest scrutiny by probably a majority of the country's population. For 444 days the American people have focused on us, most of the time without seeing us; only on a few occasions such as the Christmas services had some of us been seen by an intensely curious and sympathetic public. Now we would be tested, watched to see whether we would measure up to the high expectations that surrounded our tragedy and now our freedom. How would this collection of diplomats look close up? Were we as strong in spirit and character as we had been made out to be? Or were we nothing more than a hapless bunch of fellow Americans victimized by misguided, or at least unrealistic, national policy? The answer would not be immediately apparent, but I was confident of the answer myself as I looked at these colleagues of mine who had not lost their spirit, who seemed to have bounced back so quickly in esprit and good health. They were, I thought, a remarkably attractive group of fellow Americans, and I congratulated myself for the thousandth time for my good fortune in having been so ably supported.

Hundreds of journalists want to ask as many questions and more, though there is time in an hour and a half for only a few to be put to us. One asks one of the Marines what his plans were, and he responds that he intends to get back to his normal pursuits—"chasing women"—as quickly as possible. That answer relaxes us all, and more than any other perhaps is evidence to a concerned public (and particularly to an immensely curious psychiatric profession) that we are not as bad off for the wear as had been generally feared. At one point I am reminded by the way a question is posed that I have forgotten to include in my opening remarks the positive reference I had planned to make about President Carter for the role he had played in making possible our release. I do that now. Later I receive perhaps a dozen letters criticizing me for seeming to slight Jimmy Carter. I regret my lapse and can only hope that it will not be misinterpreted since I respect the former president for the patient discussions and diplomacy that had resulted in our freedom. Regrettably, first impressions are difficult to correct, and I fear that this is the case in this instance.

We board our buses to travel again along our freedom road back to the airport but not before an immensely poignant farewell from the cadets of West Point. The entire corps, the "long gray line," is in dress formation along our departure route, their leaders saluting, the rank and file breaking the rules with broad smiles and near waves themselves. Probably there are some tears as well, certainly there are from us as we wave at these beautiful men and women so symbolic of the finest in a country that had supported us so fervently and was opening its heart to us in this remarkable journey home.

Along those country roads of New York, we see again the signs and posters and placards that express a nation's relief and pride. Governor Carey is at the airport to see us off, presenting each of us with gold pins for our lapels: "I Love New York." We do indeed, but we are quickly aboard four aircraft of the president's fleet that carry us and our families on this last leg of our flight to freedom. Each plane proudly bears the name Freedom One.

Looking out our windows as we approach Andrews Air Force Base, it is apparent that this is no routine landing of the presidential fleet at its home port of Andrews—evident when the door of the aircraft is opened and I look down the ramp at a long receiving line headed by Vice President and Mrs. Bush. This time there is no question that, as chief of that hapless diplomatic mission in Tehran, I should be the first down that ramp with my arms raised in a V for victory salute, the first to be welcomed by a government whose servants we were, and the first to express to that government the gratitude we feel. Penne and my sons follow me down. The vice president bids us welcome in that relaxed style and spirit of friendship that is so typical of George Bush. I say a few word of thanks, but words do not come easily in the awe and emotion I feel as I move from an embrace by Barbara Bush to a bear hug from House Speaker Tip O'Neill, handshakes from Secretary of State Haig, the Secretary of Defense, and many others, the line ending with Dennis Hayes, president of the American Foreign Service Association. Beyond are the terminal buildings, their flat roofs covered with people and their banners bidding us welcome. Security officers direct us along cheering crowds, the blare of military bands, and rows of press photographers. It is difficult to spot anyone without a camera.

There are my in-laws, Fred and "Mother B." Babcock, stalwart supporters through all that pain in Tehran. There too are brother, Arvid, and sister, Norma—by now adept with a constantly inquiring media, Arvid is called the Walter Cronkite of Odin, Minnesota—and nieces and nephews who have flown to Washington to be part of an event they will never forget, most of them guests of Northwest Airlines. Behind our aircraft the three others line up to discharge the rest of the cast of this national drama, the tarmac becoming a sea of cheering, waving, crying, saluting, exultant humanity until finally we are moved toward waiting D.C. transit buses to begin a motorcade to the city.

D.C. transit buses—indeed, a whole fleet of them—line up to take 52 returned Americans and a host of family and friends, escorted by senior officials of government, along the Parkway, across the South Capitol Street bridge, over the Anacostia River, and up Pennsylvania Avenue to the president's house. We are joined in our bus by none other than Vice President and Mrs. Bush, who sit in the side seats at the front and seem almost as excited as we are by the welcome we have just experienced. Warm and engaging people in any event, they are accustomed to crowds and public ceremonies, but before we reach the White House, they are boggle-eyed too, professing that in all their political life they have never seen such an outpouring of love and excitement on the part of so many people in every walk of life. Before we reach the city itself, the Parkway is lined with waving crowds, from adjacent apartment developments, from government offices in the suburbs, from automobiles parked and waiting on blocked access roads. And again the placards and banners: "U.S. 52, Iran 0";

"Your country loves you"; "Buy Iraqi War Bonds"; "Government workers welcome you back to work." Many of the banners are personalized, welcoming specific hostages directly. But the faces of the crowds say it best: everyone laughing and cheering, with tear-streaked faces and expressions of relief, of pride, of love. And nothing expresses it so well to me as the sight of an elderly woman standing alone on a slope overlooking the Parkway with a hand over her heart. The vice president and his wife see it too, and there are tears in the eyes of each of us.

Entering the city proper there are even larger crowds, and as we turn down Pennsylvania Avenue there is a virtual sea of humanity, including those waving from almost every window and rooftop of the great federal office buildings on each side. Motorcycle and foot police make little effort to hold the crowds back as people press toward the buses, trying to reach out and shake our hands as we wave from the bus windows. We wish we could reach out and embrace every one of these magnificent countrymen and women. Unable to do that, I tape a page of lined yellow notepaper to the bus window with the simple words "thank you." (That piece of paper later arrives at our home by mail, sent us by that thoughtful lady, Barbara Bush.)

The crowds are a riot of color; there are flags and yellow ribbons everywhere. Great bows of ribbon on buildings, flags topped with ribbons, lamp posts tied with them; no one in the vast crowd seems without one. I look at Penne and wonder how she must feel at the sight of what had come of the yellow ribbon effort she had begun early in the crisis, tying a large bow of yellow around an oak tree in our front yard. She had told the rector of our church what she planned to do, hoping the yellow ribbon would become a symbol that would rally the American public in a spirit of hope and unity. "Nice idea," he had commented, "but I wonder if it will catch on."

Only a week before along this same avenue a new president, Ronald Reagan, had led his inaugural parade from the Capitol to the White House, a parade that had begun with the news that the hostages were at last airborne safely from Tehran. Great stretches of bleachers from that parade still stand along the avenue, overflowing with crowds that far outnumber those that had seen that inaugural parade. And now that group of hostages whose fate had so troubled and, in the view of many, massively contributed to the defeat of a president, ride in their buses through the north gates of the White House to receive the welcome of the new president.

In the entrance hall the 53 of us (joined now by Richard Queen) are directed to the Blue Room. Minutes later President and Mrs. Reagan enter, she in brilliant yellow. They are introduced to each of us a bit stiffly and formally at first, but this is relieved by Nancy Reagan suddenly exclaiming that she wasn't going to hold back, embracing and kissing each of us as she moved around that handsome room. We are escorted down the steps, out the ground entrance to a raised platform on the south lawn. It is happily an unseasonably warm winter day in Washington, and there is a great assembly of people. Our families are escorted to a special area, close behind members of the cabinet, the diplomatic corps, and seemingly almost the entire Congress, they wanting to be part of this

too. Across from them is the press corps in record numbers. Flags are everywhere, ceremonial buglers in their places, and stretching across the lawn are
military bands and the ceremonial honor guard.

The buglers signal the arrival of President and Mrs. Reagan; the Army Band,
"Pershing's Own," plays the national anthem; and I suspect there are few dry
eyes among all that throng. For me the sound of that music and the sight of the
flags trigger almost overwhelming emotions. Now it is all in place—my colleagues standing safe and proud and at attention, the nation's leadership welcoming us with respect and admiration, the people of this capital city cheering
from the streets around us, our families watching with pride and relief this
culmination of a long and wearing trauma. And all about us the sounds and color
that symbolize the sense of unity and patriotism that pervades the city in an
intensity rarely seen or known in its history. I think of what a long and troubled
voyage all this has been, my words of silent prayer tumbling about in the pride,
exhilaration, and awe that fill my heart and mind in this time and place that I
will never forget.

The ceremony is simple and short. The president expresses a nation's welcome home in an eloquent speech that also speaks firmly of policy regarding the
terrorism that has triggered all of this. Let those who would attempt to repeat
such acts in the future know, he warns, that there will be swift retribution, a
statement implicitly critical of his predecessor's policies in handling the crisis in
Iran. The president turns to me, saying he understands that Bruce Laingen
(inaccurately identifying me as "the deputy chief of our mission in Tehran") will
speak for the group of former hostages. I look out on that unprecedented scene
and beyond, to a nation watching on television. I should be faint with nervous
tension; I will never know why I am not. Long months of knowing in my heart
that such a time and responsibility might come and a silent prayer now for
support leave me more confident and relaxed than I think I have ever been in
a public forum. I take from my pocket a scrap of paper with scribbled notes and
speak of the thanks and gratitude of my colleagues, of "the love affair we will
always feel for this country," of our pride in our families, and of our special debt
to those who sought to help us win our freedom, above all to those who gave
their lives at Desert One. I recall one of the hundreds of signs and placards that
had greeted us—a quote from *Man of La Mancha:* "And the world will be
better for this." I turn and say, "We pray, Mr. President, that this will be so."
The president returns to the podium to present a gift (that each of my colleagues would later receive separately) in the form of a rosewood box containing
a miniature American flag—symbolizing the actual full-sized flags on their
separate standards that stand on the south steps (these flags reach us eventually
as well).

The president leads a spirited singing of "God Bless America," and with that
our freedom is official. President and Mrs. Reagan lead us to a reception in the
East Room, so crowded that movement is difficult. It is a noisy, exuberant
crowd, each of the hostages caught up in knots of the curious, family, and
friends that swirl about. There, too, are members of the families of several of
the men who died at Desert One; they tell us that they are as glad as our own

families that we are back, safe and well. I look at them, controlling their emotions better than I, and I marvel at their strength in being so genuine in their welcome when their hearts must be so heavy. Colonel Beckwith, leader of the rescue mission at Desert One, is there, telling me that they would have had no difficulty had helicopters not failed them. "We knew exactly where you were . . . we had looked beforehand even into the room where you were held!" He refers presumably to the quality of intelligence on the ground. I choose not to say anything about my own reservations, taking the opportunity instead to try to say to Beckwith and the families of those who had died what it means to me to know that others felt so deeply about my freedom as to put their lives on the line in that extremely difficult rescue attempt. In another corner of the room is Ken Taylor and his wife, Pat, those two magnificent Canadians who had made possible the escape of my six colleagues almost a year to the day earlier. No truer friends for Americans exist, and yet they are Canadian to the core and deeply proud of it.

Our schedule calls for yet another event this afternoon, and we are signaled to reboard the buses lined up along the roadway sweeping up to the north portico. Outside the high wrought-iron fence are still thousands of people, many shouting at us by name. The White House is but six or eight blocks distant from the Department of State, a glass and limestone building of little architectural merit that sprawls over two square blocks. Within its walls our colleagues in the business of diplomacy had shared vicariously in our long ordeal. The hostages did not all look to the Department of State as their home agency; almost as many were military. But the Department of State had been the center of all that bureaucratic and policy action that had sought our release, and it was entirely appropriate that our odyssey include a drive past to symbolize the special connection between hostages and their government. So our buses move slowly along C Street, stopping in front of State's diplomatic entrance, and there those of us for whom State is the home office get out and walk. There is Delores "Tiger" Mann, the epitome of the career service secretary and a colleague from an assignment in Afghanistan, swooping up to swallow me with an enthusiastic embrace. There, too, are hundreds of others, waving, shouting, and clapping, with many more waving from behind windows in the faceless facade of that building.

There is yet one more stop before we are home, and that is an overnight stay at the Marriott Hotel in Crystal City, that complex across the Potomac River in Virginia of block after block of bright and shiny but singularly uninteresting office and hotel construction. Across the river the skies light up with fireworks on the Mall to celebrate our return; around the Lincoln Memorial 53 laser beams point skyward in a great cone of light. In the hotel there are drinks and talk, dinner and more talk in a hotel restaurant set aside specially for hostages and their families. But there, too, at a table nearby, is Congressman Hansen of Idaho, that indefatigable gentleman who in the first month of the crisis had journeyed to Tehran, convinced that he had a contribution to make to its resolution, aware as well that publicity would not hurt him politically. He seems tonight to continue to feel the need to be seen in our midst. I am groggy with fatigue, increasingly hoarse with a throat that promises to worsen. A State Department doctor produces pills; he is there to cope with a half-dozen of my colleagues fallen victim to the same bugs that threaten me—bugs that find us lacking some of our immunity after all those months in Tehran; bugs that probably find their task easier as well because our vocal cords are abused by the almost constant talking that catching up has asked of us.

The next morning there is one last motorcade. Penne, feeling deeply about my status as chief of the mission in Tehran, asks the State Department for a limousine for the trip to our house in Bethesda. No, says the department, we are now on our own. When the news reached that redoubtable friend Joyce Brown, she went to work with connections more promising than State; waiting for us as we come through the hotel lobby are three long, black, dignified limousines. These and several less imposing vehicles of family origin form a motorcade that takes us back across the Potomac, up Rock Creek Park and Massachusetts Avenue, and to the Maryland state line, where a squad of Maryland motorcycle policemen wait for us and escort us fore and aft on the last leg of our journey. Our route takes us to my family's neighborhood schools, where students wait to give us a noisy welcome home. We stop first at Radnor Elementary, where several hundred bouncy youngsters squeal and yell and wave their flags and posters. One of the policemen hands me a bullhorn, and I attempt a little speech of thanks and love for the prayers and support these youngsters have given me and my family. Then we are off to Thomas Pyle Junior High School, almost smothered by an enthusiastic student body. Next to Whitman Senior High School, where several thousand students and faculty line the street in a demonstration that is as close to a political rally as I suspect I will ever be the center of, and then a swing through the broad grounds of the Landon School, where a jazz band joins in the welcome.

And then the last and the biggest surprise of all. Across Bradley Boulevard at the foot of my own street is a great yellow banner proclaiming "Welcome home Bruce Laingen"—the work of the Bethesda–Chevy Chase Rescue Squad. And up the street, 5627 Old Chester Road, at last is home. There are several hundred of our friends and neighbors, crowded behind a yellow restraining rope. On the front lawn is the band from Pyle Junior High, pounding out— what else?—"Tie a Yellow Ribbon 'Round the Old Oak Tree." Penne and I and our three sons stand there, a huge American flag held in place behind us, and we shake our heads in amazement and delight, with a few tears too, to see this incredible welcome, on a street where community spirit had never before seemed exceptional. But today it is, and so I pick up that bullhorn for yet one more speech, in a voice by now scarcely audible, and salute my neighborhood for this example of the best in America's tradition of community spirit. I say that if the hostage crisis has taught my country anything perhaps it has reaffirmed for all of us the strength of that spirit in our society and its worth.

Penne and I walk over to the oak tree, where Penne's yellow ribbon is in its second winter, ceremonially removing it and holding it aloft as a symbolic end to our odyssey. But not before the band whips into another patriotic piece, and I dance a jig with Penne, swoop up a neighbor child in a photo session, sign a few autographs, and finally receive from a good neighbor and old friend, Sherman Poland, a bouquet of dried flowers—a reminder of my penchant for flowers in a bachelor house that he and I and six others had shared in our early years in Washington.

Our flight to freedom is complete. I am home again; Penne, too, can finally begin to relax. Three equally hyped-up sons join us for a final flurry of photo-ops at what for me is convincing evidence that my freedom is real—an open front door. Inside is more family—all manner of them, all waiting for the inside story from this member so long and so curiously caught up in a drama of such consequence. A floor-to-ceiling Christmas tree, alive with yellow ribbons, still commands center stage. No such tree ever looked more beautiful or more symbolic of the hope and light of the Christmas message. As I look at it, I pray a final thank you to that God who had been with me in those long and lonely dialogues in Tehran. And there is Duchess, my dog, delighted to join in the welcome—not yet aware but shortly destined, as Penne had told one TV interviewer during the crisis, to be kicked from the place on our bed it had taken over during my absence.

Outside, the band packs its instruments and our neighbors slowly disperse—a bit reluctantly perhaps, for they too are fellow travelers on my cloud nine. And in 52 other neighborhoods across the country, there are similar welcome-home celebrations. Our long dark trial is behind us. America is no longer hostage; the country can breathe a collective sigh of relief. Walter Cronkite's anchor line of remembering the hostages on the evening news had stopped at Day 444.

19

Epilogue

It is now 11 years since our flight to freedom ended on that south lawn of the White House. Despite President Reagan's warning of swift retribution should Americans again be taken hostage in the Middle East, our citizens were bombed, hijacked, murdered, and held hostage throughout the decade that followed. Only in December 1991, with the release of Terry Anderson from the Hezbollah dungeons of Beirut, could it be said that no Americans were held hostage in that troubled corner of the world. In that sense, only now can those of us held in Tehran say that we too are finally free.

Much of the 1980s saw Iran in continued war with Iraq—a grievous conflict that arguably began because of the hostage crisis, Saddam Hussein sensing an opportunity in Iran's isolation to launch his aggression, and that ended only with Ayatollah Khomeini's reluctant acceptance in 1988 of a UN-supervised cease-fire. The Ayatollah died in 1989, succeeded as Faqih (supreme spiritual leader) by the then President Hojjatol-Islam Ali Khamanei, who was in turn succeeded as president by Hashemi Rafsanjani. Ghotbzadeh was eventually executed, on charges of plotting against the regime. Ayatollah Beheshti was killed in a bomb explosion 1981, as was Mohammed Ali Rajai in that same year. Bani-Sadr was driven from office in 1981, went into hiding, and now lives in exile in Paris.

Only now, and in good part because of the new strategic balance in the area that has followed the end of the cold war and the American victory in Desert Storm, has President Rafsanjani seemed to be seriously trying to demonstrate to the world community that if he is not a "moderate," he is at least a pragmatist about the course of Iran's Islamic Revolution. And yet the British novelist Salman Rushdie continues to suffer under the threat of execution imposed on him by the Tehran regime, and in 1991 the last prime minister under the Shah, Shahpour Bakhtiar, was brutally murdered in his own exile in Paris. Those like myself, who continue to believe that the Iranian Revolution has in important respects been incompatible with that country's history and traditions, can only hope that Rafsanjani's pragmatism deepens.

In that "Policy on Iran" telegram that I was able to spirit out of the Foreign Ministry in December 1979, I included this observation: "Whatever the evolution of the political scene in Iran, we should follow a general policy of leaving it to the Iranians to set the pace in future U.S.-Iranian relations, but responding to initiatives from them that demonstrably serve our interests." . . . I went on to say:

> We cannot overemphasize the positive effects on our interest in Iran of progress on the Palestinian issue. Nor can we fail to note our hope that all of us, Congress included, will have learned from the hostage experience how much our interests in the Middle East have been hostage to the shortcomings in our national energy policy over many years.

Thirteen years later, in 1992, surely those views are even more valid than they were then. Regrettably, I was not able, given the course of our energy policy, to be true to one of my personal commitments on my return from Iran, i.e., that I would never buy another automobile until I could buy a battery-operated one. Today we are as dependent on Middle East oil as ever, and General Motors has yet to introduce its battery-operated car on the market.

Those we knew in Tehran as the Students following the Line of the Imam are by now older, presumably wiser, but no longer a political force as such. That was not, however, before they completed publication of some 70 volumes, complete with Farsi translation, of documents recovered from our embassy— many pieced back together, strip by shredded strip. A bookstore near the entrance to our embassy compound has them on public sale. Some of the militant "students" found martyrdom on the front with Iraq, one became a deputy foreign minister, one served for a time as chargé of Iran's embassy in Beirut, and the current Iranian ambassador in Bern is believed to have had his own connections with the unfortunate events in our embassy compound in Tehran. None is believed to have entered the United States.

Today, almost half of our hostage group remain on active duty in government service, including both Ann Swift and Kate Koob. Victor Tomseth is our deputy chief of mission in Bangkok; Michael Howland is on Washington assignment after service at our Consulate General in Lahore, Pakistan. Three have died: William Keough, Col. Lee Holland, and John McKeel, Jr. In Tehran our embassy compound remains a training center for Revolutionary Guards, its outer walls still a place for revolutionary zealots to post their vitriol against the United States. The former Iranian Embassy in Washington has served as State

Department Annex #2. Our interests in Tehran continue to be represented by the Swiss Embassy, where my former driver, Hicaz, found employment as well. And before the crisis was over in Tehran, the good people of that embassy somehow were able to extricate Andy Sens's dog Tom from that compound and get him home to his master.

Among our diplomatic friends in Tehran, Canadian Ambassador Ken Taylor retired from his Foreign Service after an assignment as consul general in New York City and began a career in the private sector. British Ambassador Sir John Graham is also retired and has spent the past several years as director of a major British think tank, the Ditchley Foundation. Swiss Ambassador Erik Lang served later as ambassador to Canada and is now his country's ambassador in Portugal. Papal Nuncio Annibale Bugnini died in 1982.

At Arlington National Cemetery in Washington, a memorial honors the eight men who did not return alive from Iran—lost in the tragedy that struck the Hostage Rescue Mission at Desert One—"Victims of the Desert," as my papal nuncio friend movingly spoke of them in a letter to me at the time. In 1983, I joined with Secretary of Defense Caspar Weinberger in unveiling that memorial, saying in my remarks: "Fifty-three fellow Americans, who did not and now can never know you, reach out to you in a spirit of undying respect. . . . We will not forget."

My son Bill graduated from the Naval Academy in 1982 and served three years on active duty until forced to retire because of rheumatoid arthritis. He is now a senior design engineer at McDonnell Douglas in St. Louis. Chip, a graduate of NROTC at the University of Minnesota in 1983, is back at that same university as a lieutenant and assistant professor of naval science. Jim, a Naval Academy graduate in 1988, is a lieutenant with a Hawkeye E-2 squadron, now on the carrier *Independence*. Both Chip and Jim served with the USS *Midway* battle group in the Persian Gulf during Desert Storm. Jim, on the carrier *Midway*, and Chip, then a helicopter group commander on the destroyer USS *Fife*, by ironic coincidence sailed into the Persian Gulf via the Strait of Hormuz on November 4, 1990, the 11th anniversary to the day of the seizure of my embassy in Tehran.

Eleven years later, the Iran hostage crisis has receded into history, and in time it will probably be little more than a footnote in the larger record of our troubled relations with the Middle East. But few Americans—and certainly not the hostages themselves—will easily forget its human dimensions. Fifty-three Americans gained a profoundly new appreciation of themselves, of their capacity to cope, of the power of faith, and of the freedoms they enjoy as Americans. The human spirit proved again to be something of remarkable resilience, already evident among the POWs who suffered far more in Vietnam. Human beings, the old adage has it, are like tea bags: they don't know their own strengths until they get into hot water.

At home, the American public saw reason to reach out to those 53 Americans in distress in what was an unprecedented example of the best in our country's tradition of community, a strength we too often forget. After the guilt trips of Vietnam and Watergate, here was a crisis, whatever one's view of its origins and handling, where right and wrong seemed crystal clear. For 444 days, the American public responded with flags, prayer vigils, bell ringing, and—in abundance—with yellow ribbons. And on our return the nation celebrated with us in a remarkable surge of national patriotism. For at least a brief time, Americans felt better about themselves. Perhaps some of that remains a part of our collective national psyche.

The lesson is clear and has been throughout our history. When Americans sense agreement on a cause, we are capable of responding as a community, and we are the stronger for it. Desert Storm is only the most recent example. Again there was reason to unite and, with success in that effort, to celebrate and to remember with yellow ribbons. We can again unite as a national community to learn and to build from the tragedy of the Los Angeles riots.

My wife Penne's identification with the yellow ribbon as a symbol of caring and remembrance continued throughout the 1980s and especially during Desert Storm. In April 1991, a Washington ceremony saw her present the original "Mother of All Yellow Ribbons," the one she had wrapped around the oak tree in our front yard during the hostage crisis, to the Library of Congress. There it is today, on permanent exhibit in the Library's Folklife Center.

Index